Together We Stand Forever

Laura L. Drumb

"The grass withereth, the flower fadeth: but the word of our God shall stand forever."
Isaiah 40:8

Copyright © 2024 Laura L. Drumb

www.lauraldrumb.com

All rights reserved. No part of this book may be used or reproduced by any means, graphic, electronic, or mechanical, including photocopying, recording, taping or by any information storage retrieval system without the written permission of the publisher except in the case of brief quotations embodied in critical articles and reviews.

Because of the dynamic nature of the Internet, any web addresses or links contained in this book may have changed since publication and may no longer be valid. The views expressed in this work are solely those of the author and do not necessarily reflect the views of the publisher, and the publisher hereby disclaims any responsibility for them.

Certain stock imagery © BigStock Images

Any people depicted in stock imagery provided by BigStock are models, and such images are being used for illustrative purposes only.

This book is a work of fiction. Names, characters, places, and incidents are either the product of the author's imagination or are used fictitiously. Any resemblance to actual events, locales, organizations, or persons living or dead is coincidental and not the intent of either the author or publisher.

Prepared for publication by www.40DayPublishing.com

Cover design by www.40DayGraphics.com

Printed in the United States of America

TABLE OF CONTENTS

TRANSITION i
DEDICATION iii
AUTHOR NOTES v
CHAPTER ONE 1
CHAPTER TWO 9
CHAPTER THREE 20
CHAPTER FOUR 28
CHAPTER FIVE 36
CHAPTER SIX 43
CHAPTER SEVEN 49
CHAPTER EIGHT 57
CHAPTER NINE 66
CHAPTER TEN 74
CHAPTER ELEVEN 82
CHAPTER TWELVE 88
CHAPTER THIRTEEN 94
CHAPTER FOURTEEN 102
CHAPTER FIFTEEN 112
CHAPTER SIXTEEN 122
CHAPTER SEVENTEEN 130
CHAPTER EIGHTEEN 143
CHAPTER NINETEEN 152
CHAPTER TWENTY 163
CHAPTER TWENTY-ONE 174

CHAPTER TWENTY-TWO	185
CHAPTER TWENTY-THREE	196
CHAPTER TWENTY-FOUR	208
CHAPTER TWENTY-FIVE	220
CHAPTER TWENTY-SIX	229
CHAPTER TWENTY-SEVEN	239
CHAPTER TWENTY-EIGHT	252
CHAPTER TWENTY-NINE	263
CHAPTER THIRTY	275
CHAPTER THIRTY-ONE	287
CHAPTER THIRTY-TWO	301
CHAPTER THIRTY-THREE	311
CHAPTER THIRTY-FOUR	323
CHAPTER THIRTY-FIVE	336
CHAPTER THIRTY-SIX	346
CHAPTER THIRTY-SEVEN	356
CHAPTER THIRTY-EIGHT	366
CHAPTER THIRTY-NINE	376
CHAPTER FORTY	387
CHAPTER FORTY-ONE	397
CHAPTER FORTY-TWO	410
CHAPTER FORTY-THREE	421
CHAPTER FORTY-FOUR	429
ACKNOWLEDGMENTS	437
QUESTIONS FOR FURTHER STUDY	441
MEET AUTHOR LAURA L. DRUMB	443

TRANSITION

from first book to

Together We Stand Forever

When readers left Mandy (Prayer Woman) and Ken-ai-te in 1853, their wedding had been interrupted by a vicious attack from their enemy who had sworn death for both of them. During this battle, the warrior finally managed to kill their enemy and end the tragedies that resulted from his hatred. Later that day they not only committed themselves to completing their wedding vows but also to sharing the Gospel with their people as God led, from now until forever.

Fast forward to 1867. The couple have a family now and have established a ministry to the Kiowa people to share Christ on the prairie of Indian Territory. Through both of these, God has blessed them in a powerful way. However, when the buffalo begin to disappear from the Plains due to the indiscriminate slaughter of the majestic animals by white men encroaching on ancient tribal lands, the crisis erupts into catastrophe. As starvation looms, God steps in and provides the perfect solution. Yet, Mandy hesitates at the enormity of the task ahead of her. Can she and Ken-ai-te continue to stand together against this new enemy they must confront, and trust God to save their family and the Kiowa people from certain destruction?

Sept, 2024

To Jamie,

Enjoy reading the story!

The Word of God stands true forever!

Laura L. Drum

DEDICATION

This book is lovingly dedicated to my husband Gary, who has become my main cheerleader with this relatively new writing career. Without your patient support and kindness in accepting many take-out meals and quickie dinners, not to mention laundry undone and errands never run, because I have been writing all day and have tuned all else out, this novel would never have happened. Truly, we have stood together to face with God's help whatever life threw at us for more than fifty years now, and I pray we can do so for many more to come!

And, also to our two daughters who have always been there for me in this calling from the Lord to write. Holly and Angela, you will never know how much your encouragement has meant to me over the years, and now from each of your husbands as well. I am so proud of both of you and am humbled by your love and appreciation of history and reading as adults. And now you have helped shape a whole new generation of readers who are enjoying my books as well, in our seven grandchildren!

Praise be to God Almighty who has given me the gift of this amazing family and inspires me as He continues to call me to write for Him!

With all my love,

Laura and Mom

Called to Hope…To Live In Joy! ~ Ephesians 1:18, Romans 15:13

AUTHOR NOTES

By the end of the Civil War, the buffalo, often called the "Thunder of the Plains," had begun to disappear from the mid-section of the North American Continent, called the Great Plains. This forced the Native Americans living there to follow the remaining herds further west or to turn to other food sources to continue their way of life. It would not be long before the majestic creatures were gone completely, along with the way of life the Kiowa and other Native American tribes had enjoyed for generations.

The railroads undoubtedly re-shaped American history forever, in more ways than one. However, there existed a dark side to this revolution in industry and commerce. During the building of the thousands of miles of tracks criss-crossing the endless prairies, executives who had never visited the area hired frontiersmen to feed the large army of workers doing the backbreaking labor, using local wildlife and game. Once the hunters learned they could often get as much as five hundred pounds of meat from a single buffalo, these massive beasts quickly became their favorite quarry. Although they butchered whatever they shot, the end result was a horrifying loss to those natives who were as desperate for the food as were the white men.

When the tracks were finally completed and passengers began traveling west into regions never before seen by most white people, the curiosity of those folks for this unusual type of wildlife everywhere they looked was equally matched with that of the ones who were the object of such attention. Capable of running across the vast expanses at speeds up to forty miles per hour, they could easily outrun most horses, let alone a locomotive held captive to its tracks. For some insane reason, people thought it great "sport" to shoot them as fast as they could do so. Sadly, none of the animals had a clue what was about to happen when they ambled alongside the trains or gathered to rest on the tracks. The result: rotting carcasses that dotted the prairie in every direction from one horizon to the other, a tragic symbol of culture clash at its worst, and signaling the end of an era.

Of the roughly sixty million American Bison that once roamed the area from modern-day Montana south to Mexico—an area of more than a million square miles—almost the entire species was wiped out within a relatively short time. Given the fact they had been a major part of life on the Great Plains for hundreds of years, this fact is chilling, indeed. From 1872-74, for example, it is estimated that more than 7.5 million of them were killed in those two short years alone!

This seismic shift in society cannot be ignored but needs to be understood in its place in history for tribes such as the Comanche, Cheyenne, Apache, Pawnee, Sioux, Kiowa and many others. One can easily imagine the devastating impact on the way of life for them, as they heavily depended on the buffalo for its meat, hides, bones, fur, horns, hoofs, teeth, and countless other parts for everything from food, sewing utensils, and weapons, to their tipi covers, clothing, and rawhide ropes, to name only a few. Even their religion changed because they honored the buffalo with their prayers to the Great Spirit while making use of its benefits to them as a gift from Him. The loss was overwhelming and difficult to comprehend for its long-reaching effects.

Warriors became restless and then enraged as their families began to starve, and simultaneously they were pushed further away from ancient tribal lands. Eventually most were forced to move to isolated Reservations set up by the government to contain them so the white men could have more space to build their towns. That fury spilled over more times than history can record into violent conflicts between settlers and the various tribes, resulting in vast numbers of atrocities on both sides. The Native Americans were fighting a losing war with Progress, and of course over time the tragedy played out on the pages of American History in the West, with ramifications still felt today. Any time a pocket of peaceful villages dotting the prairie could hold out against starvation, disease, hopelessness, and defeat, it was considered a victory.

Thus, the stage is set for the story in this novel, set in 1867 shortly after the close of the American Civil War. Starvation is a powerful motivation for moving far beyond the normal into more drastic solutions, especially when it affects children. God gives Mandy and Ken-ai-te an opportunity to obey His leading to stop this tragedy and save their people. Their choice to follow Him, even without understanding, offers us an example to follow when faced with our own dilemmas in life.

Even if you have read the first book, be sure to read the Transition Section in the opening pages of this one. It is intended as a bridge from one to the next. While the primary action of *Together We Stand Forever* takes place far from Indian Territory, its flavor and richness are woven throughout the time Mandy is in Ohio and serves as a vital backdrop for the entire story. The goal, of course, is to provide a way of survival for the Kiowa people back home. But as God often does, His steps can lead in vastly different directions from what we have planned. Uncovering secrets from the past as well as revealing those in the present becomes Mandy's focus as she struggles to understand it all but tries her best to leave those "why's" in the hands of the One who is far wiser than any man ever has been.

Researching the Underground Railroad for this story fascinated me, as I learned so much about it I never knew before. For one thing, I realized I had never read *Uncle Tom's Cabin*, so I checked it out of the library and poured over every page, taking copious notes as I did so. Then I studied up on the life of its author, Harriet Beecher Stowe, and discovered she not only was from Cincinnati, Ohio (only a few miles from Trenton) but she also was a contemporary of Harriet Tubman. Conveniently, in the middle of all this research, the movie *Harriet* came out, based on the life of this runaway slave who was called Moses for her untiring rescues of those held in the bondage of slavery. And more studying took place. One note here: I found several of Mrs. Stowe's speeches and statements recorded for posterity and used them in shaping the one she made at the fictious rally attended by Nan and Ida. In addition, the movie was meticulously researched by the producers, and I used the spirit of Harriet's fiery speeches in that movie to create the words read by the other Harriet at said rally. I pray the literary license I employed in creating this whole scenario has honored these two heroes of our nation, as well as all those who sacrificed so much to end the tragedy of slavery long ago, as Nan and Ida did. Not to mention remembering the brave souls who risked everything to claim the freedom they believed they deserved to experience but which had been cruelly denied to them.

The scene where Ken-ai-te tracks Lily is firmly based on research I did into this fascinating skill. Tom Brown, Jr. has written a book called *The Science and Art of Tracking*, and he actually has a tracking school as well.

There, he trains people, especially law enforcement officials, how to do this difficult task properly and without destroying evidence in the process. I became utterly entranced with his methods and incorporated several of them into that scene. Many thanks to my Facebook friend Paty Norman Jager for pointing me in the right direction on this!

A fascinating piece of history came to light as I read about the Trenton area, regarding Reverend L.L. Langstroth and his extensive work with honeybees. The more I read, the more convinced I became that this info had to be written into the plot somehow! Thus, was born the Honey Garden on Ida's property, and preserving this vital link between flowers and bees that became so important to this story.

One last note about research has to do with the characters Bessie and her brother Samuel. While in the throes of writing their backstory, my husband and I went to eat one night at our local Cracker Barrel restaurant. These charming establishments are decorated with countless historic and vintage photographs and items from the past. That evening we happened to be sitting under a photo of a striking black couple from the mid-1800s, by the look of their clothing. The longer I stared at them, the more I realized this was my Bessie and Samuel! Taking out my phone to snap a picture, to my husband's embarrassment, I rejoiced that I finally had a vision of these two very important people in my fictious story. Although I have no idea who the couple in the portrait was, I nevertheless hope I have done them honor with this novel. Thank you, Cracker Barrel!

Be sure to read over the Questions For Further Study, found at the back of the book. They provide an excellent resource for individuals and group discussions alike, as we reflect on our own emotions and beliefs about these difficult topics Mandy faces. No one is immune to the need for this introspection, as our faith is perfected in weakness, through His strength. Even a fictional story may help us uncover that which is hidden and allow the light of His Word to reveal what He would desire to restore.

Not all bondage is found behind bars but of course will always be found in the seeds of prejudice, bitterness, jealousy, and blind hatred. And those are not restricted to the past. If not identified from there, however, they can never be fully defeated and will continue to yield fruit that is poisoned from the roots, sometimes for generations to come. We may justify them and rationalize them constantly, but Jesus says only the Truth found in Him can ever set a person free. Ignoring history or attempting to rewrite it in order to hide any aspect never works, in fact can even compound the destruction. Only as Christ transforms lives through true repentance can His power be unleashed to bring victory in the present out of despair from long ago.

Mandy learned this lesson in the first novel and now must re-learn it in the current book from a very different angle. With help from the prayers of her faithful husband, she embarks on an emotional and spiritual journey of discovery to confront and find the truth of her aunt's escape from that bondage and how it now impacts her own life. Relying on lies never accomplishes what is hoped but only delays the inevitable. Many themes emerge from this story, but the most powerful one comes as Mandy is told over and over by many in Trenton of how her aunt changed as a result of that new-found freedom. Rather than living in regret, Mandy seeks to bring it to light for everyone and allow God's purpose to be revealed. Perhaps readers will find the same redemption and restoration for themselves. At least, that is my prayer!

As always, if you have any questions about the spiritual truths contained herein, do not hesitate to contact me. I would love the opportunity to share more in detail with you about any or all of them. All Scriptural references are from the King James Version, as that is the only translation of the Bible that Mandy and Ken-ai-te would have had in their time period. Refer often back to the book verse, found at the front of the book—"The grass withereth, the flower fadeth: but the word of our God shall stand forever." Isaiah 40:8 (KJV). And so it shall!

Thank you for your continued interest in Mandy and Ken-ai-te's story, and may God receive any and all glory and praise that is due for the messages He has laid on my heart to prayerfully share with you, my dear readers. How I do thank Him for each one of you!

Blessings,

Laura L. Drumb

Called To Hope…To Live In Joy! ~ Ephesians 1:18, Romans 15:13
AuthorLauraLDrumb@gmail.com
www.facebook.com/lauraldrumb
www.lauraldrumb.com

CHAPTER ONE

"He shall not be afraid of evil tidings: his heart is fixed, trusting in the LORD." Psalm 112:7

April 10, 1867
Indian Territory

"Hacho, Jacob! We did not know you were back from the fort. Come sit with us. Did you have a good journey?" Prayer Woman smiled in greeting, as did her husband Ken-ai-te, when the man reined in and hopped off his horse in front of their tipi.

"Hello, my friends," Jacob replied, and shook hands with the warrior. He nodded at his friend's wife and children and ran his hands through his unruly shock of red hair to smooth it down after the ride. "Good to see all of you, too. Don't mind if I do. Yes, it was a good trip this time. I only returned to the Trading Post a couple of hours ago and got here as quickly as I could manage. Any chance you might have some bread and the plum jam you are so famous for? Sure have missed that and have a hankering for it today."

"Actually, I do. I will get it ready while you and Ken-ai-te visit."

"Thank you, but it is you I have come to see this time."

"Me? Whatever for?" She noticed her husband's questioning look and was certain she must have an equally puzzled one on her face as he strode toward them. Jacob spent a great deal of his rare spare time in the camp whenever he could get away from the Trading Post, but he always came to see his closest friend rather than his friend's wife. How odd that he came to see her this time.

The food forgotten, Prayer Woman took the item he held out to her.

"I came to bring you this because I knew how much it would mean to you, and I wanted to deliver it as quickly as possible. It's a letter I got from Two Peaks while I was at Fort Granger. He was going to bring it to you himself, but since I was there that saved him from having to get leave to come home solely for that, which would have further delayed its delivery into your hands. He asked how his mother was and I told him much better since his recent visit. I trust that she continues to heal?"

"Yes, she is doing better, although still quite weak. His coming to see her did a great deal to perk up her spirits. It was kind of the colonel to allow his trusted scout the time off last week. Wait," she interrupted herself, "did you say a *letter?*" For the first time she glanced down at the small white packet in her hand. "From my aunt? I mean, it would have to be, since the one I sent to her is the only letter I have written in the last fifteen years or so! But it's rather soon after I sent my own to her! How could that happen this quickly?"

"Two Peaks told me that after he explained the situation to his commanding officer, the colonel readily agreed to help, as our friend thought might be the case. Colonel Adams agreed to send your letter in a military dispatch going back east within a couple of days. That way it would get there faster than it might even if we had mail service out here. And if you can believe, it was going to a fort in Ohio very close to where your aunt lives! The colonel put a personal note from him in with it, requesting that the letter be taken into Trenton to your aunt in person by the major to whom the dispatch was sent. And he willingly complied."

"God do that." Ken-ai-te's simple statement caught Prayer Woman off guard. He was right; indeed, the hand of their Father worked all that out as no man could have!

Jacob continued. "In addition to all this, that major graciously offered to send your aunt's reply back in another dispatch if she could write it that same day, which she obviously did. That is how you got it so rapidly, even over such long distances. Guess there are some advantages to our friend having saved the life of Colonel Adams!"

Prayer Woman nodded. "I am most grateful that Two Peaks and the colonel were very kind to do this for me, for us both." With trembling fingers, she opened the letter and glanced down a couple of lines. "It *is* from Aunt Ida! And she is still alive and doing well, apparently. If you two will excuse me, I will read this quickly and then fill you in on what she has to say."

She walked over to sit on a rock nearby while the men visited quietly about various topics. Without being told to do so, their daughter Lily brought Jacob bread and jam as her two younger brothers worked on their own tasks. Each person, however, kept an eye on Prayer Woman while trying not to stare. The curiosity from all of them was obvious in their shared looks back and forth, although they were trying to be polite and respect her privacy. Occasionally she would let out a soft gasp, but no other emotion until finally she cried out.

"No! No!" And she added with a wail, "Aunt Ida, you cannot do this to me!"

"What she say?" Ken-ai-te asked. "What wrong?"

Prayer Woman glanced up, dismay spilling over into her face, she was sure. She took note that her husband's expression reflected her own tension and anxiety. It was clear to all of them something had upset her greatly.

"She says she is quite ill and not expected to live, for one thing. Apparently, she has a cancer in her stomach and the doctor says she only has a short time left. I am deeply saddened to lose her, after having finally made contact with her again." And her voice broke. She struggled to regain control and then went on. "Doctors don't know everything and maybe they are wrong. How I pray they are!"

"But what has she done that you're this upset about it?" Jacob asked. "Your words were, *you cannot do this to me,* but surely she had no control over getting sick."

"No, no, that was because of something else, not because of her illness. She has asked that I come to see her again before she dies. I cannot do that! There is no way I can go that far, and to a white city, with me being Kiowa. What is she thinking?"

"Did you tell her," asked Jacob, "that you are Kiowa now?"

She took a moment to reply. "Well, not exactly. I knew if she read that truth in my letter it would hurt her deeply and probably anger her as well. She has no idea I married my captor, much less that I am half-Kiowa by birth. And fully Kiowa now by choice! I simply couldn't do that to her deliberately. She never has had a love—or even tolerance, for that matter—for any Indian, since her parents were killed in a raid when she and my father were young. I figured I would never see her again, maybe she was already deceased, in fact; therefore, it wouldn't matter if I bent the truth a tiny bit. Instead of my real Kiowa name, I made up a white-sounding name and used it on the envelope of the letter. Otherwise, she might have tossed it without reading it."

"She think you white?"

"Well yes, Ken-ai-te, I guess she does. That's why she didn't think about asking me to come visit before she dies, I suppose. Otherwise, she would have known how dangerous it is to expect a Kiowa to come to Trenton. Am I not correct, Jacob, that I couldn't possibly go there without creating a great deal of trouble?"

"Yes, sad to say, you are right. Everything all over the country is in a great deal of chaos right now and has been since the war ended, as I understand it. One thing that has not changed is how prejudiced people are in general against any Indian they see, especially back East. You might be shot or hanged before you could get even get halfway there. In fact, if all the newspaper stories I've been reading are any indication, it's a dangerous time for a person from any Indian tribe to be seen in towns or cities alike."

"That's what I thought might be the case. It appears people aren't any different now than they ever were, even after fighting a brutal war over setting the Negroes free. The few newspapers you have brought to us from the fort over the last several years have proven that to my heart. Even such a terrible conflict as a civil war didn't change a thing, apparently. I don't understand this at all but it seems that anyone who isn't white is suspected of being evil, and capable of horrific acts of violence. They aren't even given a chance to prove otherwise. And that goes double for Indians. Do you recall, Jacob, the one article you read to us last week about that farmer and his family who were massacred in Arkansas? And how the people over-reacted and hanged several Indians before discovering they were innocent?"

"Yes, I remember. I don't understand what's happening either, to be honest. But I do agree your aunt's request cannot be taken lightly."

"As upsetting as all that is, it is the urgency of Aunt Ida's request that troubles me. And the reason."

"Reason?" her husband asked, clearly confused.

She cleared her throat. "Let's see, how do I explain all this? After reading my letter, Aunt Ida decided to leave her entire estate to me, and apparently it is quite vast from what she said. She immediately called her attorney to come and help her change her will so it's already done—simply waiting on my signature for it to be legal. And of course, her, um, death." She winced at this last word and blinked back tears at the thought. "I don't want to lose her just as I found her again!" The tears came unbidden and trickled down her cheeks.

"Not know this word, es-tate."

"Oh, I'm sorry, Ken-ai-te, of course you wouldn't," she said as she wiped away her tears. "It's a white man's word meaning all the possessions that one has at the time of death. And a will is a legal paper that designates who gets what after the person dies. She has left everything to me, her house and grounds and furniture and investments and—well, everything she has. But I don't want it. I want *her*, not her money!"

Ken-ai-te appeared to be quite thoughtful but didn't reply.

"Of course you do," Jacob offered kindly. "You're under no obligation to accept her gift, you know." And he gently added, "But I do think it would be quite disappointing to her if you refuse to go see her before she dies." It was his turn to get quiet. After a moment or two, he smiled.

"What if you went as a white woman instead of as a Kiowa?"

"How could I do that? I don't own any clothing except my buckskin dresses and moccasins. Besides, it's so far away, how on earth would I get there? Even if I could figure that question out, we don't have enough money to buy food for our people as it is, let alone if I spend our meager savings to travel all that distance merely to go visit a dying woman. No, that would be impossible."

"But that the point," said Ken-ai-te. "We have plenty money for food if you get this es-tate. Right?" He turned to Jacob for confirmation.

"Well, yes, I suppose you're right. She must be quite a wealthy woman. That money could mean the difference in starvation and survival for the Kiowa, Prayer Woman."

"But I don't *want* to go to Ohio! And not only that, but I cannot go! No way am I ever going back to a white culture that I no longer understand, and whose people would kill me if they knew the truth. I can handle the few white settlers who come through this area from time to time but I would be terrified to go to a city again, no matter the reason." She hesitated slightly.

"One more thing that concerns me is that apparently I have a cousin who lives with Aunt Ida but for some unexplained reason she is cutting him out of her will. She warned me repeatedly about him, to be careful of how vindictive he might be against me when he finds this out. How I even ended up with a cousin when Aunt Ida never married is beyond me, but what if this man's threats are more than I can handle? There is a young woman who also lives with her, a companion of sorts, the best I can understand.

Aunt Ida encouraged me to gain her trust, along with that of her lawyer who is a long-time friend. They will help protect me, she says. But what if they cannot? I'm afraid I won't know who to trust when I get there and without you beside me, well, it is all way too fearsome to consider! No, no!" she cried, shaking her head.

"Prayer Woman—" Ken-ai-te began but she interrupted him.

"No, I said! I simply cannot possibly consider it! What's more, no one can ever make me go, either. No guilt trip from my aunt and no pressure from either of you can force me into this, and that's the end of it!"

"Whoa now, I'm not trying to force you to do anything, Prayer Woman," said Jacob. "I'm only pointing out that you might want to stop and at least pray about the decision. I've never seen you so opinionated about something without a great deal of prayer behind it first! You are light skinned enough to pass for white, you know, with different clothing and hairstyle. Maybe that will give you some hope that it might work without putting you in danger."

"Now you're trying to remake me into something I am not! You've heard countless times about all the anguish I went through long ago trying to become Kiowa. And now you have the audacity to suggest I should throw all that away? I fought for it, bled for it, and I will never give up my Kiowa heritage now, not for anything in the world!"

"I wouldn't dream of suggesting that you give up your heritage, merely hide it a short time for a greater purpose. You need to look at the bigger picture, not merely your own feelings. Besides, you were the one who started this whole thing with your letter to her, right?"

Prayer Woman nodded, and her shoulders sagged.

"Stop for a moment and remember. What made you write it in the first place?"

"Over time God kept reminding me that I have an aunt whom I have not seen in years, and recently every time I prayed for her He seemed to put an urgency in my heart to contact her. Maybe she was dead after all this time? Or living in poverty? Or ill and alone? I had no idea why, just that it seemed important to get in touch with her as soon as possible. But how? In spite of my pleas, no answer came. One afternoon I was mumbling yet another prayer to Him about this and failed to notice that Two Peaks, who was here from the fort visiting his mother, had overheard me. He didn't realize I was talking to God so asked what was on my heart. He's like a younger brother to me, as you know, so before I knew it I had poured out the whole story to him. Immediately he mentioned that he might have a way to get a letter through to her for me if it was that essential. My joy overflowed! Within moments we had worked out the details and I sat down to write to her right away. Later that evening when he returned to the fort, he had my letter in his knapsack."

"So, you prayed and God provided an answer," said Jacob. "Seems plain enough to me that He planned this. I agree, I don't know why God wants you to go see her but He is offering a plan to save your people as well. How much better can it get? If you need to bend the truth a bit, as you put it, to claim this estate and get to see your aunt one more time before she dies, who cares? You are not lying about who you are nor are you attempting to commit a crime by stealing what is not yours already. Obviously, she still cares for you in spite of how much time it has been. What is the problem here?"

Prayer Woman stared with her jaw dropped open. He still didn't get it. Then the real blow struck.

"You must go." Ken-ai-te's quiet statement caught Prayer Woman off guard after her emotional outburst. Was her husband actually *ordering* her to go? How dare he!

"How could you even think about commanding me to go do this thing? You cannot possibly be serious! I'm your wife, not your *slave*, remember?"

With things clearly getting more out of control by the minute, Jacob took a step back to avoid getting in the middle of this argument between his two dear friends. This was quite uncharacteristic of Prayer Woman, to be so stubborn about something without even stopping to pray. That was usually her first course of action about any decision that needed to be made, ever since he had known her. He motioned to the children to leave the circle immediately and he turned to go as well.

"Jacob, stay," the warrior said with a glance his way. "You must help with decision."

Ken-ai-te glared at his wife as she fumed in silence, returning his hard stare. The children scattered but Jacob remained by the side of his friends as requested, although unsure what he could do to help. Except pray for peace and understanding, which he did.

"What? Now you cannot even order me to do something against my will on your own, without asking your best friend to help you with it?" Sarcasm dripped from every word. Ken-ai- te silently stood his ground.

The shock on Ken-ai-te's face reflected what Jacob felt as well. This letter had really upset Prayer Woman, so maybe it would be best to leave the matter with the two of them. They certainly didn't need his influence or advice getting in the way. He saw both sides and had no idea right now why God seemed to be choosing a course of action that so obviously had torn Prayer Woman's heart in two. At the same time, with the buffalo almost gone from the prairie, or at least their part of it, the Kiowa were facing certain starvation before long. They had to have money to purchase the food they could no longer hunt. For months now the three of them had been having endless discussions about what to do. Every one of them always ended the same way, without a firm decision. There simply were no easy answers. Life here had become much more complicated, made even more difficult by the ever-increasing restrictions on the tribes in the territory going anywhere they pleased as they had usually done in the past, even in order to hunt for food. And they were running out of options.

Why couldn't Prayer Woman see this? Obviously, Ken-ai-te did. As chief, it was his responsibility to feed his people but that was no longer possible from their traditional source. What else could he do, when faced with the possibility of a vast fortune that was theirs for the taking—and legally? But how could Jacob help these two resolve their disagreement? Or should he even try? As a rule he would stay out of it but perhaps the idea rapidly taking shape in his mind would work, and his brain raced furiously to skim through all the details so he could talk to them rationally about it once the argument was resolved. If it was. Surely it would be! He prayed they would both listen to a well-thought-out plan once they had calmed down.

"Stay away from me, Ken-ai-te," she shouted as he tried to grasp her arm and she jerked it away. Perhaps he had intended to escort her to the tipi for more privacy than they had out here in the open in front of everyone. Arguments were so rare between these two that heads were turning at their loud and angry voices.

"I am *not* going to Ohio, no matter what you say, do you hear me? And no one on this earth can force me to do so!"

CHAPTER TWO

"If I take the wings of the morning, and dwell in the uttermost parts of the sea; Even there shall thy hand lead me, and thy right hand shall hold me." Psalm 139:9-10

April 11, 1867
Indian Territory

"Ken-ai-te, may we talk?"

He glanced up from working on arrowheads as Prayer Woman approached, then returned to his task without saying anything. A twinge of remorse crunched her heart as she realized how deeply she had hurt her husband the day before.

"I know you are very unhappy with me and I am with myself, to be honest. This is all my fault and I hope you can forgive me. Sleep would not come last night as I prayed and wrestled with my emotions, asking for God's wisdom in this situation."

He finally met her eyes and she continued.

"Please know how sorry I am for hurting you and embarrassing you in front of Jacob and the children. I don't know what came over me." She stopped and took a breath. "No, that's not true. I know exactly what came over me. Fear. I was terrified at the prospect of having to go to Trenton, for whatever reason. Still am. I let the fear control me and that was wrong. But God has shown me from His Word that He is stronger than this fear and all my anxieties. I knew it in my heart of course but He had to remind me, to show me how wrong I was to allow it to guide my tongue last night."

"Forgiven. Not mean to order you to do something you could not." He smiled at her while her heart melted. How many times had that happened to her down through the years? Too many to count.

"Thank you for that grace you give to me, my husband. I certainly don't deserve it."

"Can share what God say?"

"Of course, I was hoping you would ask!" She had her Bible in her hand and sat down beside him to show him the words that had touched her heart so deeply. "Psalm 119:133 says, 'Order my steps in thy word: and let not any iniquity have dominion over me.' I had to ask God's forgiveness for listening to my fear instead of to Him."

"Good word from The Spirit."

"Yes, and there is more, another verse from the Psalms, Chapter 138 verse 7: 'Though I walk in the midst of trouble, thou wilt revive me: thou shalt stretch forth thine hand against the wrath of mine enemies, and thy right hand shall save me.' I believe He is saying He not only will save me, He will also save our people, if I am obedient even in the face of great danger and all my fears."

"Why so afraid? Not like you."

"I know. It's hard to explain in words. When I first came to the camp with you, I was terrified of having to accept the Kiowa way of life as my only future. I resented it bitterly and told God that often. And you!" He laughed, then grew more serious as she continued. "It was very difficult for me for a long time. But as you know, there came a point when I finally was able to adapt enough to be content and eventually to be happy as a Kiowa. For many weeks I cried and begged God to let me go 'home' even though I honestly had no idea where my home was any longer. Not at the mission and certainly not in Ohio. So where did I belong? Here with you, of course! And now, after all these years, God is granting the desire of my heart to go home to Ohio. But is it the right thing for me to do? I don't know. I think I'm afraid most of all of going to see Aunt Ida, not fitting in there, and that would hurt. And maybe—well, maybe I'm a little afraid I will like it *too much!* As in, not wanting to come home."

His smile faded. "You want to stay in this O-hi-o now? In house there?"

"Never! Not in a million years! I love it here in Indian Territory, Ken-ai-te, and I love our life here together. I hope you know I love you with all my heart, from now until forever." That brought a sweet smile to the face of her beloved once more. "I adore our beautiful children and all our friends and family here in the village and have absolutely no desire to ever leave our home."

"Yet people need food so we need money for that. How long this take to get es-tate?"

"Well, the way Aunt Ida made it sound, not very long. I have to go there and sign the papers and I'm sure the lawyer has some things to do legally on it all, but I assume the money will then be given to me. Of course, if Aunt Ida is still living, it all becomes more complicated to settle quickly. But if she is has passed away by the time I get there, I'm thinking a few days is all."

"Jacob's idea good one. Will it work?"

"My going as a white woman instead of as a Kiowa, you mean?"

He nodded and stared intently into her eyes. "Jacob say before he left he has clothes in store you can wear. And can pay when you get home. Save money for trip that way."

Prayer Woman blinked a moment, thinking. *Hmm, that might work. Why didn't I pay more attention to what he was saying yesterday?* The guilt came rushing back in answer: she had been so busy fuming over the idea of going to Ohio that she didn't even consider how. Jacob, on the other hand, had been clear-headed and evidently had a plan that made good sense for her protection. And her husband had agreed.

"Prayer Woman, want you to consider idea of Jacob, o-kay? And take Lily, too."

"Take Lily into that mess? You can't be serious about that!"

Her anger rose for a second but she quickly bit it back. Long ago she and Ken-ai-te had agreed that at some point in the future their daughter would need to be introduced to white society, but this way? Into all the danger and uncertainty? On the other hand, going back to where her mother had grown up might be the best way to do that. There probably would never again be as good an opportunity as this one for Lily to learn first-hand what living in the white culture was all about. Once more, her husband's cool head prevailed while her own temper had gotten the best of her for a moment. Would she ever learn?

"Well, now that I think about it, we did agree to do this for her someday and it would be nice to have some company on the trip. She is fluent in English and has a level head on her shoulders, plus she is old enough to be cautious about any slip-ups in Kiowa or about our way of life back home. Most of all, she is light skinned like I am, while the boys are darker like you. There is no way they could pass for white, but I believe Lily could. What bothers me is to go living a lie. Will God honor the reason in spite of that?"

"Not know but think starvation not His plan, either."

"True. He did protect Sarah and Abraham from Pharaoh with a lie, plus there are quite a few other instances in the Bible where He used lies for protection of His people and plans, while never condoning dishonesty. His purposes are hard to understand sometimes but we are not to seek that knowledge as much as seek to obey when He directs us. I believe He has done that, so asking why is not a good thing. Going is."

"Glad you agree. Jacob say he has clothes for Lily, too. Need to go to store soon to get those and other supplies today."

"Yes, I suppose we do need to do that in a little while. At least once we get to Trenton we will have a place to stay, with Aunt Ida. This cousin she mentioned living in the house might complicate things a bit but maybe not too much, since we are relatives at least. In addition, she has a companion there with her as well who is a woman so it's not like we will be staying in a house with a man we don't know. The important thing is that it will also save us money for the few days we are in town."

"That a good thing, to save money any way you can. You sure this okay with aunt? Is house big enough for all of you?" he asked with a frown.

"Yes, my love, it is. As far as if it's all right with Aunt Ida for us to be there, that is a requirement of her will, although a strange one, that I must stay overnight at least one night in my old room when I come. I have no idea why, but I want to do that and as I said, it will save money as well. Besides, the house has five bed chambers so there is plenty of room."

"Five? That a big house! Get lost in it?"

"No," she replied with a chuckle. "I'm pretty sure I can remember my way around!" Then she got quiet again. "Here we are discussing the living arrangements, but my big question is how will we get all the way to Ohio? There are no stagecoaches here, as we have seen described in the newspapers Jacob has brought us from the fort. Nor trains, for that matter. I suppose we will have to ride by horseback the whole way, which could be very difficult at the least and time consuming as well, not to mention dangerous for a woman and a young girl traveling alone."

"Jacob and I talk after you leave and decide trip must be by horseback to place called Fort Smith, think that the name. Not sure where that is but Jacob know and is long distance. Can ride at night and rest during day, to avoid people and towns, will take about three days. There Jacob say you catch train for this O-hi-o, maybe two more days but easier than on horseback. When he order supplies, that is how they get to him, he say, so sure it will work for people, too. Know what train is?"

"Yes, I do know what a train is, saw them in Trenton when I was a child. I have never ridden on one, but they are big machines designed to take people and supplies from one place to another in much shorter time than they could do on their own. So this Fort Smith place has a train that will take us to Trenton?"

"Trust Jacob when he say that is true. Sooner leave, sooner back."

"But I don't know the way to this Fort Smith. How will Lily and I ever find it on our own?"

"Jacob say he and I go with you that far. Rest of trip by yourselves. Too dangerous for me to take you alone but he white so can protect me. I know buffalo trails and back woods so he say I must go or he get lost."

At that Prayer Woman smiled. Imagine Jacob getting lost anywhere! He was a true frontiersman, brave and bold, years of experience behind him in living out here on the prairie, not afraid of anything or anyone. Except maybe a Comanche war party! Who wasn't afraid of that? With Jacob along, she would feel confident they would be fine, especially with her wise husband guiding them along the hidden paths and through the wilderness no white man could figure out.

She didn't say anything for a moment longer, trying to take in the enormity of what she was committing herself to. With no way to communicate with her beloved once she left him, the concept of being on her own took on an ominous tone. What lay ahead for her and her daughter in this far-off place? It had been over fourteen years since she was there. One thing for certain, it had changed, especially since the war. Could she even find her way around town any longer? Only after a great struggle had she been able to intentionally bury all those memories long ago because it was too painful to keep resurrecting them. What would happen when she dug them up again? Was she prepared for that? She shivered involuntarily and her husband noticed.

He rose and pulled her to her feet to hold her close. Encircled in his loving arms, Prayer Woman knew she could do this with God's help, but she became overwhelmed with a desire to never leave his embrace again, and the tears came. Gently he wiped them away without a word.

How does he always know what I need, right when I need it, Lord? I am certain it is because You know my needs and he listens to Your voice! Thank You for a man of such quiet and strong faith to walk beside me through life. Even when we are apart, I know You will guide and protect both of us. Please let this whole thing be over quickly and let Aunt Ida stay alive until I can get there.

"One thing keeps coming up to crush my heart, Ken-ai-te, and that is—how will I know who to trust there? Aunt Ida warned me about my cousin being dangerous but what about those others she mentioned? How can I know for sure how trustworthy they really are?"

"God will guide, that the important thing."

"Yes, I agree. I must focus on that more than on my fears, my husband."

"We stand together here," he said kindly. "No different when apart. We stand together in God's Word, no matter what. He protect you every step. I pray and all will be good. Right?"

She gazed up into his dark eyes as all her doubts and fears about this long and perilous journey ahead melted away. Well, most of them anyway. And God would handle those for her, she knew, with her husband's prayers from back home holding her up.

"You always say the right words, the ones I need to hear. I am deeply blessed to have you in my life, you know that, don't you? Pray for me while I am gone?"

His smile told her all she needed to know. Further words were not necessary. He was right, there was no difference in facing this together even though they would be hundreds of miles apart for the first time. God was in charge, so what did they have to fear?

At that moment they heard the plaintive cry of a baby from somewhere in the camp. Their heads jerked around in that direction. Prayer Woman's heart sank. She knew that family and knew this little one wouldn't survive much longer without more food. Many here were in the same predicament but somehow it seemed more heart-wrenching for an infant. Any doubts she had that this whole scheme was necessary flew away like the lark on the morning breeze. God's plan had to be for the child to survive, for all the children to live, and for some odd reason He placed that responsibility solely in her hands. She must get that money and do it soon!

"You know, Ken-ai-te, when we made the agreement between us to ensure our children would be fluent in speaking Kiowa and English, and additionally made the commitment to make sure they knew how to read and write in English as well, little did we know God had this day in mind."

"Yes, you right. Lily loves her books very much, learns many things from them. Glad we find money to buy those for her all this time. Believe it will help her think like a white girl."

"I'm sure it will. And she is going to need to do that a great deal in the days ahead. We both are."

By the next morning all the complicated plans were finalized for the venture so at first light a small group of Kiowa prepared to leave the camp and head toward the Trading Post to see the four off on their journey. After securing the clothing they needed, packing some away and changing into the outfit each chose to wear, Jacob mentioned a couple of other items to Prayer Woman that she would need, namely a handkerchief and a pocket watch. Then he handed her a small gold ring.

"You cannot go as a married woman without this, Prayer Woman. I know it is foreign to your Kiowa culture but necessary from this point forward."

"Oh, I hadn't given a thought to any of these, but especially the wedding band. Thank you for thinking of such a tiny yet essential detail. Why do you have a wedding ring here at the store? That seems an odd selection for your usual stock."

"Occasionally I get folks coming through who decide to get married at the last minute and need this. So I try to keep one here at least. It will complete your transformation. If anyone doubts the truth of your claim to being married, this silent symbol will put an end to those. You can return it, along with all the other items, when you get home."

Prayer Woman asked Ken-ai-te to put it on her finger, and he did so, but with a puzzled look until she explained.

"This will stay on my hand until I get back, in honor of our marriage, my husband!" And she kissed him on the cheek as he smiled.

While Ken-ai-te packed up the few items they would need, Prayer Woman gazed into the kind eyes of the couple who would be caring for the boys until their father could return, and a sob caught in her throat. She mouthed the words "thank you" and they nodded. They would be in good hands—just not hers. Her heart almost broke in two as she pulled them into one last embrace. How long before she would have this privilege once more?

Lord, take care of them while I cannot! Gulping to maintain control, she watched them walk away and called out a farewell in Kiowa as the boys turned to wave at her. They were showing such courage, certainly better than their mother felt in this moment. Was it too late to call a halt to this crazy plan? Shoulders sagging with resignation, she told herself that yes it was, reminding her heart this was not her idea but God's. Her job was to obey. She patted the small bag tied at her waist which contained her Bible. *Father, remind me often to obey You in the path ahead!*

A short time later, Jacob quickly gave his daughter Hannah a few last-minute instructions on running the Trading Post while he was away. She had done this a few times before but as a rule he was only gone overnight when he would travel to the fort for supplies. This time was different. He was unsure how long it would take them to get to Fort Smith and back, but certainly far longer than two days. So, he had enlisted the assistance of several braves from the village to agree to come as needed, and she seemed genuinely appreciative for their promised help and protection.

Hannah had returned to the territory some months before, after finishing college back east, and while Jacob was a jolly, friendly person his daughter was another matter. She had grown up with her mother, as the two had separated when their daughter was quite young. After her mother's death, she decided to head west in order to get reacquainted with her father. The reunion had been strained and at times tense. Yet, the young woman shouldered this task bravely and showed only confidence this crisp sunny morning in handling things in her father's absence. What a relief to Prayer Woman, as she couldn't imagine having to make this journey without Jacob's presence with them.

"Don't worry, Father. I will be fine with all the help I will have here!" She gestured at the small crowd gathered around them, as several eager braves nodded to reassure him.

When they were finally ready, Ken-ai-te led them in prayer, to ask for God's protection for the two going to Ohio and for those left behind while they were gone. And that all would go well with God's plan to prevent starvation for the Kiowa people, citing one of his favorite verses, Psalm 37:5.

"Commit thy way unto the LORD; trust also in him; and he shall bring it to pass."

Hearing those blessed words calmed Prayer Woman's heart considerably and she determined to cling to them often in the days ahead. Already armed with three specific verses to guide her, she felt ready to take on the world. Patting her Bible at her side for reassurance, she thanked God once again for His eternal truth in that book.

Prayer Woman reminded Lily that they would not be speaking any more Kiowa from that point on, no matter what. No one must suspect they were not white women. With sadness Prayer Woman reminded herself and the others that she was now Amanda again, or Mandy, but would not be able to use her Kiowa name until she returned home. *Please, Father, make that soon!*

The grueling trip was long and difficult but without major incident. One thing that highly disturbed all of them, however, was the level of destruction they witnessed, the further east they traveled, presumably from battles in the war. They never got very close to any towns but could see from afar the devastation of farms, churches, schools, and many other buildings that had been burned. Most still were not rebuilt. What would Mandy find in Ohio? She blinked back tears of sadness but also recognized they were tears of fear and prayed fervently for that to be banished.

Reminding herself often that she must concentrate only on the hard ride they were making, she found reassurance in the steady rhythm of the ponies' hooves as they raced across the mostly empty prairie, clambered over rocky places, and wound through mazes of wooded areas as well. They scarcely had time to feel pity for those who had lost so much in the terrible conflict, but she did pray each time another scene came in view for those affected and asked for God's provision and healing to be evident.

Mandy thanked the Lord often for the split riding skirts Jacob had found for them, as they proved far better than the large, cumbersome ones they would have to purchase once they arrived. She had forgotten how much more comfortable a deerskin dress was than one with a bodice. They had not worried about the corsets they would normally have had underneath as the two of them certainly wouldn't survive the many miles on horseback if they wore those, too. The constraints of the uncomfortable material around her middle, however, nearly stifled her at times and she hoped her daughter was faring better than she was with this. Lily kept up well with the adults and her mother couldn't help but feel some pride in that, as though she did this all the time. She couldn't wait to introduce her daughter to Ida. Would she be as pleased to meet them? From her letter, it sounded as though they would be welcomed with open arms and Mandy prayed that would be true, even after all these years.

When they made a stop at one point on the second day, they all pitched in to water and feed the horses and secure them in some heavy underbrush within a large thicket as they had done before a couple of times, where the four could stretch out in the shade alongside their mounts the remainder of the day. That way they would be able to see without being seen, should anyone happen to come along while they were resting. The sun was high overhead but no one mentioned food. They could eat while they rode but they all needed sleep for now and to stay hidden until dusk. Riding hard through the night should put them close to their destination by the next day, and Mandy found herself alternatively filled with excitement in anticipation of seeing her aunt again soon, and terror at what she would find when they arrived. Right now, she was far too tired to care. The ponies were not even whinnying, obviously as exhausted as their riders. Ken-ai-te laid out blankets for his wife and daughter and lay down between them, with Jacob on the other side of Lily. Within moments after settling into her husband's strong arms, Mandy drifted off for this much-needed break in their arduous journey.

She had no idea how long she had been asleep when she felt the Kiowa chief tense up next to her. Immediately she was on the alert. Putting fingers to his lips but not making a sound, he nodded in the direction from which they had come earlier and took his bow in his hand as he sat up. Jacob silently leapt to his feet to keep the horses steady and quiet. Mandy thought surely the riders could hear her heartbeat, it pounded so loud in her own ears, as the men came perilously close to where their group was hidden. Lily stirred; Mandy calmed her with a hand on her leg, but the girl's panicked eyes spoke volumes without a word. *God, protect us! Don't let them see us!*

After several moments, the cowboys casually rode on past without ever knowing they had been carefully watched from the bushes nearby. At long last, Mandy slowly let out her breath, not even realizing until then that she had been holding it. No one spoke, just settled back down again. But who could sleep now, even with the danger long gone? What if it happened again and they failed to hear? She scolded herself for borrowing trouble and tried to release it back to the Lord as her drowsiness finally took over.

Thank You for keeping us from being discovered and I ask for Your continued watch-care until we reach our destination. Be with my boys and...

CHAPTER THREE

"...Be strong and of good courage...fear not, nor be dismayed: for the LORD God, even my God, will be with thee; he will not fail thee, nor forsake thee..." I Chronicles 28:20

April 14, 1867
Fort Smith, Arkansas

"Whoa, hold up a minute!" Jacob's voice, barely above a whisper, warned the others to be as quiet as possible.

Their guide rode through the heavy underbrush ahead of them while the rest waited to see what he would discover. After a moment, Ken-ai-te urged his pony on over to where Jacob had come to a stop on the edge of a clearing, barely visible through the leaves.

"Fort Smith," Jacob said quietly and motioned the ladies to join them. "At least I believe that it is, from the descriptions I've read of the place."

"We are here," Ken-ai-te said with a smile.

"Finally!" Mandy added and he nodded at his wife.

"As we discussed earlier," Jacob said, "I'm going on into town to make the train reservations and ensure it is safe for the ladies. I will leave you to look after your family, Ken-ai- te, but I should return shortly. You all stay quiet and under cover while I'm gone."

The three of them dismounted as he left, and they watered their horses, then drank from the water bags and canteens and munched on a bit of pemmican while they rested, although Ken-ai-te was on the alert the whole time with his bow in his hand. He wondered while they slept when he would again have the privilege of watching over these whom he loved so much, and he prayed for them in every way he could think of for what lay ahead of them, recognizing only God could know the exact needs they would have. Now, His Heavenly Father alone would be the defender of his beloved family. His trust in this Great Spirit to whom he had dedicated his heart long ago grew immeasurably as he considered all this in these quiet moments.

A short time later the sound of hoof beats announced the return of Jacob. Maybe. In one swift motion the warrior pulled an arrow out of the quiver on his back and loaded it in his bow, prepared to attack if it was not his friend. With a sigh of relief, he finally spotted a flash of red hair and then Jacob's familiar face through the brush. He relaxed, laying the weapons on the ground next to his things.

"*Hacho,* Ken-ai-te! I'm back. Are they sleeping?"

"Yes, but I will awaken them. You bring good news?" His friend nodded in response as Ken-ai-te gently nudged his wife and daughter.

The ladies sat up and stretched, eager to hear what Jacob had to say.

"Tell us what you learned, my friend," said Ken-ai-te, as he clasped Jacob's hand in greeting.

"I got the train tickets without any problem, much cheaper than I imagined they would be, which means I have some money to give back to you, Prayer—um, Amanda, for you to use on the journey. Two are for St. Louis, the other two for on into Trenton. I'm not sure if you have to change trains anywhere else along the way but the conductor can explain it to you if required. At least you already have the tickets purchased so that should lessen the confusion for you. Of course, guard them carefully."

"I'm sure I can handle this, Jacob, thanks very much. I will put these here in my handbag where they won't be out of my sight. They are much too valuable to risk having them stolen or lost."

"When does train leave?" Ken-ai-te asked.

"Unfortunately, not until 7:30 tomorrow morning. Therefore, I also secured you and Lily a room for the night, Amanda, at a safe and reliable Hotel For Ladies close to the depot. The owner was friendly and kind, told me she had plenty of room for the two of you even at the last minute like this. The rate was surprisingly reasonable, thus you easily have enough to cover the cost, with money left over. I also talked to her about you staying with her on the return trip, until you can get word to us that you are here and we can come get the two of you."

Mandy frowned. "How am I to do that?"

"Well, I got that worked out as well, or I should say, God did. I said a quick prayer over that question and He reminded me of how this all began, with a letter in a military dispatch. Why not try that again? So, I rode over to the stockade to talk to the commanding officer and explained our dilemma. I mentioned Colonel Adams' name to him and he knew him! Can you believe that? I figure that could only be a gift from God to us."

"Really? That is a miracle, that of all the military commanders, they should know each other!"

"I agree. His name is Colonel Morris and he said he would be glad to send a dispatch to Fort Granger as soon as you get back here to Fort Smith and include your letter in it. I don't know how God did it, but He did! And our problem is solved. We should be here in a couple of days at most after your message arrives. I will alert Two Peaks when I get back home so he can be watching for it."

Mandy grinned. "I feel much better knowing all this. God be praised for working everything out, and for your wisdom in knowing how to handle it!"

"Way I look at it, if you don't ask, you don't get, thus why not ask if you have a need? And God answered. Kinda what the Bible teaches us, isn't it?"

Lily took the lull for a chance to ask a question. "Mama, what's a depot?"

"Oh, child, that is a building where the train picks up passengers and lets them off again. We will board it there so it is good that it is only a short walk. Gathering wood every morning for the fire requires more walking than this will be. Think you can handle it?"

Her daughter smiled and nodded. This simple exchange reminded Mandy afresh that Lily heard all that was said, even though she knew better than to participate in an adult conversation—except when curiosity overwhelmed her! Mandy would need to remember to explain things better to satisfy her inquiring mind. Everything from now on would be a whole new world for her. And perhaps for her mother in some ways!

Ken-ai-te hugged his wife gently at the great news and his smile tugged at her heart, knowing she would not see many more of these for some time to come. How long would it be? Would she be able to bear this separation, now that it was upon them? Only with God's help, she knew, and she fought back the rising panic.

"Another thing, Ken-ai-te, this lady seems like a real no-nonsense woman who has some rules in place to protect all her boarders, such as no men allowed. Which means you don't need to fear they might be bothered tonight. They will be perfectly safe. But we are losing daylight fast so best if you go ahead and say your goodbyes now in order for me to get them settled and back here before dark. I appreciate your willingness to hold the horses for me because I know your heart would push you to be the one to safely deliver your wife and daughter in town. But of course, you mustn't be seen by anyone for obvious reasons. Once I get back, we will need to put some distance between us and this fort before we can rest."

The warrior nodded his thanks to his friend and pulled Mandy even closer with a few quiet words for her ears only. While hugging his daughter, he solemnly reminded her that for the Kiowa there are no "goodbyes" because their people only say, "see you later." That is also true for those who believe in Jesus, and therefore he refused to use that word to his family. Lily smiled and buried her head against his chest. Mandy knew what she was doing, something that long ago she had taught her children: to make special memories by breathing a scent, staring long at a scene, or holding tight to an object to help remember a little longer. Tears sprung into her eyes. When would they next be reunited as a family?

Ken-ai-te pulled his wife close to him once more and began, "Prayer Woman—" but she abruptly interrupted him by putting her fingers up to his lips.

"No, my name now is Amanda once again, remember?"

"Always Prayer Woman to me," and he smiled bravely at his wife. She wished she felt as confident as he appeared to be. "God say we stand before fear together, not as bad as alone. You facing much ahead but I pray for you at home. Do not forget that. Hold it in your heart no matter what. Prayer Angel will be close by, too, whenever God sends love and peace. And with boys and with me, too." He stopped and reached inside his shirt and drew out a small folded paper. "This message for you when you get on train tomorrow. Jacob help me write it from Bible, but also from my heart." She took it from him and tucked it in her handbag, eager to see what he wrote but content to wait as he asked. "Now, go in His Name."

Then he placed one hand on her shoulder and raised the other above his head, lifting his face to the sky, and prayed in Kiowa. He asked for protection over his family and the mission that took them far away and praised God for His promise of watch-care over them, no matter what lay ahead.

Mandy's heart overflowed. *Father, thank You for this moment. I know I shall remember it always.*

When he finished, the finality of it all hit Mandy and by the time the warrior had kissed his wife, her tears were flowing. She knew he would not be happy with her behavior but she couldn't help it. Grateful he had adopted long ago at her request the white man's way of greeting between husband and wife with a kiss, she took great pleasure from knowing that each time he seemed to relish it more! Today was extra special, however, and she clung to him even tighter which did not help her hold back the emotion.

"Take care of your mother, Lily," Jacob said to his beloved Goddaughter. "You know she needs looking after!" Lily giggled as he grinned and ruffled the top of her head.

They mounted up and Jacob led the way. But to what? That thought terrified Mandy and she fought back the panic once again. With God's help she managed to ride away with her back straight, head held high with pride as she had been taught, without looking back. But inside? That was a different story. Her stomach threatened to upend itself and she fought back the bitter taste in her mouth without flinching outwardly, taking big gulps of air to keep her head from spinning.

This really is happening, God! Go before me and be my guide, as well as my rear guard against all dangers. As Ken-ai-te has asked, now help me to be wise and to listen for Your voice above all others. Take care of my husband and boys while we are gone and thank You again for allowing Jacob to help us as he has done. None of this would be possible without him. Protect them both from all harm on the return journey. Please let the time go quickly so we can get back home in time to save our people!

In spite of the peace she felt from talking with her heavenly Father, she fidgeted on the horse's back, her muscles tensing up, as they rode down into the settlement. Far larger than their little place around Jacob's Trading Post, the noise and confusion unnerved her. Lily seemed to be taking it all in with a big grin on her face, but Mandy tried not to look around too much as they rode down the dirt road between buildings. She was grateful they had not had to do this by themselves, as she would have been unable to cope with all of it, for sure. As it was, only prayer held her together. What about the next several days? A tall order, even for God, given their circumstances. Yet, she knew He was capable. Would she be able to follow Him in obedience and be like Peter walking on the water toward his Savior, not looking at the fierce waves on either side but gazing only on His face? She felt the eyes of her beloved on her back the whole way down to the main road into town and it comforted her a bit. *God, don't let me be afraid! Help me!*

They turned the corner around some buildings. A quick glance over her shoulder confirmed that the stand of trees on top of the hill they had just left was out of sight. Never had Mandy felt so alone! Well, at least not for many years. A small sign swung gently in the breeze in the front of the place Jacob seemed to be headed for, a lovely frame house painted a soft blue with white shutters and a broad front porch. The sign read simply Ma Wolf's Hotel for Ladies. Mandy's stomach lurched again and she fought for control.

Moments later, Jacob rapped on the door of the hotel as the three of them waited on the porch, filled with large white rocking chairs. It had been a long time since Mandy had seen those and with a start realized she had forgotten what they looked like. Apparently, boarders often sat out here to rock away while observing the lovely gardens in front as well as the activity in the street beyond the gate. Mandy thanked the Lord they would only be here overnight, then it was off on their great adventure by train.

A creaking door shook her out of her thoughts.

"Hello, Ma Wolf. It's me again, Jacob Murphy. I brought my friends Mrs. Amanda Alton and her daughter Lily."

"Welcome, Mr. Murphy! I am delighted to meet both of you, Mrs. Alton. Come in, won't you?"

They walked into the parlor just inside the front door and Mandy instantly felt at home here. Yes, this would do nicely for their first night in "civilization" until the train departed the next morning.

"Mr. Murphy, you failed to tell me how lovely Miss Alton is!"

Lily blushed, lowering her eyes to the ground. *I need to remind her to look people in the eye here and say thanks, otherwise it appears she is hiding something. For a Kiowa lowering the eyes is acceptable and preferred for a young maiden of course, but not in the white world.* They weren't even on their own yet and already Mandy could see how difficult this crazy idea might prove to be for both of them.

The woman's greeting had been cheery but Mandy wondered if she would be this quick to accept them if she knew the truth of their heritage. She tried to put that dark thought aside and focus on what her landlady was saying.

Ma Wolf began rattling off her rules of the house, including that no gentlemen callers were permitted after 5:00 PM. *Odd how long it has been since I have heard anyone refer to time in that manner. I had almost forgotten.* She thought about the watch in her handbag and was grateful Jacob had insisted she take it along. It represented another step of the transition back to a white society obsessed with time, far away from the Kiowa who marked it only by the position of the sun or phase of the moon.

"No problem, Mrs. Wolf," said Mandy. "We don't know anyone in town and won't be here long enough to meet anyone. As Mr. Murphy told you, we simply need the room for a night. Where is the Railroad Depot located?"

"About three blocks south of us here. I see you have very light luggage so the walk won't be too difficult. I serve breakfast at 6:00 AM. What time does your train leave in the morning?"

"At 7:30, I believe, which means that will work out fine. And yes, we only have these two valises with us, as our trip won't be an extensive one."

"Mr. Murphy said you all will need to stay here again on your return journey, until he can come to fetch you home. Is that right?" She looked to Jacob for confirmation.

"Yes, that is right," he replied. "It should be next week sometime, if all goes well. Mrs. Alton will need to send a message through the commander of the fort, since we have no mail service out in our part of the territory yet. It should only take us a couple of days to get here."

"Us?"

"Oh, I meant me," said Jacob. "I will come as soon as I get word that they have arrived, so if they could stay until I get in town that would be most helpful." He deliberately avoided glancing over at Mandy after this obvious mistake. And prayed Mrs. Wolf didn't question it further.

"Certainly. I will look forward to having the two of you back with us as guests soon. Seems to me like an awfully long journey for such a short time. Of course, that is none of my business, is it? What is my business, however, is to see that you are cared for while under my roof, and that I can do. If you follow the rules, we should get along famously! Shall we take leave of the gentleman now and I will show you upstairs to your room?"

The farewells to Jacob were short and he walked out the door. They were truly on their own now!

"This is your room, Mrs. Alton," she said as she unlocked the door and handed Mandy the key. "I'm sorry it's not bigger but it's all I had this evening with two beds. I do hope it will be comfortable for you both."

"No problem, Mrs. Wolf. Better than we had on the trail the last two days!"

Suddenly every muscle in Mandy's body ached to get into bed. How could she be so tired, and without warning like this? Perhaps the let-down of bidding farewell to her beloved, plus the anxiety about the next few days, had overwhelmed her at last. Would her body take to the soft bed after many long years of sleeping on the buffalo rug in their tipi? She hoped so!

"Please, call me Ma, like everyone else does. I will leave you to get freshened up before dinner. There are two other ladies staying with us at the moment, one is our teacher in town and the other is a young widow. She may be leaving on the same train as you two in the morning, am not sure yet. But she is going somewhere back East now that her husband passed. We eat dinner at 7:00 PM sharp. Any questions?"

After a few more directions they would need to know about staying overnight and the door had been closed firmly behind their landlady, Lily squealed in delight.

"I love it here! Look at these! They are beds, right? You told me about them but I had no idea they would be this soft!" And she bounced up and down on each of the beds several times, giggling with glee.

"Yes, my dear, I had forgotten about that myself! They do look quite comfortable, don't they?"

With a start, Mandy realized how much she had missed hearing her daughter laugh. There had been precious little to be joyous about lately, since the starvation began in earnest and all the hard times that came with that. A heaviness of heart had hung over all of the village and pressed in on everyone there, day and night, even on the children, robbing them of so much. She shuddered, praying those days would soon be behind them permanently.

Please, God, let that be true! I cannot take much of this loneliness I already feel for our way of life as well as dread for what is ahead of us in Trenton and how I will have to live during this venture. But equally as terrible is what our people are facing right now, tonight. Ease their pain and suffering, Father!

"Mama, I don't want to ever leave if this is what white civilization is like! Please tell me we can stay forever!"

CHAPTER FOUR

"The LORD is good, a stronghold in the day of trouble; and he knoweth them that trust in him." Nahum 1:7

April 14, 1867
Fort Smith, Arkansas

As tired as I am," Lily giggled, "I believe I could easily sleep in this for two days!" She plopped down on the bed nearest the small window overlooking the back garden, though she didn't stay there for long.

Mandy wearily headed for the washstand in one corner of the room, pouring water out of the pitcher into the large matching bowl with delicate pink roses painted all over it. Her heart ached over Lily's words about not wanting to go home. She had neatly sidestepped for the moment her statement but knew it would remain in her daughter's heart and it stabbed deep. It was all Mandy wanted at that moment, to go home!

"It will be good to be rid of some of the dust from the long journey," she managed to say, choking back her emotions. "Then we must rest until time to eat." Could she as easily wash away her loneliness and discomfort, as the dirt from the trail?

Lily flitted to and fro in the room, chattering nonstop about every little detail she encountered, from the soft green wallpaper to the lace curtains in the window to the charming pictures on the walls to the rose garden outside to the colorful quilts on the beds, fingering them carefully with great awe.

I hope she does not get too used to these luxuries. That will make going home to the camp very difficult. But that is what this trip is all about for her, seeing all these sights for the first time. Thank You, Lord, for Ken-ai-te's wisdom in insisting that I not make this journey on my own. May it help Lily accept her life as a Kiowa more and appreciate it all without any regret. And may the same be true for me!

Mandy collapsed on her own bed after a few minutes and snuggled down into its softness herself, relishing the feel of sheets on her skin, with the feather pillow under her head. Oh, how she had missed these little things!

"Mama, is that what this thing is used for, to cushion the head?" And she held hers up in front of her.

"Yes, it is. It's called a pillow."

"Such strange customs these white people have! But I sure do like this one!" More laughter exploded across the room as she tucked her own under her head and nestled down in it.

"Soft?" her mother asked with a broad smile.

"Yes! I already love sleeping in a bed, and with real sheets, too! You told me how they felt but I never believed they could feel this wonderful against my skin. How did you ever get used to being on the buffalo robe in our tipi, after growing up sleeping in a bed?"

Mandy chuckled. "It was hard at first, I have to admit. But when I fell in love with your father, I no longer cared where I lay my head, only that it be next to his. Even on hard ground, I will be thrilled to lie beside him for the rest of my life. I must admit that I had forgotten how luxurious all this is, though."

Mandy closed her eyes and basked in the warmth of her daughter's delighted squeals and soft giggles. How long had it been since she had heard that lovely sound? Far too long, sadly.

And the same for her sons as well. Heart heavy with this burden, she prayed for them to once again discover the joy of having laughter bubble up naturally from inside due to pure contentment. Was that too much of a gift to ask for? She hoped not, figuring Jesus Himself must have loved to laugh. *Hopefully soon, boys!*

A short time later the two dove into a table filled with all kinds of delicious foods, along with the other two boarders. Lily had the common sense not to ask what everything was, thank goodness, but Mandy also made an extra effort to graciously identify it all for her so she wouldn't be tempted to inquire about something as basic as mashed potatoes or fried chicken. Ma Wolf was an excellent cook! They chatted after the meal with the others for a bit but because they had to catch a train right after breakfast, they slipped out early to retire for the evening.

Back in their room, Mandy frowned upon noticing a decided difference from Lily's mood earlier.

"Do you feel all right, Lily? You seem quieter than usual since dinner. Did the food not agree with you?"

"Oh, I'm fine, and yes, the food was very tasty, even the things I've never had before. My first real meal in a white home! But the sorrow of all Mrs. Anderson has been through bothers me."

"Yes, it is such a sad tale, isn't it? Imagine how awful it must be, to lose your husband and your baby the same night, burned up in a fire like that."

"You said you and Papa lost a baby, too. I recall you telling me briefly long ago but don't remember many details, in fact, had forgotten about it until you brought it up to Mrs. Anderson."

"Yes, we did. You were only a year old when she was born, and because of how sad it was I really don't like to talk about her death. As Kiowa, we are forbidden of course to speak again by name of one who has gone to Heaven, unless that name is passed on. We probably would have given another daughter part of her name, but we only had the two boys. Therefore, we do not speak of her any longer. But God knew her and our Father Creator never forgets a precious life, no matter how tiny she was. Quite frankly, the hole in my heart will never be filled up again, nor in your father's."

After several moments, Lily added softly, "And I will never forget my sister, either. Even though I have no memories of her, the fact that she lived is what I will choose to remember. Is that why you and Papa did not have another baby for a few years? Because of the hurt?"

"Yes, I had a difficult time but needed to care for you. Your father struggled with his love for God because of the daughter we lost. Almost three years went by before we wanted to have more children, then we had the boys one right after the other, as we had with you girls. I believe God taught me a depth of compassion for others through that sad time which I never would have experienced without walking that pathway. Your father learned to trust God like never before due to it. So now we can see God's purpose behind the loss, though at the time all we could think of was our empty arms. Our lives are so full of the three of you children today that it almost seems like the sorrow was that of a friend instead of my own heart. Until..."

Lily glanced up at her mother and held her breath. Mandy's eyes were closed, her face raised to the ceiling, a position that Lily knew well. This was a holy moment of prayer between her mother and the Lord. She would speak no words out loud to break the precious quiet in the small room, respecting her mother's need to commune with her Father.

Slipping under the covers, a sigh escaped from the lips of the young girl and she picked up the one book she had brought with her to continue reading for a while. It had been a gift from her parents for her twelfth birthday and a cherished one. In fact, she was on the third reading of it! There had been a few books over the years, yet never enough for her voracious appetite for reading. But she knew her parents scraped together the money from time to time to order her one through Jacob because she found so much pleasure in new ones. Lily never ceased to be deeply grateful for this privilege.

After a few minutes Mandy finished her prayer time and smiled at the sight of her daughter nestled down in the covers reading.

"You certainly have enjoyed that book, child."

Lily frowned and put it down.

"Yes, Mama, I have and I am very appreciative of this gift. But could you please stop calling me 'child'? I really am not, you know, at least by Kiowa standards. Many of my friends are already pledged to young braves in the village and are eagerly learning skills necessary to become a Kiowa wife and mother."

"You are right, I am sorry. Old habits die hard. Others have given their daughters in marriage when they are young, but your father and I promised ourselves we would wait until you were old enough to help choose with whom you would spend your life, instead of being forced to marry one you do not love. Marriage traditions for our people are quite different from the white ones and we both agree that a nice blend of the two cultures is best for you and the boys. That is why we wait. Now, tell me a little about this story."

"Just so you know that I really am quite grown up now. Thank you for allowing me a choice in my future husband. I am very blessed to have you and Papa as my parents. Please forgive me for being impolite but you brought me on this trip because you felt I was ready to embrace a part of our heritage that I've never known before. Therefore, it is important to me to do it right."

"You are correct, dear, and I apologize." She smiled at her daughter. "I'm waiting to hear about your book."

"I've read it through twice already but every time I read it, I find something new in it to treasure. That is what Papa told me one time about books, that they are priceless valuables and should be treated as such. This one is no exception. It is about a young woman who dreams of marrying a farmer but is terrified of Indian attacks and doesn't think she has the courage to do what God seems to have planned for her future. Farming is hard work she discovers, which is fine with her, but it is the danger of living out on the frontier that scares her."

"I see. You are right, the perils of living away from civilization when you are white can be overwhelming. But when isolated like that you have the opportunity to make friends with the various Indian tribes nearby and learn from them, and then they can learn from you as well. The very definition of neighbor, in fact. That is how I believe God wants us to live in this country."

"Is that why you and Papa have been so adamant about us learning to speak and read English as well as knowing Kiowa?"

"That is precisely why. As you grow up, you will need more and more to learn about the white man's ways and how to live peacefully in your heart with both cultures. Especially since they are part of your heritage. All blood is red, Lily, never forget that. But cultures and their traditions are strong which can make life pleasurable or miserable, depending on how you view them. Our prayer for you and your brothers is to learn to respect all men and embrace them as brothers through Christ. You don't have to approve of every attitude or behavior of course, but you do have to learn how to love them in the Lord."

"Mama, do you think that someday Indian Territory will be a part of the United States of America?"

"To be honest I do. However, it may be a long time coming yet. The eastern half seems far more settled than the more remote western area, where we live. I'm sure you noticed on our journey here that there was much devastation from the recent War Between The States throughout that part of the territory. No telling how long it will take to rebuild everything.

I was shocked to see how busy and crowded with people Fort Smith is. That is what scares me!"

"Yes, I understand. Why don't people like the Kiowa? They only defend their hunting grounds against those who would steal the buffalo and deer vital to their way of life. Wars are rare, right?"

"Well, we see few where we live, but in truth given the right circumstances even the Kiowa can be fierce warriors when they need to be. No group of people is free of sin, Lily. Jesus died for everyone, remember? That means we all sin and need His forgiveness and redemption. Some whites seem to think they are above that while the Indians are the evil ones. We know that is not true, but it can seem to be true at times."

"Your aunt felt that way, didn't she?"

"Yes, and with good reason. She witnessed the deaths of her parents and a younger sister at the hands of a band of ruthless Indians when she was only fourteen years old. She and my father barely escaped with their lives, leaving her alone in the wilderness to rear her brother all on her own. My father was too young to remember the attack itself but did well remember crying for his mother and having only his sister to comfort him. How on earth Aunt Ida managed to pull them both through that terrible time is beyond me. Neither one ever even told me where they lived then, since she never would talk about it in much detail. Her bitterness at anyone with red skin was legendary, however. I cannot blame her but certainly wish we weren't having to go to see her with this ridiculous lie shielding us from her wrath. The longer I think about it, the more uneasy I become."

"How did they end up in Trenton?"

"I truthfully don't know. I think a couple of years after the massacre she heard about the chance to own land in that area and took my father to go check it out. And they ended up settling there. Such courage! It wasn't much more than a frontier town itself when they first came but it grew larger rather quickly and soon, they had a bustling community around them. My aunt opened a general store at first, I think she said, and it made her a great deal of money. They worked long, hard hours to build it up, then she sold it for quite a handsome profit and bought another business. They continued to do that for several years, in fact. Each one made them more money until they had a tidy sum to take care of them for many years to come."

"How interesting. But how did they manage to do that if it was such a small place?"

"Many people were on their way west at that time and came through there so they never wanted for customers. She was a brilliant businesswoman long before women were supposed to do that. Having my father's help made a big impact on her success as it gave her a respectability she might not have had otherwise. But she made it in spite of the odds, and because of having to work exceptionally hard and still care for my father, she never married. After some time, she ended up building a nice house on the outskirts of town and decided to stay home to care for her brother rather than working such long hours in a store. There was a large amount of land around it as well and when I was growing up, she had a gardener who took care of it so I wasn't allowed to play out there very much. I had lessons and plenty to learn inside. But I always longed to be free enough to roam around the place on my own."

"It sounds incredible, Mama. I envy you for those memories."

Mandy frowned at her daughter's words.

"Have you not been happy living as a Kiowa with our people?"

"Well, to tell the truth, not completely. I read in the books you buy me about a different way of life and have always dreamed of finding out about it for myself. Now, I'm getting to live my dream and I cannot tell you how exciting it is to me!"

"Just don't get carried away. Remember, we are only going to be gone for a few days and then we go back to live in the village with our family. Enjoy the visit but don't ever forget for a moment who you are: the daughter of a Kiowa chief. You have a purpose in life to fulfill and God will walk with you through it, but it is your responsibility to focus on that, not on wild dreams of another world."

Lily did not say much else for a while, kept her nose in the book, but Mandy knew her mood. She was not happy with this reminder. And it had not settled well with her own heart, truth be told. Her stomach clenched as she recalled the days of her childhood as well as the town where she grew up. Mandy had been happy and content as long as her father was close by, in spite of her aunt's strict and sometimes even harsh manner. Being a spinster meant she truly had no idea how to rear a young lady, but she certainly made a good effort at it.

Perhaps I should not have thought so badly of her after I left her home but focused instead on the blessings God gave me through her lessons and example. It really was a good life in most ways and many of my memories were quite sweet ones.

She winced, sighing as the conviction arose in her heart more with each passing moment.

Lord, forgive me and help Aunt Ida to have forgiven me after all these years, too. I'm thinking right now You are showing me that maybe I was a bit too harsh on my own daughter, so help me find kinder ways to speak to her. But I am afraid she will not want to go home! Take away this irrational fear, Lord, and help me get to know my daughter's dreams as well as her feelings about them while we are on this journey together. And help her learn to respect mine.

After a short time, Mandy told Lily they both needed to get to sleep because they had a long day ahead of them starting in a few short hours, and she extinguished the lamp on her bedside table.

With the room plummeted into darkness for a moment, Mandy was surprised at how bright the moonlight illumined the shadows around them as it streamed in through the window.

"Mama, can you tell me—"

"Sleep, Lily! I just said we must be up early in the morning in order to get to the train on time. We can talk later. Now, say your prayers and think of God's Word as you drift off. I love you very much."

"I know. That's what you tell me every night and I never fail to end my day that way. I love you, too." She heard her daughter yawn. Sleep tiptoed around them both as Mandy felt her body slowly relax.

Thank You, Father, for all the blessings that have come my way this day. My heart is empty without Ken-ai-te next to me, knowing he is riding hard in the night for home instead of enjoying a delicious meal and soft bed as I have tonight. Protect him and Jacob and help them get back safely. Go before us tomorrow every step. Give me wisdom to keep our secret and to get us to Trenton without any problems. Let Aunt Ida know I'm on my way and please care for her until I can see her again. Amen.

CHAPTER FIVE

"Thou art my hiding place; thou shalt preserve me from trouble; thou shalt compass me about with songs of deliverance."
Psalm 32:7

April 15, 1867
Fort Smith, Arkansas

"Mama, is this a train? It's enormous!"

Seized by a fresh wave of panic, Mandy could only nod. It had been years since she had seen one of these up close and had forgotten how massive the beasts were. Standing there on the platform, she wondered whatever possessed her to think they could possibly do this venture on their own. All she wanted to do was run away and hide somewhere. *God, help me!*

How many times had she prayed this same prayer in desperation? Yet she knew He heard her cries and would honor them with peace, if she would push away the fear to allow Him to do His part. No better time than right now to step forward in faith and let Him work.

"But Mama, how do they get across the prairie?"

"They move on iron rails called tracks. See them there on the ground, side by side? They keep the train moving straight, and of course that means it cannot go where there are no tracks. Before you ask, yes, this is what some Indians call an 'Iron Horse' and for good reason. But come, we must hurry before they leave without us!"

Taking a deep breath Mandy glanced around. Spotting a group of passengers boarding a short distance away, they headed that direction. Mandy carried both their valises while Lily eagerly clutched the small basket of food that Ma Wolf had given them as they left the hotel that morning.

She had explained to them there would be no food available for the most part while on the train, plus the stops were short and the food far too expensive at those stations to count on that for meals. Her hope, she said, was that this basket of goodies might come in handy for them—and then she firmly refused all payment for the gift. What a blessing her insight was! Without this food, they might have become quite hungry on their long journey. Once more, God's provision was nothing short of amazing.

With the aid of a man who called himself a train conductor, whatever that was, they soon were on board and he tossed the valises up to them, hopping up right behind as the train began moving with a lurch. This kindly man took their tickets and walked them to their seats, then pointed out the small washroom at one end of the car for their use when necessary. Lily mouthed the word to her mother, "Inside?" and Mandy almost laughed. Would wonders never cease?

As the two of them settled in, the car moved slowly out of Fort Smith, leaving all semblance of towns and homes behind them, gathering speed as it did so. Lily's eyes went wide and Mandy's weren't far behind! For a short time, Mandy was nervous about releasing the armrests. She clutched them with such a strong grip, she thought her fingers might shatter into tiny pieces. Little by little, however, she relaxed and felt more confident the car wouldn't crash any moment. Soon she was able to breathe deeply again and began to enjoy the sight of the receding buildings through the large window beside them. Finally, wide pasturelands and farms opened up on both sides as they clacked down the tracks, speeding away from civilization at the fort.

"When will we get to Trenton, Mama?"

"Not until sometime late tomorrow, ch—that is, *my dear.*" Lily's eyes twinkled with this sweet gesture from her mother and it warmed Mandy's heart. "That's after we change trains in St. Louis and again in Cincinnati. We have to pray we will not miss those connections, or our arrival will be further delayed. Trains don't wait on passengers!"

"You mean we have to spend the night on the train? Where do we sleep?"

She laughed again. That same question was one the station master had patiently outlined for her as he helped her with the tickets earlier. They both had much to learn!

"There are no beds so we will sleep in our seats. With our cloaks to cover us we should be comfortable and with our goodies to eat, the trip should be pleasant enough. I have never ridden a train before, so this is as much of an adventure for me as it is for you!"

"If the train goes through Trenton, why is it you never got to ride on one growing up?"

"They didn't come to our little town until I was almost grown, but in any case, we didn't have money for it. As a rule we used a horse and buggy for our transportation. Trains were for long-distance trips. When Papa and I left for Indian Territory, he wanted to save our money as much as possible to rebuild the mission, so we rode by covered wagon to get there. That was quite an adventure as well, and I think I already prefer riding by train than in one of those. They bumped with every rock in our path and we had to walk a great deal of the way, to take the load off the horse team pulling the wagon. It took many long days, while this will only take two days by locomotive."

She stopped and swallowed against the lump about to choke her. Clearing her throat and forcing herself to smile past the pain of the mention of her dear father, she continued.

"Why don't we watch outside while we are here, and see what beautiful things God has made for us to observe that we cannot see back home?"

Her emotions threatened to overwhelm her all of a sudden, and she needed the distraction to stop remembering, for the moment. Long ago she left the memories behind in order to hang onto her sanity in those dark days after her capture. Going "home" would force them to the forefront now. Was she ready for that? How many times in these past couple of days had she asked herself that very question, with the answer still eluding her?

Palms moist with anxiety and with a knot deep in her stomach, she pretended to see all the beauty outside that Lily was discovering, in the hopes her daughter would not sense the turmoil in her mother's heart. *What was I thinking when I agreed to this crazy plan? God, You have no idea what I'm walking into here and*—she stopped abruptly in mid-thought. Of course He knew!

It was Mandy herself who faced the unknown, not her Heavenly Father. She struggled to regain a measure of confidence that whatever lay ahead, He already knew about it, had a plan for it, and had given her all she needed to walk through it with His victory. How she needed His help! A Bible verse came to mind at that moment, one she had memorized long ago—Psalm 32:8. Why was she only now remembering it regarding this journey? Whatever the reason, its words calmed her spirit. "I will instruct thee and teach thee in the way which thou shalt go: I will guide thee with mine eye." He had already done this for her so far, and she knew He would continue to answer her pleas for direction. *Thank You, Father, for these words of encouragement from Your heart to mine.*

The remembrance of the folded paper Ken-ai-te had handed her right before they bid farewell came rushing in. *He said I was to read it once I was on the train!* She pulled it out of the spot where she had been carrying it, opening it carefully. It was a Bible verse which he had printed out carefully in his own handwriting. How difficult that must have been for him! Because the Kiowa do not have a written language, he had not learned how to write the alphabet until Mandy entered his life. *Thank you, Jacob, for helping my beloved to set these words to paper. I shall cherish them forever!*

It was Psalm 61:1: "The Spirit of the Lord GOD is upon me; because the LORD hath anointed me to preach good tidings unto the meek; he hath sent me to bind up the brokenhearted, to proclaim liberty to the captives, and the opening of the prison to them that are bound."

Powerful words for the journey Mandy was undertaking right now! *I wonder who will need to hear the good tidings? And who will be brokenhearted? And whom might I meet who will be in need of liberty because of being held captive for one reason or another? And where will I encounter a prison that needs to be opened for those who are bound?* She stared at the words. Although they were familiar to her, she had never memorized them. Now, she worked hard on that. *I would like to hide these words in my heart, Lord, that they can be used by you in the days to come to bring You honor! My husband felt they were given to him for a blessing and I quite agree. Bring them to full fruit and help me remember them well.*

As she committed the words to memory silently, she also nodded from time to time in response to Lily's excitement over the gorgeous scenery whizzing by. What a joy to watch her taking it all in, not missing a single thing! Mandy's confidence grew with each phrase she repeated, that God had a purpose for calling her to Ohio. Discovering that filled her with a sense of anticipation at first, then slowly more of a sense of apprehension, and eventually her eyes blurred, her focus jerked off the Scripture passage. Tiny thoughts nipped at her heels as a wild dog might do in trying to sink his teeth into her flesh.

What if I actually like being there more than living on the prairie? What if I truly don't want to go home? What if I am reluctant to once again give up civilization for the wild frontier of Indian Territory?

No answers jumped forward. But one thing became crystal clear as she finally shoved all these what-ifs into that dark box where they belonged, alongside the errant thoughts of abandonment and despair that had lain dormant there all these years. She loved Ken-ai-te with her whole being, knew she was in the center of God's Will for her future as his wife, and felt accepted for herself by the Kiowa people. That is something she knew would never happen with white society once everyone knew she had been living with Indians for more than fourteen years.

They treat it like a foul word—Indians—and would sooner scrub mud off their shoes than look me in the eye! At least that is what Jesse told me happened as a rule to those who fell prey to capture by them and later tried to return home.

She had not given him a thought in many long years but now, her curiosity aroused, she pondered for a moment what might have happened to him after Pete was killed and she was taken. Even though he had been the other foreman at the mission, he never came looking for her. This had hurt deeply for a long time back then. Today, it no longer seemed to matter. But his words of warning had made the conflict a difficult one to overcome every time she considered running away. But to where? Mandy shuddered with the bitter memory that had frequently torn her apart in those early days of her captivity. Only God could have resolved all that pain!

No, the best place for me is and always will be with the people for whom God created me, so I can share His love with them and watch lives transformed for eternity. From now until forever.

Peace once again settled around her as did a warm buffalo robe on a cold winter night. Comforting, protecting, encouraging, and filling her with thanksgiving for His provision. Nothing could ever be better than that. Except maybe being in her husband's arms! She glanced down at the verse and surprised herself at how much of it she had already learned. *Thank you, Ken-ai-te! I love you so much! And thank You, God, for how Your Word always meets my every need. Always.*

"Mama," Lily's words interrupted Mandy's thoughts, "I feel in a way as I do when riding on my paint across the prairie, where I can see from one end of the, um, horizon to the other. The only thing missing is having the wind in my hair!"

"With the windows open, you can do that even, at least a little, as the breezes come through the car. I agree, it does feel a little like that." Unfortunately, with the fresh air came also the ash and soot from the engine's smoke, blowing in through the windows, quickly coating everything and everyone. The dust blew in as well, choking out attempts at conversation for the most part, unless one enjoyed getting a mouthful of dirt! The pair settled in for the long ride and eventually stopped trying to carry on a conversation except when necessary. It was not worth the effort or discomfort.

Moving about the car was difficult at best, so for the most part the two of them remained seated the majority of the time, only standing to stretch muscles from time to time or when using the washroom briefly. Because the car was pretty full, walking could not be accomplished easily without bumping into others, and the jostling of the train's movement also complicated things. It would be a boring trip, apparently, but at least they would get there far faster than on horseback.

Mandy glanced around the car at her fellow travelers. She spotted a couple of families, quite a few rough appearing characters in cowboy boots and hats whose stares she tried to avoid, along with several men who might be termed as gentlemen by white standards. They were dressed up more than the cow hands, as though they had somewhere important to be. Sitting across from the two of them was a lone cowboy who appeared to be asleep, she observed with some relief.

One lady sitting by herself across the aisle had two small children to keep corralled as well as a babe in arms. She struggled to keep them occupied and in their seats, as well as reasonably quiet. But the noise levels around them were loud enough that she need not have worried about their squeals, chatter, and occasional cries for attention. From the chugging of the engine and the clack of the wheels on the tracks, little about this trip could be described as quiet! In fact, it amazed her the man by them could manage to sleep with all the din on every side.

A short time later Lily whispered to her mother, asking permission to help the lady with the three young children, and her mother of course granted the request. When the young mother eagerly accepted the help, Lily moved across the aisle to sit with them and began playing a simple game with the two older children while the mother fed the baby. In no time she had them giggling at the stories she made up to keep them occupied. The mother glanced over at Mandy and mouthed the words *thank you* repeatedly. Perhaps this was one small way God could use Lily to share His love, and the emotion swelled in Mandy's heart at her daughter's unselfish act of kindness.

She noted how tender Lily's touch was with the children. The pride of seeing her daughter's joy with those little ones reminded her how much the Lord loved her as well. Mandy thanked Him that her child was discovering a servant heart toward others through such a simple act.

When the children began yawning, Lily helped their mother get them settled down for a nap. Upon retaking her seat next to Mandy once more, she picked up her book again as though she had just laid it down.

She really is growing up, Lord. Thank You for helping her to mature in her love for You most of all.

After some time, the train stopped at an isolated depot without a town close by, and the only passengers who boarded were a small group of about ten US Army soldiers. Tension threatened to rise up again in Mandy's heart at the sight of them as they managed to squeeze into their seats at the back of the car, rifles slung over their shoulders. She was grateful they didn't know the true identity of two of the passengers. Merely having them that close made her nervous for some other reason. But why?

Mandy's mind raced backward in time, searching for an answer as the train began once more chugging on down the tracks. *If only they did not have those weapons, I could relax and enjoy this trip much better!* Her heart raced and she felt beads of perspiration on her upper lip. What was the matter with her? She fought the rising panic, but it wasn't working.

God, why did they have to board this particular train, and why now? Can You please get them off at the next stop? Please, I beg You!

CHAPTER SIX

"And thou shalt be secure, because there is hope; yea, thou shalt dig about thee, and thou shalt take thy rest in safety." Job 11:18

April 15, 1867
Somewhere On The Prairie

*P**lease don't let my emotions destroy my calling to be on this trip!*
    Why would soldiers make her feel this way? Then a painful flashback reached out from long ago to help explain her reaction. A similar group to these men at the far end of the railroad car had come to the mission to return Josiah's body to her after he was killed by renegade Indians shortly before she was captured. Tears stung the back of her eyes and she blinked hard to keep them from forming. How could she possibly have forgotten that, one of her most traumatic moments up to that day?
    Remembering…the sense of abandonment she felt that morning. Knowing her Papa would never again smile at her or hug her or laugh with her. And confusion. What was she to do now that their dream to share Christ with the Kiowa could no longer be realized? Why would God have allowed this horrible, senseless tragedy to occur? Josiah had ridden out the day before to take a Bible to a new Believer in one of the camps not far away and when he didn't return by dark, she had an uneasy feeling something was drastically wrong. Still, she had clung to her hopes that God would protect him and take care of them both out there on the frontier. After all, they were in that place on God's commission; therefore, surely nothing dangerous could happen to them, right?
    The harsh reality had been harder to bear than she imagined, but rather quickly God reaffirmed to her that His calling on her life to this place had not changed. Convincing the others who helped them with the work to keep the mission open was another matter, namely Jesse and Pete of course. *Oh, Papa! I miss you still. Constantly I long to see your handsome face again. The reunion with you and Mama someday in Heaven will be twice as sweet. I can't wait!*

Even after having reviewed that scene in her past, Mandy was still quite unsettled upon considering the presence of the soldiers on the train. Was there more to this bitter memory that she had stashed away and now failed to recall? Her heart raced for a few minutes. Would it ever return to a more normal rhythm?

What a childish reaction this is! Lord, I call on You to either help me recall the root of this so we can talk about it, or to help me bury it permanently and stop fretting over it. Today, these men seem to be friendly, in no way a threat. I simply must release this feeling, once and for all.

Mandy's mind scrambled for something better to say by way of casual conversation that wouldn't imply any relation to her real thoughts, and she cleared her throat.

"I wonder when the next stop is coming up. As far as we can see in any direction, no buildings or towns or even farms are in sight. This is truly a desolate part of our journey."

"I know what you mean, Mama, but I think the flat part of the prairie is rather pretty. However, I would hate to live out here away from other people."

Without warning, something jolted through her as if she had been struck by lightning and she swallowed hard. Another difficult memory caused her to shiver.

When she and Ken-ai-te had been planning their wedding ceremony at the start of their new life together years ago, word came that soldiers were searching for any white captives of the various tribes in the territory. She had panicked at the thought of now being separated from the people she had grown to love—and the man with whom she wanted to spend the rest of her life. For two terrible days, she cried out to God to wake her up from the nightmare. If the Lord had heard her pleas all those months for rescue, as He surely had, why wait until *now* to answer them? Now, when she no longer wished to be rescued!

Ken-ai-te had been ready to fight to the death to keep her, even suggesting they flee deeper into the wilderness where they could never be found by any whites, soldiers or not. Mandy had been devastated at the thought that her honor might mean others would die, and she told him she would rather go back with them than place her beloved in danger. It was truly an untenable situation with no easy answers. The bitter taste in her mouth choked her again right now from the vivid memory.

God had a better plan, though. Using her adopted mother Sleeping Bird, He presented it to Mandy at precisely the right moment. Soon Mandy was reading her father's words in his own handwriting, explaining the secret he had carried to his grave that would release her from the bondage of her present sorrow. Without that journal, Mandy would never have known the anguish her father had suffered her entire life as he wrestled with how and when to tell his daughter the truth of her heritage. And she would never have known that now she was free to choose for herself the culture with whom she would live the rest of her days. No clearer answer could ever be heard from Heaven than this one!

With no hesitation whatsoever, Mandy chose the Kiowa people, also of course choosing to remain as Ken-ai-te's wife, a decision she had never regretted for one single moment. As the soldiers came through their village a few days later, she stood proudly next to her chosen husband while the chief explained there were only Kiowa in their camp. And that was the truth!

Those soldiers could have ripped me from the arms of my husband and forced me to return to a white culture that didn't want me, would never accept me, and would not respect the circumstances of how I came to be with the Kiowa. Yes, Lord, that is the reason for my anxiety regarding those in US Army uniforms! They have never meant good news or protection or safety to me. Maybe today You can finally change that into an appreciation for them. Or at least a tolerance of their presence.

"I'm hungry, Mama." Her daughter's practical statement interrupted her thoughts once again, but in truth she was grateful to be pulled back from the moments of recollection that put that knot in her stomach. The mixture of sadness and joy would be difficult to explain to anyone else.

Lily continued, "I didn't think this morning after our delicious breakfast, I think they called it, that I would ever say those words again! But it's true. Will we have a meal stop soon?"

"Don't you recall what Ma Wolf said when she handed us the basket stuffed with all kinds of snacks that she prepared for us?"

"Yes, she did say the railroad food was undependable and expensive, didn't she, and not of the best quality, provided you could even buy any of it along the way. I thought perhaps she exaggerated a bit. But we have been riding for several hours now, the sun is high overhead, yet not one food stop so far."

"And none in sight, either. I think it's time we checked out this feast here and not be concerned with waiting until the train stops long enough to buy something to eat. It's not like we can leave the car whenever we are hungry to purchase food in between towns. I agree with you, I'm getting empty myself."

They decided to only nibble for the mid-day meal and save as much of the rest as possible for later. Having the blessing of that large morning meal would definitely tide them over with only a light luncheon now. Who knew when they would have the opportunity to eat like that again? Near starvation on the prairie for the past several moons had taught both of them to appreciate the food they had and trust God to provide where the next meal would come from. Both had learned they could survive even if their stomachs rumbled with hunger from time to time. This was no different simply because they were in a railroad car instead of in a tipi.

Mandy prayed a quiet grace over the cheese and crackers they picked out, along with a couple of pieces of fruit tucked in alongside them, and they proceeded to eat. Out of the corner of her eye, she saw the young cowboy sitting opposite them had awakened and now stared at her with an odd expression on his face. Being under this much scrutiny with no choice but to endure it made Mandy quite uncomfortable. She smiled at the man and he nodded. Her heart skipped a beat but not out of delight by any means. How she wished fervently he would turn his attention elsewhere. Uh-oh, too late to hope for that.

"You really believe in all that *God stuff,* Missy?" he fairly shouted to be heard above the noise around them and stared right at her.

"Yes, sir, I do. Don't you?"

"Nah, religion is for kids and old ladies. Not for men."

"My husband is very strong in his faith. In fact, most of the men I know are. They find it helps them get through the tough times to pray and listen to God's voice guiding them."

"Huh, thought only preacher-men would do that. Where do you live?"

"Way out on the prairie in Indian Territory, in the far western part. There are no real towns anywhere around us but we are about a day's ride from Ft. Granger if that helps."

"Never heard of that place, sorry. So, how does God help your man?"

Mandy breathed a quick prayer for guidance as to what she should say, her mouth suddenly dry as a swirl of dust blew past her face. This always happened when she spoke of the Lord's goodness but she had learned to not let it stop her. Even when she had swallowed a mouthful of dirt! She also needed discernment for how to answer without giving away their secret.

"Well, he is a leader among those we live around and they look to him for guidance and advice in providing for their families, with food and shelter, for instance. Food has become quite scarce in the territory with the buffalo disappearing from the prairie. Therefore, the men spend their time constantly hunting antelope, deer, and other wild game for us to have enough to eat. Not like we can get it from a store, you know!"

"Yeah, rough country out there. I served in a regiment during the war that at one point had to go into the territory to chase some Rebs out of the area. We were there long enough to encounter quite a few of the natives in a couple of skirmishes, too, and for me to discover I really hated the flat prairie. I've been in Ft. Smith since then and when I was discharged a couple of days ago, I decided I'd head back home to civilization in St. Louis, where things aren't so hard."

"I see. I hope you find what you are looking for, Mr.—"

"Oh, sorry, I didn't give you my name, ma'am. I'm Bart Conrad, at your service."

"Nice to officially meet you, Mr. Conrad. My name is Mrs. Alton and this is my daughter Lily."

"Where are you folks headed?"

"We are going to see my aunt in a little town right outside Cincinnati, Ohio. She has been ill and asked us to come so we are on our way there. It's a long journey from home."

"Yes, I would say it is. Bet that man of yours was none too happy to see you leave him behind. Why didn't he come with you?"

"We have two young sons at home and he needed to stay there with them. The trip would have been far too hard on them, I'm afraid."

She stopped a moment, uncomfortable with continuing to give this stranger any more specifics regarding their life back in Indian Territory. Best to switch topics rather than possibly add to the lies.

"I do hope, Mr. Conrad, that you will seek God's guidance as you make this new life of yours. I know He would love to give it to you if you will ask Him."

He gave her another odd look and said, "I think what I will do is take a nap for a bit. That sun was mighty hot this morning and has me plumb wore out."

Mandy nodded in reply, curious why he needed to sleep when he had just awakened from a nap earlier. But she said nothing while the two of them finished up their meager meal, stashed the remaining snacks back in the basket, and pushed it under their seat out of the way.

"I think Mr. Conrad has the right idea, that a nap might be nice this afternoon in spite of the jostling of the car. Are you going to read for a while?"

Lily nodded and Mandy rolled her cloak up to use as a pillow and closed her eyes. She was grateful for the break in the conversation with Mr. Conrad, frankly. It took great effort to speak to anyone due to the noise levels. In addition, the thin layer of grime that had formed on everything in the car also plagued the tongue when one spoke, she had discovered. Plus, she was uncomfortable in giving personal details to strangers, in case she said something that betrayed the lie she and Lily were living now. *God, help me keep more to myself and not be rude about it. I need to be more private than I tend to be by nature.* She wondered if she was thinking like a Kiowa in that, or more as a white woman. *Lord, remind me I must discard the former for a time and cling to the latter as much as I can.* The rhythm of the train rolling over the tracks soon had lulled her to sleep.

No telling how long she had been resting when suddenly a commotion arose in the car. Excited voices cried out the same word over and over, one that immediately brought Mandy to full alert.

"Indians! *Indians!* Look, there they are, riding down the hill in the distance toward us!" Mandy stared in horror where everyone was pointing. They were right! A small band of warriors rode fast toward the train, their shrill war cries echoing on the empty prairie around them. Fear gripped her heart as she realized they were attacking!

She couldn't make out what tribe they might be from, but this far from Indian Territory she was fairly certain they were not Kiowa, much to her relief. Several children began wailing, recognizing the danger they were all in, and some of the women added their cries to the growing din.

Mandy's heart sank as a woman near her shrieked.

"We are all going to die!"

CHAPTER SEVEN

"So shall they fear the name of the LORD from the west, and his glory from the rising of the sun. When the enemy shall come in like a flood, the Spirit of the LORD shall lift up a standard against him."
Isaiah 59:19

April 15, 1867
Somewhere in Missouri

"Men, move to the windows, quickly! If you have a weapon get it out and make sure it can be seen by the savages."

One of the soldiers who appeared to be in charge barked out the order even as the speed of the train increased dramatically, lurching from side to side as it did so. He commanded two of the men to move forward to the car ahead of them to warn those passengers as well, while the others took up their stations at various windows closest to their attackers.

"Ladies, these men will help you take your children and move now to the inside seats, or better yet, crouch down out of sight on the floor in between the seats. They are probably looking for captives so the fewer women and children they see, the less likely they are going to be willing to challenge all these guns to get them."

"Yes sir, Captain," one of the men answered and moved to help the women to a place of safety, such as it was.

The women scurried to do as directed, huddling together on their knees mostly in the aisle, their children under them or using their cloaks to hide them. The whole sight struck Mandy as bizarre. It was obvious these brave frontier women had been through an attack from hostile Indians before—and probably more than one. Kiowa mothers shielded their children from danger in much the same way as the white ones were doing now. But many of the Kiowa women also fought alongside their husbands, sons, and fathers rather than trembling in fear and helplessness.

She instinctively reached to her waist to draw her knife out of its sheath, then recalled it had to be left at home. Therefore, completely at the mercy of the ability of the soldiers to repel the attackers, she prayed for each man that his bullets would find their marks and defend all of them from a deadly defeat.

"Save your ammunition, men," the Captain shouted, "as we have no extras, make every shot count!" The chilling words sank deep. She felt as the prey of an eagle must when the talons pin it to the earth, helpless and terrified. *Father, deliver us from this danger!*

As the war whoops grew louder and more fierce, they mixed with whimpers and crying from those crouched on the floor around Mandy, and she clapped her hands over her ears to shut it all out while clamping her eyes tightly. When she opened them a few seconds later, her daughter was staring at her with an odd expression on her face.

"Mama, are you scared?" Lily whispered.

Mandy nodded.

"Good, because I am scared, too, and I wasn't sure it was right for me to feel that way."

"Don't talk—pray!" she whispered back frantically. Lily nodded her head, closing her eyes and shrank even further toward the wooden floor she knelt on. Mandy's heart pounded in her ears. She gulped short, ragged breaths along with the sobs she fought to hold back. What would happen to them? But she saw her daughter's example and claimed it for her own.

Somehow, that simple act of faith on her daughter's behalf gave Mandy the courage she needed to reach out and grasp God's peace to throw around her shoulders and shake off the panic that threatened to engulf her. *Thank You, God, for letting my daughter lead me in faith. How I need her child-like trust at a time like this!*

Something else that helped her was watching first-hand the bravery of the men in the railroad car, especially the soldiers, who were risking their lives to protect women and children they didn't even know. These men, whom she had mistrusted so deeply only a short time ago and had begged God to get them off the train and away from her presence, now appeared more as protectors of them all, rather than ones bent on revenge against her personally. It was all quite confusing, to say the least. There was little time to consider this for long, but one thought came to the forefront: these men were acting very much like the Kiowa people do in a battle! *Thank You for blessing me with Your courage through them.* The expressions on their faces showed determination rather than panic and that fact alone calmed her further. Ken-ai-te would have no cause to be ashamed of her this day!

As the Indians got closer, shots rang out first from the other car and finally from their own. Mandy shielded her daughter as best she could with her own body, stretched out on the floor with several other women and a handful of children attempting to stay out of sight as long as possible. With every breath, she pleaded with her Heavenly Father for their deliverance from this potential catastrophe. Screams were on every side and she didn't dare raise her head up to see the battle raging around them. Mandy stared mindlessly at a dark stain on the floor of the car, at least until it dawned on her it was most likely blood. Closing her eyes, she could now literally smell the fear all around her, as years of experience with her people had taught her. Was most of it her own or only part of it? She continued to pray with all her heart to stay composed—at least on the outside. The more she spoke with her Savior, the less panic she felt inside. No matter what lay ahead, He was in control. *God protect us!*

A moment later she peeked one eye open, glimpsing out the closest window. In that instant she spotted three warriors as they came alongside the car. And gasped! They were wearing war paint and their quivers were full! The firing continued from the soldiers and civilians alike, then arrows began whizzing around them. One found its mark in a man right by Mandy and he collapsed almost at her feet. She immediately reached out to check the wound. Seeing it was not deep, and buried in his shoulder as it was, she also knew it would be fairly easy to remove without too much damage.

Her mind jerked back to the day her heart shattered with the death of her beloved friend and second mother Sleeping Bird. She had taken an arrow meant for her adopted daughter, but unfortunately that one went deep into the gut area. There would be no removing it. Mandy fought back tears as she recalled the pain-filled look in those blue eyes of hers that told her she knew full well the seriousness of her wound. But it was that horrible knowledge that brought the older woman finally to the point of reaching out for Jesus' love with her dying breaths. The bittersweet memory warmed Mandy's heart, knowing that someday she would see her beloved friend again, along with both her parents, all of whom awaited her arrival in Heaven. Would this be the day that might happen? She prayed not!

The man groaned and that shifted Mandy's thoughts back to the present. She wished she had some of her healing herbs to help him but of course they had been left behind in the village. Although she had a couple of things for small wounds and upset stomachs and so forth in her valise, there was nothing to aid in this situation. Besides, what would everyone think if she did try? There would be questions from all of them along with raised suspicions, especially given the attack still going on. This definitely was not the time to be facing that!

Instead, she grabbed her handkerchief and dabbed at the blood bubbling out around the arrow shaft to try to keep it contained a bit. Until that moment she had not seen the need for the small cloth that Jacob had insisted she carry with her, as all white women did. How grateful she was for his insight! Mandy had forgotten this tiny detail of a lady's outfit after all these years. Shaking off the brief memory, she lifted the man up to God's healing hand as she and Lily worked to hold him as still as possible between them there on the floor, against the jostling of the car as it raced down the tracks. Was their flight a futile attempt to outrun the attackers? Would there be enough bullets to stave them off? Or would any moment bring some of the warriors climbing through the open windows to kill them all? Mandy shuddered at the terrible thought. Death would be better than capture, of that she was certain. But one glance at her daughter's face reminded her of how hard she would fight, doing anything possible to keep them both alive, if it came to that. *Please be merciful, God!*

Minutes crept by in an agonizing wait for victory or defeat, but in reality the whole episode was probably over relatively quickly. Finally the Indians fell back further and further as their cries grew more faint. At long last someone called out.

"They are leaving! We have beaten them! Thank God, they didn't win!"

Cheers went up from all sides and the tension relaxed considerably. Sniffles could still be heard from some of the youngest children as their mothers brought comfort by reassuring them the "bad men" were gone. *Bad men? They are just Indians, not the bloodthirsty brutes you seem to think they are!* Mandy wanted to scream these words but swallowed them instead. They would not be welcome ones right now.

After a few more minutes, the Captain gave another command, one far better received than his earlier ones.

"Folks, they have given up and ridden off, all right. I guess we were too much for them. They likely have gone back to pick up their dead and slink on back to the hole they came out of. Everyone is now welcome to return to their original seats if you would like to. The danger is over. Thank you to all you fellows who helped us out. Don't think we could have repelled those redskins like we did without your help."

One of the soldiers came over to attend to the injured man, saying he was what passed for a doctor with their unit so Mandy willingly relinquished care over to him. He agreed with her assessment that it was not a serious wound but best to leave the arrow where it was for now to prevent further blood loss until they could get him to the next train station. The wounded man thanked her softly through clenched teeth due to the pain, and she smiled in reply. Mandy returned to her seat, along with her daughter, both heaving big sighs of relief, as did everyone else. Within moments, smiles filled every face in the car.

Gradually the level of chattering increased as everyone calmed down. However, the once peaceful country outside now seemed a little less serene somehow, with this graphic reminder of the dangers that lay hidden out there beyond the windows of the train car. Not to mention the fact they were nevertheless close enough to reach out and bring destruction in a heartbeat when least expected.

Mandy shivered but it wasn't solely because of that thought. Harsh remarks she was hearing from everybody around her caused her blood to chill and her stomach to lurch.

"We sure showed them, didn't we?"

"They won't be taking any white scalps today!"

"The only good Indian is a dead one, all right!"

"You bet! If I could get my hands around the throat of one of those thieving redmen, they wouldn't be able to kill any more of our decent hard-working people!"

"Our menfolk managed to kill most of them, while the rest of those cowards took off! They should have stopped the train and chased them down and shot them, too!"

"Yes! Wiping them from the face of the earth is the only way to deal with those demons from you-know-where who are bent on butchering innocent people like they do!"

"Why does the government even allow them to live? Why not kill all of them before they kill us?"

Glancing over at Lily, it was obvious she heard every word as well, because her cheeks flared a deep red even though she glared down at her book, holding it with white knuckles that betrayed her outwardly calm expression. Mandy's heart pinched with sadness to think that her daughter had to hear all these hateful words being said. Looking down at her own lap, she was shocked to see her fingers trembling, and she fought back her anger at the ignorance that triggered that fury. Knowing more of this lay ahead of them when they arrived in Trenton did not ease the pain now. There, it would be all around them. Most likely, she would be unable to protect Lily from the hurt coming. *God, forgive them and put Your arms around my baby! While You are at it, comfort my heart from all this wickedness.*

Finally, Mandy clapped her hands over her ears briefly to shut it all out. Her heart couldn't take listening to this any longer! One part of her almost wished the attackers had been successful, because of these mean-spirited words being shouted around her with such glee. *You wouldn't be laughing and rejoicing if they had! You would have been screaming for mercy by now.*

Reality, however, quickly overtook the ire she felt and she regretted her vicious thoughts. In truth, the two of them had been in as much danger as all the rest of the people on the train. If the raiding party had been successful, they would have shown two Kiowa women no more mercy than they would have for the whites, and perhaps even less. The irony of how close they had come to being killed here today, by Indians who mistook them for whites, was too overwhelming to consider right now.

Thank You, Lord, for preventing that disaster, for taking care of Lily and me in the midst of this horror. Please stop the cruel words tumbling out of these ignorant mouths. My heart cannot take much more of this!

Little by little the pounding in her chest returned to a more normal rhythm, to match the slower pace now of the train itself. But a knot formed in the pit of her stomach. Her palms became damp. Would the Indians return if they were still around? She hoped not and tried to breathe deeply to steady her shaking hands. Her trust was in her Heavenly Father, after all, not in the hands of the soldiers or other men who had defended them earlier.

How grateful she felt to those who had protected the strangers around them, showing remarkable courage as well as such kindness to the women and children on board. But she didn't want to confuse things and give credit for their ultimate deliverance from disaster to anyone but God Almighty! What a strange twist of fate God had permitted here. Mandy knew it would haunt her for some time.

Turning her attention back to the scenery out the windows, Mandy breathed deep of the fragrance of a strange yellow flower she had never seen before, growing alongside the tracks in endless fields stretching as far as the eye could see. Suddenly a conversation behind her caught her ear in spite of the chaos in the crowd, pulling her out of the beauty and back to the ugliness of reality.

"One of the soldiers said the Indians were probably after the cattle the train is carrying."

"Oh, I didn't know they had cattle on this train as well as people."

"Seems there is a cattle buyer on board—the gentleman in the back there—" and he gestured with his head in that direction, "who came to Fort Smith to purchase some cattle for his ranch. The Indians, he told me a few minutes ago, were probably runaways from a reservation somewhere in Indian Territory. Apparently, they are starving there so often slip away and steal whatever they can get their hands on to fill their bellies. Why can't they just buy food like everyone else? Why do they feel they have to murder and steal to get it?"

"I don't know. I agree with you. They have food on those Reservations, right? Why do they insist on invading our lands to steal it from decent folks?"

Mandy's anger rose once more with every word being uttered! Oh, how she wanted to stand up and shout to everyone on the train that they cannot help it if they are starving! It was the white men who stole land from them in the first place! That is what started all the years of wars and killing, including of the buffalo. Not the other way around. Her fury bubbled up and threatened to choke her. How dare they say those things against her people?

God, I cannot be silent! Yet, I know I must not say anything. Help me control my anger and forgive me for the hatred burning in my heart against this ignorance! And forgive these people who don't know what they are talking about. I'll bet they have never gone to bed with an empty stomach the way the Kiowa do every night right now. Or heard their children cry in the night for something to eat. Will there never be justice or peace for my people? Or enough food again? Do You hear our pleas, our death wails? Please, Father, do something to help us before it is too late!

CHAPTER EIGHT

"For we are his workmanship, created in Christ Jesus unto good works, which God hath before ordained that we should walk in them." Ephesians 2:10

April 15, 1867
Somewhere in Missouri

"Mama, what are those men talking about? What is a cattle buyer?"

Mandy's heart sank. She had hoped her daughter had not overheard those idle words that stabbed like daggers. Lily lived every day with starvation at the door of their tipi. How could her mother hope to soften this pain when she could do nothing for the other one?

"A cattle buyer is a man who travels around buying stock for a ranch, sometimes his own and sometimes one he works for. My Papa told me one time about how they do this but I'm afraid I didn't pay much attention, therefore know little about it beyond that."

Silence greeted her explanation. But the expression on Lily's face said it all. There was no way to completely cushion this blow she had suffered with simple information.

Softly she spoke so only Lily could hear. "I hoped you hadn't heard all that. We both know the truth, and that is what is important. You mustn't pay attention to what others say, when they have no idea what life is like where we live. Release the anger, the pain, the sadness to our God, is my advice. We cannot respond, no matter how much we wish to do so. The ones who are talking are ignorant but you are not. You live it every day. I'm proud of how you do this, by the way, with dignity and courage. We honor our God with our silence at this time."

Lily looked at her mother, nodded with a smile, and returned to her reading. Mandy sighed, grateful she could lose herself in a book instead of struggling inside the way her mother did. What a tough battle her young daughter was having to face! But Mandy meant every word she had said. *Now, if I can live it as well! Help me let it go, Father. I want to allow You the privilege of setting things straight at some point, and without my help!*

Mandy claimed one Scripture after another for a while, anything she could recall, that would help calm her heart, ease her anxiety, and keep her mind on God's words instead of someone else's. Interesting how they weren't even in Trenton yet, but she already found herself living life from both sides, as a white woman and as a Kiowa. Neither set of traditions was perfect; nor was either flawed to the point of breaking. The confusion made it hard to concentrate on gaining strength from the verses. *Perhaps if I read them instead of relying on my memory, they will come alive more.*

Mandy picked up her Bible, randomly searching through some of the well-worn pages, taking nourishment from the words, then moving on to the next passage. God spoke to her gently and with kindness, bringing comfort and encouragement to her heart. Not willing to let go of either part of her heritage, yet unable to fully resolve the two, Mandy with determination merely accepted the peace slowly filling her heart right now with deep gratitude. There would be a time someday to address all that. Today was not that day. He had met her need once again right now, as He had countless times before. And would on many more occasions in the future, she knew.

Taking a deep breath, she finally laid the precious book aside and decided to embrace the beauty of the scenery outside instead of focusing on such heavy topics. More of the yellow flowers whizzed by on both sides now, filling the car with their aroma. Along with the ever-present dust, of course! After a short time she felt her eyes growing heavy. *Perhaps I should rest for a bit now.*

As Mandy settled down with the cloak under her head, she caught the eye of Mr. Conrad across from her. Why did he keep staring at her like that? It made her uneasy and she clamped her eyes shut. Shivers rippled down her arms, slithering across her back.

Please let him stop this, Lord. I don't want to be rude but I really don't appreciate his attentions. Ken-ai-te, I need you so much! Why did I think I could manage even one day without you by my side? We are supposed to be taking a stand against evil on the prairie together for the rest of our lives, not separated by hundreds of miles!

She peeked through her eyelashes across the way and sure enough, he spotted her spying on him! And almost smiled. Almost. She popped her eyes open, returning his stare with what she hoped he would see as the irritation she felt. To her shock he asked an abrupt question.

"Where was your God, Mrs. Alton, when those Injuns attacked?"

Was his inquiry a genuine seeking, to gain comfort and understanding? Or a deliberate berating of her faith in His protection? She couldn't be sure but knew she must respond. Praying for wisdom, she took a deep breath.

"He was right there with us. Didn't you feel Him? I certainly did. He and I had quite a few words exchanged between us, believe me! Just because I wasn't crying out didn't mean I wasn't afraid, I must admit. But I also knew who was in charge which made it easier to endure. Maybe you didn't have time to pray while you were shooting but I certainly did where I crouched on the floor on top of my daughter during the attack. For one thing, I prayed for you and for all the other men who were protecting us so bravely."

Ignoring the compliment, he got right to the heart of what bothered him.

"Yet, He allowed the danger. I don't get it."

"Well, you recall at the Crucifixion His own Son was brutally killed for us on the Cross, right?"

Bart nodded but said nothing. Mandy's heart stood still. In an instant she knew he earnestly sought an answer as his eyes bored into hers, his expression a mixture of pain, defiance, and fear!

Father, give me the right words! I never expected to be sharing the Gospel with a white man on a train far away from the Kiowa people like this. Are You sure this is what I should be saying right now? He is white! I thought You called me to minister to the Kiowa. What are You doing here?

Peace settled over her in place of the turmoil of a moment before. Of course this was what she was to be doing! In the same way that Jesus had gone to the Temple as a young boy to be "about his father's business" so she should do the same, no matter where she was or what color the skin of the one needing Christ! Share, and let God do the rest regardless of the circumstances, she reminded herself gently. Another gulp of air to clear her head. With a quick prayer. Again. *This needs to be about You, Lord, not me!*

"God was in the same place today as He was on that day long ago. Watching over us all from Heaven and watching over His Son while He took His final breaths on earth. He was ready to receive Him once the sacrifice was complete. When Jesus said, 'It is finished' and took his final gasp of air, He gave up His life for us. It wasn't taken from Him against His will. He willingly gave it up for me—also for you. But, His Father was there watching every single second of that ordeal His Son endured for all of us. Today was no different. He knew the outcome ahead of time, and whether it ended in disaster or not, He still would have been there. He wasn't going anywhere, no matter what happened."

She waited breathlessly. And prayed for the young cowboy, that he would not reject the love that reached out to hold his heart in these moments. Would he accept it? Or reject it once again as he apparently had done before?

Mandy never took her eyes off his. Slowly a tear silently slipped out and slid down his cheek. *Mercy abounds! Mr. Conrad, please reach out to grasp it!* She had seen this many times in her years in ministry to her people. The heart has no color but darkness, until the Light of the World comes in to change everything!

He appeared to struggle for control over the emotions obviously welling up inside, and Mandy felt a nudge to speak up.

She leaned forward slightly. Gently she spoke so only the two in front of her could hear.

"He is here right now for you, if you desire to speak to Him. No fancy words are necessary, not even ones spoken out loud if you prefer not to. I can pray with you, or you can simply talk to Him yourself."

"You prayed for me? While I was killing men, or at least trying to? That is so hard to understand, a God who would listen while that was going on. And you, a stranger? Praying for me? You don't know me, have no idea what all I have done, lady. Yet you prayed for *me?*"

She nodded and remained silent but never broke eye contact with him. Even more softly he continued.

"Could you—would you do that, for me? Now? I'm astounded that even though you don't know me, yet you have said what I needed to hear this afternoon in a way I've never heard it explained before. I think I feel Him, as you said, that He is here in this train car. Do you think He really will listen to this ole sinner?"

"Of course He will listen, Mr. Conrad. He is always ready to hear words of confession and repentance. Always. Do you admit that you have sinned? We all have, you know. Even sins only He can know about. But His blood on the Cross covers them all, no matter how black the heart may be."

The cowboy nodded, his face a glum mask as he stared at the floor. Mandy saw his anguish in how he wrung his hands, though, and recognized the battle going on inside him. Oh, how he needed Jesus!

"Yes, I have sinned. Why I'm telling you this I don't understand. But it's true."

He took a deep breath, closed his eyes as another tear made its way down his face. Then Bart opened his eyes and glanced down at his rugged hands where they were now clasped tightly together in his lap as though they might fly away if he let go. He studied them as the silence dragged on. Mandy waited. Finally he broke the spell and cleared his throat, raised his head and stared intently at her eyes, perhaps searching for a hint of hypocrisy or ridicule. He would find none there!

"Do I have to, to say, in, in so many words what all I have done?" For a moment, Mandy thought Bart was about to break into sobs! This obviously pained him deeply, the remembrance of his transgressions, and the possibility he would need to bare his heart even more in front of this stranger and her daughter seemed to unnerve him. She asked for courage to bolster him in these critical moments.

"In your heart you need to before Him, but not out loud to me. It is none of my business and He already knows. You simply need to agree with Him on this, so He is freed to offer forgiveness as well as the opportunity for you to spend eternity with Him in Heaven. Is that what you want, to be with him from now until forever?"

He nodded, his eyes already closed. She waited a moment, glanced at her daughter, and caught her breath at the sight of tears glistening in those dark eyes. Lily smiled at her mother with pride mixed with joy. What a sacred moment this was for them to share!

"Please pray with me, will you?" the young man asked without opening his eyes. The hand-wringing continued, indicating the depths of turmoil he was feeling at this time.

Mandy took a deep breath, bowed her head, and led him in prayer. And right there on that train, in front of everyone, Mr. Bart Conrad gave his heart and life and future to Jesus!

When they finished, the cowboy had a broad grin on his previously tense face that radiated a peace not of this world—matched only by the expressions on Mandy and Lily!

"That was incredible! I had no idea I could feel this way! I believe what you said, that He freed me from my sins. I don't pretend to know why or how but in my heart I know it's true. Thank you for talking to me. Not many folks would bother to speak with a beat-up cowpoke like me, but it didn't seem to concern you one bit. Guess there was a reason for that Indian attack, after all, to get my heart in the right place."

"Yes," Mandy laughed. "For all of us, in fact. A little danger always reminds us of who is in charge, doesn't it? We are both very thrilled for you."

"You are? I mean, I feel I need to know so much more. How do I learn?"

"From the Bible." Mandy picked up her own from the spot she had laid it earlier while reading it and handed it to him.

"I saw you reading what looked like a Bible a while ago. My mother used to do that every morning, but I have never understood anything I have read in it. Nor what anyone has ever said about it, either. So, is this your magic key?"

"No magic involved. It is the presence of God in what He calls His Living Word. It is unlike any other book in the world. If you don't own one, you need to get one as soon as possible. I'm sure you can buy one in St. Louis or wherever it is you are going today."

Mandy's breath caught in her throat as he leafed through the book while she spoke. An expression of wonderment slowly spread across his entire face. She shivered slightly. People discovering the Word of God always affected her like this! And she continued.

"Read the book of John first. It was written for new Believers like yourself. This day you will remember for the rest of your life and even throughout eternity. Oh, and the angels are singing now, did you know that?"

"They are? Angels? Really? Because of *me?*" His jaw dropped in shock at the thought.

"Yes, God's Word tells us that when a new soul comes to Him, the angels rejoice in Heaven. Another thing, you need to spend time every single day in prayer, that is, talking to Him. Not *about* Him but *to* Him. From there you need to learn to listen to what He has to say to you. He will guide you in your decisions because His Holy Spirit now lives in you. In addition, as often as possible, it is important that you begin attending regular worship services, to learn more about Him and be with others who are searching for more of Him as you are."

"Well, my mother will be very happy to hear that at least. That's where I'm going, to see her after a long absence. I suspect she will be thrilled about all that's happened to me. She used to tell me when I was a boy that she prayed every single morning and night for me to know Him. I doubt that has changed any. It will be a pleasure to accompany her to church now. I used to dread it, every time I went home for a visit. She will never believe this! You think God really answers prayers like hers?"

"Of course He does! You are the proof of that. One last thing I want you to remember is that we will see each other in Heaven someday. That is His promise. Forever."

"What was that you said a moment ago, something about forever?"

She and Lily laughed out loud, and her daughter spoke up for the first time.

"Mama said *from now until forever*. It is something my father used to say to her before they married. We all use it a great deal now. It means for all eternity."

"Hmm, from now until forever. I like that. Sounds like your father is a wise man, all right."

"Oh, he is! And he loves God, as my mother explained earlier to you."

"He is a very lucky man, too, to have the two of you on his side."

"He is *blessed* to have God on his side, as you are now," said Mandy. "Our Heavenly Father created you and has loved you all your life. Everything He has done has been to bring you to this moment. Now you are united with Him through His love for you. From now until forever."

Bart shook his head repeatedly, smiling from ear to ear.

"You know, I kept eyeing you during the attack and I could tell you were upset but not as frantic as the other women were. There was just something, well, different, about you. And your face."

Mandy smiled. "What about my face?"

"It was completely serene, even in the midst of the danger we all faced. That is why I asked you where God was. You seemed to know, somehow.

All the rest of us were merely hoping He was around here somewhere. But you knew."

His words startled her for a moment. Not solely because he had been watching her in spite of the danger all around them, but because she had been in her own personal war with her feelings versus her faith throughout the attack. She had prayed for protection and survival but there was a far greater battle going on than she had realized. Now, she saw with spiritual understanding the truth, and it overwhelmed her momentarily. Suppose she had surrendered to her natural reactions? Yielded to her panic? But her complete trust in God's protection deep inside, forged through many trials during her life so far, had apparently overtaken her fear even without her recognition of what was happening, and confirmed by her daughter's own faith. At the least her facial expression had radiated the comfort being shared from God's heart to hers as she prayed. That one thing made all the difference for this one man. What a miracle! Yet, she knew the source of her confidence and it was not in her own strength. Never in her own, not for one moment.

"The presence of the Holy Spirit brings peace. That is why He is called the Prince of Peace, in fact. No matter what we are facing, we can know His peace, even when it makes no sense with what we are going through right at the moment. It is described in the Scriptures as a 'peace that passeth understanding' because it truly is. It cannot be explained in earthly terms. It takes experience with Him to learn to claim it in difficult times, but it can happen for you, too. I get my power to do this through prayer, talking with my Father. At times, such as during this recent chaos, I am every bit as afraid as the next person. But He holds me up through the storm. As I said, trying to put it into words is difficult but I hope you can understand at least part of what I am saying."

He continued to look squarely at her but said nothing. Would admitting her terror become a stumbling block to him? Oh, how she prayed not! Mandy felt so undeserving of the honor this man, a virtual stranger, had paid her by allowing her to introduce him to Jesus. She couldn't bear the thought he might see her as hypocritical in any way. The event they had just gone through together, however, followed by his acceptance of Christ, had knit a piece of God's hope into each heart with their deliverance from certain disaster and this young man's own eternal rescue. Could he see this, grasp its intricacies from the few words she had spoken? Or be pushed further away from the One who reached out right now with that peace?

Lord, thank You for keeping me faithful even in the midst of an Indian attack. You are my peace and I'm deeply grateful You are now Mr. Conrad's as well. Help him understand!

The radiant smile that came from him once more warmed her heart and gave her the answer she had hoped for.

"Oh, I understand all right. Now. And forever. Excuse me, *from now until forever!*"

CHAPTER NINE

"...I am the way, the truth, and the life: no man cometh unto the Father, but by me." John 14:6

April 15, 1867
St. Louis, Missouri

"St. Louis! Next stop St. Louis!" bellowed the Conductor as he moved down the aisle, coming to a stop next to Mandy.

"Mrs. Alton, the next stop is St. Louis, where you two will need to change trains. I will point out the right one when we get into the station. Should be another fifteen minutes, more or less, if you want to get freshened up a bit."

"Thank you very much, sir. We will do that."

They asked Mr. Conrad to keep an eye on their things and they made their way to the washroom. It only held one person at a time so Mandy waited while her daughter was in there, then she took a turn. At least her hair could be smoothed down with the dust brushed off her clothing. The cool water poured from the pitcher felt good on her parched, dry face. The wind and sand had left it feeling rough. This was far better than dirty!

Returning to their seats, Mandy stuck her hand out to shake with Mr. Conrad as they both bid him a fond farewell.

"Remember what I told you about getting a Bible and going to church," she said kindly. "It is imperative that you don't try to do this all on your own. Do not get distracted from this, and let Him lead every step you take. We will be praying for you!"

"Thank you, thank you both. I can never say thanks enough and I will pray for you, too. I have a feeling that my mother will be very happy to receive me now!"

And he tipped his hat to them. It had been a long time since Mandy had seen a polite gentleman do this and it stunned her for a moment, leaving her a bit breathless at the gesture. Maybe being back in civilization wouldn't be so bad, after all!

At the Train Station—for it was far larger than a mere Depot out in the middle of nowhere—Mandy was shocked how many trains were there at the same time. It was all quite confusing and she greatly appreciated the Conductor's kindness. He helped ensure that they reached the right train for the next part of their journey and reminded them to be sure they had all their belongings upon leaving the car.

Before long, they were on board, clacking down the tracks once more, this time headed for Ohio! Mandy's excitement mounted, mixed with apprehension.

What if Aunt Ida does not survive until I arrive? How will I know what to do?

After they settled in, Mandy's mind began wandering back to the letter from her aunt. Much of it seemed very unlike the woman who had reared her, whose speech had always been precise and no-nonsense. This was more like the ramblings of a complete stranger. Had she changed that much in fourteen years? Emotion had muddled many of the words until now, as Mandy began trying to sort it all out in her mind. She pulled out the letter to look it over once again and realized that several points simply didn't make sense.

For one thing, Ida urged her niece to seek counsel from a man named Matthew Grayson, the attorney who had drawn up her will, then changed it for his client upon receipt of Mandy's letter. Seems there were some papers she would need to sign with him to complete the legalities of inheriting the estate, so this appeared to be the first priority once she arrived. For Mandy, she wanted nothing more than to visit with her aunt and get caught up on the lost years since she left for Indian Territory. The idea of wasting precious time she may not have dealing with the lawyer instead upset her terribly. Yes, the money was why she came. It would feed her people for a long time. But it wasn't the only reason, not by far! The closer she got to home, the more eager she found herself to be there.

Wait! Had she just called it *home?* The thought struck deep. Yes, it would always be her home, the one where she grew up, the one where she was loved and nurtured by the two people who meant the most to her in the whole world. But God had led her far from Ohio and now she had a new home. One where she was completely content, to love the four people who now meant everything to her. Was that normal? Did all people feel that way—loving two or more "homes" at the same time? The houses themselves couldn't possibly be any different from each other, and in many ways the love within was as well. Yet, it had all originated in the heart of her Heavenly Father, planned from before the foundation of the world. *My goodness, I am certainly sounding rather philosophical this afternoon, aren't I, Lord? All I know or care about is that where You are, there is contentment, whether in a mansion in Trenton or in a tipi on the prairie—or on a railroad car in the middle of nowhere.* She glanced over at her daughter, happily absorbed in her book, and thanked God again and again for all her many blessings. Including those back "home" in that tipi.

Mandy reluctantly pulled her mind away from the territory and forced it once more on the letter from her aunt. Skimming through the words, she saw the next area of concern was in the form of a caution against trusting her cousin Alex.

Cousin? I have a cousin? How can that be? Aunt Ida never married yet he apparently is related to her, which makes absolutely no sense at all. If he is a relative, why warn me about him? It seems he ought to be the one fulfilling the role of my confidante and protector while I am visiting, but apparently not. Aunt Ida sounds almost fearful of him, but surely I read too much into her words. It's all so confusing!

Mandy would certainly be on her guard against this cousin but figured that since he lives there with her aunt, he cannot be too much of a threat. Nor could she avoid encountering him if she also were to live there, even for only a few days. She hoped he would at least be agreeable to working with her to get all the affairs straightened out quickly and not cause any trouble with the fact that he was being cut out of the will, with it all going to her. Would she be as amenable, were she in his place? The truth behind this question made her squirm a bit inside.

That was the next thing on her mental list of questions. Why leave it all to Mandy? Ida hadn't heard from her for more than fourteen years—then suddenly decides her vast estate would best be served if it went to her long-lost niece? *I am most grateful, Aunt Ida, believe me, but I really don't understand any of this. I can definitely see why Cousin Alex might be jealous or even angry. You certainly have put a great deal on my shoulders, all right. Glad God's shoulders are strong enough to carry the weight for me, as I am afraid mine are not!*

But, she wondered if this whole thing shouldn't be the other way around? To trust a relative but use caution with a stranger? Yet, in truth they both were strangers to her. If her aunt trusted this Mr. Grayson, she supposed she ought to as well. Cousin Alex was another thing altogether.

The third curiosity was the odd request by Ida that her niece stay at least one night in her old room in the house, in order to claim the inheritance. Mandy was grateful to have a safe place—at least she hoped it was—to stay while in town, and one that wouldn't cost any money. She would need to be quite frugal with her expenses for the next few days, in order to have enough funds to pay for their return tickets. This provision in the will had solved the issue of where they would stay the first night at least, and she hoped for the entire visit. *I wonder if my bedchamber has changed any at all?* A great deal had happened to her since she last was there, and she certainly wasn't the same person as before. How would she feel, seeing it again?

The last curious point concerned a young woman by the name of Nan. Ida had mentioned that she took care of her now that she was gravely ill, but who was she? Another spinster friend, perhaps? Or maybe a nurse or possibly a servant hired for that purpose? Would Mandy have to assume all those duties herself or would this woman stay on for a time? So many questions! And few answers or hints at what might happen when they got there. The one thing she did know, however, was that God had it all firmly under control, even if she could not see how or why. Did she have enough confidence in Him to release all these unknowns into His keeping? Including herself and her daughter? *I will just be glad when this whole fiasco is over and I'm back home on the prairie again with my beloved!*

Mandy vaguely noted that while she had been lost in her thoughts, they had passed numerous farms and small communities sprinkled with endless pasturelands surrounding them, as far as they could see on either side of the train. She tried to rein in all the swirling concerns and focus on something tangible and up close instead.

I wonder what crops they grow here in—where is it that we are now? Oh, yes, Illinois, that was our next state to cross. Glad I stressed geography to the children as much as I did all these years. But it keeps changing as the country grows. I am grateful Indian Territory has remained pretty much the same, although I heard through Two Peaks that since the War ended, there would most likely be many changes coming even for our area. Wonder if that includes the Reservation we keep hearing about?

"Mama! Look, there is a corn field! I recognize the plants from the pictures you showed us of the Pilgrims. You said you used to grow corn close to where you lived in Trenton, right?"

"Yes, it is corn, you are correct. Soon the ears will appear on those stalks as they get taller through the coming summer. But we did not grow the corn, farmers outside the town did."

"Well, that is what I meant. I knew you and Aunt Ida didn't grow it in her back garden! That would be silly! I love to eat the corn that Mr. Murphy brings us sometimes from—well, *others,*" and she emphasized that last word to cover her near-slipup about other tribes on the prairie who cultivate and share it with them. "Roasting it in the campfire," she continued, "makes it very tasty. Yum!"

"You are right, it is fresh when he brings it to us, after others have brought it to the Trading Post to barter for various goods they need. Jacob cannot begin to eat all that by himself, even with Miss Hannah now living with him. We are blessed to get to have it, especially when there is so little food to share with our people."

"Um, Mama, I think you mean with the Kiowa people, right?"

Mandy caught her breath. She had slipped up but her daughter kindly reminded her without missing a beat. She had been concerned that Lily would be the one who might say the wrong thing, when she had done it!

Nodding, she agreed. "Yes, with the Kiowa who need it to survive. There should be plenty of corn here in a few months now, if these plants are any indication. I am sure the same will be true back home."

"What are those other plants in the pastures on the right side of the train?"

"I really don't know but would imagine it might be wheat. It is hard to tell until it is ripe, then it is easy to spot with the bushy tops waving in the wind."

"Speaking of all this makes me hungry, Mama. Is it about time for us to have our evening meal?"

"Yes, I believe it is. Why don't you get the basket out from beneath the seats and we will see what we have in there for tonight. We will need to save some back for the morning meal and to stretch through to the midday meal if possible, as we won't arrive in Trenton until later in the day. Or maybe we can get something to eat while in Cincinnati. I think there won't be quite the rush to get to our next train at that point. But we'll see. I know God will show us how to make this food last."

"Kind of like the boy with the loaves and fishes did, the one whom Jesus blessed, right? He fed thousands with that small lunch."

"You are exactly right, my dear. God works miracles when we pray and believe."

They spread out the food, Mandy gave the blessing for it, and they both ate enough to satisfy their hunger for the night. After that the two of them spent some time praying quietly together. The noise level of course made this difficult at best but they tried. They also prayed for Mr. Conrad, especially that when he got home his mother would be kind to him about his decision to follow Jesus.

The two watched in wonder as the sun set in the west a while later. The red, orange, and yellow streaks across the sky displayed God's handiwork, and they had the perfect vantage point from which to watch it all.

"I miss our sunsets in the territory, Mama, but this one is breathtaking, too."

Mandy nodded and basked in the beauty until the last light left the sky.

The seats across from them this time remained empty most of the night, much to Mandy's relief. Sleeping among strangers was stressful enough, without the proximity of being right next to them. This car was not quite as crowded as the one earlier had been and there were fewer stops, since it was nighttime. Maybe not a feather bed in sight nor even padded seats but still, this was better than sleeping on the ground!

"Tomorrow night," Lily said to her mother, "we will sleep in beds again, right? In the house where you grew up, in fact."

"Well, I hope that we will at least. Let's not get too excited about it for the time being. Only God knows what we will find in Trenton, my dear. For now, we need to get some rest, as it will be a long day again tomorrow to get to our final destination."

Maybe not a good night's sleep for them, by any means, but at least they would have the chance to get some rest, as the Conductor announced he would be turning down the lamps after 9:00 for that purpose.

As this took place on schedule, Lily became quite excited, pointing out the window.

"Look, Mama! See all the stars out there? It's much like on the prairie back home! We couldn't see them while the lights were on in the car. They are beautiful!"

"Yes, the stars can be seen from all over the world, Lily. It is, indeed, a majestic sight."

Mandy recalled a special night long ago when the village had to be moved to follow the buffalo shortly after she had come to live with the Kiowa. Sleeping Bird related one legend after another about the stars that kept them all entertained that evening as they slept under the twinkling lights overhead, without the tipi to obscure their view. Echoes of coyotes in the distance lulled them to sleep, knowing they were far off and not a danger. At the time Mandy was concerned that she would never find her way back to the mission once escape became possible. Moving farther away from it as they were increased her anxiety greatly, so she tried to replay every step they had taken and remember landmarks for later. Her concern kept her distracted for most of the stories, but she did hear them many more times in the ensuing years. However, right now, for some reason her brain was coming up empty on recalling them. How she wished she could remember all the details, to share with Lily.

Suddenly out of the darkness came Lily's soft voice, barely loud enough for her mother to hear above the clacking of the wheels of the car on the tracks, as she related to herself, one after another, those very stories! *Thank You, Father, for a daughter who can carry on our heritage as Kiowa women and for future generations not yet born. I am so humbled and blessed!*

Snuggling down against her cloak under her head listening to those words brought her heart much comfort. What was her beloved doing right now? Perhaps he was also gazing above him at the heavens and praying for her and their daughter. When would she see him again and feel his strong arms around her, protecting her and reassuring her that all is right in their world, as long as they stand together? She hoped her sons had food in their stomachs this night. But how many more nights would that be true? *God, take care of them!*

The words soon faded as Lily became drowsy but Mandy continued to stare out into the darkness, now thinking about growing up in Trenton with her aunt. Her stomach clenched a bit, but she forced herself to relax. For the most part, she had been happy and content there if her father was close by, in spite of her aunt's strict and sometimes even harsh manner. With Ida being a spinster, it meant she truly had no idea how to rear a young lady, but she certainly made a good effort at it. Mandy wished she had not thought so badly of her during those years.

Leaving civilization behind had taught her how precious those times had been to the shaping of her mind and heart for what lay ahead of her in Indian Territory. It really had been a good life in most ways and many of her childhood memories had been quite sweet ones, she had to admit. Why had she allowed her heart to wall them off as though they were all painful? One stone at a time she felt that mythical wall begin to crumble, a bit at least. Perhaps that is the very reason God was bringing her back, to confront her past as it really had been. Was she ready for that? Ready or not, if it was God's will, she would embrace it and knew He would be with her every step.

After a few minutes, instead of going on to sleep as Mandy expected, Lily began peppering her mother with questions on several topics since they were basically alone. After dodging the answers for a few minutes, Mandy firmly put a stop to it.

"Lily, we cannot talk right now. It's been a very long day and both of us need sleep more than talk. When we finally get to Trenton, there should be plenty of opportunity to answer all your many questions."

"I'm sorry, Mama. I know you are right. I feel as though I'm a pot about to bubble over at any moment and am not sure I can even sleep at all for thinking about all the new sights I have encountered today! Of course, the stars overhead and the moon now rising are helping me feel more at home."

"And more relaxed, I hope?"

Lily nodded, eventually closing her eyes. Mandy stared out the window a while longer before she, too, surrendered to her fatigue.

Thanks be to You, Jesus, for providing us with safety so far, and I ask that You will keep us from harm in the days ahead as well. Help me overcome my fear and guard my tongue as You keep the danger away. I want to be as confident as Lily seems to be that all will be well in Trenton. But somehow, I do not share her optimism. Do You warn me with this or is it my own reluctance to even be on this journey, causing me to fail to trust You, leaving me confused? Show me, Father! Keep Aunt Ida alive that I might see her soon, and please help to ease her pain as death approaches. Flood my mind with Your Word as I surrender to sleep. Be with my family in my absence, especially Ken-ai-te. Let him know how much I love and miss him. Hold my boys close...

CHAPTER TEN

"And the LORD, he it is that doth go before thee; he will be with thee, he will not fail thee, neither forsake thee: fear not, neither be dismayed." Deuteronomy 31:8

April 16, 1867
Trenton, Ohio

"Which way is the house, Mama? I hope you remember or how will we find our way?"

Mandy glanced around and nodded toward a street leading away from the depot. "That way, I think," pointing to their right, "a short distance is all."

They gathered up their valises and walked between two buildings, to emerge onto a wide street as dust swirled around them. Mandy coughed.

"This is as bad as the train ride! They must not have had rain for a while but from the looks of those clouds behind us there will be rain before long. And this will all be a sea of mud. We need to hurry, else we might get caught out in the downpour. It would not do to show up drenched to our skin. Definitely not the way to impress my aunt after all this time. To the right, Lily."

Her daughter's jaw dropped open from the sight of the buildings they passed and, indeed, the whole scene took Mandy's breath away as well. Trenton had certainly grown much larger since she lived here, with the houses and businesses having increased in size and number as well. She tried to remember to keep her mouth closed as proper ladies should, even when in awe. Was she truly standing only a block away from the house where she grew up? Or was this a dream? Rounding another corner, Mandy stopped abruptly. Lily, who had been following her mother, almost ran into her.

"What is it?" She followed her mother's stare across the street to a large two-story house with an expansive front porch framed by four white columns. Spacious grounds on every side set it apart and deepened the grandeur since the other buildings they had seen since arriving were simple and much smaller, plus all crowded close together. Surrounded by tall trees on each side, even with long-neglected bushes along the fence line in front, it was impressive, no doubt about it. Again, Lily's jaw dropped.

"*That* is your house, Mama? Or rather, the one belonging to Great-Aunt Ida?" she asked, eyes wide. "I never dreamed it would be this big and so grand!"

Mandy nodded as her eyes misted over for a second. She quickly blinked away the tears threatening to fall, steeling herself for the first of many memories that might overwhelm her if she wasn't careful to control her emotions.

"Yes, that is Wellington Oaks, named for those trees on that side," and she pointed to a stand of large trees off to one side of the house. How did they get to be that tall? Fourteen years of growth makes a difference, apparently.

As they stepped out into the street to head in that direction, a wagon appeared and raced straight toward them! The driver appeared to be having great difficulty maneuvering around the pair, maybe due to the large load he carried. Frozen in place, Mandy could only gape in horror, expecting him to slam into them any second. At the last moment he managed to avoid hitting them, but just barely. As he flew by, he shot an angry warning over his shoulder.

"Look out! Watch where you are going, you two!"

He kept on without slowing down, much less stopping to ensure they were all right. Shaken at their narrow escape, Mandy grabbed Lily's sleeve and dragged her to safety on the other side, coming to stop right in front of their destination.

Mandy silently chided herself for failing to watch for danger the way she should have, being so taken at the sight of the place where she had lived long ago. What other problems would they encounter here that the responsibility would be hers for their safety? She must be more watchful and less overcome with this busy and imposing town. Where was Ken-ai-te when she needed him to protect them both? *Certainly not here,* she reminded herself. *Lord, help me take care of my daughter better!*

"Are you all right, Lily?" Mandy brushed dust off her daughter's skirt to cover her own nervousness. At Lily's nod, Mandy took a deep breath and turned to look at the front gate. How often she had stood here in years past, in a whole other life in fact, before entering her home! Everything was different now, however. Everything. Her anxiety heightened as she rehearsed silently once more what she would say at the door.

"Come, Lily, we are here." With an air of far more confidence than she felt in reality, Mandy walked down the long, winding pathway and right up to the door, knocking firmly.

Nothing. No answer. No sound whatsoever, in fact. Was anyone even home?

"Your aunt doesn't know we are coming, does she, Mama?"

"No, she doesn't as I had no way to let her know we were on our way. Or my cousin, for that matter. But that's all right because this gives us an advantage our hosts will not have, that of surprise."

"A battle tactic Papa taught all of us before we could walk!"

"Hush, dear, do you want someone to hear you speak of battle tactics?" But inside, Mandy was proud of Lily for recalling this important piece of advice from her father. *I hope it works, Ken-ai-te! May your godly wisdom help us now!*

She tried again, this time rapping harder and longer. Shouting came through the heavy door in response. Although the words were a bit muffled, clearly someone was angry. Mandy tensed up. Should she continue knocking? Before she had a chance to decide, the door suddenly jerked open and a tall man, with a red face mostly obscured by a bushy dark beard, fairly screamed at them.

"What do you want?"

Taken aback at being addressed in such a rude manner, Mandy's words failed her for a moment. But she quickly found her voice.

"Cousin—Cousin Alex, I presume? I am your cousin, Amanda Clark Alton, and this is my daughter Lily. We have come from Indian Territory to see Aunt Ida. Is she home?"

Before he could respond, a lone woman with long blonde hair in curls appeared at the top of the staircase behind Alex. She rushed down the steps calling out as she ran toward the visitors.

"Amanda! How wonderful that you came after all. I feared you might not be able to make the trip."

When she got to the doorway, she added, "Alex, for heaven's sake, let the two of them in before they get soaked from the rain! Or maybe it's not raining yet but it certainly appears to be about to drown us all."

She elbowed her way in front of Alex to where Mandy stood, pulling her inside, with Lily right behind. Then she slammed the door shut. When she turned to face Alex, his expression crunched into an ugly mask of fury and irritation, finished off with a rolling of his eyes.

"Oh, not *you* again! Why can't you stay upstairs where you belong?"

"I came down here to see what all the commotion is about. It is disturbing Miss Ida and you know we cannot have that. But she will be delighted to have company and especially these two."

"Not company, *intruders* are what I would call them. The same goes for you. I swear, I will see that you are banished from here yet. And you know I can do it!"

He swirled to glare again at Mandy. While she hadn't expected him to welcome a stranger with open arms, she was a bit shocked at his anger and highly offensive manner. After all, they were related.

"And I will stop you as well!" He shook his finger right in her face. "There is *no way* you are going to get your hands on one penny of this estate, I guarantee that. You might as well go right on back to your Indian tipi or wherever you live, do you hear me? I won't have you on the grounds of this place one moment longer! Out! Do you not hear me?"

He leaned in as he screamed and now was inches from her face. Mandy instinctively took a step backward. Inwardly, she gasped at his words, for they were closer to the truth than he could have imagined.

How did he know? Oh wait, he has to be guessing! Simply because we are from Indian Territory, he thinks we must live in a tipi. How ignorant can one get? But I do live in a tipi! And what is so terrible about that?

A chill rippled down her spine. There would be no easy way out of this tangle, she feared. All hope evaporated of getting the inheritance and returning home quickly with the money they so desperately needed. What would happen to her people now? Words failed her and she stood there staring at her adversary, feeling as though she had been physically whipped. *God, help me!*

As if in swift response to the prayer, the beautiful blonde lady, whoever she was, intervened on her behalf again, deftly stepping between them, glaring up at the man's imposing height as though it meant nothing. With her lips pursed in obvious anger, hands on her hips in a confrontational manner even an imbecile could not miss, *he* was the one forced to step back. Mandy's heart leapt at this raw courage by such a delicate person as she appeared to be. Immediately she liked this woman, and they hadn't even been introduced yet!

"Alex, stop being so rude!" It was her turn to shake her finger in his face. "They didn't come to see you. Go on back into your study now, or wherever the rock is that you crawled out from under to answer the door, and leave us alone. We won't be bothering you further." To emphasize that, she whirled around and turned her back on him, then reached out to draw Mandy into an embrace as though they were the long-lost cousins!

Mandy couldn't help but smile at this turn of events, given the caution her aunt had given in her letter about the cold reception she might receive from her cousin. It finally dawned on her that this must be the woman Nan her aunt mentioned, but who exactly was she? Far different from the one she had expected, certainly. Why did Cousin Alex dislike her that much? Mandy felt confused by it all, but she did return the kind hug. At least it gave her a chance to tear her attention away from the man who had towered over her with such a menacing glare and hateful words. After a moment she released Mandy and stepped back, nodding at Lily.

"I'm absolutely thrilled that you could come. Did I hear you say this delightful young lady with you is your daughter Lily?" Before Mandy had a chance to answer, she continued. "We'll have time for proper introductions soon enough. Your aunt will be so pleased to see you as well. Come, let us go up to see her right away and get you both away from this unpleasantness as quickly as possible. We can get you settled into your room later. Just leave your valises here in the vestibule for now. She was so positive you would be here that she left orders saying no matter what time of day or night you arrived, she was to greet you immediately. Please, follow me."

Mandy hesitated a moment. How much she wanted to see her aunt after all these years! But under these circumstances? She still needed a clarification of who it was she now followed upstairs. As long as this person took her away from the horrid Cousin Alex, however, she really didn't mind who she was, and the two followed her without looking back.

Behind her, she heard Alex stomp back into the study and slam the sliding doors closed behind him. Mandy winced at the sound. *Aunt Ida would have your head on a platter for doing that if she had witnessed it! One time when I got angry and pulled that same stunt, she nearly took mine off with her cutting words!* At least he wouldn't be bothering them any longer for now. She admired how he backed down in the face of this determined and mysterious young woman. Mandy knew she must learn her secrets to handling this difficult man!

"Good riddance," the woman muttered under her breath without turning around. "Wish he'd stay in there all the time."

"Excuse me," Mandy called out as she hurried to catch up, "but who are you? My aunt told me Alex would be here and mentioned in passing in her brief letter about a friend named Nan who was caring for her. Is that you, by chance?"

"Oh, I *am* sorry!" She stopped on the stairs and turned to face the two of them. "I should have introduced myself properly to you both and I do apologize. That scene we just experienced had me a bit rattled there for a moment. My name is, indeed, Nan, Nan Brewster. I'm a friend of your aunt's, and yes, I have been caring for her the last couple of weeks."

She extended her hand and Mandy grasped it eagerly in her own. *What do you know, a friend of Aunt Ida's but one even younger than I am!* Mandy loved the twinkle in her blue eyes and returned the broad grin with one of her own. Out of the corner of her eye she saw Lily curtsy slightly and took note of how easily she stepped into the good manners she had been taught.

As though she could read her mind, Nan added, "I'm really more like family than friend." Her warm smile quickly eased any concerns Mandy had entertained about this person. "I heard you tell Alex that this is your daughter Lily. What a blessing it will be to your aunt to not only get to see you after all these years, but also meet your daughter!"

She turned to Lily. "That is such a lovely name, to match a lovely young lady!"

"Thank you, Miss Brewster," Lily replied.

"No, I insist you both call me Nan. Now, as to my presence, I am certainly more family than that creature Alex is to her." Her face colored slightly. "Sorry, I didn't mean to criticize him like that. I understand he is kin to you. But he is without a doubt the rudest, *meanest* one individual I know! But let's not talk about him. Come along, I know your aunt is anxious to see you, as you are to see her."

Mandy swallowed what she was about to say, an agreement of that assessment of this strange man to whom she was related but had no idea how. *Maybe Nan knows and can tell me. At least, I hope so.* This question had haunted her ever since receiving the fateful letter that brought them all this distance. The answer she sought would have to wait for now but she did intend to find out soon, whether from Nan or from her aunt.

The three of them hurried up the rest of the long flight of stairs to Ida's bedchamber, still located in the same place Mandy remembered from her childhood. In fact, as she glanced around, little seemed to have changed since she lived here. As they climbed the steps Lily's mouth was open the whole way, head turning one direction and then the other to admire the massive wooden bannisters, crystal chandeliers, and impressive artwork on the walls.

Mandy finally whispered to her daughter, "Please close your mouth. A young lady does not gape like a fish!"

"Sorry, Mama! This is incredible!"

"It's a staircase, daughter. For walking on. Not an art gallery."

As they arrived in front of the heavy door before them, Mandy asked their guide a question in a hushed tone.

"I know my aunt is gravely ill, but I am excited that God granted the prayer of my heart to keep her alive until I could get here. How is she doing, really?"

"She is in a great deal of pain most of the time now but fortunately only occasionally is conscious. However, I believe she can hear what I say to her even when she has her eyes closed and appears to be asleep. Feel free to talk to her because I want very much for her to know you are here at last. This is her heart's prayer, you know, to get to see you once more before she goes to Heaven."

Mandy had never been the object of someone's heart prayer before, except to her husband. It gave her cold chills to think that her aunt wanted that much to see her niece, and she thanked God again for making it possible for them to come. And in time.

Shock must have registered on Mandy's face when she lay eyes on her aunt.

"I know, it's a bit of a jolt to see her like this, isn't it?" said Nan. "I forget that others are not prepared since I am with her all the time. Come on over here closer to the bed."

Ida's shrunken body seemed almost lost in the soft bedding around her. The ashen appearance of her face startled Mandy. *Is that what this cancer does to a person? I knew it was deadly but was not prepared for this.* Blinking back tears, Mandy rushed to one side of the bed, with Nan on the other. Lily found a chair in the room and quietly settled into it. It consoled Mandy to know that her daughter would be praying for all of them right now, unbidden but recognizing the need. Goodness knew, they could use the prayers.

"Miss Ida, look who I have brought to see you! Amanda is here, and her daughter Lily came with her. Can you open your eyes so you can see them? Please try!"

CHAPTER ELEVEN

"For God is not the author of confusion but of peace..."
I Corinthians 14:33

April 16, 1867

"That's right! You can see them, can't you? They are so excited to be here with you." Nan's urgent words to Ida touched Mandy's heart. Nothing could have been more true at the moment!

Slowly, one eyelid came open, then the other one. Mandy's heart leapt when a hint of a smile appeared on her aunt's lips.

"Aunt Ida, it's Amanda. I'm right here, squeezing your hand. Can you squeeze it back?"

"Of course I can, my dear. I may be dying but I'm not stupid, you know."

Mandy laughed as did Nan, and they smiled at each other.

"That's my girl," said Nan. "If there is one thing I would agree with you on, it is that you are not stupid! Would you like a sip of water?"

"Yes, please, that would be lovely, Nan."

She poured a fresh glass from the bedside table and lifted Ida's head up so she could drink. However, she was unable to get much more than a sip down before she coughed deeply and waved her away.

After a moment she said, "You got my letter, I see, and came as I requested. I'm so pleased. I never expected you to bring your daughter as well. Where is she?"

Mandy motioned for Lily to step forward. She took her great-aunt's frail hand in her own, gently caressing the long fingers.

"Aunt Ida, this is Lily."

"Hello, Great-Aunt Ida. I'm glad I finally got to meet you. Mama has talked about you all my life."

"Has she? Well, I hope you don't believe everything you hear. You know, you are every bit as lovely as your mother was at your age. Don't let that go to your head but it is meant as a compliment, young lady." And she chuckled softly.

Ida closed her eyes and didn't move. Mandy's heart froze. Was this it? Had she slipped away right in front of them while speaking? Perhaps the effort it required of her had been too much. *Oh, Father, please, not yet! I've just gotten here!*

Nan must have seen the stunned look on Mandy's face and knew what she was thinking, because she smiled kindly at her.

"She's merely gone back to sleep for now. Hopefully she will awaken again soon. She has so much to talk to you about and knew it would be difficult, perhaps even impossible, for you to get here in time. Apparently, she has written you some letters but for the life of me I cannot find them anywhere. One day she mentioned something in passing about hiding away the memories where Alex couldn't get to them, so maybe that is what she was talking about—your letters. Perhaps you can think of someplace where she might have hidden them and can do a better job than I have in locating them. It would be a shame to lose all those priceless thoughts that she said she committed to paper for you alone."

"Well, I will think about it. I would certainly hate to lose them as well. They are all I have left of her now, or soon will be. What is the doctor saying about how much longer she must endure all this pain and suffering?"

"Any time, frankly. It's all right to speak of it in front of her as she is fully aware. That's why she changed her will and wrote that letter begging you to come see her before it was too late. About two weeks ago she became dramatically weaker and very ill so I moved in here, to look after her. Alex certainly wasn't doing it. I couldn't bear to think of her being here in pain and all alone without proper care. I work at the Emporium here in town and they have been kind enough to give me some time off. It would be a disaster if I were to lose my job of course. Now that you are here, perhaps I can go back to work because being without any income has been very hard on me, having to depend on Alex to give me money to live on. Of course, it's Miss Ida's money but you'd think every penny was his own the way he fusses over it. Disgusting man."

"Can you tell me how he is related to my aunt? She never had children, so I'm confused about how she now has a grandson."

"I'll be happy to but let's move to the drawing room adjacent to the bed chamber, if that's all right with you. I can still hear her if she needs me but our talking won't disturb her sleep, either." Mandy glanced over at her aunt before exiting and thanked God once more for ensuring her safe arrival from Indian Territory, before taking Ida to her heavenly home.

A few minutes later they were settled into the cozy space, one Mandy remembered fondly, with the door between the rooms ajar. Lily settled into a comfortable wing-back chair and pulled out her book from the bag she carried, intending to read while the two ladies talked. But suddenly she rose and walked over to a large bookshelf on one wall which was packed with books from floor to ceiling.

"May I look at these?"

"Of course, my dear. They are all of Miss Ida's favorites. From the look on your face, I would say you love books as much as she does. If you spot one you are interested in, feel free to take it to read while you are here. Sadly, she certainly won't have further use for them. I know she would be thrilled to share her collection with you. Besides, soon it will belong to you anyway, well to your mother technically." Mandy saw her daughter's eyes widen at that thought, however premature it might be, but she wisely said nothing.

How on earth will we ever get all those back home by horseback? There must be several hundred of them, at least! Where will we put them in our little tipi? I'm sure God has a plan for that, too, but it will be interesting to see how He works that out. I couldn't possibly tell Lily she cannot have all these books!

Lily nodded, silently walking up and down the rows, occasionally pulling a book out to take a closer look. Finally, she found one that did not go back in place, and she took it over to the chair. Within moments she was absorbed in its pages. Mandy's heart fluttered at the sight of her daughter reading here in Aunt Ida's sitting room, where she herself had spent many an hour doing precisely that long ago, and she sighed deeply.

"Cup of tea, Amanda? Is it all right if I call you Amanda? I have heard enough about you, I feel that I know you. But I don't want to be too presumptuous."

"Oh, my no, that's fine. I would feel awkward if you did not use my first name."

"Good! Please remember, my name is Nan, to you both," and she smiled over at Lily.

"Thank you, Nan," Mandy replied. "Tea would be very welcome. It has been a long day."

Nan scurried around to fix enough for both of them, pouring some hot water from a kettle simmering on the small stove in one corner.

"I use this area for preparing many of Miss Ida's meals and snacks for myself, as it means I don't have to go downstairs to the kitchen as often, where I risk running into Alex. I try to minimize contact with him, or I would be upset all day long. Do you wish to have sugar and cream with your tea?"

How long has it been since I had a cup of tea? I drank coffee at the Boarding House for our morning meal a couple of days ago, but I have not had tea since I left this house, frankly! We had none to fix at the mission those few weeks we were there, only coffee. I'm not even certain how I take it after all this time! She cleared her throat against the emotion of all the memories flooding her mind.

"One lump of sugar with a little bit of cream, if you please. I am not used to such luxury as to be waited on like this!"

With the first sip, her taste buds leapt to life! *Yumm, this is so tasty, I had quite forgotten.* She savored every drop as its warmth helped relax her inside.

"Back to your earlier question, Amanda, about how Alex is related to your aunt, it is a bit of a complex story. Let's see, how shall I begin? Some years back before the War Between the States began, Miss Ida took in a young woman by the name of Catherine Osgood because she was quite destitute with no means of support. Her husband had died, leaving her with three young boys to rear on her own. In addition, she had fallen quite ill and could not care for them adequately any longer. Within a few weeks Miss Ida decided to legally adopt all of them."

"That was awfully kind of my aunt to do something that generous. I'm certain it wasn't their preference, to be so dependent on a stranger like that."

"Yes, you are correct but she never hesitated. It surprised all her friends and alarmed a few skeptics as well. Miss Ida felt deeply sorry for her, such a lovely young mother she was, too. The boys were very sweet also. Tommy and James were the younger ones, and the older one was Alex. She gave them a home along with all the love in her heart, and they lived quite happily here with Miss Ida for some time, giving her the loving family she had always desired. After the adoption became final, they even took her last name for their own."

"Aunt Ida used to tell me her biggest regret in life was never marrying, that apparently God had a different plan for her life than the usual one through the stability of marriage. She spent too many years caring for my father and then supporting the two of them with several businesses when she was younger, which left very little time and energy remaining to pour into a husband. I suppose this was His way of providing a daughter and grandchildren for her in a respectable manner but without that commitment."

"Yes, it definitely did that for a short time. However, Catherine was never very strong after her illness. Tragically, before long she died."

"How perfectly sad! Those poor little boys!"

"Miss Ida tried to rear the three of them the best she could, ensuring they got a good education and knew right from wrong. They all three were good boys, kind, obedient, and respectful in all their ways. It was obvious to everyone they loved their grandmother very much. Eventually, Miss Ida apprenticed them out to the local blacksmith and that way they could learn a trade. All three had been hanging around the livery stable in town in all their free time anyway, so she figured why not let them earn some money doing what they enjoyed?"

"Makes sense to me," said Mandy. "They would need some way to make a living when they got a little older."

"Exactly. A short time after this, however, the War broke out. It wasn't a month into it that the Union Army commander at the nearby fort came here to enlist the blacksmith into the military. For the first few weeks he was stationed out at the fort and the boys stayed with him there. That way, they got to see Miss Ida often. But when the blacksmith was sent off with the army to another part of the state, as hard as it was, Miss Ida parted with the boys, sending them with the smithy along with her blessing. She gave the man money to care for them and made him promise to let her know if they needed her for anything."

"The war must have been terrible, even here in Ohio."

"Oh, it was. But that is another story for a different day. A long story, in fact, but one I will be happy to share with you at some point when there is time, if you really want to know about it. Back to the boys, though. A few weeks later Miss Ida got word that their camp had been overrun by

Confederate soldiers and they were all killed—the smithy, all three boys, in fact most of the men in the whole unit. It was a really difficult time for her."

"How horrible! I'm very sad to hear that. But, wait a minute—if they were killed, how can Alex be here now?"

"That is the most astounding part of this whole bizarre affair!"

CHAPTER TWELVE

"For the king knoweth of these things...for I am persuaded that none...are hidden from him; for this thing was not done in a corner." Acts 26:26

April 16, 1867

"You are serious? There is *more*? My head is about to explode with all this as it is!"

"Oh, I do apologize, Amanda. After you have come all this way, here I am dumping these terrible events on you without allowing you to rest first. We can finish this tomorrow, if you would like. I'm a terrible hostess!"

"Please don't apologize, Nan. I am eager to know all the details, believe me. It has been a long several days but you can't stop now! Please, go on. Obviously," gesturing toward her daughter, "Lily is content and I do want to hear what has happened to my aunt, to understand what she has been through."

"Well, if you are sure. Where was I? Oh, yes, a week after we heard about the boys' untimely deaths, Miss Ida received a letter stating that her grandson Alex had not perished in the attack as had first been thought, but had, indeed, survived. However, he was badly wounded and it would take some extended time for him to recover from his injuries. The good news was he would be sent home as soon as he had recovered well enough for travel. She was overjoyed!"

"I'm sure she felt great relief! What a blessing that he was alive after all."

Nan had an odd expression on her face Mandy couldn't read. *Why not a blessing that he was not killed? I'm confused!*

"The thing is," Nan continued, "when he finally did come home no one even recognized him, including his grandmother. He had grown a big, bushy beard that hid much of his face, for one thing. For another, he appeared to be much older than 18, which was Alex's age by that time. There were several little things that didn't add up, but Miss Ida wanted desperately to believe he was her grandson, so she never seriously questioned any of them. But the biggest discrepancy is that this 'Alex' was cruel and mean-spirited, whereas Miss Ida's Alex had been kind and tender-hearted. It did not take long before several of Miss Ida's closest friends, including me—well, we, that is, the truth is that we all saw through the thinly veiled disguise to recognize him for what he was: an imposter after her money and property. But we couldn't prove anything and because it upset Miss Ida to talk about it, we remained silent for the most part. However, we were not happy, let me tell you. She deserved so much more."

"An *imposter*? My word! What happened when she became ill? Did he take care of her?"

"Not at all. That was sickening, seeing how he neglected her at the time when she needed someone the most. I did what I could but not being around all the time, it was tough. Even long before she found out about the cancer, none of Miss Ida's friends were welcome here. She and I would see each other at church or occasionally meet for lunch or go for a stroll in the park, perhaps. But I quit coming over because of how unpleasant it was to have to see this man, even briefly, especially if he was drunk—which he usually was."

"Drunk? But Aunt Ida was always adamant about not allowing spirits of any kind in her home!"

"I know. He defied her, saying she didn't understand a man's needs and he wasn't giving up his whiskey for any woman, let alone an old one. She finally told him he must keep it in the study at all times, never drinking in front of her. And—" She abruptly stopped, chewed her lower lip a second, then with a gentle shake of her head continued.

"Well, never mind that, but his behavior when he had been drinking heavily was despicable, beyond words at times. It broke my heart. The only good thing was that Alex frequently left town for extended business trips, demands of his freight hauling company he said. Life was much happier for everyone when he was gone. Unfortunately, he always came home eventually. I resented him because he was not fighting in the war, frankly, but he used the excuse that his wounds, suffered in the battle that took the lives of his brothers, kept him from being able to re-enlist. I think it was hogwash, to be honest. I never saw any evidence of an injury and truthfully believe he made it up to get out of the Army and keep out of the military in the future."

"If he is an imposter, what happened to the real Alex?"

"I have no idea but if asked to speculate, I would imagine the earlier report was the more accurate one, that Alex was killed along with his brothers. Maybe this man, whoever he is, wrote the second letter himself, who knows? Certain aspects of life were quite confusing during the war. Frequently wrong information was reported about deaths and injuries as well as other details because of possibly giving away secrets about troop numbers and other vital information to the enemy. Therefore, it was often difficult if not impossible to confirm anything with certainty. So we believed it, at first. Miss Ida put a lot of stock in that young man, refusing to hear of any rumors or gossip about him, period. I finally quit trying to tell her that something was not right. We all heard many whispers about his activities and behavior, in fact enough of them that it was hard to ignore altogether. But she wouldn't listen."

"That's despicable. This had to have been deeply disappointing for my aunt. Apparently, she loved him a great deal."

"Yes, she did. She had adopted all of them, as I said, making Catherine her heir. Later on, her boys were to inherit a sizeable amount when they reached adulthood. It about crushed her to lose Catherine; the thought of all three boys dying as well was more than she could bear. Her denial overtook her common sense. Until she got the cancer diagnosis, things were not great with Alex around but at least tolerable for the most part. However, that devastating news changed everything and threw her into great despair."

"But why? I mean, I am certain she was not thrilled in any way to discover she was dying but in *despair* over it? That doesn't sound like the aunt I knew."

"I agree, an attitude like that was not in character with Ida Clark! Although I have only known her a little more than ten years, in that time often she has told me of various ways in which she had matured a great deal from what she was like when younger. While I find that difficult to believe, I am aware how time often changes people, certainly has me. For instance,

I do know first-hand that the war brought dramatic change to her in several key ways. Even still, her lack of ability or desire to fight off the cancer, to simply give up and want to die without even trying to survive, wasn't like her at all. She told me these differences in her heart were what she most wanted to chronicle with the letters she wrote to you, to assure you that she would not end her life as she started out, lost in bondage to sin and darkness. Such important messages! I cannot believe they are lost! Surely there is a secret hiding place here somewhere that only you would know about."

"As I said earlier, I will certainly give it some thought but nothing comes to mind immediately. Back to Cousin Alex, or whoever he really is. Why did you move in here with Aunt Ida? Was it when she became ill or did something else happen to make her ask for your help?"

"Oh, yes, that. Well, she started having all kinds of strange hallucinations. The doctor said it was from the medication he was giving her for the pain, made her have odd dreams, sometimes even while fully awake. One of those that recurred often is difficult to even say out loud—that Alex was trying to kill her."

"*Kill* her? Oh, my! That is just unbelievable. How? And why?"

"For her money of course. She believed he was poisoning her with the food he prepared for her. When he got around to cooking, that is. I rather doubted the truth of that accusation at first but knew it could be possible. The coincidence was too much to ignore, as that is when she really became ill, with more pain than she could tolerate, requiring a constant increase in the laudanum to keep her somewhat comfortable and allow her to sleep. Finally, I realized Alex had fired the cook and then refused to prepare meals! On top of it all, he was starving her, in other words."

"Oh no! This gets worse by the minute! My poor, sweet aunt!" Mandy's heart squeezed tight and wouldn't let go, making it difficult to even breathe at this awful news.

Nan continued. "As I began listening to her complaints, I finally realized they were more than mere delusions. I promptly moved in here to look after her properly, determined to get to the bottom of this whole ugly mess. Although Alex was furious, I think he also was secretly relieved he didn't have to pay any attention to her after that, could go about his normal day and ignore both of us. Which he did. He didn't even come in to check on her for days at a time."

"What? That is terrible! Some grandson he turned out to be. If only I had known…."

"How could you? Anyway, the doctor eventually told me that he believed she was being poisoned, confirming my earlier fears, in addition to being starved. With the pain from the cancer plus the medication in her system, it was a terrible combination. However, she actually improved for several days after I moved in!"

"Not surprising, given all this. There is much to be said for a good diet when one is ill. One's spirits often perk up as well when physical strength returns."

"Exactly. She became more like she had been before she found out about the cancer, more like her old self, in fact, only somewhat weaker. But the blows she had suffered were too strong for her complete recovery. Between losing Bessie and fearing for her life from an imposter claiming to be her grandson, it was all too much."

"Who is Bessie?"

"I think your aunt wants to share about her with you herself and probably did in those missing letters. But if we cannot find them, I will tell you about Bessie. She was a dear friend, too, who disappeared a few weeks ago. It really hurt your aunt deeply that she left without telling her goodbye. It's a long story and I know you both are tired this evening. I assume you plan on staying here at the house, right? I know at least one night here is a condition of the inheritance, in fact in your old room. Therefore, I put fresh linens in there for you, in the hopes you would come. Will it be all right if the two of you share the room, or would Lily like to have her own bed chamber?"

"No, that will be fine for us to share. We are not used to such finery as it is. I had hoped we might stay here while in town, if that is all right. I'm not prepared to pay for a hotel room for several days. Aunt Ida told me about the request I stay here at least one night but warned me that might be difficult because of Alex. The way he acted downstairs a while ago makes me nervous about my decision to stay."

"Don't worry about him. He just stays permanently angry these days. If not at Miss Ida, then at me, and unfortunately now you will probably bear some of that brunt yourself. But don't let it get to you! Of course, you both are welcome here as long as Miss Ida is alive. When she passes, we will need to leave the house, I'm afraid, for our own safety. But Miss Ida also said you are to go to see Mr. Grayson, her attorney, as soon as possible and sign some papers for him. He might have some ideas about where you should go. The Boarding House where I normally stay is holding my room, thank goodness. I'm quite certain the landlady can accommodate the two of you there, if you like."

"Yes, she did mention his name as well. My thought was to go see him first thing in the morning to get those papers signed. Aunt Ida will rest easier and frankly I will as well, once that task is done. After that we can decide about where we will stay for the few days it takes to get the money so I can go home."

"You are right, that does not have to be decided tonight. However, you do need to go get something to eat at the hotel restaurant down the street before time for it to close. I don't have anything to offer you for dinner, unless you are hungry for clear broth, which is what I'm preparing for your aunt. I'm praying I can get a few sips of it in her at least."

"I think we'll pass on the broth but thank you all the same! It's down the street, you say?"

"Yes, you cannot miss it, in the next block in fact. The name is The Trenton Arms and the dining room is right inside the front entrance. They are very reasonable, with decent food. Lily, would you mind running downstairs to get the valises from the vestibule while I show your mother where you all will be staying?"

"Of course. I'll be—"

Suddenly from the other room came a shriek that chilled Mandy's blood.

"Imposter! Liar! Thief! He is no good and—"

The two ladies raced to Ida's bedside. She thrashed about in the bed with a strange trance-like expression on her face, screaming her accusations over and over.

"Murderer! Watch out! He's a murderer!"

CHAPTER THIRTEEN

"He discovereth deep things out of darkness, and bringeth out to light the shadow of death." Job 12:22

April 16, 1867

"Aunt Ida! Please, calm yourself! I'm right here as is Nan."

"Amanda? Is that really you? You are here at last?"

"Yes, Aunt Ida, I'm here. We spoke earlier but maybe you don't recall. You've been asleep for a while giving Nan and the two of us the chance to get better acquainted."

"Alex—he's—be careful. Not trust—"

"Miss Ida, I've told her all about Alex. She knows. You must rest for now. Don't excite yourself or you will start coughing again."

"Yes, rest. Must rest." She closed her eyes one more, her breathing shallow but regular. Without warning, they popped open once more, a panicky look on her face.

"Matthew! You must talk…Matthew will know…papers to sign before…" Her eyes slowly closed again.

"Yes, Miss Ida, she will get the papers signed in the morning. Before Alex can find out, I will make sure of that. Please stay calm so your body can rest."

Mandy glanced up and her heart broke for the tears streaming down her new friend's cheeks as she gazed at the pale, still form against the sheets before them. How hard this must have been all this time on poor Nan, day after day of watching Aunt Ida's mind and body collapse like they have! Nan swiped away the tears and sighed, glancing across the bed at Mandy solemnly, as each held one of Ida's frail hands in her own.

After a few minutes with Ida resting easily, Nan gestured with her head toward the sitting room and they quietly slipped out. Lily was still reading but glanced up when they came in. Mandy noticed her daughter had come to the doorway of the bedchamber to overhear some of the rantings by Ida as well as part of what Nan said, then apparently returned to her reading. She was grateful Lily was able to absorb herself in the book and shut out everything else around her. Or at least enough to avoid the drama and pain. How she longed to be able to do the same!

Mandy now knew there was good reason to believe her so-called cousin was an imposter who had caused her aunt all sorts of problems since his return. But a thief and murderer, too? Her head reeled. What had God gotten her into, bringing her here to this house, to this situation? *Oh, Ken-ai-te, where are you when I need you beside me, for your wisdom, not to mention your protection?*

Mandy collapsed into her chair, covering her face with her hands.

"Mama, are you all right?" Lily asked, as she rushed to her side and knelt in front of her. Mandy pulled her daughter into her arms, assuring her she was fine.

"Is it always like this, with her wavering between knowing and not knowing?" Mandy asked Nan.

"Yes, I'm afraid it is now, has been for most of the past couple of weeks. As I told you, I have been here, night and day for that long, with each hour becoming worse than the one before. I'm very relieved that you have come but I'm sorry you had to see her like this. One part of me prayed you would not arrive until after she—"

"Yes, I can understand. Had I known, I would have prayed the same thing. You are so kind to her. I feel awful you have had to bear this all alone."

"That's what friends are for. Although, she is much more than a friend to me. More like a mother and certainly a mentor who has taught me much. About life. About faith. About courage. About so much! How will I face life without her now?"

This time it was Nan who broke down in sobs. Mandy held her for several moments while she wept. Finally, spent, she dabbed at her eyes with her handkerchief and took a deep breath.

"As I said earlier, I am a terrible hostess! Here you come all this way and I have not offered you even a room where you can rest. Come, let's get you settled because you need to go eat before it gets any later. I'm certain you both must be exhausted by now."

As they got to the top of the stairs, Lily spoke up.

"Mama, I can run down to get our valises now if you like."

"Yes, that would be most helpful, my dear. Thank you. We are going to the second door on the right there."

"That's right," said Nan. "I had forgotten for the moment that you know your way around the house as well as I do! You don't need me to show you where your own bedchamber is!"

"Well, you are very kind to want to do so. We will be fine if you want to get back to my aunt."

"I will in a moment," she said as Lily scampered down the staircase. "Miss Ida insisted that the room be kept precisely as you left it. Of course, we had it cleaned regularly but otherwise, it is untouched since you last stood here. As I said earlier, I put fresh linens on the bed yesterday, in the sincere hope you would be coming soon to occupy it."

When Mandy stepped into the room, she gasped. It looked as she remembered it from the morning she left Trenton for Indian Territory more than fourteen years ago!

"It's a bit like stepping back in time! I need to catch my breath a moment."

Lily returned with the cases and Nan left them to get settled. She told the two of them she would go back to the sitting room to prepare a bowl of soup for Ida should she awaken again and want to eat. After Mandy closed the door behind her, she turned to see her daughter staring in awe at the room.

"Mama! I had no idea it would be this beautiful! No wonder it was hard for you to leave here."

"Actually, I was thrilled to be leaving, truth be told. Let's get our things unpacked quickly, such as they are. Afterward, we need to get some dinner, as Nan suggested. I hope that restaurant she mentioned will still be open."

It didn't take long to get washed up and freshen their clothing. Lily plopped down on the bed, thrilled at how soft it was. All the "girlie" things on the shelves around the room delighted her as well, from the porcelain dolls to the delicate hair ribbons on display to the lace on everything in sight. She had never seen anything like all this, and each was a little piece of heaven to her as she gingerly fingered every one with squeals of delight!

Mandy's mind focused on the tragedy playing out down the hall, also briefly touching on the cruel man downstairs who now was far more than merely a stranger to be dealt with. In truth he was instead a cunning adversary who apparently would stop at nothing to get the inheritance for himself. *Lord, I am going to need all the help You can give me to get through this venture. Give me wisdom and courage in as large a measure as You can!*

A short time later the pair was in the hotel dining room awaiting a scrumptious-sounding meal to be served momentarily. They needed something substantial after two days on the train with their light snacks, and only pemmican for the two days on the trail before that.

"Mama, was this hotel here when you lived in Trenton?"

"No, my dear, it was not. This would have been considered way too grand for the tiny community I grew up in. I'm amazed enough people would stay here in this town to justify its existence, frankly. But it appears to do a brisk business. The food smells delicious and seems not too expensive. We shall have to figure out a more economical way to eat, however, if we are to be here very long, or we will use up our money before time to return home."

"It all smells heavenly! What does this 'pot roast' you ordered for us taste like?"

"Much like buffalo stew, except it is made with beef instead of buffalo of course."

"Yum! I cannot wait for every delicious bite!"

The waitress brought their meals before long, and they ate quickly before it had time to get cold. Every bite was savored because who knew when their next meal would be?

"Mama, who is Matthew? Do you know? I heard Aunt Ida talking about him."

"He is the lawyer who handles my aunt's affairs. In her letter, she told me to go see him as soon as I got in town because he would have all the paperwork for me to sign to claim my inheritance. Since Aunt Ida is still alive, I'm not sure what I will need to do about all that now."

"Will she live long? I have not seen much sickness in my life but I have seen some, especially have seen death several times in the last year or so in the village. And—" she stopped, looking at her mother with a face full of compassion. "I don't think your aunt can last much longer, don't you agree?"

"Sadly, yes, I do, and obviously Nan does as well. Yes, dear Lily, your eyes have witnessed far too much from the difficult conditions at home. We mustn't speak of that here, but I do want you to know that your presence already has made the awkward circumstances at the house easier for me to bear. I'm deeply grateful you came along on this trip."

"I am, too! I never expected to see anything like this!" She looked around at the elegant surroundings in the dining room. At least, elegant to them.

They were used to a Kiowa village out on the prairie, living in tipis, and preparing their meals on open campfires. Lily was already an accomplished cook and Mandy was proud of how her daughter was learning all the skills necessary to take her place as a Kiowa woman someday soon. Those thoughts seemed oddly out of place in these surroundings with the elegant chandeliers hanging overhead, along with delicate candles flickering on each table covered with a white linen cloth. Gentle tinklings from around the room reminded them that real crystal and china were in use here, plus the knives and forks were there for a reason! It was far more than a mere Inn along a rural roadway, all of which seemed to represent quite a step up for Trenton.

Mandy glanced up the stairs as they left. *I suppose that is where the guests stay. A small but comfortable place. I wonder if we shall be here shortly ourselves.*

They hurried back to the house, grateful it had not yet started to rain, though it appeared it might at any moment. The sunset was hidden from view by the dark clouds in the sky and the wind had picked up.

"Should we just go on in, do you think?" asked Lily when they arrived.

"Given that we might be soaked any second if we do not, yes I think we should. I dread the thought of a repeat of the earlier scene with Cousin Alex." The last words stuck in her throat as she said them.

If he isn't the real Alex, then I wonder who he is? I guess for now it is best to pretend that I don't know all about him and continue to address him as my cousin. But in a way that seems a gross disrespect to Aunt Ida. Lord, show me how to handle this. I don't think I can face him right now. How I need Your courage!

Mandy tried the door and it was not locked. They stepped into the vestibule. To her great relief, there was no sign of Alex. The study was dark and empty, the downstairs quiet. They quickly went up the stairs and directly to Ida's bed chamber. Nan was sitting on the bed again, holding her friend's hand, singing quietly to her. A strange song for the situation, something about chariots.

She stopped when they entered.

"Did you have a good dinner? I truly regret I had nothing to feed you here. But I trust the food was acceptable to you?"

"Oh yes, it was delicious and quite reasonable in price. And no sign of Alex when we came in. How is Aunt Ida doing?"

"No words since you left. I couldn't get her to rouse or eat anything, either. She hasn't had enough to feed a bird for two days now. I'm going to ask the doctor to check on her tomorrow. I will go down and lock up in a bit before I retire for the night."

"I think we will do the same ourselves. Remember, I'm here if you should need me."

"Thank you, that means a great deal. I will call if I need help. Be sure to let me know if you need anything. I'm not exactly the world's best hostess right now. Oh, I think I've already said that more than once, haven't I?"

She rose and hugged Mandy who returned it enthusiastically. Had they only met a few hours ago? It seemed they had known one another forever! Mandy offered thanks to the Lord for this new friend and for her loving care for Ida. What a relief for Mandy's heart, to know she wasn't facing all this alone!

As mother and daughter got ready for bed, they chatted about the trip Mandy and her father made to Indian Territory long ago. The reality of what they found when they arrived had been quite different from what she expected of course, not to mention how dramatically their lives changed very soon after they got there. The story was one often told over the years but had taken on new meaning for both of them, now that they were in this house.

Before getting into bed, Mandy decided to poke around a bit to see if she could figure out where her aunt could have hidden the letters that Nan mentioned. It made sense they might be secreted in this room and certainly would be the one place Alex would never look.

After several minutes of searching she said, "No luck on the letters. Maybe tomorrow when I am more rested I can look again."

"What are we going to do in the morning, Mama? The book I'm reading is quite intriguing, and I would be happy to stay here to read if that is all right with you."

"No, I don't want to leave you alone here in case Cousin Alex makes more trouble. I would like for you to go with me but you may bring your book. It is exciting to see you interested in a book that my aunt owns."

"Yes, it is marked up, too, which is odd for a novel. Almost like she had studied it in a way, rather than merely leafing through its pages."

"What do you mean, *marked?*"

"Many of the words and sentences are underlined. With a number of notes written in the margins, too. It must have been a favorite, as it appears that several comments are older than others—almost as though she re-read it more than once."

"That is interesting. Well, I will look forward to hearing more about this later. For now, we must get to sleep. In a real bed!"

"With real pillows!" exclaimed Lily. At that they both giggled like little schoolgirls!

Just as Mandy climbed into bed, a spot over by the fireplace caught her eye. And she jumped right out again.

"Mama, are you all right?" Lily asked, alarm lining her face.

"Yes! More than all right, in fact. I think I know where she may have hidden the letters! I had almost forgotten, but I had a secret hiding place here in my room where I kept a handful of my dearest treasures as a child. I didn't think my aunt knew about it but maybe she did, after all. Or found it after I left. I took the box with me of course but the empty space is exactly right for hiding letters."

Mandy rushed to the fireplace hearth and bent to pull at one brick on the corner down at the bottom. After tugging on it several moments, the brick gave way and came sliding out!

"Something is in there!" she cried as she pulled a box out.

"What is it, Mama?"

"The box is full of letters! From my aunt! Look, a few appear to be very old, too. One group is held together with a blue ribbon and has the name Bessie on top. Wasn't that the name of that other friend Nan mentioned had lived here for a while before she left?"

"She did more than simply leave, she disappeared. How mysterious!"

Lily yawned as Mandy spread out the letters on the bed to get a better look under the lamp light. The young girl picked up her book to read while her mother glanced through the messages from her aunt.

"A few of the letters were written to me right after I left, and others appear to have continued for several months after I was captured. Oh my!" Mandy was lost for quite a while in the memories the letters brought up to her.

When she looked again at her daughter, she smiled to see Lily had fallen asleep while reading. Mandy tenderly put the book up and tucked her daughter under the covers. *Imagine my doing this for Lily, in my own childhood bed!* Then she gathered up the letters as well, taking them over to the desk instead. There she sat for a long time, reading well into the night. Finally, her eyes became heavy as she searched for a stopping point. Suddenly one passage she read made her sit upright and cry out softly.

"Oh, my! Here is our proof!"

CHAPTER FOURTEEN

"But my God shall supply all your need according to his riches in glory by Christ Jesus." Phil. 4:19

April 17, 1867

"Nan, I found the letters!"

She glanced up from the pie crust she was working on. "Really? Where were they?"

"They were hidden in my room, in a place Aunt Ida knew I would check out when I came back and stayed in there. That must have been the whole reason she made that request a part of her will. Anyway, you will never guess what I read last night in one of Aunt Ida's letters! It was quite late and I was tired from having read so many of them, that at first I thought I surely had read the words wrong. But I did not. I believe you will agree, this is the proof we were hoping for about Cousin Alex!"

"What on earth are you talking about, Amanda? What proof and of what, exactly?"

Mandy glanced around for a moment, checking to see if Alex lurked close by, eavesdropping. *No sign of him, thank goodness, but I cannot take that risk.*

"Um, could we go out into the garden for a little stroll?"

Sensing the need for privacy in Mandy's request, she hesitated only a moment.

"That should work if you think that Lily could possibly stay with Miss Ida while we take a brief break outside. I really don't think she should be left alone for long. I only came down because the two of you were up there and I knew you could hear her if she called out. While you go ask Lily, I will finish up this pie and load the tray for breakfast. That way, when we return we can get up there quickly. Will it take us long?"

"Not long at all. It is for your ears alone, however. I am certain Lily will be happy to keep Aunt Ida company for a few minutes for us. Be right back."

She raced up the stairs, heart pounding from the excitement of what she had to share more than from the physical exertion. Within moments, she was back down, to find Nan was done with her preparations.

"Did you tell her there is a window in Miss Ida's room overlooking the garden, in case she needs us quickly?"

"I did. How well I recall that very window and how it would always get me into trouble when I was younger! I wasn't supposed to be playing out in the garden area but if Aunt Ida caught me by looking out that window, she would call out to me about my trespassing, loud enough that the neighbors could hear her!"

As they walked through the flower garden, Mandy fingered the letter in her pocket. She could feel the tension rise from her toes up to her head. Would Nan believe what she was about to learn? She hoped so! Once they were out of direct earshot of the house, Nan stopped and asked what Mandy had read that was urgent enough to warrant all this secrecy.

"I have a letter here that was in response, apparently, to one Aunt Ida wrote to Alex's commanding officer, or at least the one over him after the other one died in the attack. She asked if Alex survived or not."

"And…"

"And the answer is that Alex did survive briefly but his wounds were far too grievous for him to live long-term. Within a few days, he passed away in a field hospital not far from the site of the disaster. 'Our Alex' is not really *ours* at all!"

"Oh, my word! How on earth did she manage to send that message right under Alex's nose, without him finding out about it?"

"I'm not sure of course but I would guess she made up a pretense to have Mr. Grayson or another friend carry the letter to the fort with a request to send it through official channels. That is how I got mine through to Aunt Ida, and how she replied back to me as well."

"The big question is how she managed to keep it to herself after learning the truth! That must have been quite difficult for her. But even more, *why* keep it secret instead of confronting him with the evidence?"

"Good point, Nan. Do we dare ask her?"

"No, I think it would only cause her terrible agony if she had to face us in her dying hours and talk about how Alex deceived her and betrayed her trust like he has."

"You are probably right. I wouldn't want to hurt her like that. The truth would help my claim if it comes to a dispute of course but otherwise will only cause more harm, I should think."

"I had suspected for a long time of course that Alex wasn't who he said he was. A great many little things simply didn't add up, as I told you yesterday. But to find out for certain that he isn't Alex, our Alex, well, this is certainly shocking, all right! I can't believe she had the courage to be that resourceful, as to write to the captain of his company for verification of his death."

"When Alex showed up here how did he explain his presence to Aunt Ida, knowing she had received the official notification from the Army of the fact that he was killed?"

"What Miss Ida told me was that he merely said in all the confusion of the battle aftermath, he was unconscious from his wounds which caused him to be misidentified. He was taken to the Army Hospital in a nearby garrison where no one knew him. However, once he was fully awake he informed them of his name and told them he had been aiding the blacksmith in his job when he was injured."

"And the smithy conveniently was no longer living to contradict him," said Mandy quietly.

"Exactly. Along with his commander, who would have instantly seen through the lie long before it got to this point. I recall that Alex told Miss Ida that after he recovered, he was forced to go into battle with a new regiment, making it impossible for him to let her know he was alive. It was well beyond a year later before he showed up here. My curiosity was aroused as to where he had been all those long months. When I asked him, he said he had been busy working his freight business in Kentucky and other parts of Ohio, which kept him scrambling constantly to make a profit with it in the waning days of the war and right afterward. Life was hard back then, so it was a believable story. Now it seems all he told us was a lie. He is nothing but a big fraud!"

"How I am going to face him now," added Mandy, "knowing the truth yet not exposing it, is beyond me. Who on earth is he? And why is he here, pretending to be Alex?"

"The answer is obvious but for now, we need to focus on Miss Ida. Speaking of her, we need to get back upstairs."

As Mandy followed her new friend, she glanced around at all the plants, from trees to bushes to flowers. It was beautiful! After breakfast she would come back out to explore with Lily and perhaps Nan could walk with them as well. The fresh air would be good for her.

I wonder if I should show this letter to the lawyer when I meet him later this morning? I think not yet, because not having met the man before, I'm not sure I want to admit to him that Alex is not the person he pretends to be. Maybe later but not now. Speaking of that, I need to get ready in order to make it to his office as soon as possible. And away from that horrid imposter who dares to call himself my cousin!

Some time later, Mandy and Lily were on their way to meet Matthew Grayson, Ida Clark's lawyer. Since it was only a few blocks away from Wellington Oaks and a beautiful spring day, the two were enjoying the brisk walk.

"Mama," Lily asked after a few minutes, "why is it that you were concerned about going to Mr. Grayson's house? I heard you tell Miss Nan you were uncomfortable with that."

"A lady does not visit a gentleman in his home without a chaperone. And I do not mean her twelve year old daughter! When I was younger I thought that rule was silly. But as an adult I can see it makes perfect sense. However, this situation is a bit different. With his office in his home, we have no choice."

"Yes, Miss Nan said he uses a room in his cabin so perhaps it will be all right, especially with your daughter along!"

"Here we are," Mandy said. The red letters on the grey sign hanging out in front proclaimed to all who walked by that this, indeed, was the office of "Matthew Grayson, Esquire, Attorney at Law." Their destination. *Why am I so nervous?*

"Lily," her mother said, stopping a few steps away from the door, "I need you to be on your very best behavior while we are here. There will be plenty of grown-up talk going on and I cannot explain everything to you because much of it I'm afraid I won't understand myself. Therefore, to save any embarrassment, I'm asking that you not speak unless spoken to. If you have questions, please save them until we are out of there, all right?"

"Yes, Mama, I understand. I brought my book. Would it be rude to read while you are talking to the lawyer?"

"No, I think that will be fine once we are settled in. I will tell you when I believe it is appropriate, but you are not to pull out the book until that time, understood?" She nodded. Mandy gulped, trying to shake her anxiety.

After a brief hesitation, Mandy knocked on the door and a female voice told them to come on in. *A female? I thought he was unmarried!*

There was a small table right inside the door where an attractive young lady sat, apparently the one who had spoken to them. Mandy glanced quickly around the room and spotted a larger desk back in the corner which she assumed was Mr. Grayson's, but no sign of the lawyer himself.

"May I help you?"

"Yes, my name is Mrs. Amanda Alton and this is my daughter Lily. We have come from Indian Territory to see Mr. Grayson, if he is available."

"Indian Territory?" Her eyes widened a bit. "May I tell him what it is about?"

"Certainly. I am Miss Ida Clark's niece and I believe Mr. Grayson has some paperwork that I need to sign regarding my aunt's Last Will and Testament."

"Oh, yes, of course, Mrs. Alton. I thought when you said where you were from that it must be you. He's been expecting your arrival for a few days now. Please have a seat." She gestured toward several chairs off to one side. "He is in a meeting with a client but they should be through in a few minutes."

They had barely gotten seated when a tall man wearing a patch over one eye came into the room, followed by another gentleman, grinning from ear to ear, who addressed the other by name.

"Thank you very much, Mr. Grayson. This means a great deal to me and to my family. We couldn't have done it without your help." And the two shook hands.

"You are most welcome, sir," he said. "Happy to help."

As Mandy studied the handsome face of the lawyer, the sight took her breath away for a moment. He was not at all the type of person she had expected to be her aunt's attorney. For one thing, she thought he would be much older. And, well, nothing like he was! She colored slightly, taking in a gulp of air to steady her nerves, and lowering her eyes. *Stop being so foolish! You aren't a silly schoolgirl! The way you are reacting, you would think he was proposing marriage!*

She finally glanced back up but tried to avoid the face that had taken her by surprise. To her shock she felt drawn to it, nevertheless. Even the eye patch failed to mar his striking appearance.

The client walked toward the door, but his attention was obviously glued to the young lady at the table and he never noticed the two waiting in the corner.

"Good day, Miss Lawson," he said as he put his hat on, immediately tipping it to her.

The lady nodded and smiled at him pleasantly as he disappeared out the door.

"Miss Lawson, I thought I heard voices a few moments ago. Did someone—" He stopped as his gaze fell on his visitors.

"Yes, sir. This is Mrs. Amanda Alton and her daughter Lily. From Indian Territory." Mandy stood and faced the attorney.

"Of course, Mrs. Alton! I am Matthew Grayson, in case you hadn't figured that out by now. What a delight to get to meet you at last. And your lovely daughter, what an unexpected pleasure that she was able to come with you." He shook her hand first, then reached out to Lily, who stood as well and smiled shyly as she returned his offered handshake. Mandy could see the excitement radiate in her child's face at being treated in such a grown-up manner. *Why does that bother me like this? Is it because she is, indeed, growing up and I had not realized it?*

"Please, won't you both follow me? We can visit privately in here." He nodded toward the room from which he had emerged a few minutes before. "Miss Lawson, please let me know when Mr. Patton arrives, will you?"

Grayson escorted them into the comfortable room with a large table in the middle and a bookcase against one wall. Chairs ringed the table and he indicated they should take a seat there, which they did.

"Mr. Grayson, I didn't mean to intrude if you have someone else coming to meet with you. My aunt was quite insistent that I come as soon as possible to sign the papers with you about her will, and Nan, that is Miss Brewster, told me I should come right away this morning. Lily and I arrived late yesterday afternoon so naturally I am most anxious to find out more about this whole affair from you. It's a bit difficult to get any details out of my aunt right now, as I am sure you know."

"Yes," and his face fell visibly. Gently he asked, "How is Miss Ida today?"

"Not doing well but thankfully she sleeps most of the time. Miss Brewster has filled me in on several things, but I have quite a few questions which I hope you can answer." She stopped and turned to her daughter. "Lily, you may go ahead and read if you like."

Turning back to the attorney, Mandy was surprised when he spoke to her daughter, as children were rarely addressed in a personal manner by adults unless they knew them well. Or at least that was the case years ago and she had no reason to believe it had changed. Again, the discomfort nudged at her heart. *What is wrong with me?*

"Lily, what is it you are reading?"

"Sir, it—it is a book of Great-Aunt Ida's, called *Uncle Tom's Cabin* by Harriet Beecher Stowe."

"Ah, yes, the book that started a war!"

"What?" Lily's face paled. "A *war?*"

"Yes, did you not know? I suppose living out in Indian Territory is why. The book was quite the stir here. When President Lincoln, God rest his soul, read the book several years ago he became fired up about the abolitionists' cause even more than before. Or at least, that is what we have been told. It certainly was true for many of us throughout the nation. Are you enjoying it?"

"Yes, I am, thank you."

"I suppose I should have asked it another way. This book is not one a person really 'enjoys' but instead absorbs the lessons within it, wiping away a tear here and there or gnashing teeth where appropriate at the injustices. Wouldn't you agree?"

"I am only about half-way through but yes, already I have shed a few tears. I had no idea adults would feel the same way, however."

"Tears?" Mandy asked in awe. "My goodness!" She turned to Grayson. "She only started it last night but has been reading a great deal since. That is her big love—books—and she reads every one we can buy her as fast as she can."

"Tell me, Lily—and then I will let you get to your reading so your mother and I can visit about this will—what is your impression of all the markings your great-aunt has put into the book?"

"Uh, well, I noticed them right off, if that is what you mean. Some of the words are older than others and seem to have faded with time, thus are not easily read. Others stand out and have caught my eye, although I'm not sure what to make of them."

"We will talk about this more later, if that is all right with you. Perhaps I can explain various aspects of it if you wish. Your great-aunt and I had many discussions about this book. Did you know that it made a tremendous impact on her life and faith?"

"Really?" asked Mandy, startled. What would her aunt have been thinking to discuss something as personal and private as her faith with her attorney? What did that have to do with legal matters?

"Yes, Mrs. Alton. You will find your aunt discussed it with many here in town over quite a few years. She even had the privilege to hear Mrs. Stowe speak one time and she would tell anyone who would listen how exciting that was for her. God did a great work of change in her heart because of it as well. She bought the book and had it autographed that night."

Lily turned quickly to the front of the book and leafed over several pages until she found the words inscribed to her great-aunt from the author. Her eyes wide, Lily smiled.

"She met the woman who wrote the book, Mama! How I wish I could meet an author some day!"

"Why don't you get on with your reading, dear? We will talk about this further at a later time. Mr. Grayson is a busy man and we mustn't waste any more of his time."

"Oh, this is not a waste of my time by any means. However, I know you did not travel thousands of miles in order to talk about a book! If you will excuse me a moment, I will get the papers you need to sign."

He ducked out of the room briefly, returning with several documents, a pen, and a bottle of ink. He took a seat next to Mandy, shuffling through to find the right page.

"As I believe you know, your aunt is leaving almost her entire estate to you. What you may not know, however, is that this is minus a small bequest to her church as well as one to her beloved friend and companion, Nan Brewster."

"How wonderful! I know Miss Brewster will use it wisely. That was very kind and generous of my aunt to do this for her. It is humbling to know she also cared about her church. They always need money so I'm quite certain they will be most appreciative of their gift, too."

"Yes, I agree with you. She was most insistent on doing this and I assured her that it would not diminish the impact of your own inheritance, to include them also."

"Of course not. God's work must go on, whether in Trenton or in Indian Territory. In addition, from what I have seen in the one day I have been here, my aunt could never have survived this long without the loving care provided by Miss Brewster. I cannot imagine what would have happened to Aunt Ida without her. Their friendship is quite special, to say the least."

"It is, indeed. At any rate, normally, I would be barred from discussing the contents of the will with you or anyone, for that matter, until Miss Ida passes away. But she specifically asked that I talk to you about it when you arrived, even if she is still living. Do you understand all this?"

"Yes, sir, I think I do. I must say I'm a bit overwhelmed at her generosity. In her letter to me, she told me it would be quite a bit of money but wasn't specific beyond that. Regardless, it will mean life itself to the Kiowa people, among whom my husband and I minister in Indian Territory. They are starving right now; therefore, it is most urgent that I return home with this inheritance as soon as possible to help keep them alive. I only hope it will be enough to buy the food they no longer can hunt for, since the buffalo have disappeared from the prairie."

"I'm sorry to hear of this misfortune for the Kiowa people and I am pleased I could play a small part in providing for their needs. What happened to the buffalo? I thought they numbered in the hundreds of thousands out there."

"They used to and were a major portion of the livelihood for the entire tribe, indeed for many of the tribes, for generations. But over the past few years they have been killed indiscriminately by people coming into the territory and hunting them for sport, not for food. The carcasses by the dozens are often left to rot for the most part, which has been particularly painful for the Kiowa to watch, knowing how much they need those animals to survive. Everything from their shelter to their clothing, to their tools, to of course their food supply for the winter months, all depend on having a good hunt every fall. Sadly, that is no longer possible. The deer, rabbit, squirrel, and a bear they might occasionally find doesn't begin to sustain an entire village of hungry people for months on end. I apologize for rambling on, but it is a situation near and dear to my heart." *If you only knew how much this means to me and to my family!*

"No apology needed. Yes, I can see the dilemma all right. I keep hearing that the Reservations out west where all the Indians are being moved will mean they don't have to hunt for their food any longer. Is that true?"

"We have heard the same stories but so far there is no Reservation in our area. Therefore, I cannot answer your question with any degree of certainty. However, I can tell you the Kiowa were not meant to be 'kept' or taken care of like children or pets. These proud people have always been free to roam across the prairie in pursuit of the buffalo. They move their villages, in fact, to follow them as they migrate from one place to another, especially in the fall of the year when the fur is the thickest and the meat on the animals has increased from the summer feedings. Hunting is their lifeblood. If they can no longer hunt, the loss of dignity will be even harder to accept than the lack of food has been. With this money, therefore, my husband and I plan to purchase beef to feed the people as well as cowhides to provide shelter and clothing. Although not a great solution, it is far better than sitting on the prairie watching their children slowly starve to death. But tell me, Mr. Grayson, will the estate give us the money we need for this? I'm concerned that it might not be enough."

"Oh, believe me, it will more than cover that cost! In fact, Mrs. Alton, you are about to become an extremely wealthy woman!"

CHAPTER FIFTEEN

"For I am the LORD, I change not..." Malachi 3:6

April 17, 1867

"Excuse me? What did you just say?" Mandy could barely get the words out. She swallowed hard. *Wealthy, did he say? No, extremely wealthy! I cannot even comprehend this.*

"It's a lot to take in at once, isn't it?" Mr. Grayson's voice broke through the fog.

"Yes, sir, to be honest, it is. I had no idea! You mean that house is worth that much money?"

"She owns far more than merely a house, Mrs. Alton. The extensive grounds around the house also belong to her and are quite valuable in themselves, with the large apple orchard and the beautiful gardens of course. Inside the house, the furniture and furnishings will be worth a vast sum, I should imagine, although we won't know for certain until everything is inventoried adequately. This includes all the artwork on the walls, her books, jewelry, as well as many other personal items throughout the house. And of course any of those that you might wish to keep will be up to you. Some of the financial details I cannot go into at this point but will certainly do so at a later time. Trust me, she has a large amount of savings safely protected, as well as land holdings and investments that can all be sold rather quickly. In spite of the war years, which cut into everyone's savings considerably of course, she has managed to increase her estate tremendously. Inheriting her cousin's gold mine out in California also didn't hurt any, either."

"Gold mine? Are you serious?"

"Yes, I am. This distant cousin apparently was touched by Miss Ida's kindness to him in staking him for his dream of going west to mine for gold. When he got out there and struck it rich, he wrote up a will leaving his share of the gold mine to her, should anything happen to him. He had an unscrupulous partner in the venture who, as I understand it, tried to squeeze him out of his half of the profits when they hit the strike. Little did he know that it was all protected legally. When your aunt's cousin turned up dead, the authorities found the will and awarded the entire half of its worth to your aunt. Even though only half, it was a considerable fortune."

"Oh, my word! I suppose Aunt Ida could easily have multiplied her assets several times over, knowing how frugal she was with money. It seems I made the right decision in coming to claim this, despite the extreme hardships it caused for us to get here. This news has left me stunned, as I had no idea the estate would be worth that much."

"I agree your coming was the right thing to do for several reasons. Your aunt sincerely hoped and prayed you would arrive in time as she was desperate to see you once more. And so you have."

"I'm grateful for God's timing in granting that prayer for it was also my own. My biggest regret is that I didn't come sooner."

"Be that as it may, at least now you are here. Another point I wanted to make with you right off is that as soon as your aunt became ill, I was flooded with inquiries regarding the possible sale of her home. I assume from what you said earlier, you have no intentions of living in the house once it is in your possession. Therefore, I also assume you will want to sell it as quickly as you can, is that right?"

"Yes, you are correct. I do hope that can be accomplished without too much of a delay."

"We shall be sorry to see you leave but I do understand your rush to get home. To respond to your concern, I feel certain the sale of the house and grounds can be done very quickly, based on the amount of interest I have seen thus far, even before she has passed away. As distressing as this subject might seem to you, it is something we need to discuss, although details can certainly wait for later. Out of those requests, I feel that you might want to consider one in particular. Mr. and Mrs. Crawford Mason work with our local Historical Society and they would like to purchase the house in order to set it up as a museum. Their intention is to preserve it so the folks in our community can enjoy it as well as learn about your aunt's essential role in the development of much of it over the years. Later on, I will be happy to arrange an opportunity for you to meet with them to hear their ideas for the project. If that is agreeable to you, of course."

"A museum? How lovely! I think Aunt Ida would be overwhelmed with such an honor. I will definitely keep this in mind, sir, and I appreciate your letting me know about this option—when the time comes."

"I didn't mean to get the cart before the horse, as they say, but I wanted to assure you there is hope for getting it sold rapidly and at a very good price. In addition, I want to let you know that I shall do all in my power to carry out your aunt's wishes to the letter. Meantime, there is the matter of a signature on these papers." He pointed out to her the places where she needed to sign her name. "All these papers do is to assign the inheritance to you, as the major beneficiary of her will. The only thing lacking is to enter the date the will is to be probated and at that point the title of everything you are owed will be transferred to you."

Why is my hand shaking so? Is it because of all the good we can do with this money for our people? Ken-ai-te, you should be here to share in this! Oh, my love! Can you imagine what this will mean for them? Or am I nervous because I'm using a false name? Why do the lies keep hitting me in the face like this? God, help me! I'm trying to obey You. Why do I remain confused and fearful over this?

She took a deep breath and signed the false name. The result would be in God's hands.

"Would your hesitation have anything to do with concerns you might have about a woman being able to inherit real property? Because if it is, you need not worry. Ohio recently passed a law making that legal in our state. In fact, we are the first one in the nation to have such a ruling on the books."

"Oh, I hadn't even thought about that being a problem. Well, good to know." She deliberately avoided answering his question, hoping he wouldn't press her. That truly was the least of her worries at the moment. Mr. Grayson rose and gathered up the papers, excusing himself for a moment. Mandy breathed a sigh of relief. *That was easy enough. Hope the rest of this process goes as quickly. All I want is to go home!*

While Mr. Grayson was out of the room, Mandy sat quietly, studying her hands on the table before her.

You are not even in the ground, Aunt Ida, yet we are sitting here calmly talking about disposing of all your possessions. With these hands I have signed all you own away, even though it is what you want. Somehow, that doesn't seem right! In spite of the fact it needed to be done, in fact has been done at your insistence, I don't like this one bit. What was it you used to tell me, something about the cycle of life continuing on, whether we are ready for it to do so or not? At least your money will serve a greater good. I can take great solace from that.

Tears sprang into her eyes. She honestly wasn't certain if they were more for her suffering people back home or for her pending grief over losing the aunt she only now was beginning to know and understand. Perhaps it was both. Blinking them back she cleared her throat, glancing around the room to distract herself from the deep emotion.

Mandy's eye landed on Lily whose attention was firmly fixed on the book in her hands. *We need to discuss that book more carefully. I want to know more about what kind of an impact the story had on my aunt. Apparently, that same power is now drawing my daughter ever deeper into its depths. Never when I taught her to read did I dream it might lead to something like this!*

When the attorney returned, he let Mandy know that he had spoken with his next client and asked him to come back later that afternoon, which he readily agreed to do.

"This way, we will have more time to talk. There is another matter concerning the will I haven't mentioned yet but you need to know about it, again at your aunt's specific direction. I take it that because you spent the night at your aunt's home last night as she requested you do, you have met your cousin, Alex Clark. Is that correct?"

"Yes, I did. He was most disagreeable, even rude and threatening at one point, in fact. What have I done to make him so angry at me?"

"It's all very complicated, I'm afraid. Has Nan told you how he came to be the grandson of your aunt?"

"Yes, she did explain all that to me. It's hard to understand how my aunt's kindness could have resulted in such an obnoxious boor as this man living with her but it seems it has."

She almost said something about having learned he was not the man he pretended to be but wasn't quite ready to reveal that to him. Not yet, if at all.

"When he first came back from the war, she immediately changed her will to ensure that he would be the sole heir to the entire estate, as she had promised to do when his mother died years ago. Upon word that the three boys had died in battle she had named several charities to inherit, instead of them, but naturally wanted to put him back in when he showed up. He seemed a little too, um, shall I say *eager* to complete the legal paperwork for my liking. But I couldn't argue with Miss Ida that it needed to be done."

"That makes perfect sense to me. Was that a problem? You sound a bit hesitant about it."

"Well, over time your aunt has increasingly had her doubts about whether Alex is who he says he is, that is, if he really is her grandson. She wisely told me one day that with everything in life there are changes. We should not be surprised when they come but instead embrace them, adapt to them, with God's help. The good news, of course, is that He never changes, only people experience that. Yet, she was deeply troubled as the discrepancies regarding Alex piled up, one after another. When he first returned for instance, she said the pants he had left at the house, instead of being too short, which she fully expected them to be since he had grown older and thus taller, were too long! When Alex left, he towered over quite a few his age and we could all tell he would be a tall man when fully grown. Thus, this quirk was very odd, to say the least. He claimed it was due to the trauma of war, together with his leg injuries which never had healed properly, or some such nonsense. Miss Ida dismissed it as unimportant at first but after a while it increasingly bothered her. Along with several other inconsistencies, most of which were quite inconsequential and easily explained away, she became quite disturbed over this one thing. Every time she had to hem up another pair of his pants it would upset her further. Not surprisingly, mentioning it irritated him, so she finally dropped it."

"How did you find out about it, then? Are you saying she finally told you about her suspicions?"

"That's correct, she did. I had to agree with her after hearing what she had to say that he appeared to be an imposter. How I hated having to hurt her as I did but I had to be honest. Without proof, however, beyond him having forgotten a few key memories from his childhood and pants dragging on the ground, there was little she could do but to accept him for who he was: her grandson and thus heir to her estate."

He stopped, appearing to measure his words carefully before he continued. Mandy tensed up, the fluttering in her stomach indicating to her that something dreadful may be coming.

"In addition, I expressed some concern to her about a rather delicate matter, that of living in a house with a man who had nothing to gain from her staying alive and everything to gain if she did not."

Mandy's eyes flew wide. "You feared he might try to harm her?" The lawyer appeared to hesitate again in replying, as though checking every word before saying it.

This is why Nan was so certain that harm had already come to her beloved friend. I was afraid she exaggerated with her charge, but it appears in truth to have great merit!

He cleared his throat. "As much as I disliked saying the words out loud—and still do right now—yes. She asked me several times about possibly changing her will yet again, to leave the estate to others in order to prevent him from getting it. Although I explained how easy it was to do this, she always hesitated and never seemed quite ready to take that drastic of a step. However, recently she seemed to become more upset than usual over this topic and I figured she was close to the decision.

"When she received your letter, that seemed to be the impetus she was waiting for. Immediately, she sent for me to ensure you would have the bulk of it, not him. Whether he truly is Alex Clark or not, his attitude, let alone his treatment of her, left a great deal to be desired. At last she had an option that made perfect sense and gave her great peace as she faced her terminal diagnosis."

Mandy had been praying while he spoke and decided it was time to share what she had learned with the attorney. He deserved to know the truth. Hearing herself repeat the words out loud made cold chills break out on her arms. When she finished, he seemed genuinely anxious over this revelation.

"Perhaps," he said, "it was upon receiving this letter from the commander that she changed her mind about defending Alex because what it contains is the proof she had been seeking. Not the answer she wanted but at least iron-clad proof he is an imposter. This letter, do you have it?"

"I have Aunt Ida's letter explaining about it but not the original one from whoever she wrote to. Maybe it is in with the other letters, I'm not sure. Will her words attesting to this be enough to constitute proof?"

"It won't be as effective as the original but yes, I believe it will work. It all depends on how far we have to push this point of truth, and that remains to be seen."

"Frankly, I wasn't sure I should tell you about it but after hearing you relate everything from the past year or so, I knew God was urging me to reveal it to you. The letter is back at the house with all the others."

"Others? As in other letters? Your aunt wrote more than one to you?"

"Apparently as soon as I disappeared years ago she began writing to me, as a way to handle her grief. She kept them in a secret hiding place I had as a child, in the brickwork of the fireplace hearth in my bedroom. Nan said as Aunt Ida's illness progressed, she had often rambled on about letters to her niece, even how they had some sort of connection to her 'pretend grandson' as well. They seemed to be part of the frequent hallucinations, though, so she dismissed them as not being real. At least at first she did, but after a few days began to wonder if it might all be true. Her searching turned up nothing. When I arrived, she insisted that I try to find them to solve this mystery. After wracking my brain all evening, I suddenly remembered this spot but I honestly didn't think Aunt Ida even knew it was there. Apparently, she had discovered it at some point after I left and had been filling it with letters for years out of sentiment, long before Alex ever entered her life. Once he returned, it became a perfect place for hiding something she didn't want him to see. Thus, she felt free to write about her deepest feelings without fear of repercussions. Indeed, all this time she has been sharing her love on paper, a love she could no longer express otherwise."

"What a special way to look at it!"

"Thank you. It's true. I can see her love on every page I have read thus far. She reared me, you know. While the two of us didn't always see eye to eye, she meant the world to me as the only mother I knew." *Until I met Sleeping Bird, that is.*

"Yes, I know the story of how your father showed up with you when you were only a few weeks old to ask his sister for help in caring for you. Your aunt told me about it many times, with great pride as a matter of fact. She loved both of you very much and was devastated when the two of you left. Upon finding out he had been killed and you had been captured by Indians, the despair almost overwhelmed her."

Mandy's heart warmed to this man even more. No longer a stranger, she realized he knew a great deal about her. In addition, her aunt had obviously valued his friendship highly, far beyond his legal advice, to confide such details to him. She hoped he wouldn't be dismayed to consider that she had lived with the Kiowa for a time, as some whites certainly would be. Little did he know *how* long she had been with them! His attitude, however, seemed the same after saying this so she relaxed a bit. Yes, Mandy liked this man very much!

"Thank you, Mr. Grayson, for your kind words. I'm certain that was very difficult on her." *And on me, for that matter! I must change this topic or my heart will get bogged down in too many sad memories.*

"I'm not trying to pry but I would love to know more about these letters and what your aunt said to you. If you feel comfortable sharing anything from them."

"Of course I would be happy to do that, as there is nothing terribly personal in them. The thing is, there are quite a few and thus it is going to take me a while to get through all of them. But I'm working on it. It is interesting that you should ask this, as after Nan and I talked about it, we both realized that I might be able to find important information about Alex from them. But more than that, I hoped they might help me better understand my aunt and why she had undergone such a drastic change the past fourteen years. Perhaps that is one of the reasons God brought me here, besides honoring Aunt Ida's bequest, to discover this fact and the events that caused it all."

"I think you could be more right than you know. This explains at least why she insisted on including in the directions about her will the rather odd request for you to spend at least one night in the house and specifically, in your old room. She must have hoped you would recall the hiding spot and find her letters to you. They must be very important for her to go to all this trouble."

Mandy nodded. Why not entrust the letters to Mr. Grayson or to Nan instead of hiding them away? *Maybe I'll find the answer by the time I finish all my reading.*

"Mr. Grayson, do you believe God can change a person's heart, turn him from evil and bring good out of chaos?"

He smiled. "I'm not a theologian, Mrs. Alton, but yes, I do. He has done it for me. You are referring to your so-called cousin, right? In his case, I'm not sure even God can do that for his hard heart. God is in the business of changing lives but that is one soul I think even He has given up on."

"I'm not thoroughly convinced of that—yet. Perhaps, with enough love and compassion, the tiny spark of humanity that has to be there could be brought out. After all, Christ died for him the same as He did for you or for me."

"Yes, He did. But to be perfectly blunt, Nan and I both have reached out to the man repeatedly over time and Clark has not once responded to either of us. What's more, I truly don't think he ever will. If he could have been persuaded by love and compassion, as you say, I believe your aunt would have been able to exact a change in him, in spite of the evil intent he apparently had in coming here, pretending to be a person he is not. Instead, he has only gotten steadily worse!"

"You probably are correct but I can't shake the feeling that at some point he is going to need God. I sincerely hope it will not be too late for him. Perhaps my aunt will share in one or more of the dozens and dozens of letters she wrote how she saw the same thing, had the same hope. Obviously, I haven't had time to read all of them yet. I started with the oldest ones but quickly switched to reading the newer ones instead, where I learned of the confirmation of her suspicions about Alex. Along with a great deal more, to be honest, much of which has surprised me. She was quite different in these later years than when I was growing up and I'm having a difficult time absorbing all that."

"From what I know and you have told me today, I believe you will find she had good cause for those changes. That book your daughter is reading is one of the keys to that puzzle, but my guess is those letters will explain even more. You might keep an eye out for a deep secret I know she wanted very much to tell you in person. Because she couldn't be certain you would get here in time to do that, my guess is it is in one of those letters, or probably a series of them because it would take too much effort and paper to tell it in only one."

"Now you have my curiosity up! Obviously, you know what it is but I suppose I will have to wait to hear it from Aunt Ida, one way or the other." He nodded, smiling.

"It is a piece of the past worth waiting on, believe me."

"I hate to switch subjects but if you don't have anything further, Lily and I need to leave. I appreciate your time and all your kindness to my aunt throughout the years. I pray this matter can be concluded rapidly, as we discussed."

He stared at her intently. "There is one other thing I wish to discuss with you." Instead of continuing, he glanced down at his hands before him and was silent for several moments.

"Mr. Grayson? Is something wrong? What else did you need to talk about?"

"Oh, I'm sorry. I was trying to decide how to state this. I truly do not wish to frighten you but feel obligated to caution you, nevertheless." He glanced over at Lily who was still absorbed in her book, then back to Mandy and made eye contact with her, deep frowns wrinkling his forehead. Again, Mandy felt a sense of dread overwhelm her. What could be so awful that he had such difficulty saying the words?

"I really think you need to make plans to get out of the house as soon as possible after your aunt passes away. Grief may seem your first priority at that point but I'm far more focused on your safety. Especially after your confirmation that Alex isn't really Alex, I feel it is essential that you follow my suggestion carefully, you and Nan as well. The moment that your aunt is gone, pack your things and get out. Otherwise, I fear for your very lives!"

CHAPTER SIXTEEN

"Call unto me, and I will answer thee, and shew thee great and mighty things, which thou knowest not." Jeremiah 33:3

April 17, 1867

"You really are serious about this, aren't you, Mr. Grayson?"

Mandy felt the color drain out of her cheeks and she worked to control her irregular breathing, to keep it calm and measured. Her heart pounded. If Alex presented that much danger to them, how could they continue living under the same roof with him even one more day? Who knew how long it would be before the Lord finally called her aunt to Heaven so this nightmare would be over? She had to protect her daughter! What if something happened to her? How would she ever explain it to Ken-ai-te? Or to herself? It was bad enough considering the harm Alex intended for her aunt, but to realize it might very well extend to Mandy herself and the other two as well—that was a whole different proposition that shook her deeply.

He nodded but again his eyes darted over to Lily and right back again to her mother. She got the message not to scare Lily but that was all right because Mandy was terrified enough for both of them!

Her head spinning, Mandy fought to recall what she had on her mind before this specter arose to smother her.

God, help me manage this fear in order to focus on the business questions I have. I'm not used to this and cannot seem to keep my mind on anything. Yet, it is up to me to do so. I know I was going to leave but there was something else I needed to ask him first. What was it? Oh, now I recall, his fee. We have never discussed how much all this is going to cost me!

She gulped and cleared her throat. "I understand and will certainly keep your caution in mind. One last thing before we leave, however, is that I do need to discuss a little matter of money with you, sir. How much is your fee for handling this case for me? You see, I don't have much cash with me as I had counted on staying at the house and eating our meals there while in town. Now, it appears that won't be an option. On top of everything else, I must save back some money in order to afford for the two of us to get back home once we are done here in Trenton. As much as I regret saying this, I don't know how long we can afford to remain here, frankly."

He laughed. "As I told you earlier, the one thing you do not have to worry about is money! The inheritance is vast and should easily cover all your expenses while here, plus get you back home safe and sound."

"But I don't have that money yet!"

"I realize that but am quite confident that this will be over within a few days, with the proceeds from the estate in your hands very soon. Until that time, I will cover it all for you. Thanks to your aunt's wisdom and encouragement some time ago, I now have the funds to help clients in this manner out of my own pocket. It is my turn to help you. When the whole matter is settled, at that time I will take my expenses out plus my fee and the rest will be yours."

"I'm not comfortable with having to depend on a total stranger's kindness, sir. Won't people in town notice this and perhaps get the wrong impression?"

"Folks will talk no matter what, but that shouldn't be your concern. They are used to me doing this for others and most will think nothing of my doing it for you. For the few who might attach any sinister motive to the situation, that is their problem, not ours. I assure you I will be doing all I can to protect your reputation every step of the way, however. Leave it in my hands. Your aunt entrusted this situation to my care, and I intend to see that her instructions are carefully followed in the most minute of detail."

"Stating it that way sounds much better to me. I suppose I truly don't have a choice. If my aunt trusts you, I shall do the same."

"Good! Then that matter is settled. I will set up an account for you at the Emporium right away for you to purchase whatever goods you might need while you are here. It is like a general store of sorts. All you will do is make your selections and the owner, who is a friend of mine, will charge everything to me. Keep your cash. Or I can hold it for you, if you prefer. I have the only safe in the town, where I keep my money and important papers that are vital to my business."

"A safe? What is that? I've never heard of such a thing, but the name intrigues me."

"It is a fairly new idea, a type of a large steel box, if you will, but I decided because we have no bank in the village yet, this was essential. Quite a few folks in town have used me to store their money, in fact, since I installed it here in my office. I can assure you, it would be safe in my safe!" And they laughed together.

"Perhaps that is a good idea. I hate to carry it around but also do not trust leaving it in the house when I am not there to protect it." Opening the small drawstring cache she carried around her wrist, Mandy pulled out the few bills she had in it. He counted them out and gave her a receipt. Her eyes were wide as he proceeded to open a door in the back of the room to reveal the presence of this safe. Lily jumped up to inspect the novelty as well. Both were in awe over its immense size. Lily touched it, then jumped back and blushed.

"I'm sorry, Mr. Grayson! I wondered what it was made out of."

"That's okay, Lily. It won't bite! As I said, it is made from steel, a very strong metal that is not easily breached. That means the contents remain secure through most attacks, such as robbers trying use explosives or a storm blowing it away or a fire that might otherwise burn it up." He finished securing the money within its walls and clanged the door shut, causing Mandy to jump at the harsh sound. "There, all tucked in until you need it."

"Thank you for securing my money, Mr. Grayson. You are most kind to do this for me."

"My pleasure, always glad to help. Another place I will set up an account for you is at the hotel dining room. When you need to eat there, you can also charge that instead of paying individually for the meals."

"My goodness, you are one step ahead of me with all of this! I didn't know such a thing was possible, but it would be a nice convenience, all right. I keep thinking we are ready to leave, yet more questions come to mind that I need your advice on."

"Fire away! I am happy to answer all of them, or at least try."

"When we move out of the house, where on earth will we go? Nan said she lives at a boarding house as a rule and that the landlady held her room for her when she moved in with Aunt Ida. Her plan is to go back there. But where will Lily and I stay?"

"I took the liberty of speaking with Mrs. Betsy Wilson, in case you did come to Trenton. She owns the Wilson Boarding House over on State Street, where Nan usually lives, and I asked her about availability. She has graciously consented to have you there as well. Of course, I didn't know there would be two of you but I am certain that will not be a problem, especially if you are willing to share a room. Once you are officially residents, you will take your meals there. Until that time, your meals will be covered at the hotel dining room or you can of course eat there at your aunt's with Nan."

Relief flooded Mandy's heart. God was providing for their every need, one step at a time!

"That sounds ideal, thank you. We stayed one night in Fort Smith on the way here at a hotel for ladies and the landlady was very sweet to us, also was an excellent cook! I'm sure Mrs. Wilson is equally as nice. But–but—"

"Please tell me you are not about to protest the expense of all this. It will be fine. Simply accept it and stop worrying." His smile melted much of the anxiety in her mind as she sat back into her chair, trying to relax and believe he truly did have everything covered.

How soon can You get me home, Lord? I don't fit in here very well! But it seems You have sent this kind man to help me do exactly that for now. Thank You!

He continued. "When the time comes, I can arrange to have your things moved for you if you need me to. Nan in particular may need an extra hand since she has been there for several weeks now and may have more to move than the two of you will. In addition, I have to caution you that you must not remove anything out of the house that is not yours personally until after the will is probated. But anything of sentimental meaning to you, say from your bedchamber, is another matter. We don't want to give Clark any reason to get pushy about the fact that under the law, possession counts for a great deal."

"Understood. Always, I will continue to pray that my cousin—or whoever he really is—will decide to change the course of his life and reach out to God for the salvation only He can provide. In my life I have met many who were transformed when they embraced Christ's love, while others resisted, refusing to have any part of Him. On the way from Fort Smith, in fact, I met a young man who decided he needed Christ. He chose a radically different direction for his life right there on a crowded train in the middle of the cornfields of Missouri. Oh, how I do wish Alex could experience that."

"Well, until he does, please exercise extreme caution whenever you are around him, will you do me that favor? I don't trust him as far as I can throw him!"

"I promise. And now, Lily, we really must get out of Mr. Grayson's hair. I want to go by this Emporium on the way back to the house to pick up a few things we might need for the next few days. We couldn't bring much baggage with us by horseback and train of course."

"Great idea! Before you leave, I will write a message to the owner of the store and you can take it to him. That way, he will know how to charge your purchases."

"Of course. After we go there, we need to get back to the house as the doctor was supposed to come this morning and I'm hopeful he has better news for us today about my aunt."

"I hope to come over there this afternoon myself to check on her. Please know if I can help either you or Nan out in any way, I would be happy to do so."

"Then, I guess we are ready to take our leave, Mr. Grayson. Thank you very much for all your kindness and help. I feel much better now about the task ahead. With these details taken care of, I can more easily put my attention on my aunt's situation rather than on money and arrangements. I hope to see you this afternoon at some point."

"One last thing before you leave, Mrs. Alton. Would you consider calling me Matthew instead of Mr. Grayson? I mean, I know you haven't known me long but after all I have heard about you from Miss Ida, I feel I know you well. My relationship with your aunt has been a dear one to my heart for quite a few years now. It just seems a bit awkward to have to go by last names. People here are less formal than back East, and I would imagine folks where you come from are more casual still. I don't want to be presumptuous here at all or indicate a personal relationship. However, I do want you to feel more trust in me than you normally would for the lawyer handling your aunt's will. Look on me as a family friend, if that helps."

"Of course, I think that would be entirely appropriate, given all this. What you have said explains, I suppose, why you have referred to Nan by her first name, instead of as Miss Brewster. I wondered about that as we have been talking."

"Yes, you are correct. Nan and I have known each other for several years and have been on a first name basis for most of that time."

"I see. In that case, please, do call me Amanda. No one ever calls me Mrs. Alton!" As soon as the words were out, she realized the truth of them. *No one did* because that was not her name, except here in Trenton!

"I will be happy to, *Amanda.*"

"Excellent! And may I ask yet one more question, if you don't mind?"

"Of course. I'm in no hurry at all."

"You said it was through my aunt's wisdom and encouragement that you were able to finance our stay here. I don't understand. How did she do that?"

"Well, it goes back to before the war. When I first met your aunt, she kind of took me under her wing, I guess you would say. My parents had recently been killed in an accident and I was at a loss in my grief for a short time. I inherited their holdings of several farms but had no interest in managing them. One thing led to another, and I ended up confiding in her one day that my dream was to be a lawyer instead of a farmer, especially not a large landowner as my father had been. Miss Ida encouraged me to follow that urging from God, pointing out that if I sold the farms, I could live on that money while reading law. There were no attorneys here at the time, but I moved to the county seat over in Hamilton and took a year to study under the guidance of one she knew over there. By the time I was done, the war had broken out. I immediately enlisted, putting aside my dream for a time."

"That was very noble of you to serve your country during such a difficult time."

"Thank you but it really wasn't anything noble, merely my duty as an American and I make no apologies for doing so. When I was injured, they sent me back here to Trenton to recuperate but I had nowhere to live, since I had sold my childhood home before going to Hamilton."

"You were injured?"

He smiled and pointed to his eye patch. "Yes, I was, about two years into the war. In addition to losing an eye, I also received a nasty wound to my leg that left me limping for a while. I still do sometimes when I am tired. Miss Ida immediately stepped up, allowing me to recover in her home.

During that time, we had many long talks about my future and prayed together often as well. She became almost like a second mother to me. Her advice, not to mention her tender care for my wounds, was invaluable to getting me back on my feet, physically and mentally. I can never thank her enough for all she did."

"How wonderful to hear this! Seems there is a great deal I don't know about my aunt but I am learning of her generosity from others now that I'm here."

"She is a very special lady! Mostly, she encouraged me to use my small fortune, which I had barely touched since my parents died, to help people who needed a lawyer but couldn't afford one. Not for charity, you understand, but for getting what they deserved but for one reason or another could not pay up front to hire proper representation. Therefore, I have set up my practice doing exactly that. The deep satisfaction I have from helping others who find themselves in such a predicament has far outweighed the minor inconveniences I have suffered along the way, of paying out money and leaving it to God to recover my expenses. He has never let me down!"

"How exciting to hear such a special testimony to God's watch care!"

"Indeed. And to your aunt's encouragement. That is why I said it is due to her that I have the funds to help you now. God has blessed and expects me to pay that back to others as I can. From this point on, you are *not* to worry about money, do you hear me?"

"Yes, sir, loud and clear! Now, I really do need to get out of here and allow you to get back to work. Thank you for all you have done thus far plus are going to do to help Lily and me with all we are facing."

"You are most welcome, Amanda. Please take care of yourself around 'Alex,' and tell Nan hello for me."

"I certainly shall. Do you want to write that message to the owner of the Emporium now?"

"Yes, give me a minute to do that." Moments later, he handed her the note.

"Goodbye, Mr. Grayson," Lily said and returned his offer to shake her hand, then he did so with her mother.

"Enjoy that book. We really need to talk about it soon."

"Yes, sir. I have a few questions so maybe you can answer them later."

Within a few minutes they were at the Emporium, thanks to the directions given to them by Miss Lawson. As they entered, they were startled to hear someone shouting gruffly with caustic words that stung, given their special circumstances.

"I don't care what you say, you owe that amount and until you pay your bill, you are not taking those supplies out of this store! Now get out or I will use this shotgun on you!"

CHAPTER SEVENTEEN

"For thou hast been a strength to the poor, a strength to the needy in his distress, a refuge from the storm, a shadow from the heat..."
Isaiah 25:4

April 17, 1867

"What on earth is going on?" Lily whispered to Mandy.

"I don't know. Maybe we should leave. I wonder if that is the owner?"

The man in question rushed past them without a glance their way, a grim look on his face, while the one who had spoken just glared after him. Slowly he lowered his weapon as he realized several customers stared in his direction. Clearly, he was the store proprietor.

"Sorry about that, folks. Happens sometimes in this business. Didn't mean to frighten anyone. Now, who was next?"

He calmly went about the task of adding up a customer's items as though nothing unusual had taken place while everyone else continued to look at various goods on display. *Does this happen that often, that no one is upset in the least? I am petrified enough for all of us!*

"Let's select what we came for and get out of here quickly, Lily." Mandy's heart raced as she thought about the note in her pocket. What would be the owner's reaction to not getting paid when she gave it to him? Surely he would not be angry with them for refusing to pay! *Oh, Father, get us out of here safely! If this were not so essential I would skip doing it, but we must have some clothing.*

"Oh, Mama, look at that gorgeous blue dress!" Lily rushed over to where it was hanging on the end of a counter with some others. "It's my favorite color and I think it would fit me, don't you?"

"It is beautiful, I have to agree, and yes, it appears to be about your size. But you really have no use for something this fancy, dear. We need to think about attire suitable for the funeral we have coming up soon, for instance. This most decidedly would not be fitting for that event."

"What about for church?" Lily asked, fingering the delicate lace at the neckline. "Would it be too much for that? You said we needed something to wear there. I do so love this!"

"We'll think about it. Meantime, why don't you pick out some undergarments? We discussed this morning what all you need. You need to stick with that list, and I will do the same." She managed to divert Lily's attention away from the dress, while she discreetly checked out the price and gasped. *That's ridiculous for one dress! Oh, wait, I have to remember that things have different values here than what I am used to. But oh my! What would Ken-ai-te say about my spending this much of our meat money on clothing as extravagant as this?* Immediately she knew the answer. He would be thrilled to see his daughter in that dress, even if he had to do without meat for a month to pay for it!

They spent several minutes picking out night clothes as well as the more personal items that would be needed for their short stay here. They certainly couldn't wear only the two travel outfits they each had been able to pack!

Mandy looked over several bolts of fabric and longed to be able to take them back to the territory with her to make some bright colored clothing for the Kiowa women in their village. Since they no longer could depend on having hides to tan and turn into the buckskin dresses they were used to, she knew these would excite the ladies beyond words! But alas, how on earth would they ever get them back there? She recalled the years she spent learning to sew by hand as a young girl and actually became excited at the thought of doing that again in order to share the lovely materials with her friends back home. For years, all she had sewn had been with tanned hides, adding elaborate beading to brighten and decorate. But this was different!

What am I thinking? I cannot possibly take the bolts with me, along with everything else I would need. Indeed, they would be offended deeply even if I managed to do it somehow. Centuries of tradition thrown away, just like that? To dress them as white women? But what else can they do without the buffalo any longer to provide the hides they require to make clothing for their families? We may be able to use the cowhides from the cows we hope to purchase but I've never sewn on those and have no idea if they will even work for this purpose. God, please help me use wisdom here. Maybe before I leave You will have given me an answer on all this, but not today. Right now, I need to concentrate on the needs in front of me for myself and for Lily.

Suddenly it dawned on Mandy that she had no clue where her daughter was! The answer came quickly to calm her anxiety, when she heard girlish voices giggling behind a tall display of various household items. It had to be Lily! But who else was with her?

Mandy came around the corner, catching sight of Lily bent over a large group of hair ribbons spread out on a table in front of her. Another young girl about her age stood next to her, dressed in a very pretentious outfit for one so young, complete with gloves and a bonnet. The girls whispered together again and laughed at their secret joke. How it warmed Mandy's heart to see Lily this happy! And with a total stranger, no less. She had always made friends easily and it appeared this was true here as well as in Indian Territory.

"Oh, Mama, guess what I found? A beautiful blue ribbon that exactly matches the shade of the dress I saw a few minutes ago! Wouldn't this look stunning in my dark hair?" She held it up for her mother to see.

"Yes, it is lovely, dear, but we haven't decided to buy the dress yet. Who is your new friend?"

"I'm sorry, I forgot to introduce her to you. Her name is Ginny, that is *Genevieve*, Cordon. And she's French! Well, American now, but she was born in France. Imagine my meeting someone born on the other side of the world, right here in Trenton! Ginny, this is my mother, Mrs. Alton."

Lily said that as though she used that title every single day! Mandy was proud of her daughter for remembering. Or was she adapting a little *too* quickly? The thought troubled her but she shook it off.

Ginny curtsied slightly. "Nice to meet you, ma'am. My mother is here as well. I think she is looking at some lace shawls over in that corner." She nodded with her head toward the back of the store.

"Good to meet you, Ginny. Lily, we need to finish our selections as we must get back to the house as soon as possible. Did you find the items I sent you after a few minutes ago?"

"Yes, Mama, I did. I put them up on the front case in order to browse around some more. I saw one lady do that so thought it would be all right to leave them there for a few minutes while I looked at other things. But then I met Ginny!" And the girls were off into more giggles.

"Genevieve! Whatever are you laughing about like that?"

The stern voice in a strong French accent made Mandy's heart freeze. She still wasn't over the scene they witnessed as they entered the store, with the owner chasing that man out for non-payment. This jarring sound added to that underlying anxiety.

"Mama, my new friend Lily and I were laughing about, well, something private between us."

"That is no way to introduce someone, Genevieve, and you well know it. In addition, there is no cause for rudeness. You should be ashamed of yourself." She glared at her daughter and Ginny's face fell.

"I'm sorry, Mama. This is Lily Alton, who only arrived in Trenton yesterday. Lily, this is my mother, Madame Cordon. Uh, *Mrs.* Cordon, I mean." She turned to Lily and added, "I am supposed to use American titles since we live in America now. But sometimes I forget!" And she giggled again while Lily joined her.

"Mrs. Cordon, it is good to meet you," said Lily as she curtsied politely. "This is my mother, Mrs. Alton."

Mandy extended her hand toward the other woman. When she didn't immediately respond, she wondered if maybe in France women did not greet one another by shaking hands? After only a brief hesitation Mrs. Cordon did respond in kind and the awkward moment passed.

"It seems our girls have struck quite a friendship in these last few minutes, Mrs. Cordon."

"Yes, it would seem that way. I have taught Genevieve not to address strangers without permission, but it appears she ignored my advice in this, as she often does in many ways."

The frown on her face disappointed Mandy. *I seriously doubt if we will become friends with that attitude! It's not like Lily is going to harm your precious daughter, you know!* Mandy scolded herself silently for being so harsh. She hardly knew the woman, certainly not enough to form such an unpleasant opinion of her like that. But her words did seem a bit of an overreaction. They were girls shopping in a store and giggles were to be expected at that age. And very welcomed, given the difficult circumstances lately at home on the prairie. Lily deserved some laughter in her life!

"Well, Genevieve, have you finished picking out what you wanted? We need to get home and I'm certain the Altons do as well."

"Mama, Lily and I were talking a minute ago about how wonderful it would be if she could come over tomorrow to see all my beautiful dresses from France, as well as my porcelain dolls. Oh, also the gorgeous doll house Papa brought me on his last trip back to France. Could she? Would that be all right with you if she came to play?"

"Well—"

"Oh, *please,* Mama? I get so lonely without any friends my age. We are both twelve and have already discovered that we have much in common. Please?"

"I really am not sure it would be appropriate for us to intrude on the Cordons' lives, Lily," said Mandy. She hoped to smooth over yet another awkward moment before Lily's feelings could be hurt by this rather hostile woman's potential rejection of the invitation her daughter had suggested.

"Oh, it's not an intrusion at all, Mrs. Alton. It's just that Genevieve stays very busy with her tutors and all her lessons, meaning there is hardly time for play, as she puts it."

"That's exactly my point, what I keep trying to tell you and Papa!" Ginny seemed on the verge of tears and Mandy felt rather sorry for the poor girl.

"I need to make friends, you have said so, but how *can* I if you fill my days with endless lessons that don't matter and don't allow me time to play with other girls?"

Mrs. Cordon visibly bristled at her daughter's outburst. Mandy assumed this was rather out of character for Ginny as well as violating the rules of etiquette that seemed rather important to her mother. But she was thrilled that this young lady wanted to be with Lily enough to stand up to her mother for the right to have friends her age.

After a long moment of staring between the two, Mrs. Cordon finally relented.

"All right, Genevieve, if you promise me that you will complete your French lesson before Lily arrives, you may invite her to come for a while before your piano lesson tomorrow afternoon."

"Really? Oh, Mama, thank you *so* much! Lily, can you come over at 2:00 tomorrow? My piano tutor comes at 4:00. That way we will have *two whole hours!*"

Lily turned to Mandy. "Mama, may I go? Please?"

"Yes, of course, you may, if it means that much to you, Lily. I will need to know how to get to your house, Mrs. Cordon."

"Anyone can show you the way in this little hamlet, I'm certain. It's the large house up on the hill at the end of Castle Street."

"I know the street but not the house but am certain we can find it."

"Mama used to live here in Trenton long ago, but it has changed a great deal since then," Lily told the others.

"Oh, really?" Mrs. Cordon asked.

"Yes, I left about fourteen years ago and only recently returned to visit my aunt. Perhaps you know her, Miss Ida Clark?"

"She is your *aunt?* Of course I know her. Everyone in town does, in fact. Such a kind lady but she has been quite ill, isn't that correct?"

"Yes, she has," Mandy replied, not sure if she should say more about her aunt's condition or not. It seemed many knew each other's business here, but some things needed to remain private. The fact that her aunt was dying was one of those. At least for now.

"I do hope she is doing better now that you are here. It is my understanding, however, that her illness is quite serious. You two are staying in her house, I take it?" she asked.

"I am afraid your information is correct. Her illness is not fleeting but thank you for your concern. Yes, we are staying with her. My aunt asked that we visit before she, well, before she passed away. We are only here for a few days, though." *Should I have said that she is dying? Too late now! She probably already knows.*

"I see, and I am sorry to hear this news. That is a beautiful home she has. And those trees are enormous! We tried to find a lot with trees on it when we built our house but weren't that fortunate. I admire her property every time we walk by there."

"Thank you. It is lovely, isn't it? Lily, we need to hurry. Aunt Ida will be expecting us soon. Mrs. Cordon, Genevieve, it was good to meet you. We shall see you tomorrow at 2:00. Thank you for the invitation."

"Yes, thank you, Mrs. Cordon," said Lily. "Ginny, um, that is *Genevieve*, I am excited to get to see all of your things! See you tomorrow!"

As the Cordons walked away, Mandy pondered at the conversation.

Was it my imagination or did Mrs. Cordon seem to soften to the idea of the girls becoming friends when she discovered who my aunt was? And where we live? Is that a good thing or not? She is certainly eaten up with her snobbishness but apparently her daughter is not, or Lily would see through that in a second. I'm grateful she has made a friend, as I have with Nan, but hate to see that based on what part of town we live in.

Ken-ai-te, please pray with me that we can return home soon, back to the simple life of the Kiowa. I do not belong here!

The two hastily worked to finalize their clothing selections, including the blue dress Lily wanted so badly and of course the blue ribbon to match! Mandy agreed, it would be perfect for church. They also picked out a pair of white gloves for each of them as well as a cute lacy bonnet that matched the dress. With her daughter's approval, Mandy picked out a lovely dark grey shoulder scarf for herself to go over a light grey dress she selected, figuring the scarf would dress it up for church sufficiently. And the dress would work for the funeral. They got a dark green plaid dress for Lily for that event as well as a white lace shawl to wear over it for everyday. All of a sudden, Mandy was seized with an overwhelming sadness, realizing that Ida would never see her great-niece in it. *I cannot allow my heart to be drawn into sorrow before she has even passed from this earth! Now, what else do we need?*

Soon they had all the other items ready to take to the front of the shop, where they faced the biggest challenge of all: convincing the owner to accept Matthew's note with his request to set up a charge account for them, to be managed by him. Would this man do so and allow them to leave with their purchases? Or chase them out of the store as well at the point of a gun? Mandy's knees shook as they walked up to the counter.

"Sir, I have a note from Mr. Matthew Grayson, who is my attorney. He requested that I give this to you when my daughter and I had completed our shopping." She shoved the paper at him, holding her breath to see his reaction.

He glanced over it quickly and smiled, putting Mandy's heart at ease finally.

"That will be fine. I do this often for that young man. Let's get these added up and I will set things in order for you, so that the two of you can be on your way."

Just like that! Mandy was floored but thrilled. Within moments, they were, indeed, on their way back to the house, arms loaded down with all kinds of packages. She was overwhelmed at the total cost of it all but reminded herself to trust Matthew's judgement and stop worrying so much.

I could get used to this kind of situation, not having to pay for something when I buy it! But I shouldn't. Right, Lord? Thank You for taking care of all my panic and nervousness. And thank You, again, for Matthew's kindness.

As they left, Lily said to her mother, "I'm excited about getting to go to Ginny's house but a little nervous, too. If I end up sitting in on any of her classes, I wonder if it will be too advanced for me. All my schooling has been from you, whereas hers is from tutors."

"It's a lot the same, though, Lily. She does not attend a traditional school, and neither do you. But I think you will be able to keep up with her and perhaps learn a little from her at the same time. Because we expected this to be a very short journey, I did not plan on doing any teaching while we were here, yet God has provided an excellent way for you to stay up with your lessons anyway. If it comes to that."

"Hmm, I had not thought of it that way. I suppose you are right!"

Upon arriving back at the house, Mandy was dismayed to see the doctor's buggy sitting outside in front. She had figured the man would be long gone if he had been able to come by early this morning as Nan had hoped. Perhaps he had been delayed with another patient. They raced up the steps and into the foyer. To Mandy's great relief, the study was once again dark and empty.

"Let's get upstairs to deposit all these things in the room and go see Aunt Ida," she said to her daughter. "I'm eager to hear what the doctor has to say."

A few minutes later, upon entering the bed chamber, Mandy instantly knew the news was not good. The doctor was bent over his patient, listening to her heart, then straightened, with a rather grim expression on his face.

"Oh, Amanda, I'm relieved you got home in time!" Nan rushed over to hug her. Lily retreated to her chair and Nan took her friend's arm, pulling her toward the bed.

"Dr. Banning, this is Miss Ida's niece, the one I was telling you about. Amanda, this is Dr. Joel Banning and he is finishing his exam of your aunt."

The doctor nodded and gestured toward the sitting area. The two of them followed him in there.

"I wish I could be more encouraging, ladies, but I'm afraid we are at the end of the long journey for Miss Ida. I cannot see any way she will survive more than a few more minutes, or perhaps a few hours at the most. Best if you both say your goodbyes now. She should be able to hear you at least, but don't expect any response from her, as she is too weak to speak or perhaps even open her eyes. Her breathing will get more shallow toward the end and most likely at that point she will slip into a coma. Her heart will keep beating until God says it's time, and then it will be over, most likely without further pain or suffering. I'm not trying to be brutal here, merely practical. You both need to know what you are facing within a couple of hours, or in several of them, hard to say, but I'm guessing definitely today. I'm very sorry about this but I have done all I can. The rest is up to God Almighty, now."

"And you are certain there is nothing more you can do?" asked Nan.

"Positive. It is out of my hands. I need to go see another patient who is experiencing a difficult pregnancy and unfortunately am not sure how long I will be detained there." He paused as he saw the alarmed expressions on their faces. "However, one thing I would like to do before I leave is have some time alone with Miss Ida, if that would be all right. She has been my patient for many years now and I would like some time to pray for her and say goodbye in my own way. Why don't you all go for a stroll in the garden? I doubt if Miss Amanda has had time to see all of it. Even under these circumstances, it is worth taking the time to walk through it. And has she seen the cemetery, Miss Nan?"

"No, sir," answered Nan, "we haven't had time to even get out there for more than a brief talk early today."

"Well, if that is the case, by all means indulge an old country doctor with this final request. And go enjoy the beautiful sunshine and all God has provided in the garden. I believe Miss Amanda needs to view the heart of her aunt out there among those beautiful blossoms."

Within minutes, the three of them were downstairs and making their way through the lush flower beds outside the back door. Almost immediately, Mandy swiped at a bumblebee that buzzed around her head.

"What was that?" she cried, dodging him repeatedly.

"It was a bumblebee is all, which is to be expected because this area is called The Honey Garden!"

"Well, I knew it was a bee but I have never seen one like that before! A Honey Garden? How unique!"

"Your aunt had a gardener, Michael Simpson, who kept things out here well cared for until he enlisted in the Army and left to fight in the war. Sadly, he never returned. But long before that, he had referred Miss Ida to a man by the name of Reverend L. L. Langstroth who lives over by Oxford. He built quite a reputation as one who not only kept bees but also nurtured them by building a Honey Garden where they could find a wide array of flowers with the sweetest of nectar for them to enjoy. We rented a buggy one Sunday afternoon and the three of us drove over there to spend some time learning how to do this right. When we returned home, we worked feverishly to create our own version of it here in her yard. Mr. Simpson told us his goal was to transform the whole area into a gorgeous array of flowers of all types and colors, because the bees are attracted by color as well as scent. Folks came from all over the county to see the garden once it was finished. The curious thing is, Mr. Simpson said other plants would benefit throughout this whole section of town from the pollinating the bees did here. Isn't that amazing?"

"How fascinating! I cannot believe anyone would actively pursue having bees close by. We collect wild honey in the woods from time to time back home but it is far from a pleasant task. I discovered from doing it that I am not a fan of bees or wasps of any kind. However, I certainly do like to eat the honey!"

Nan laughed and continued. "Reverend Langstroth is a Presbyterian clergyman by profession. This pastime of his soon became an all-consuming hobby for him. Eventually he became known to many as the Father of American Beekeeping, in fact. You should have seen the huge gardens he had! He even created a special place for the bees to live, called a hive, and would regularly harvest the honey from it. Very brave man, in my estimation. We didn't go that far here, so don't worry, you won't find any hives, only the bees busy collecting their pollen. It is a fascinating study in nature, frankly."

"I love to smell the fragrance of all these flowers and no wonder you so enjoy the beauty of their vibrant colors. The beekeeping, however, I will leave to others!"

"One interesting but sad sidenote to this is that during the war we gathered many of these blossoms to use for funerals of those men who were killed in battle. There were many in those sad days, of course, and often no body to bury, as most of the soldiers were laid to rest where they fell. But the families needed to have a funeral and a grave marker, so we provided flowers for them. It wasn't much but a little something we could do to help ease their terrible grief."

"How kind of my aunt to do that. She mentioned this briefly in one of her letters, but I didn't quite understand when I read it. Now I do. In fact,

I'm learning that her heart had depths I never knew as a child, but it is gratifying to hear what an impact she had on the people here in Trenton. One passage I do recall is that she said the more she cut for funerals, the more blossoms God seemed to grow in greater abundance. She called it her 'flower miracle'!"

"I haven't heard that term in a long time, but yes, she credited God for inspiring her to create this huge garden, thinking she was doing it for the beauty alone. In truth, He had other plans, for when the need was great, the supply was greater still. He promised to provide for *everything* we need, and this is one small way she could contribute to the dire needs of others, by sharing the flowers."

They walked a little further in silence and Nan pointed to a fenced area in the back where they were headed.

"Over here is the cemetery. You might find this a bit morbid, but I truly think you will find the place particularly interesting. Miss Ida was deeply disturbed that your father never had a resting place, at least one she could visit. Therefore, she put up a marker for her brother, even though his body was not there. Shortly afterward she added the one for your mother, saying that a Christian deserved a decent burial, body or no body. About a year after your disappearance, she decided to give up hope you were alive and would return someday, so she placed one out here for you as well. At the same time, she had three markers made for her parents and sister, too. Their bodies are not there, either, of course, but she needed that link with them somehow."

The three stood now gazing down at the six markers Nan indicated. Cold chills swept over Mandy's heart in realizing that her own grave was represented here! How grateful she was that she could now have it removed. Walking only a few steps further, another marker caught her attention, and she froze on the spot.

"She put one up for herself?"

"Yes, she did. Miss Ida said it would save me having to do this task whenever God called her Home. I told her I didn't mind but she insisted so I backed off. It seemed to mean a great deal to her, to have it here waiting. All we have to do is add her death date. Next to her is Catherine's grave, and beside her are markers for her two sons who died. At one time, of course, there was also one for Alex, but when he returned, it was removed."

God, is that really going to be today? Help me accept that, whenever it comes!

Mandy walked on a few more steps to two other small wooden crosses off to one side, reading the names softly.

"Bessie Langston. And Samuel Langston."

"Yes, Samuel is here but not his sister. You haven't heard the story about Bessie and her brother yet, but it was important to your aunt to honor the two of them with these markers, bodies here or not."

Abruptly, Nan turned and walked away without another word. Even Lily noticed her odd behavior at the mention of Bessie and frowned as she watched her leave the cemetery, but respectfully said nothing until she was out of earshot.

"Mama, I had no idea I would get to see my great-grandparents' graves and also those of your parents! This is very exciting. Can I say that about a cemetery? The Kiowa have such different ideas about burial of the dead. I find it a little strange that here we can talk freely about people who are deceased, since that is forbidden in our culture. Oh, excuse me, in *their* culture."

They hurried to catch up with Nan, who waved her hand over a large orchard off to one side of the property, explaining these were the apple trees.

"We spent a great deal of our time for several years putting up the apples as well as we could, storing countless jars in the cellar. During the war, many products from the simple apple kept a great many folks alive when food was scarce. These included apple butter, spiced apple rings, and applesauce, among quite a few others. Miss Ida also became known for her apple pies, breads, cobblers, and cakes, whenever she could get her hands on sugar for those, since it was rather hard to come by at times. It gave us something to do to keep from becoming too sad over the tremendous loss of life for many here in Trenton due to the conflict, while waiting for more passengers to arrive."

"Passengers?" Mandy asked.

"Yes, for the Underground Railroad. Didn't your aunt explain about all that in her letters, about Bessie and how God changed her due to the book Lily is reading?"

"She did mention it in one letter in passing but I did not understand all she said and have a million questions about it. When I have finished the rest of the messages, perhaps I will get those answered without having to bother you with it."

"Well, I certainly don't mind, just don't want to bore you by going on about events from the past. All you have to do is ask. Perhaps we should get back upstairs now. Dr. Banning will be eager to get to his next patient, I'm sure. I'm nervous leaving Miss Ida for too long at a time. I desperately want to be there when she leaves us..."

Tears sprang into Nan's eyes and she blinked them back, as Mandy fought her own. Forget Kiowa courage at a time like this! She was white for the moment and chose to behave as any white woman would under such a circumstance. A twinge of guilt tweaked in the pit of her stomach. *I'm quite certain Ken-ai-te would not be happy with me right now, but somehow I believe he would understand and be kind in my grief. Right, my love?*

"Dr. Banning," Nan asked anxiously as they entered Ida's bedchamber moments later, "is there any change, any further hope you can give us?"

He smiled and said, "For once, I'm glad I was wrong! She only moments ago awakened, asking for all three of you!"

"Of course I am awake, Dr. Banning. I have a last message for each of my loved ones and I have asked God not to take me Home until I get to deliver them." She frowned. "Is Matthew not here?"

"He told me he would be coming over a little later, Aunt Ida, but no, he's not here now. Did you have something to say to him as well?"

"Yes, I do. He is like a son to me, and I want a chance to speak to him once more if possible. But for now, let's get on with this. The doctor may have been wrong in his dire prediction of any minute, but he wasn't far off in the fact that I'm going Home at last and very soon!"

CHAPTER EIGHTEEN

"Let us therefore come boldly unto the throne of grace, that we may obtain mercy, and find grace to help in time of need." Hebrews 4:16

April 17, 1867

"Aunt Ida, I really don't think it is wise for you to talk right now. Why don't you lie still and rest instead of trying to speak?"

Mandy sat next to her, wringing her fingers in anguish. Close to tears, she fussed over the pillow under her beloved aunt's head. She had to have something to do with her hands besides wearing them out!

"Nonsense! I shall go out as I have lived my life, on my own terms but with the Lord's leading. And He has made it imperative that I say these things to those who mean the most to me, before it is too late."

As Mandy opened her mouth to protest, Ida continued.

"Don't say another word, Amanda. And close your mouth. You are not a fish!"

At that, Lily giggled and her mother smiled at her.

"Private joke?"

"Sorry, Aunt Ida. I told Lily the same thing earlier when she was gawking at some things. I don't think she believed me that I grew up hearing that. Maybe now she does!"

"Nan, be sure the door is closed so you-know-who cannot listen in to what I have to say. This is not for his ears."

"He is not home this afternoon, thank goodness, but I need to leave it open so I can hear the bell when Matthew arrives. You can speak freely, don't worry."

She smiled and closed her eyes for a moment, leaving Mandy to wonder if her aunt had fallen asleep again, or maybe—no, she would not consider that. Yet.

"Good," and the eyes popped open. "First of all, don't you three *dare* go about for months after I'm gone dressed in black mourning clothes! I always thought that custom was macabre, to say the least. That does not honor me and is not easy to maintain when you are young people such as yourselves. Same thing with not attending social events, ridiculous custom! When folks criticize you for not keeping this tradition, I want you to tell them that I demanded you not do it. Understood?"

And she gazed from one to the other of them with that intense stare only Ida Clark could give to another when making a point she didn't want forgotten! They all nodded and she smiled in response.

"Nan, you have been like a daughter to me, with all that entails. I don't have the strength to relate everything, but you know how I feel about your friendship. We faced some dangerous times and some funny times, always together and always with God as our guide." A short coughing spasm interrupted Ida but it passed quickly. "Use the bequest I am leaving you to start a new life away from Trenton, wherever your dreams take you. Don't hole up in a house in this place as I did."

"Oh, Miss Ida! Thank you for that chance. I am going to go out to Indian Territory to visit Amanda and her family soon, if they will have me. And I can't wait!"

Mandy's eyes widened in horror as her heart sank. The truth would come out about Mandy's life with the Kiowa if she did that! Somehow, she *must* prevent Nan from coming, whatever it might take.

"What an adventure that will be!" said Ida. It was obvious her strength was fading fast as she struggled to finish her thought. "Just don't get yourself captured by an Indian, as Amanda did."

"No, I certainly do not want to do that. But yes," said Nan, blinking back tears as she continued, "an adventure of a lifetime. And who knows, perhaps I shall like it enough that I never want to come back home! Regardless, I benefitted far more from our friendship than I ever gave to it, believe me, and I am deeply grateful for all you did for me over the years." Within a moment Ida had drifted off to sleep.

The tears flowed as Mandy patted her friend's hand in sympathy. From a distance below came the sound of the bell at the front door.

"Oh, Matthew must be here," she said as she wiped her face. "Excuse me a second while I run down and let him in. Miss Ida, if you can hear me, please hang in there so you can say goodbye properly to Matthew."

Nan had barely disappeared when Ida said quietly, "Amanda, from what Nan has told me I gather you do not intend to remain here in this house after I am gone."

"That's right, Aunt Ida. I love this house but I love my family more, and they need me. God has called me to Indian Territory and I must go back home."

"Good for you! Take Nan with you and show her the world where you live out there. Don't let her bury herself here in Trenton as I did. Oh, did I already say that?"

"I promise, Aunt Ida. We will protect her as much as we can and support her decisions as to where she wants to settle. This bequest means everything to her." Her aunt closed her eyes and smiled, a content expression on her face. *Somehow I will keep this promise. I am not sure how, but God will give me that answer when the time comes.*

A moment later Matthew came rushing into the room, concern lining his handsome face.

"Miss Ida, I understand you were asking for me. I'm here now. Can you hear me?"

She nodded and opened one eye to squint at the man.

"That really you, Matthew?"

"Yes, Miss Ida, it really is me. Are you dreaming about me again?" And he chuckled. Mandy was startled when her aunt did the same.

"Always, my dear, always. If only I had met you when I was younger...."

Mandy found this line of conversation strange at such a time but interesting to note the obvious love between these two, much as mother and son would be. In any case, the bond between them was far stronger than Mandy had realized earlier when visiting with the attorney.

"Matthew, I have already told you everything I wanted to say, but I wish to ask you to look after my niece and Nan for me, will you? They need a man to take care of them right now. Especially against The Great Imposter!"

Matthew said, "Amanda told me about finding a letter from you confirming his false identity. Believe me, I will be watching for his crafty schemes to try to steal the inheritance. I promise you that it shall be

Amanda's, and your two other bequests will be honored as well. You can rest easy with me caring for them."

"Thank you, I knew you would. But I wanted a chance to look you in the eye, in that one good eye of yours," and they both smiled, "and hear it again. You did get her signature on all the papers, right?"

"Yes, never fear, all is in order, precisely as you desired."

"Excellent. You are the son I never had and I love you dearly. But you already know that!"

"Yes, ma'am, I do. I love you as well, Miss Ida. Watch for me when I enter Heaven someday! Yours will be one of the first faces I hope to see."

He stepped back from the bed and moved to the corner next to Lily, wiping his eye as he did so.

"Lily, where are you, girl? I have something to say to you, too."

"Right here, Great-Aunt Ida." Lily came forward and crouched down beside the older woman where she could easily see her, tenderly taking her hand in her own. "I was here all along but I've been reading my book. Or rather, one of yours. I hope you don't mind."

"Mind? Why should I mind? Books must be read to be of any value. They do no one any good sitting on a shelf. I am delighted to hear this. Which one did you select?"

"It's *Uncle Tom's Cabin*."

"Ah, the worst of times but the best of the best in books about it."

"You underlined whole paragraphs and wrote notes in the margins, some with dates. Was there a reason you did that? I mean, it's a novel, not a textbook."

"I read it several times and in each experience God would speak to me in a different manner about the horrific events it related. He had so much to teach me. Learn well, my child. Cherish its words, no matter how painful. It was no coincidence that you picked that book. Don't let the word *fiction* scare you off from finding God's Word on every page. Because it is there. This story is true in every sense of the word. I watched it happen, right before my eyes."

Another coughing spell followed but within moments Ida continued, her voice strong once again.

"When God said to me, 'Ida, now that you know the truth, what do you intend to *do* about this tragedy?' I knew He meant business. He wouldn't let go of my heart, even when it threatened to strangle me. Share that book with as many people as you can. The books are all yours, my child. They need to be owned by someone who will appreciate them, and I believe you are that person. And remember me..." Here her voice trailed off as she drifted back to sleep.

It took several moments for Lily to regain her composure, as she thanked her great aunt over and over through the tears. The same was true for both ladies. Even Matthew sniffled several times in the silence.

Finally, Lily said quietly, "You can be assured that I shall do that, Great-Aunt Ida." And she gently kissed the back of the frail hand that gripped her own, reluctant to pull away one second earlier than necessary.

As unexpectedly as they had closed, Ida's eyes opened once more.

"Amanda, are you still here? I didn't dream that you came all the way from Indian Territory to see me, did I?" Lily returned to her chair as her mother came forward to take her place beside the bed.

"No, Aunt Ida, I'm right here." She gripped her aunt's fingers and was surprised at the strength in them. "How can I bear the guilt of having procrastinated contacting you all those years, only to lose you right after I finally found you again?"

"Please don't focus on that, Amanda. Think about the years we had together and the heritage of faith that embraced you as a child. I would hope it sustained you during those dark days of living in captivity with the Indians."

"Oh, it did, most assuredly, and gave me the strength to lead many to Christ as well. I am deeply grateful for all the years you insisted on regular church attendance and daily prayers, along with memorizing Scripture. You cannot know how much that meant to me!"

"Oh, I see that you still have your gold cross around your neck. Your father was so thrilled when he picked that out for you on your birthday long ago. And of course it pleased him that you liked it well enough to wear it all the time. How special that you still cherish it today."

"I wouldn't dream of taking it off, Aunt Ida. And it has been an opening for many who have seen it over the years to ask me about the Gospel it represents." *Such as Ken-ai-te but I can't share that right now!*

"Did you find the letters?"

"Yes, I did. Very clever for you to hide them in my room and then require me to spend one night there. You knew that would be one of the first places I looked, didn't you?"

"It was the only place I could think of that *he* wouldn't look. And I didn't want him intruding on my heart like that. At first I wrote to you out of my own grieving spirit, not certain if you were alive or dead but convinced I had to pour out my hurt on paper anyway. I suppose it was my way of connecting to you, in case you had survived somehow. Later, it became a way to keep my sanity when my world began to crumble. Have you read any of them? I lose sense of time, confined to my bed as I am. Maybe you haven't had time to do so yet."

"I actually have read most of them. It is my hope that I can finish later tonight."

"Did you read the Bessie ones? I certainly hope you have."

"Not yet, but I did see them, all wrapped with the blue ribbon. She must have meant a great deal to you to have preserved the memories like that. Nan said she was a special friend; therefore, I'm eager to learn all about her."

"She represented hope and freedom to me. Every day I was around her, God reminded me of how He had delivered me from the bondage of my sin. Took away my heart of stone and gave me a heart of flesh, one that felt deeply and grieved hard, one determined to stop the travesty of slavery wherever I encountered it. In the fields and streets and in the hearts of man as well. Did you know…"

She began coughing hard again and stopped.

"Aunt Ida, you don't have to talk if it causes you pain."

"Yes, I do! I *have* to say this, Amanda! God demanded that I set things right with you and has given me a second chance to do precisely that now. Where was I?"

"You said, 'did you know' but stopped."

"Oh, yes. Did you know you can experience bondage and never enter a cotton field? Because I did. Let Nan describe later in greater detail than I can what we experienced. My memory is failing but she will recall every vivid detail, I'm certain, because we walked through it all together. Through the pain I learned that only Jesus could set me free. Bessie reminded me of that and loved me in spite of who I used to be. That meant so much, still does. And I hope that you can forgive me as well. As I pray Jesus can see how I changed, too."

"I know He can! Ever since I arrived, I keep hearing about how much good you have done to help others all these long years."

"Miss Ida," Nan added, "Bessie and her brother are only two of those whom the Lord honored because of how you served them in the Name of Jesus. And I am another one of those. For now, however, you need to go with Jesus when He calls you, and stop fighting the pain and leave the suffering behind. That is where you belong, with Him, not in this world. Someday I shall hug you again and we will never be parted! Forever together."

"Aunt Ida, I hope you will heed Nan's words because they are true. As I said, I wish I could have shared more of those lost years with you. For now I have only memories and your letters to console me. But in truth, you are not mine, never have been. You belong *to* Jesus and *with* Him. I shall look forward to worshipping our King with you someday, where there will be no more regrets or tears or sorrow. *From now until forever.*"

And just like that, in the quietness of the room and surrounded by her loved ones, Ida Clark took her last breath on earth and slipped into the arms of her Savior.

A short time later, the four people emerged from the room already feeling the deep loss. Yet somehow, they also were at peace. The world seemed very empty for them, the house echoing their hollow steps on the stairs.

Upon reaching the vestibule, Nan glanced over at the darkened study and said, "Thank goodness he appears to be gone. I honestly don't think I could face him tonight, with Aunt Ida's body still warm upstairs. Let's go into the Parlor and talk about how to arrange it for the service tomorrow."

A short time later they walked Matthew to the door to bid him goodnight. He informed them that he would notify the undertaker of Ida's death and ask that he send over some women to prepare her body for burial, moving it to the Parlor that very night. He would also stop by the church to let the preacher know and request a couple of men come dig the grave the next morning. They would stay to finish up after the funeral. In addition, he would bring a black wreath for the front door when he returned the next day.

Mandy was shocked that Matthew had all the plans for the service under control and she realized that he and her aunt must have discussed them multiple times in great detail. She was too numb to do this herself and figured Nan felt the same way, as he quickly briefed them on what to expect. What a blessing to have Matthew there to help them!

"We will do the Reading of the Will immediately following the service tomorrow. That way, hopefully none of us will have to deal with Alex, as he most likely won't be here for either event. But in any case, I can handle that if he shows up. Remember, if he does return, do not say a word to him about the estate or the will, understood? We don't want to rile him unnecessarily. Just ignore him if you can."

"I can *happily* do that," said Nan with a bite of sarcasm.

"And remember, too, that all three of you must be packed up and out of here by tomorrow afternoon. I will hire a wagon to come fetch you at 4:00 and take you both to the Boarding House. Amanda, Mrs. Wilson does have a room for you and Lily. It's not large but the two of you should be quite comfortable there for the few days you are here, if you don't mind sharing accommodations."

"That sounds lovely, Matthew. How on earth can we ever thank you for taking care of everything for us like you have?"

"Your aunt is the one who thought of all the details. I am merely her messenger. But I am here if you should need me for anything. See you all about 9:30 in the morning."

And he turned to give Nan and Amanda a quick hug, then shook Lily's hand. She opened her mouth as though to speak, but closed it again.

"Did you have something to say, Miss Lily?" he asked.

"Well, it seems kind of silly right now, but I was supposed to go to the Cordons' home tomorrow afternoon. Would it be possible for you to let them know why I will not be there?"

"Of course. I didn't realize you knew the Cordons."

"Well, we met them today at the Emporium," said Mandy, "or at least Mrs. Cordon and her daughter. And the girls got along very well in that short time, which resulted in Lily being invited to come over to spend time with Ginny."

"Not a problem, Miss Lily," he said, looking back at her. "I will be happy to let them know what happened. Perhaps you girls can get together on Friday."

Lily smiled at him. "That would be perfect, sir."

And with that, he was gone.

"How can one woman make such a deep impression on everyone around her, like Ida Clark did?" asked Nan to no one in particular as she closed the door behind him.

"Anyone hungry?" asked Lily. "I could fix something light if you are."

"No, thanks, honey," replied her mother. "At least nothing for me. Suddenly I am utterly exhausted and would prefer sleep to eating. But if you want anything, help yourself."

"Not really, Mama. I was concerned about the two of you."

Mandy asked, "How about you, Nan?"

"Thanks, but I am fine. I will be up for a while yet, packing up some things and preparing for tomorrow. The ladies will be here any time to move Miss Ida's, um, body, so I need to listen for them to arrive. But at any rate, I would like to get upstairs as soon as possible and stay there, in case Alex comes home. I certainly don't relish having to see him tonight. Can you imagine how angry he's going to be when he discovers that he has been cut out of the will altogether? He imagined himself the Lord of the Manor here," and she paused to look around her, "but in truth he is going to be on the street this time tomorrow when Matthew informs him that he has lost all this to you, Amanda! I cannot wait to see his face!"

CHAPTER NINETEEN

"The LORD is slow to anger, and great in power, and will not at all acquit the wicked: the LORD hath his way in the whirlwind and in the storm, and the clouds are the dust of his feet." Nahum 1:3

April 18, 1867

"What a day this has been so far, and it's not over!" declared Mandy as she and Lily packed the last of their things in the valises. They had been forced to purchase a third small one to hold the new clothing they had bought since coming to Trenton. She stepped back to survey the room to ensure they had not left anything behind.

"I think that's all of our possessions, Mama. I wish we could have taken a couple of the dolls you had as a child with us. It would be fun to show them to Ginny."

"Matthew cautioned against removing any items from the house, remember? Perhaps before we leave you can bring Ginny over here to see them. I have an idea her mother would love to see the whole house, the way she looked around as they left this morning. How kind it was of her to bring Ginny to the funeral."

"Yes, it was. I appreciated having a friend sit by me during the service. She is the only friend I have here."

"Are you two ready?" asked Nan, joining the others. "I already took a load downstairs so if you need help, I have a couple of extra hands. I think I heard Matthew's wagon pull up in front as I came up here."

"He said 4:00, didn't he?" asked Mandy as she pulled the watch from her pocket to check it. "Right on time! I was saying goodbye once more to my room. Many fond memories here."

"Well, it all belongs to you, now. The trick is going to be keeping it out of Alex's hands. But that is up to Matthew. Our job is to get out of here before Alex returns! Wonder where he was that was important enough for him to miss her funeral, when he knew his grandmother was dying?"

"Whatever kept him away, I'm grateful he was not here for the service or the Reading of the Will. No telling what might have happened, had he been present." She paused for a moment. "Lily, I know what I said about not taking anything out of the house, but I have reconsidered on one thing, of which I am quite certain Aunt Ida would approve. Why don't you slip into the sitting room very quickly and select one more book to take with you? That way, when you complete the one you are reading now, you will have another to start."

"Oh, Mama! Could I?" She looked eagerly from her mother to Nan, who was grinning as broadly as Mandy.

"Of course, that is a delightful idea!" said Nan.

"I know exactly which one I want, too, so it won't take me long to grab it and put it in my bag. There is a book of poems that caught my eye that first day."

"Poetry?" asked Mandy in amazement. "I had no idea you were a fan of it."

"Well, I have read a little but not much. Imagine a whole book of nothing but verse! I'll be right back!"

She scampered from the room and down the hall. When she returned she clutched the small book tight in both hands, a glow on her face Mandy hadn't seen in some time. *Thank You, Lord, for putting that thought in my heart at the last moment like this. I pray You will use it to touch her heart as only You can!*

"Thank you, Mama!" she cried as she tucked it carefully into her valise.

The three struggled down the stairs carrying their things and were nearly at the bottom step when the door suddenly was thrust open. Cousin Alex had returned, with a bluster!

"What the devil are you doing still in my house?" he demanded. Right behind him, visible to the ladies but not to him, Matthew strode up the steps onto the porch. "You better not be stealing any of my property!" Alex thundered.

"They are moving out right now," said Matthew calmly. Alex whirled around in his direction, then immediately swung back to glare at Mandy as the attorney dodged him to help the ladies. How could Matthew speak in such a controlled voice when face to face with this man? Mandy imagined this was difficult at best for him and was certain she could not have done so with such boldness! "Give them time to remove their things and they will be out of your way. Don't worry, they are only taking what belongs to them."

"Where is my grandmother? Upstairs sleeping again while all this noise is going on?" he smirked.

"She died last night, for your information," snapped Nan over her shoulder as she swept past him and out the door. "Not that you care."

"What? The old bat finally kicked the bucket? Well, hallelujah!"

"How dare you profane her memory like that!" shouted Matthew, his face bright red as he defiantly positioned himself between Alex and the three ladies. Quite obviously, he had had all he could take as his restraint came off. "Have you no decency? It is apparent that you are without any compassion whatsoever for these women who have lost a beloved one."

He didn't wait for the man to respond. Taking a few of the things from Mandy, Matthew gestured to Lily to go ahead of him and stomped out the door behind her. Mandy quickly followed, leaving Alex standing there by himself.

But he didn't remain long, as he hastened to catch up.

"Wait up! When is the funeral?"

Matthew stopped, turning slowly to face him. "For your information, it was held this morning. Your grandmother was buried out in back, if you care to visit her grave in the Clark Family Cemetery. You were nowhere to be found and no one knew how to reach you to let you know. You should have stayed closer to home if you were wanting to attend her services. You knew she was critically ill and that the funeral would be held quickly after her death. If you have more questions, contact my office. We are busy at the moment, not to mention *in mourning*. Did you not see the black wreath? When that is displayed on a home's front door, it is common decency to respect the grief of those who live there."

As Matthew helped Lily into the wagon up in front, Alex called out, "In case anyone is interested, I was away on business. You know, that *thing* that puts food on the table? Of course, you wouldn't know anything about that, would you Grayson, having been kept by my grandmother for years now so you don't have to earn a living!"

Matthew turned on his heel abruptly, fury lighting up his face, but he didn't say a word, just glared. Mandy held her breath. Would the two come to blows over that horrible insult he had hurled at the attorney?

But again, Matthew restrained himself. He turned back to the wagon to finish loading it, swallowing any harsh words he might be tempted to say. He helped Nan up, who offered to sit in the back to ensure nothing fell out. Mandy hopped up beside her before Matthew could assist her and within moments they were off. As they drove away, Mandy glanced back at the house, wiping away a few tears. She saw Alex go back inside and slam the door hard, causing the wreath to shake a moment before falling with a crash to the porch floor. Nan gasped but said nothing at first.

At last she said quietly, "I think we may have stirred up a hornet's nest with that man. But I believe Matthew is up to the challenge, don't you agree, Amanda?" She nodded but was far too emotional to go to the effort to talk to her friend over the noise and movement of the wagon as it bounced along the ruts in the dirt road.

During the short drive, Mandy reflected on the large crowd that had shown up that morning for the service honoring her aunt's life. With little notice, folks had set aside their busy lives to pour into Wellington Oaks from every direction, to remember and commemorate a life well lived. The standing room only crowd had overflowed from the Parlor onto the expansive porch, where they could hear through the large open windows. She had shed many tears for that fact alone. But it was the dozens of flowers and even food they brought, along with the sweet comments people mentioned to her about the impact Ida Clark had made on them over the long years, that truly touched her. The preacher did an exceptional job of sharing Scriptures and stories that her aunt had requested be used. After that, Matthew did a superb job with the eulogy he gave for his beloved friend. Mandy only hoped that when her time came, she would have as many friends to come to her funeral as her aunt had.

Oh, what am I thinking about? When I die, I will be buried out on the prairie according to our Kiowa customs, with only my immediate family to acknowledge my passing.

The discrepancy in her thinking, if only for a moment like that, made her uneasy for several hours every time she thought about it. Was she slipping too easily into the white culture and all that entails? She simply *must* remember why she came here in the first place as well as the dire need back home, that called her even this very moment to return in time to save her people! *Ken-ai-te, where are you when I need you? How often do I say this now? But it's true. You should be here by my side to comfort me, instead of my having to depend on others to do that.* And caught herself again! Not a very Kiowa reaction, to expect comfort in her mourning. She had been taught to hold in her emotions, never showing them outwardly and to expect others to do the same. *Lord, what is wrong with me? I am getting so confused! Please get me out of here soon!*

She forced her thoughts back to this morning's events once more. After all the guests had departed, Matthew sat them down to officially "read" the will, though most of them were fully aware by that point of its contents. Aunt Ida's preacher was thrilled to hear of the amount of the small bequest for his church and promised to use it to purchase a bell to put in front, to announce the services. He figured Ida would be proud to be a part of calling the faithful to worship, and Mandy agreed. Of course, Nan was ecstatic to officially learn of the amount of her bequest, which should more than cover the cost of her trip out to Indian Territory. The *how*, she would work out later. But at least now she could dare to dream that this would someday be a reality for her. Mandy's heart warmed as she considered again the deep impact her aunt had had on many people, even after her death.

One verse the preacher had used especially touched her for many reasons, as Scripture often has a way of doing when it is read with an open heart. Proverbs 12:14 clearly states that the work of a man's hand comes back to him at some point. The preacher enumerated how her aunt's dedication to Trenton and her people was now blessing her memory for all of those who had gathered to honor her. Most Mandy had been aware of but a few were a surprise to her, even after hearing so many share with her the last couple of days how God had used her aunt for such a long time in often unusual ways.

Father, please allow me the gift of influencing my family and friends the way Aunt Ida did— even beyond the grave—to point them to You and to let them know how much they meant to me. I would be most humbled if You chose to do this, but I am in awe nevertheless of how You did it for my aunt.

That evening after getting settled into the Boarding House and meeting the other residents over a delicious dinner, Mandy settled down in the

Parlor to read the rest of her aunt's letters while Nan taught Lily how to play checkers. Everyone else had gone on to their rooms.

"I cannot believe you have never played this game before, yet you are beating me!" exclaimed Nan after close to an hour. "That's three games in a row you have won!"

"It's a lot of fun! Mama, we really need to take one of these back to the boys. They would enjoy it immensely, don't you think?"

"Uh, yes, dear, I am sure you are right," she said without looking up.

"Mama, should I not have interrupted you?"

"Oh, I'm sorry, dear. I'm just a bit flustered right now. What was it you asked?"

"About the checkers game. It wasn't that important. Why are you so upset?"

"I'm sorry, dear. The game would be a lovely gift to take to your brothers. I'm not really upset, just rather confused. I'm almost done with the letters but several things aren't making sense and I'm a bit lost. Aunt Ida rambled quite a bit in her writing, so my brain is running off in several directions at once with a dozen questions, making it difficult to concentrate. Perhaps I'll finish these ones about Bessie later. Or maybe you could clear up some of my confusion, Nan. If you two are through with your game, that is."

"I certainly will try, Amanda. As for our game, your daughter has whipped me soundly, so I think this would be a good time to quit!" And she and Lily laughed. "What is it you want to know?"

"For instance, I read about the Underground Railroad and yours and my aunt's involvement in it, and it is fascinating. But I don't know why she would have done all that, given her intense dislike for people of color. It just doesn't sound like her at all."

"Well, although you know she changed a great deal in that respect, your not knowing the story behind it would naturally leave you questioning her reaction. I think what might help is if I start at the beginning and share precisely how God took her through this dramatic confrontation. It is a long tale with many parts, but I will tell you how it all unfolded, step by step, because your aunt very much wanted you to know. We might not have time to go through it all tonight so you will need to bear with me. But you are right, it is important that you know the truth. It all started as we headed home from a shopping venture to the Emporium…"

March 22, 1860
Trenton, Ohio

"Nan, what is going on up there?" Ida nodded ahead of them to a small group of people on the opposite side of the street. A woman screamed and pulled on the arm of a man with one free hand, an infant wrapped up in the other one.

"I'm not sure," she replied with a low voice, "but it appears to be another runaway slave family. Don't you think it's best not to get too close right now? I mean, one of the men has a marshal's badge on, and his dogs do not look too friendly, to say the least!"

Several others had stopped along the street as well to stare at the scene. Although their full attention remained on what was happening to these unfortunates, no one moved to help. Instead, they merely watched in mute horror as the tragic drama played out before them as if part of a macabre play.

The couple's young boy tried at one point to come to his father's aid but was soundly smacked across the face and cried out as he fell at his mother's feet. Ida instinctively reached out toward him, then pulled back but the expression on her face troubled Nan greatly. Her friend was not known for being exactly compassionate to the runaway slaves, yet she appeared to be close to tears at this scene.

"Please, sir," the woman cried over and over, "my husband has done nothing wrong! I beg you not to beat him like that! We'll go with you but please stop!"

The poor man fell under the weight of the heavy chains each of the men were slinging repeatedly onto his back, head, and arms. He glanced up at his wife, their eyes meeting briefly, before he bowed his head to the dirt and reared it no longer. The pitiful expression in the young mother's eyes, tears streaming down her face, seemed to have no effect on any of those brutalizing her husband. It was clear they were completely without compassion. One after another stomped, kicked, and hammered the man's limp body repeatedly. After their savagery seemed spent on him, they turned their blows on the woman.

She screamed and dropped to her knees, hunched over her baby to try to shield the little one from the beating. Her son rose from where he had fallen moments earlier and valiantly again tried to help but was tossed aside like a sack of potatoes. He did not move any longer, either. The hysterical mother could do nothing to stop the nightmare happening to her family. Before long she also lay in the blood-soaked dirt at their feet, her baby limp in her arms as well. It was all over within a very few minutes, an entire helpless family destroyed simply because of who they were and the color of their skin.

"Why did you have to do this?" one man demanded in a loud voice. He had been standing closer to the scene than were Ida and Nan, yet did nothing until the folks were all dead. But at least he spoke up for them. "They weren't doing anyone any harm. Surely women and children don't deserve this! Ours is a peaceful town, sir, not one that tolerates violence or bloodshed. We are in a free state, too."

"When you harbor runaway slaves," the marshal sneered, "your town can expect more of this to happen. The law is on our side. And if you don't step back, *you* will be next!" The lawman glared, brandishing his rifle in one hand, while holding a bloodied chain in the other. His menacing stare left no doubt to anyone on the street that day as to his willingness to follow through on his threat.

A wagon lumbered down the street and pulled up to the bloody scene. The men tossed the bodies into the back of it like they were bags of grain, loaded the dogs, and clambered on at the back. Without a single word further from anyone, the wagon raced down the street and out of sight in a whirl of dust. The silence left behind was deafening in more ways than one.

Ida realized she had been holding her breath, for who knows how long. Once the ghostly scene emptied, she let it out, reeling from an attack of dizziness. From the sight itself or from holding her breath too long? She knew not, nor cared. Only that her heart had been shattered with a reality that up until now had only been whispered about in shadows or behind closed doors here in their community. These men, indeed, had the legal right to chase runaways from place to place in order to recapture them, hunting them as they would a dangerous beast. But these were *people,* not wild animals! Why *kill* them so brutally, in broad daylight? And then intimidate the people of Trenton in such a ruthless manner if they dared to interfere or even protest? How on earth did their country get to such a *sickening* point, where life itself had become this cheapened?

Slowly, she and Nan continued their journey down the street, but the former excitement of their shopping trip had evaporated now. When they passed the fateful spot, both glanced over there almost in unison. Ida halted in her tracks and pulled on her friend's arm to stop her as well. Without a word to each other, both ladies bowed their heads and Ida led them in a brief prayer.

"Father, we ask Your forgiveness for those who committed this terrible act today. Convict them of the evil that drove them to take the lives of four people who only dreamed of being free. I don't pretend to understand how You can forgive them of this, but I know you have, even from the Cross You did that. We—" Ida's voice broke. She couldn't continue so Nan did, choking back her own soft sobs between words.

"Lord, we ask that You receive the souls of these four, for we know their suffering is over. These evil men will see Your judgment someday, that we also know from Your Word. Father, do whatever You must in order to bring about the end of this horrible tragedy called slavery. Show us how we can be involved in that effort."

Ida glanced up at her friend as she continued her prayer, surprised that she would be that bold out here on a public street like this. But Nan never opened her eyes, just kept pouring out her heart before the Lord. In that moment, Ida knew God was speaking directly to her through her young friend. He wanted something done! No more talking about it, or discussing it endlessly, or even praying about it. Instead, it was time to *do* something. The question was *what*.

They finished praying and after Ida's loud "Amen" the two hurried on home without another word. As soon as they were safely inside the house, however, it was much like a dam bursting.

"Nan, we simply have to get involved somehow in this new movement everyone is talking about. What is it called?"

"Abolition. To abolish slavery. And to do it legally because it is such a moral affront to God's heart."

Ida paused, studying her young friend's animated face. "You know something about this, don't you?"

"Yes, Miss Ida, I do. I have been to a couple of meetings to hear people speak about it. They meet in secret as a rule because it is too dangerous to discuss these matters in public, for those speaking as well as those attending. For months now I have been praying for a way to talk to you about the subject, but because I knew how you felt about people of color—*any* color—I decided it was best to keep my feelings to myself."

"Please, can I go with you to one of these meetings?"

Nan's jaw dropped. "Are you *sure?* Are you willing to risk your freedom and all you own for this? Because those animals we saw on the street earlier may come after you, those or others like them. That is what could happen, you know."

Ida took a deep breath, meeting Nan's intense stare with one of her own. "I understand. And I want to go. When is the next one?"

"I am going to one tomorrow night, in fact, over in Cincinnati, assuming the weather will permit me to travel that far. This one is in a church, so it might be a little safer than some of the others I have attended. Things got a bit scary at the last meeting, in fact. God protected me, however. My intention was to rent a buggy in the morning and go over there by myself, but I would love it if you would like to go with me. There is a ladies' hotel close by that I know about where I planned to stay overnight, as the journey is too long for returning that same evening this time of year. Because the rally is on a Saturday night, I thought I would go to church the next morning and return that afternoon. Several other times I have done this but prefer not to go that far on my own if I can avoid it, especially if it is snowing. It would be wonderful to have company."

"Then it's decided. I'm going, too. What time do we need to leave?"

March 23, 1860
Cincinnati, Ohio

By the time the pair got to the church where the rally was being held that next evening, the air of excitement was contagious. They could hardly contain themselves while they waited for it to begin! The snow had held off so far, fortunately, but inside the building, no one seemed to care about anything as mundane as weather.

"Who is supposed to speak tonight, Nan?"

"There are several but the one I especially want to hear is a lady by the name of Mrs. Harriet Beecher Stowe. She has written a book, apparently about this crisis of humanity caused by slavery, and I am eager to hear about it and what she has to say. She has many important friends who are all supposed to be in attendance. One of them apparently even has a price on her head, if you can believe. Therefore, they are not sure if she will get to come or not."

"A *price* on her head? Oh, my! What on earth has she done to warrant that?"

"Be a slave. Survive. Be a runaway who has rescued many others from the evil clutches of slavery. Her nickname is 'Moses' because, as her namesake did in the Bible, she leads her people out of bondage and into freedom!"

"I *knew* God had a reason for me to witness what we did yesterday, as sad as it was. He is providing the answer to my prayers right here, right now!"

CHAPTER TWENTY

"For thus saith the LORD; we have heard a voice of trembling, of fear, and not of peace." Jeremiah 30:5

April 19, 1867

"Mama, what a terrible story Miss Nan told us last night. I found myself praying for those people, even though they are long ago dead now. It was so real but also scary. How can people treat each other like that?" Lily's soft voice floated over from the bed to Mandy where she sat in the rocker, Bible in her lap, praying for her family.

"Yes, I hated for you to have to hear of such horrors but apparently that happened often back then. War is a terrible thing for everyone who is touched by it. You have experienced only a small taste of it which you may not even recall as you were quite young. The Kiowa were attacked by the Comanche several years ago and a bloody conflict erupted between the two tribes for a time. They finally were able to smoke a peace pipe between them, but it was a difficult time for us all."

"I only remember being afraid whenever any stranger came into the camp but I think I was too little to understand why."

"I'm grateful you only recall peace with our people. The war here was horrible in that it split everything, from towns to states and even families. Sadly, the bitterness is far from over. Have you read anything of all this in that book?"

"Yes, I have, Mama. I know it is fiction but as Great-Aunt Ida said, it reflects true events. Maybe that is why she read it multiple times. To learn from it, as she challenged me to do. It is all rather confusing, however. For instance, do you know what a mulatto is?"

"To be honest, I'm not entirely certain. Perhaps a person of mixed race?"

"I think it is one who has both Negro blood and white blood in them. Seems a bit silly to me, since all blood is red, as you have often pointed out!"

"How right you are, Lily!"

"But in this book, it's a disgrace to be this." She hesitated a moment. "I wondered if *I* am a disgrace, since I'm of mixed blood. Just not Negro, of course."

"Oh, my dear, *never,* not to your father and not to me! This has never mattered before. My heart is broken that now it does. If our lie were to be exposed, for instance, it would change the outcome of the court case and completely change Aunt Ida's will, simply because I am also of mixed blood. According to the laws of the United States that would mean I am unable to inherit property. Such a tragedy. Will this country ever get it right, I wonder?"

"Mama, do I not belong here *or* in Indian Territory? I mean, our village accepts me and both of my brothers, as well as you, but I have heard of others that turn out all white captives and their children."

"The important thing I want you to learn from this book is that the root cause of all of this confusion, contradiction, and sadness is *sin*. One that resulted in slavery being accepted as normal, which of course required it to be defended, with an entire country being formed to preserve it. You can never justify sin in God's eyes. Never. All that grows out of it is tainted as well. He will never tolerate sin nor look the other way while it is being committed. You have heard me say more than once that you can go to worship and pray to receive forgiveness, but that does not make it right to go straight out from there and lie or cheat or steal from others. God looks on the heart, whereas man looks on the surface, at the words, at the actions. I believe Aunt Ida finally learned the truth of that and wanted anyone who read her book later, for instance, to know that she did. It is time you learned this lesson as well."

"Why do people continue to hurt each other, over sometimes the smallest of offenses? I do it from time to time myself, but that doesn't mean I understand why."

"There are no easy answers for that, Lily. The cruel and hurtful ways in which people defy God or mock Him are not His ways. They are invented by man, who without Christ is fallen and without redemption. Simply because we call something normal or accept it as such does not make it truth in His opinion!" She paused and smiled. "I sound like I am teaching a Bible lesson, but that is not my intent here. We need to talk about this book more later! You bring up several good points, and I am eager to know what you think about it all, as well as what my aunt had to say. You know, perhaps this is one main reason God brought us here, so you could help us both see more clearly the travesty of slavery, not to mention come to understand her struggles, too."

Lily was quiet but Mandy felt she had listened well to the conversation. *That book really is a powerful force for freedom of all kinds!*

"Well," said Mandy, "we have a busy day ahead of us but we can talk more about what you are learning from that story tonight, perhaps. Right now, I need to get to Matthew's office this morning. I know you must be excited to finally get to go to Ginny's home. Please be on your best behavior there! If you slip up and say something about our secret, I won't be there to cover for you."

"Don't worry, Mama. I'm not about to tell Ginny she is spending time with a girl who is three-fourths Kiowa! Bet her mother would die if she knew the truth!"

After a delicious breakfast with all the residents, Mandy set out with Lily to take her to Ginny's house. They were both astounded at the size of the villa when they found the address, thanks to the directions from Mrs. Wilson. She indicated to them these were important people who did not offer invitations to just anyone to visit! Mandy worried about this but at the same time was thrilled her daughter had a friend to occupy her time, so she didn't have to drag her along on a boring business meeting. She expected this to be a brief one, however, focused on finishing up paperwork for the inheritance to come to her. Mandy hoped to come back and read the last of Ida's letters while waiting on Lily to finish at Ginny's. Perhaps by then she would have a definite time when they could go home!

Mandy was touched when Ginny received Lily with open warmth. Even Mrs. Cordon was friendlier than at first. She assured Mandy that they were glad to welcome Ida's great-niece to their home, saying she mustn't feel rushed to get back to pick her up. What a difference from the coldness she had first sensed from this woman!

At Matthew's office, his secretary also seemed a little kinder than before. Maybe it was her imagination but regardless, Mandy's anxiety overrode everything else for the moment. She would be glad to talk briefly with Matthew and get out of there!

As soon as they were seated in the conference room with the door closed, he said, "Amanda, I am sorry to have to bear bad news, but it appears that Alex discovered the details of the will that we hoped would remain hidden for a while yet, and he did not take the news well. He has now filed a lawsuit in the county seat to stop the performance of Miss Ida's Last Will and Testament."

"What? Oh no! How does this all work now? I mean, will I not inherit her property, after all?"

"No, no, nothing of the kind. Unfortunately, it is going to take a little longer than I had hoped. I cannot disburse the funds from her estate now, until the judge rules on this matter."

"A judge? You mean it has to go that far?"

"Yes, but Judge Adams, who has been assigned to this case, is a kind man with whom I have had quite a few dealings over the past couple of years. It is my firm opinion that you will get a fair hearing from him. In addition, when he reads all I am going to put in my supporting documents, I don't believe he will hesitate to award the entire estate to you immediately."

"Oh, you had me concerned there for a moment. How much longer will this take now? Like a few more days or what?"

"More like a few weeks, I'm afraid."

"*Weeks?* I cannot possibly stay here several weeks! I mean, I, well, I don't have provision for that long of a stay, for one thing, and I simply cannot afford to do that. There has to be a way to cut this shorter. I need to go home!"

"The law often seems to move slower than any of us would like, sad to say. Some things can be worked around but for the most part, there are laws in place to protect people in a lawsuit, on both sides, and it takes time to wind through the court system. Even though it is only a will involved here, the estate is quite sizeable, as I told you. Thus, the judge will be a little more cautious to ensure his ruling is a fair one, perhaps more so than if it were a smaller amount of money. You recall, I warned you this might happen, but I had hoped and prayed that Alex wouldn't dare try to intervene. But now he has."

"And of course for my *cousin*, it is all about the money, right? I mean, that is why he is doing this, I assume?"

"Certainly it is. Especially since we now know he is an imposter. That won't help his cause, believe me, but it certainly will help yours."

"I have a, a—a *cause?* This is all so confusing to me! I thought it would be simpler, that this morning perhaps I would walk away with the money. That way, Lily and I could leave for home right away. Whatever will we do now?"

"You will trust me, is what you will do. Please, Amanda, stay calm and hear me when I say that I have this under control. No, it won't be days but yes, it won't be impossible, either. You will have to be patient a little longer is all."

Mandy fought back the tears that threatened to spring up at this devastating news.

"Will Mrs. Wilson be all right with us staying longer at the Boarding House, do you think?"

"I know she will. When I first talked to her the other day, I told her the time frame was highly fluid at this point and she saw no problem with the two of you staying as long as it takes. Relax! I know what I'm doing and you must learn to trust me."

Reluctantly, Mandy agreed, but inside she was a quivering mess. *How will I let you know that we have been delayed, Ken-ai-te? I don't want you to think we are not coming home at all! God, what am I going to do?*

"So, what happens now?" she asked quietly.

"There will be a series of hearings and a ton of paperwork to be filed in proper order for us to prove to the judge that you are who you say you are. Additionally, we will urge the judge to consider that Miss Ida's will should be probated as quickly as possible. I will need to spend time with you on all this every day, for the most part, to get this to work as quickly as we can push it through. How about if you plan on coming here each morning around 10:00 for us to lay out that day's strategy? Will that work for you?"

"Every day? Oh my word! What will I do about Lily?"

"She can stay at the Boarding House if she likes, where she would be perfectly safe and protected, if that is what you are concerned about. Or accompany you here, I certainly don't mind. They won't be long meetings, I don't think, but I will have papers for you to sign most days, as well as we will go over Alex's responses to everything. Occasionally we will have a court hearing we must attend together but most of those only I will be present to argue certain points before the judge and you won't need to go. I promise you I will constantly seek ways to cut this down to a shorter time."

"A lot depends on how things go today at Ginny's house. I appreciated your making the arrangements for her to go over there this morning. It was my understanding that Mrs. Cordon wanted her daughter to complete certain lessons before Lily arrived, which is why we originally set the time for mid-afternoon."

"As I told you earlier, when I explained the situation, Mrs. Cordon was very kind and agreed that Lily would be a delight to have there as often and as long as it was convenient. But as you say, a lot depends on how the girls do today. Let's worry about that tomorrow!"

"I wish there was a way to get a message to my husband about our delay but that is impossible. It is my sincere hope he does not give up on us returning!"

"If I can be of any help with that, I would be most happy to do whatever you need. But as you said, without mail delivery out there, I'm not sure there is a thing we can do. However, I wanted to tell you one piece of great news: the Masons are eager to meet you this morning. They should be here any time now to lay out for you their plans for the house and grounds, if you decide to sell it to them."

"The Masons? Oh, that's the couple you mentioned who are interested in Aunt Ida's home, right?"

"That's correct. I think you will enjoy meeting Crawford and Alyssa. They are such nice people. They have no children but have dedicated themselves to creating a historical society that rivals those of much bigger cities than Trenton. Their efforts, as you will soon see, will not be complete without honoring Miss Ida. But I want them to explain all that to you instead of me doing it."

"I appreciate your efforts to move forward with the sale of the house, but it isn't mine to sell now. Maybe it never will be."

"Don't talk like that! Of course it will be, and soon. We are going to stay positive on that point. That is why I wanted you to meet them now, to encourage you that when the time is right, selling it to them will be an easy decision for you."

A soft knock sounded at the conference room door, and Miss Lawson informed her boss that the Masons had arrived.

Instantly, Mandy took a liking to the personable young couple. They were a striking pair, with her stunning beauty only rivaled by his rugged good looks himself. Why were they burying themselves in a small town, digging up details of the past, instead of creating a business of some kind that would impact many others? In any case, she found it easy to visit with them both. They were quite down to earth and excited to meet her. She thought they looked vaguely familiar and, indeed, they confirmed they had attended the services for her aunt, though out of respect made no attempt to meet or speak with her on such a sad occasion.

"First off, Mrs. Alton, I want to say on behalf of Alyssa and myself how very sorry we are for your deep loss in the death of your aunt. She was a wonderful lady who did so much to help many in this town."

"Thank you for your condolences, Mr. Mason."

"Please, Crawford, if you don't mind. *Mr. Mason* is my father! And while I love him dearly, I am not ready to *be* him quite yet."

"Of course. And I am Amanda."

"Amanda," said Alyssa, "we have a beautiful vision of how Miss Ida's home—*your* home now—could be a perfect historical museum setting for how we wish to honor your aunt as well as all her many contributions over the years to our community. People today in Trenton know many things she did but we want to ensure that future generations will know, too. Some folks are completely unaware of how she impacted the lives of so many in one way or the other, not only here but in surrounding areas as well."

"Having only recently returned here after a long absence," answered Mandy, "I am interested in learning all this as well. However, we may be rushing things a bit. Matthew told me a few minutes ago that my cousin, Alex Clark, has filed a suit against me, to stop the will from being enacted and thus the inheritance from being awarded to me, after all. While I am eager to hear your plans, please know that I cannot make any promises about selling the property to you, since it is not yet mine to sell."

"Yet," Matthew interjected. "*Yet* is the important word here. I have every confidence the estate will go to you as your aunt desired, Amanda. But yes, you are correct to express caution in this transaction. For now,

Why don't you all explain to Amanda how you wish to use the property, Crawford? That way she can see why you are eager to get your hands on the house and grounds, once she is free to sell it to you."

For the next half hour or so, they explained in vivid detail all their dreams and Mandy was amazed at how exciting it sounded. No wonder Matthew had wanted her to talk to them! Yes, this would, indeed, be such an honor to see her aunt's house used for this purpose. How she hoped it would become a reality. Soon. Very soon!

Selling not only the house but the furnishings as well would solve a desperate problem she had lost sleep over—of what to do with all the artwork and furniture, for instance, all of which must be worth a great deal of money. She thought Matthew had mentioned doing an inventory in order to determine the items to be sold at auction, along with their value. If she could come to terms with the Masons over a price for all of it, she would have the money immediately instead, with no hassle or delay. After she and Nan had taken what they wanted from the house, they could have the rest. What use would she have for artwork in her tipi? The thought was ludicrous! It would be hard enough to tell Lily she couldn't possibly take all the books with her back home.

"I am not sure if you wish to include this or not, but apparently my aunt was heavily involved in the Underground Railroad during the War Between The States and used her home as a Depot. She had a hidden room built in the cellar that was used to secrete the passengers when they were resting overnight in her home."

"That is incredible news!" said Alyssa and clapped her hands in glee! "We had heard rumors to this effect and yes, we were planning on hinting at that possibility in the museum. But if you have proof of this, that would greatly enhance some of the things we hope to use the property for."

"Primarily, that goal," added Crawford, "is to teach folks and especially children about the heritage of this town and her people, specifically Miss Clark, along with how history played such a valuable role."

"How wonderful!" said Mandy. "Yes, there is much to be said about this and other such contributions she made, I suppose. As far as *proof* is concerned, I have her letters relating all the details. Miss Brewster, my aunt's companion for years, was an eyewitness and active participant in this effort. She could share other specifics for you as well, I'm certain. And then there is the hidden room. Visitors could perhaps view it, for a better perspective on what the folks who used it experienced while there."

"What an excellent idea! This is astounding, Amanda," added Crawford. "Far more than we dared hope for. But it will be a great addition to the dream we have had for some time. Having her actual home for the museum would help with its cost but with Wellington Oaks already being well known in this area, it is a natural focus for this effort. I am absolutely delighted to hear this but also to get to meet you and share our vision with you. Our commitment to you will be to work with you on determining the selling cost of the property, so please know that should not be a problem from our standpoint. I look forward to completing this transaction very soon!"

Had God really used her aunt this powerfully, that now even after death, there were folks desiring to honor her obedience to Him during tough times and good ones, to help so many? It was a bit overwhelming to her mind. But apparently it was true!

When the couple left, Mandy felt more upbeat than she had in the last three days. Would God bless this endeavor?

Aunt Ida would blush a thousand shades of red to think of anyone honoring her for any reason, but her contributions need to be displayed for all to see. It is a part of history, plain and simple. These two have the money, the time, the knowledge, and the desire to do exactly that. Thank You, Lord! There could not possibly be a better way to make my own small contribution to Trenton's history than this one. What an incredible legacy Aunt Ida has left behind. And like it or not as a child, I am part of that now as an adult. It makes me all the more eager to learn every detail I can of how the Lord changed her heart so dramatically.

"There is one more thing, Amanda, that we need to discuss before you leave," said Matthew. "In order to show the folks in this town that you deserve this inheritance and the will should be honored the way your aunt wrote it, I feel it is imperative that you be seen often in social settings, so people can get to know you better. That is one reason I am supportive of Lily spending time with the Cordons. Though French, they are well known here, and Mrs. Cordon in particular has worked hard since moving to Trenton to be a part of the community. Building that big house and then paying for tutors for their daughter has not exactly endeared them to many but at least everyone knows who they are and that they are wealthy. For many, that is all that counts, sad to say."

"Social settings? What exactly do you mean by that?"

"At dinner parties given by various people eager to meet you, at church every Sunday, in the Park which is a center of social activity for everyone especially on Sunday afternoons when the weather cooperates—that sort of thing. We don't have a real 'society' here of course, that is for Cincinnati folks, such as the opera, theater, balls, and other such events. But for our little place, there are still plenty of ways for you to show people that you care about Trenton, even though you live in Indian Territory and plan to return there soon. You can bridge many of those gaps in the minds of some folks if you are willing to let me escort you to these places as they come up."

"But I'm a married woman. Is that appropriate?"

"It will be, the way I plan to handle it. Lily will be our chaperone much of the time, I'm sure, and I hope Nan will come with us as well, at least occasionally. People here are a little more laid back about things like that, but I would never do anything to damage your reputation in my efforts to build it up. I would like to start by taking you, your daughter, and perhaps also Nan to church this Sunday. At least, I'm assuming you would be interested in going back to the church where your aunt was such a prominent member and where, I believe, you attended when you were growing up."

"Yes, my father was the pastor there for quite a few years, in fact. Until he decided to go back to Indian Territory, that is. The minister at the church did such a great job of Aunt Ida's service, it would be a pleasure to hear him preach. What time will you call for us?"

"Let's say 10:00 as the service is at 10:30. That will give us plenty of time to visit with folks before it starts and not risk being late."

"I cannot speak for Nan but I will ask her if she would like to go. She had indicated to me at one point during the funeral planning that she was very pleased with the preacher too, so I assume she goes there."

"Yes, she does, in fact until Miss Ida became ill, she rarely missed a single week."

Mandy checked her watch and said, "Now, sir, I really need to get going as it's almost time to pick up Lily at Ginny's house. I know they said there wasn't a specific time but I told her I would be there before luncheon. If you don't have further business to discuss at the moment, I assume we can wait until Monday for anything more."

Within minutes, Mandy was back outside headed toward Castle Street to the Cordons' home. The meeting with Matthew had taken longer than she anticipated so there wasn't time to go back to the Boarding House before getting Lily. As she walked, she wondered how her daughter would take the news they would be staying longer than expected here in Trenton. Although she hoped today had gone well between the girls, if they had enjoyed themselves, leaving would be harder. But at least not as soon as Mandy had hoped. She wasn't paying much attention to the few others out walking around town, until a voice behind her abruptly caught her attention.

"There she goes, the Princess of Indian Territory! Preening like a queen when she is nothing but a guttersnipe who does not deserve one penny of my inheritance!"

Mandy whirled around to face her tormentor. Alex stood there with a smirk on his face, as though challenging her to defy him! Fear clutched at her heart. She gasped at his next words.

"You had best get back on that train you came on, lady, before something happens to mar your beauty you are so proud of. Or you might be going home in pieces!"

CHAPTER TWENTY-ONE

"A new heart also will I give you, and a new spirit will I put within you: and I will take away the stony heart out of your flesh, and I will give you an heart of flesh." Ezekiel 36:26

April 19, 1867

"Why are you saying such a horrible thing to me?" Mandy couldn't catch her breath. Had Alex really threatened to assault or even kill her? Surely her ears betrayed her!

"You heard me. Get out of Trenton, now, or you will live to regret it. Or die. Your choice."

The cad pushed past her to walk away without another word, leaving her shaken and anxious. Even with the Kiowa, she had never encountered this level of hatred. As soon as the thought formed, she realized that was not right. She had been surrounded by it in the early days of living in the village, not to mention all the hatred spewed by her mortal enemy and his wicked schemes to destroy her. Only with God's help did she endure it, eventually experiencing triumph over it.

Father, help me now to rest in Your presence as You have in the past, not in the evil I just witnessed! She closed her eyes for a moment, tuning out the normal sounds around her and soaking in the quiet of His peace. Taking a deep breath, she looked around to see if Alex still lurked nearby but he was nowhere to be seen. Quickly she walked on toward her destination. With each step her heart slowed to a more normal rhythm but the sick feeling in the pit of her stomach took longer to resolve.

Should I tell Matthew what happened? No, I am depending on Your protection, Lord, not that of any man. Oh, Ken-ai-te, I do wish you were here to give me the courage

I need to see this through, for you are the one man whose prayers I can rely on! Pray for me, that I will endure this well!

Seeing Lily's happy face a short time later made up for the anxiety she had felt earlier. Obviously, the morning had gone well. After they thanked Ginny and Mrs. Cordon, Mandy was pleased to hear the older woman invite Lily to return each morning if she wished. What a blessing that "chance" encounter in the store had been for them both!

"We will have to see about that, Mrs. Cordon, but I do appreciate your kind offer. I have a meeting each morning with my attorney for the foreseeable future so we might take you up on that invitation."

Lily bubbled as they walked back to the Boarding House, going on and on about how much fun she had with her new friend, describing in great detail one by one the delightful moments of her morning. She told her mother all about the four-story dollhouse that was made in Paris and the tiny pieces of furniture in it, from the chandeliers to the lace curtains at each window. Even the fancy set of dishes on the dining table and the rugs on the floors caught her attention. Lily couldn't stop chattering endlessly about every single bit of it!

"You should see her porcelain dolls with real hair you can brush! Each one has her own trunk for several elaborate sets of clothing for every occasion—from fur coats to tiny muffs and beautiful ball gowns. Mama, it was all absolutely amazing! I never dreamed being rich could be this much fun!"

To Mandy's relief, she never noticed how quiet her mother was, which she took as a blessing. How she dreaded telling her daughter of Alex's threat; indeed, she would not do so unless it became absolutely necessary. No need to scare her. Mandy was terrified enough for both of them. Perhaps the news they would be staying longer in town than originally planned would help if she had to reveal to her the threat. It was all very confusing and upsetting!

When they arrived back at the Boarding House, luncheon was being served. They chatted with the other boarders as they ate, getting better acquainted with them. One lady was full of questions about Ida's house when she learned they were related to her, saying she had long admired it and was consumed with curiosity for what it looked like inside. Mandy answered each one politely but was gratified that at least the Masons had been correct in their assumption that there would be plenty of interest in the house from the general public. To her it was merely a building where she grew up, but to others it was a mansion and automatically qualified as a place of fascination. She only hoped she would be able to sell it to them right away. If she was truthful, however, a rapidly growing part of her wanted Alex *out* of it as soon as possible. Every moment he lived there dishonored her aunt's memory more!

Once the two were back in their room, Mandy told Lily what Matthew had said and was frustrated, although not at all surprised, at her joyous reaction.

"Mama, that is great news! We get to stay here indefinitely! I'm really, really thrilled. One problem we do have is that we need more clothing. Do you suppose we could go shopping this afternoon? I want to look my best on Sunday at church. I have never been in one before, remember? Besides, I certainly cannot wear the same outfit to Ginny's every day."

"Hold on, we are not going to spend all our meat money on clothing so you can look elegant at the Cordons' home! Your brothers are starving in order for you to have new clothes! Have you no shame?"

"I never meant anything of the kind. Of course I am sad about Red Hawk and Spotted Rabbit. Soon they will eat well but for now, it seems you don't understand. You have been gone too long to remember, I suppose, but I have already figured this out. The nicer we look, the more likely the people are to accept us and if they do, then they will be on our side about the inheritance. How or why their opinion counts is beyond me, but it does. Matthew says so. I intend to enjoy this time as much as I can, but I need more dresses. Please, can we go shopping?"

Mandy sighed and sank on the bed. She couldn't fight both her attorney and her daughter. Perhaps they were right. She should stop worrying about a few extra weeks here if it meant getting the money to feed their people. *Ken-ai-te, help me have the wisdom to know how to do this!* With a sick feeling in the pit of her stomach, the thought struck her that she should be praying to the only One who could answer that plea, not asking her absent husband! But it did bring her comfort to talk to him as she would if back home in their tipi, about all the details of her life and decisions she faced. Was that terribly wrong? She hoped not.

So, off to the Emporium they went and Mandy shrugged off her doubts, refusing to give more thought to them or her confusion any longer. She would focus instead on what was real and right in front of her. What woman doesn't like new clothes to boost her spirits? Well, at least *white* women! Again, the conflict with the two cultures, but the white one won out decisively for this day. Besides, it was fun having Nan there to assist them with their selections and encourage them. She was thrilled, too, to hear they would be around longer than expected. Seemed Mandy was the only one not sharing that emotion!

Reluctant though she was to spend the money, once their selections had been made, her mood did improve vastly as they unpacked all their purchases a couple of hours later. After some rest time, Mandy sat down to record her newest thoughts and concerns to Ken-ai-te in the journal that she kept on her bedstand. It encouraged her to keep it close by, almost as though she had him at her side. Lily read while Mandy wrote. Before they knew it, the dinner hour had arrived, so they went downstairs. Nan would be coming home in a short time and Mandy found herself eagerly looking forward to seeing her. Until the remembrance of her encounter earlier that day with Alex came to mind. It once more stopped her cold.

I suppose I should tell Nan about this but not in the hearing of others. Lily truly deserves to know first but I don't know how to tell her right now. Maybe Nan and I could go for a walk after we eat, to have some time alone. She would probably prefer to get off her feet after a long day working at the Emporium, especially since this was her first day back, too. But I have to tell someone or I shall burst!

About an hour later Nan and Mandy set out for a walk in the nearby park. Lily begged off going, saying she wanted to do more reading as she was almost finished with her book. Mandy hesitated briefly but knew her daughter would be fine there at the house, lost in her own little world, yet with everyone else around. She *must* have the time to talk to Nan! As they walked the couple of blocks, she discussed in more detail with her friend the distressing news from Matthew as well as his strategy for the coming weeks.

She replied, "The approach Matthew suggested sounds intriguing as long as, well, as long as he does respect your married status. Not that I think he won't. Oh, don't listen to me, rambling on like this. The exciting part is that you get to stay here longer! Well, maybe not really for you, Amanda. I'm glad we have more time to get to know each other, but I'm sure you are disappointed to not be able to head for home in the next couple of days."

"Yes, I am, but I also have mixed feelings. I want to know more about Aunt Ida and all those lost years, for instance, before I leave here for good. There's so much I don't know yet. Every day seems to bring more stories of her generosity, and it means a great deal to me to hear them. Oh, look! We are already here at the Park!"

A short time later Mandy said, "This place is lovely, Nan. I have seen it from the street of course but not gotten to walk through it." Glancing around, she continued, "Seems everyone in town agrees that it is a nice evening for a walk!"

"Yes, it is one of my favorite places in town. Very private areas throughout, even when many are here. I gather you must have something to talk about that you don't want anyone else to overhear, not even Lily?"

Mandy looked around again.. "Yes, as a matter of fact, I do. This morning on my way to pick up Lily, I had a very frightening encounter with my so-called cousin."

"Really? What happened?"

"He threatened me is what happened."

"What? How? What did he say? Did he harm you?"

"No, he didn't touch me. Merely unnerved me with what he said. He told me to leave Trenton or I might end up leaving in pieces!"

"Oh no! How horrible!"

"It left me close to tears, with my knees shaking. I couldn't even think how to answer him, but thankfully he disappeared so I didn't have to. What am I going to do, Nan?"

"You are going to tell Matthew, for one thing. Right?" When Mandy didn't immediately respond, she added, "This is no longer a question. You *are* telling him, and as soon as possible!"

"I'm afraid to for fear of what he might do, but I suppose that is best. When he told me that Alex had filed the suit, I was dismayed but figured it would be a legal matter, nothing more. Certainly not something personal. But now I'm truly terrified! What if he makes good on his threat? I mean, I have no intentions of going home without the money but how do I evade seeing him around town, for instance? How do I protect myself? And Lily?"

"You are going to tell Matthew and let him handle it. In truth, this probably will strengthen your side of the case. I don't imagine the judge will take kindly to him threatening you."

"I would tend to agree. At least, I hope so."

"Please don't worry too much about him. I would love to say that he is all bark and no bite, as the old saying goes. But I cannot, with any level of confidence. I don't trust the man nor would I never turn my back on him. Neither should you, which means no taking any unnecessary chances. You shouldn't be alone on the street, for instance, and neither should Lily. I'm not much help to you with my work schedule, but perhaps Matthew will have some other ideas. Thank you for telling me. I know it must have been difficult for you to admit Alex could be this ruthless. It's a shock to me, too, yet I cannot say I'm too surprised. He's a horrid man and it's only a matter of time before he will get what is coming to him."

"Speaking of Matthew reminds me that he intends to call for us in the morning to take us to church, and I'm hoping that you will come as well. I'm a little nervous that it is inappropriate for me to be with him, since I'm a married woman, but if you and Lily are there, you two can provide an adequate chaperone. You will come, won't you?"

Nan hesitated but then replied, "Of course. I mean, after all, it is church. I was planning on going anyway, so it will be nice to be escorted by such distinguished company."

"Me, distinguished? Are you joking?"

"Not really. You are a celebrity of sorts around here, though, in case you haven't noticed."

"Now I know you are kidding me!"

"Didn't you say that Matthew wanted to ensure you would be seen and get to know many people, to strengthen your case? This is part of that, I'm sure. But in any case, you will want to be in church while you are here, I assume, so accept his kindness and do not worry about it."

"Perhaps we ought to get back to the house, as the sun is setting. In fact, we need to hurry because we don't want to be out after dark." She stopped to glance briefly at her watch. "Also, Mrs. Wilson's deadline is coming up soon in a few minutes and we don't want to get locked out!"

When they returned to the house, Lily was settled in a chair in the Parlor reading.

"Are you still working on that book, my dear?" asked Mandy.

"Oh, I finished it but decided to re-read a few of the pages. This story is truly heart-stopping in places. No wonder it is known as the book that started a war. You really ought to read it for yourself, Mama."

"Perhaps I will. Are you going to start on your book of poetry soon?"

"Probably at bedtime after while. Did you two have a good walk?"

"Yes, we did," answered Mandy and Nan nodded her head in agreement. "I was just going to ask her to continue some more of her story about Aunt Ida, if she is up to it. Are you interested in hearing it?"

"Oh, yes, Mama, I certainly am. Would you mind, Miss Nan? You aren't too tired, are you?"

"Well, I'm not sure how long I might last this evening, but I certainly will be glad to share more details with you both. How about if we do it up in your room, so we don't disturb the other residents?"

A few minutes later the three settled in the small but cozy room that Mandy and Lily shared, eager to hear what Nan had to say.

"Let's see, where was I in this? Oh, yes, I remember now. Miss Ida and I had just arrived at the rally in Cincinnati and were discussing Mrs. Stowe's friend who was supposed to speak that evening, along with several others. But this woman had a price on her head; consequently, she was unable to come at the last minute. You may recall I told Miss Ida that being a runaway was one thing, but one who came back to rescue fellow slaves from the clutches of slavery, as this woman had done, was even worse. It was for that offense the bounty was offered on this woman's head."

March 23, 1860
Cincinnati, Ohio

"To the slave owners," said Nan to her friend, "the very existence of one who does this right under their noses is an affront to their way of life. Consequently, they are determined to catch her in order to make an example of her, to frighten and intimidate other slaves throughout the South. So far, she has managed to evade capture, and many abolitionists are praying the authorities never find her.

"To think that merely being who God created you to be could become a crime!" said Ida sadly. "It's an outrage, is what it is! What is the woman's name, do you know?"

"Her real name is Harriet Tubman," said Nan, "but as I said earlier, she is called 'Moses' because she calls for masters to let her people go, as her namesake did in the Bible. Her life's work has become to lead slaves out of bondage and into freedom—that, and staying free herself."

"Oh, look, it's about to begin," Ida interrupted. "That must be Mrs. Stowe up there with the preacher, I assume."

For the following hour, Ida sat mesmerized as one speaker after another took the podium and shared from the heart about why abolition was the only answer to the travesty of slavery, not tolerance or looking the other way or even passive disobedience. Their answer was that it must be eradicated from the face of the earth before a Holy and Just God! Words that stirred Ida's blood like never before resounded in that tiny packed chapel, arousing her to shame, guilt, remorse, and finally genuine repentance for her own long-standing prejudices. At the same time, she exulted in joy over the eloquently stated solutions being painted that night. She wiped away tears often but could feel God's power at work in healing her from the inside out. How freeing it was!

One man proclaimed loudly to the crowd hanging on his every word, "Whether or not war comes, as most assume it must, we absolutely cannot ever give up our fight!" He was met with thunderous and sustained applause by all in attendance.

Clapping in the house of God? What a strange way of showing approval but it somehow seems appropriate at the moment. Ida was startled at first but soon joined in, enthusiastically and without reserve. Nan kept glancing over at Ida and smiling. Several times their eyes met. Ida was surprised that her dear friend was moved to tears as often as she was!

When Mrs. Stowe was introduced, Ida was taken with how forcefully she spoke, to be so small and dainty appearing.

"Ladies and gentlemen, I am humbled to appear here tonight with these great giants of the abolitionist movement in this state. I fear I have nothing to say that is nearly as important as they have been sharing. To be honest, I am far more comfortable writing than speaking! But God has put a message in my heart so please listen to what He has to say rather than to my words.

"A few years ago when I wrote my book *Uncle Tom's Cabin*, I had no idea it would be as popular as it is. Some folks buy a copy to burn it and show their extreme displeasure with my story. Others buy it to share with everyone they know. When I had the humbling privilege of recently meeting our great President, I was shocked when he called me the woman with the little book that started a war! Since the war has yet to be declared, I assumed he meant a war of words over this topic. But even for that, I never intended for it to go that far, only to tell a simple fictional tale that might open a few eyes to the evils of slavery, leaving the pains of war to others. It seems God has accomplished that purpose for me, and far more. If you are interested in having a copy of this book, please see me after this event is over.

"That is not why I am here, however, to sell books. I came to emphasize to all of you how important it is to pray for the overturning of slavery by whatever means we can. Several of our speakers have already explained to you how you might become involved, and I urge you to include in your prayers a petition seeking whether God is asking you to do this.

"In addition, I have one other reason to come tonight. We were to have had the pleasure of hearing from one who has been in the clutches of this evil and escaped, in fact, has escaped many times—Mrs. Harriet Tubman, also called 'Moses' by many far and wide. It is true I am partial to her because we share the same name, though we obviously are not related. But sadly, it was deemed too dangerous for her to appear so she had to flee to avoid being arrested. Before going back into hiding, however, she left us a message, asking that I read it to you. Of course, as a runaway slave she has never learned to read or write, but I scribbled down her words hastily as she spoke them. I apologize to her ahead of time if I got any of them incorrect. The spirit of them is well served, I believe.

"Folks been telling me all my life 'You can't' about one thing or the other. But I don't listen to them. I listen to the Lord. He tell me what I can do, then lead me to do it. You may not know much about slavery but I do. I was born into it. I carry its scars on my back. I still have family suffering under its evil. But I am no longer its victim. I am free! This monster name of slavery has got to be defeated, to its last breath! Spilling every drop of blood in our bodies or giving every single penny we have are not enough. Stopping it is our goal—in fact, stomping it into the ground stained with the blood of so many and burying it forever! Now, I ask, what are you going to do about it?"

Mrs. Stowe stopped while the applause roared, wiping away a tear with her handkerchief. Once quiet reigned again, she cleared her throat and continued.

"We can talk about this all night long or we can, as Mrs. Tubman asked of us, actually *do* something about this. Several people have explained how you can be involved in the abolitionist movement here in Cincinnati. If you wish to do that, I would urge you to please consult with them later. Thank you for coming and for allowing this humble woman to speak."

A while later as Nan and Ida walked out of the church toward their buggy, a couple approached whom Nan immediately recognized. She introduced Ida to her friends Mary and Henry Bell. Graciously, they invited them to take luncheon with them the next day after church, which they gladly accepted.

On the buggy ride to the hotel, the two were bundled up against the cold wind and a light snow began falling as they rode along. But their hearts were warm from what all they had heard that evening. Nan told Ida the Bells had a deep passion for abolition and she was excited they would get to visit with them the next day before heading home. Ida realized that God was, indeed, opening a door of action for her through Nan. Did she have the courage to walk through it? Ida pulled out her copy of the book written by Mrs. Stowe, leafing idly through a couple of pages in the semi-darkness.

They rode in silence for a moment. Then Ida said, "I have a feeling this story is going to bring lots of tears. But they will be worth every one to learn the truth of what slavery is all about. Living here in Ohio, I truthfully have never given it a great deal of thought. Oh, I have heard stories of course, we all have. I figured they were a bit of an exaggeration but after hearing the words tonight and especially those of Mrs. Tubman as well, I have serious doubts now whether that is the case. In addition, the horrific scene we witnessed recently has shattered all my pretense that believing the lies I have heard about this topic is acceptable to God. I can't wait to get started reading this when we get home."

The two talked well into the night, and Nan couldn't stop thanking God for giving her the courage to invite Miss Ida to come with her to Cincinnati to this rally. When they decided they better quit and get to bed or they would have trouble rising the next morning on time for the worship service, Ida asked her friend to pray for her as God reshaped her heart in many different ways. It was a bittersweet time to let go of the past and embrace the future, one neither of them would ever forget!

"If only I had understood all this better," said Ida, "when dear Josiah and Amanda were still with me, perhaps I could have been more supportive of their dream to share the Gospel with the Indians far away. I was filled with intense bitterness and hatred, though. How I do regret that now, especially since I can no longer ask their forgiveness."

"I'm sure, Miss Ida, they would not hold this against you, given that you know the truth now. Christ died for *all* people. Black, white, red, yellow, brown, every shade in between—salvation is offered for each of us, if we accept it."

"You are exactly right. Thank you for your kind encouragement. At least you don't hate me!"

"I could never hate you, Miss Ida! You have given me so much, were there for me countless times when no one else has been. I'm thrilled that God has revealed this truth to you and you have embraced it. It is my prayer that you will believe your family would feel the same, if they were able to stand before you right now. In any case it is not them you need to please, it is the Father of us all. I cannot wait to see how He will be honored by your new freedom!"

CHAPTER TWENTY-TWO

"But in every nation he that feareth him, and worketh righteousness, is accepted with him." Acts 10:35

April 21, 1867
Trenton, Ohio

"I am so excited, Mama, about going to church this morning in a white man's church, I can hardly contain my joy!"

"Hush, Lily, please remember not to say something like 'a white man's church' else others may wonder and ask questions we cannot answer!"

"Sorry, Mama, I did forget. No one is around, though. Unless a ghost is listening to us here in our own room!"

"Ghost? Oh my word! How silly! Please be cautious. Too much is at stake here."

"All right, I will. How is this church going to be different from ours?"

As they finished getting dressed Mandy tried to gather her thoughts to recall what a so-called "white man's church" might look like after all these years. Could it have changed by now?

"For one thing, it is in a real building instead of outdoors around the campfire or in—well, the place where we live once it gets cold."

"Oh, you mean our—"

"Lily!" The stern look stopped her daughter and her smile faded.

"Sorry. Please, go on."

"I'm sure the music will be quite different. When I was a young child for a while we attended at the Methodist Church in town because it was closest to our house. They had an old pump-style organ that was exciting because many people, including me, had never seen one before. As we sang our hearts out, the poor organist had quite a workout to keep it pumping with her feet to produce music!"

"When Papa preaches, I love hearing his voice booming out the Scripture like he loves to do. He sure knows a lot of verses, doesn't he?"

"Yes, my dear, he does. I'm very proud of how he has memorized much of the Bible in the years we have been together. And lives every single word as well. When I think…"

"Of what it was like when you first met?"

"That was precisely what I was going to say. Again, I must watch my words, too. But I try not to reflect on those days too often, instead focus on what God has given me since then."

A short time later they were walking into the building and a couple of times Mandy caught her daughter gaping in wonder at the sights inside. After taking their seats, the soft murmurs of other worshippers surrounded them as the pews filled up. Mandy found herself tensing up and realized it was because she wondered if Alex would be in church this morning, but relaxed when he was nowhere in sight. She supposed that was a ludicrous thought, given the lifestyle he led, but she was quite certain he had gone regularly while living with her aunt as a child. Or the real Alex had, at least.

Lily's eyes continued to widen as she gazed around the good-sized room. They were especially drawn overhead to the dark beams in the high ceiling.

Finally, she whispered, "Look up there, Mama! They are high enough to be in Heaven with God!"

"You know, Lily," said Matthew with a smile, "I never thought about it before now but I think you are right!"

He leaned over Lily to say in a quiet voice, "What do you think of our beautiful church, Amanda? I don't believe they had such a large one as this when you lived in Trenton as a child, did they?"

"Oh, my no! Ours was only a small frame building with a cross painted on the front eave and dainty lace curtains hanging in the tiny front windows. Nothing nearly as grand as this one. I particularly love these stained-glass windows. With the sun shining through them like it is, the whole place is bathed in miniature rainbows everywhere."

"What a lovely thing to say, Amanda," chimed in Nan. "I never thought about it that way. Those have only been here a short time, and I guess I never really looked around before now, to notice that you are right."

"Another of my favorite memories," added Mandy, "was of the tiny cemetery out in back that had a black wrought iron fence around it. The place gave me a spooky feeling whenever Aunt Ida wanted to go visit, but she enjoyed chatting with other people there also laying flowers on the various graves. Out of boredom, I would count the posts in the fence! It kept me occupied and quiet at least. I remember there were twenty-eight of them, in fact. Funny how I hadn't thought of that for a very long time, until now."

The service was long and a bit boring in places, Mandy thought, but overall it was about what she remembered from her childhood. Her mind wandered often, for which she felt guilty. Why couldn't she keep her focus on what the preacher was saying?

It has been many long years since I have sat through a real worship service. No, wait, that's not true! What am I thinking? Our services back home in the tipi or gathered with other Kiowa around our campfire in the middle of our village out on the prairie are every bit as valid as this one! Just different. In fact, in more ways than I remembered. I will have to share about this experience with Ken-ai-te in my writings to him this evening. He will be eager to find more ways to keep people's attention, though I honestly think his sermons are better prepared and more from the heart than this one is.

She sighed and tried hard to follow the man's rather convoluted reasoning in his retelling of the Prodigal Son returning home. Mandy prayed God's promise would be fulfilled that sharing His Word never returns void of its purpose—no matter how boring it might sound on the surface! Besides, how appropriate she found this text for her first Sunday back in Trenton.

The four of them dined after church with some friends of Matthew's who had graciously invited them over, Peter and Callie Gordon. They were a delightful family, with three children and a beautiful home. Lily enjoyed visiting with their daughter especially, quickly joining her new friend in good-natured teasing of her younger brothers. It warmed Mandy's heart immeasurably to see how easily her daughter adapted to new situations and people. Up to now, she had never seen her with others except the Kiowa in their village. Inside, Mandy was torn between being proud of her while being over-anxious that perhaps she was loving all this a little bit too much. Going home would be hard, she knew. She prayed God would clear the way when that time came to ease her daughter's hurt and sadness. It was quite apparent, however, how the Lord was using this time to grow her daughter up and strengthen her faith in small ways. Mandy's hope was they would all add up to a life-long impact that would yield much fruit among the Kiowa someday.

Following dinner, Matthew took them home to the Boarding House. Nan headed for her room to take a nap while the other two went to theirs for the same thing. After a while, Mandy began to get restless.

"Lily, let's go take a walk in the City Park, to get outdoors in the sunshine for a while this afternoon. I'm used to working as hard on Sundays as on other days of course and sitting around a great deal of the time with nothing to do seems somehow wrong. By being out among the wonders of God's creation, we can continue to worship Him even in leisure. My hands are always busy with beadwork or mending or sewing new clothing for all of us at home, and I keep remembering my aunt's admonition that idle hands are the devil's handiwork—or something along that line. I never quite understood it, frankly, until now!"

"The walk sounds lovely, Mama. You are right, you do work too hard and at times it's nice to simply relax a bit. Let me finish this one page and I'll be ready to join you."

As they strolled down the street a few minutes later, Mandy explained about the place they were going.

"It really is a beautiful location for a large park, with several ponds filled with ducks and birds of all kinds flying around. I doubt if we will have time today to explore all of it, but I wanted to share with you at least the small area I saw of it with Nan the other day. She told me there are several smaller parks like it around town but this is the main one folks gather in when they have time to visit with others. I guess Matthew would be happy if we are 'seen' by many here! When I was a child, we were not permitted to take up a knitting needle or a paintbrush on the Sabbath, so walking in the park was all we had to fill the long hours after church and before bedtime. Of course, it wasn't the same park. Ours was much smaller, not nearly as grand as this one. It seems odd that different cultures cannot find a way to combine the best of each for the benefit of all. On the one hand, we don't have enough to occupy us here, while at home we must work constantly seven days a week from sunup to long after sundown, in order to keep the family fed and clothed. Maybe someday people will work that out better."

"I hope so, before I grow up! I like to sit and read rather than having to work all the time. Ginny's family has several servants to do things like the cleaning and cooking, which astounded me! Now I am praying to have that kind of a life for myself when I grow up! You know what my biggest dream is, though? It is to go live in Paris, France someday! I cannot imagine how exciting that would be!"

"That is a pretty big dream for a Kiowa girl from the prairie, don't you think?"

She pouted a moment. "You don't think I should be reaching for that star, as Papa puts it?"

"I didn't say that at all. But it does take a substantial amount of money, dear. That is a fine dream for a white girl from Trenton, Ohio. Even for the wealthiest families, to achieve a goal like that still carries an enormous price tag. Young people can sometimes go abroad for an education, for instance, and get to travel that way. Or even live in Europe for a time, perhaps. But ours is not a wealthy family. You will be expected to take your place in our village as a Kiowa woman, not go off to school in another country or have servants to wait on you or a mansion to live in."

"With Great-Aunt Ida's fortune, I don't see why I cannot have this, same as Ginny will someday!"

"Lily! That money is not for spending on an expensive trip to a foreign country! It was planned by God to provide food for our people. Or have you so quickly forgotten *why* we came here in the first place? Do you even remember what is going on back home, with starvation lurking at every tipi?"

Mandy stared at her daughter, incredulous that those words about using the money for travel abroad could have come out of her mouth! There simply could be no defense for this ridiculous statement.

Lily met her stare defiantly but after a few seconds, it all melted away and she lowered her gaze.

"Yes, Mama, I remember. That is the problem. I don't *want* to. Why couldn't I have been born here in Trenton, instead of way out on the prairie? I want to be *white!* There, I've said it! I can't help what I feel!"

Mandy was speechless. And numb. How could she respond without hurting her daughter but also without denying their proud heritage as Kiowa?

Lily plunked herself down on a nearby bench in the silence, glumly staring at the grass beneath her feet. Mandy joined her, equally as sad. Yet also alarmed that in only two days, her daughter could have been sucked into this culture without one whit of shame or regret! How did this happen? Then it dawned on her: it was the books! They had encouraged her reading widely, as much as they could manage to provide for her, but never realized that the authors were all white and wrote about that culture as though there were no others to consider. Slowly, it apparently had seeped into Lily's mind and heart more than any of them had recognized. Now that she is living in the midst of it, how could she *not* have her head turned by it?

In truth, Mandy knew this had been one of her own greatest fears in coming back here, that she would remember and love it too much to want to go back to her simple life on the prairie. So why would her own child not fall prey to it? *God, give me the right words here to reconcile Lily's heart to her destiny! Help me resist the temptation in my own heart to take it all for granted too much. I want to go home. Now!* Taking a deep breath she plunged in, fear tugging at her mind.

"Lily, I can see your heart's desire because believe me, if anyone can understand it, it would be me. Do you know how hard it was for me to come here to Trenton? I don't know how much of the conversation between your father and me you overheard, but it was not pretty! The root of why I stomped my foot, saying an outright *no* to the idea, lies in what has happened to you since we got here. It is what I feared for myself, that I would love being here in this place, with these people, immersed in this culture again, *too much*. That I would start taking for granted having clean sheets and a soft bed, warm food whenever I was hungry without having to work for an hour to produce it, pretty clothes to wear with white gloves and a bonnet to match! What woman would not?"

"I agree! That is my point. I don't think I was created to wait on my husband as you do for Papa. I was made for greater purposes than that. Somehow, I just *know* it!"

"I do not fault you for finding this lifestyle attractive. I keep sliding into that pit myself. And must pull myself out, one foot at a time. When you met Ginny, I feared even more that this might happen, being exposed to her way of life as you have been. But you simply *must* remember at all times, dear, that this is not our life, our destiny, to live like this. I know you already want it, desperately, fervently, but it is not going to happen.

Someday when you are grown, perhaps God will take you in a different direction than your life as a Kiowa. I cannot predict the future. But to yearn for that now is to invite only misery and unhappiness to reign in your heart. Please don't let that happen! Please listen to the God of your father and to the instruction of your mother, as the Scriptures command. Know that ours is a proud heritage, too, one that is essential to the way of life on the prairie. It is in trouble, true. However, with this money God is providing, your father and I hope we can direct our people to a different pathway than they have been on before, one as full of dignity as the centuries-old one has been.

"Well, it isn't one I want to be anywhere around, thank you very much! I want more for my life than you have, Mama. Being here has confirmed it for me."

"You're very young to decide on any plan for the future at this point, Lily. It needs to come one step at a time, trusting God to reveal the next one in His timing, not yours. You will have many choices before you as you grow up, even if it doesn't seem that way right now. But living in Paris probably is not going to be one of them. Who knows? Maybe I am wrong! Perhaps God will grant that prayer and give you the dream you so desire. As your mother, I try to protect you too much at times, I know. It *is* your choice. I pray you will choose to follow God's leadership and accept responsibility as it comes. Please try not to borrow trouble and misery, for they make poor friends!"

Lily rose suddenly, stomping off toward the pond. *Perhaps the Lord can reach her through the ducks and flowers. I seem to have failed miserably at it. At least she is no longer shouting or making impossible demands. Bring us peace, Father, and help her let go!*

Mandy walked over to join her daughter at the edge of the pond. Miraculously, Lily was excited over their surroundings again, giggling at the antics of the ducklings as they waddled off behind their mother. With a smile Mandy breathed a sigh of relief.

"The Gordons seemed like nice people, didn't they?" Lily said with a smile. Mandy was thrilled that the topic of conversation had taken an abrupt turn for the better! "It was kind of them to invite us to dine with them today. I liked visiting with Ashley, their daughter. She's cute, don't you agree?"

"Yes, dear, and her red hair is gorgeous!"

Lily scampered off the path to chase a squirrel, more giggles pealing in the spring air. In spite of being hugely relieved that the argument seemed to be over, Mandy felt as though a strange darkness hovered close by, right at the edge of this bright scene. She shuddered at a horrific memory that flitted through her mind as she thought about Ashley's hair color. In one of the tipis when she was first captured, the warrior had a scalp with that color hair on his scalp pole, which he displayed prominently. How she hated having to go in there several times in obedience to the orders given to take food to the family when the mother became ill!

God, why am I reminded of that awful experience right now? Will I ever get over those nightmares? Replace this one with the joy of that sweet girl tossing her curls over her shoulder as she laughed! Without You in one's life, there is no end to the degradation that can follow. Thank You for rescuing me from living with this any longer!

It was odd to Mandy that in all the years they had known Jacob, his red hair had never connected with this terrible memory of her past. Maybe it was because the scalp was not that of a man, and it took seeing this child's locks to trigger the recollection of all this.

Mandy consciously rebuked her enemy from his hold and released the memory, choosing instead to focus on the beauty around her, relishing in the peace she felt in doing exactly that.

Spring had certainly come to Trenton, with the flowers and the leafy new growth on all the treetops announcing an end to the snow and cold of winter. Mandy recalled being in a similar park with her aunt on Sunday afternoons when she was growing up and how much she enjoyed breathing in the fragrance of everything all at once. Now, they had the Bee Garden out behind the house, but sadly, she was not permitted to be on the grounds right now while the lawsuit was pending. So this scene would have to suffice. She took it all in as much as possible. In the same way her husband had taught their children to do with breathing in the scent of a person when you parted from them for a time, now she applied that lesson as she walked. *When I go home, I want to remember this always, with God's sun shining down on all of it!*

"Mama, come see!" Lily's shriek of delight forced Mandy back to reality and out of her dreams and musings. "It's a bird's nest hidden away in the branches of a bush."

Indeed, a robin had laid her four blue eggs in the tiny nest that Lily had spied.

"Remember, we have to be sure not to touch the area around it," she said quietly as Lily pointed out the spot, "or the mother bird may not come back to sit on the eggs. That would be a tragedy to lose four baby birds due to our carelessness."

"I know, Mama, I think that's the mother bird over there, chattering away at us. She doesn't seem happy to see us this close to them, does she?"

"No, she doesn't. Don't worry, little one, we won't harm your babies. Lily, I love your sharp eyes and a mind to go with it that can sense things so easily! You could always spot the eagle flying high overheard before either of your brothers ever knew he was up there hunting. They need to learn from you how to see with their hearts more and depend on their eyes less."

"Thanks, Mama. I know Papa will teach them how to do this as they get older. He has taught me well because he is very good at that, isn't he?"

"Yes, as he is good at many things, dear. My, how I miss him, and it's only been one week today since I last saw him."

The two walked on a little further and came around a bend in the path, where they were in a bit of a secluded area with no one else around. Once more, an uneasy feeling filled Mandy's heart. *God, I asked You to take away the sad memories! Please hear me!* But it intensified with every step she took. Maybe it was something else, a warning for the future instead of remembering the past? She had the sensation of being watched and it unsettled her, but she tried to brush it away as the product of an overactive imagination. However, just to be sure, she glanced on every side but spotted nothing unusual nor anything else to warrant the urgency she felt to flee. *Flee what? Or who? Is Alex here around here, Father? I feel silly announcing our return home without sufficient reason. But should we?*

She kept looking around, but felt no better and decided to not ignore it any longer. Best to leave when not warranted than to stay and regret it. Gritting her teeth against the panic growing inside, she kept her voice as calm as possible so as not to alarm her daughter.

"Lily, I really think we should leave now. The shadows are lengthening and we need to get on back to the Boarding House."

"Oh, Mama, please, can't we stay a little longer? I wanted to go see a gorgeous flower display over there beyond those trees. Earlier I had followed the squirrel long enough to see him go through there and spotted it through the leaves. I really—" She stopped abruptly when she saw the expression on her mother's face. "Is something wrong, Mama?"

"No, not really, but we need to leave *now.*" Off she marched, hoping her daughter would follow suit out of obedience if not understanding. She had been trained to do this without question on the prairie. Would she do it now? Here? Without obvious danger?

Lily ran to catch up, a little breathless by the time they climbed the small hill to get back to the entrance. "Mama, I really think something must be wrong. Do you feel all right?"

She whirled to face her daughter.

"Lily! You have been taught to never question when given an order, even when you don't understand. Stop arguing and do what you were told!"

Her surprised expression concerned Mandy. Had she spoken too harshly for no reason? Without waiting for a response, she turned again to walk away—and almost ran straight into Alex! Where had he come from? He wasn't there a moment before! She gasped and took a step back as Lily came alongside her. His smirk made her skin crawl. God *had* tried to warn her but she delayed her obedience until it was too late!

"Out for a stroll this afternoon, are you? With your lovely daughter, no less." His eyes narrowed, in direct contradiction to the sarcastic words he uttered in his poor attempt to be charming. Fear seized Mandy's heart and she instinctively reached out to grab her daughter's arm. She did not like the way he leered at Lily. It was bad enough for him to do that to her but intolerable when directed at her little girl!

"What do you want, Alex? Haven't you done enough damage already to us? Must you torment us every time we turn around?"

"Oh, you haven't seen the half of the torment I have in mind for you, lady! And for her," nodding toward Lily who had shrunk back a little behind her mother by this time.

"How dare you! Get out of my way. I shall report you to—to, well whoever I need to. I'm sure the judge at least won't be happy to hear you have been throwing around threats at me. Stay away from us, both of us, do you hear?"

Mandy stomped right past him, half dragging Lily by her arm, to keep her out of reach of this monster. She prayed fervently God would stop him from harming them, because a quick glance showed her they were still quite alone in this part of the park.

"Don't think for one moment" he abruptly shouted at her, "that I have any intentions of backing off the lawsuit simply because you want me to! You will not live long enough to get your hands on *my house,* do you hear me? Not even to lay a *finger* on it, or I shall cut it off!"

CHAPTER TWENTY-THREE

"For the LORD your God is he that goeth with you, to fight for you against your enemies, to save you." Deuteronomy 20:4

April 21, 1867

"Hurry, Lily! We have to get to safety as soon as possible!"

Mandy raced down the street, she knew in a very unladylike fashion, but at the moment panic fueled her feet and there was no slowing them down. Lily did her best to keep up, equally as frightened from the scene that had taken place only moments ago.

One woman stopped and stared at the two as she emerged from a house, and Mandy realized she would need to slow down to avoid bringing unwanted attention to her strange actions. The last thing she wanted was to have anyone question why she was behaving in such an odd manner. Thank goodness they were almost back to the Boarding House and the security of Mrs. Wilson's locked doors!

Panting heavily, Mandy slowed her pace. When Lily caught up, she could see the terror on her daughter's face and the fear churned into anger. *How dare that creature threaten my child like that? I'll scratch his eyes out if he lays one finger on her!*

By the time they entered the parlor, they both were breathing more normally. But truth be known, neither would rest easy until that man was stopped!

"Amanda!" Nan called out. "You are the very person I hoped to see. Someone said you two had gone out for a walk. Did you have a good time? It's a beautiful day to stroll through the Park!"

She was sitting over in a corner of the Parlor with a couple of other folks and got up to greet them, but stopped when she saw the expression on their faces.

"Are you two all right? Your faces are flushed, as if you had been running. Have you? In the warm air today that is not a good thing."

"Not—not really, Nan. Could we go upstairs to talk about it, please?"

"Okay, now I demand that you tell me what is going on," Nan said firmly once Mandy slammed the bedroom door shut behind her friend—and promptly locked it from the inside!

Lily threw herself onto her bed, pulling her blanket up around her shoulders as though that could hold back whatever had frightened her so much, while tears flowed down her cheeks. Nan sank into the rocker and waited for one of them to speak. Something—or *someone*—had terrified these two and a growing suspicion in Nan's heart soured in the pit of her stomach.

"Alex just threatened the two of us! He said he would kill us if I tried to take the house from him. How could he frighten my daughter like that? What is *wrong* with that man?"

"I figured it had to be Alex again. Oh, Amanda, how awful!"

"Is there any kind of law enforcement here that could stop him? I simply cannot tolerate this any longer. Maybe it would be best to give up and go home and forget all about the inheritance. He can have it! Nothing is worth endangering my daughter's life!"

"Sad to say, there is no sheriff or anything like that, although there is a Marshall who is responsible for a large section of this part of the state and occasionally passes through town, but no one seems to know his schedule or how to reach him. It is very frustrating and something I hope changes about our community soon. Again, as I said before, I think you need to let Matthew know what is going on and let him handle it. As for giving up—no! You *cannot* surrender to this man's threats! You told me the Kiowa people are depending on that money to buy food in order to survive. How can you even think about not staying until this is over? What would those people do if you show up empty-handed?"

"They have faced hard times before and I'm sure God has a plan for them to survive. Why does it have to depend on *me?*"

"Mama, before we left you told Papa that same thing, but you remember what he said?"

Mandy hung her head a moment in shame. The words came back all too clearly. She met her daughter's level stare and nodded.

"Of course, I do. You are right to remind me. He said God has chosen a plan for survival that requires me to bring it about. Even as Moses told God he could not possibly go to Egypt to lead the people out of slavery and God refused to accept that excuse, so He will not listen to my refusal to help the Kiowa survive now." How could the words of her beloved come back to haunt her now, through this young but wise child?

Mandy sighed and sank onto the bed. "I am letting my fear override by faith, and I simply cannot do that. How does one overcome fear like this?" Yet even as she voiced the question, she knew the answer. She had faced it before, many times. In every single instance, God had met her needs and far more, showing her how to conquer the fear and not allow it to win. This would be no exception!

Nan spoke up with an unusual request. "I know you are determined to deal with this situation right now, but I think I may have some things to share with you that would help you see how to answer your own question. Besides, being captured by an Indian surely cannot have been easy! You've told me that God was with you every step, even when you could not see ahead."

"You are exactly right! He never let me down, not once. However, whatever you have to share that you think might help, I'm eager to hear it."

"It involves that book that you have just finished up, Lily," she said. "Do you have it handy?"

"Yes, I keep it here beside my bed, with my Bible." She reached into the drawer of the table nearby and pulled it out.

"I've told you that this book changed Miss Ida's life dramatically. I'm sure you've read her notes about the dates and circumstances that meant a great deal to her, Lily, and perhaps shared some of it with your mother. Rather than go over every single one, I wanted to give the two of you a quick summary of how it impacted her, emotionally and spiritually. I told you about the rally in Cincinnati but think I ended with that night. More happened the next day. The sermon that morning was based on the Good Samaritan, but it was the way the preacher ended it that hit hard."

March 24, 1860
Cincinnati, Ohio

"And so, in summary, I ask," boomed out the preacher, "who among you would leave a man lying beside the road, bleeding and wounded, regardless of the color of his skin or the country he was from?" Soft gasps could be heard all over the room as his paraphrase sank in. Nan and Ida exchanged meaningful glances. There would be much to discuss on the way home. They enjoyed a lovely meal with the Bells after church, and Nan was right, Ida found a great deal in common with these friends of hers. Their passion expressed regarding abolition startled Ida at times, and she felt more of her old beliefs crumbling. Perhaps a bit like the Wall of Jericho did when faith was applied in that old Bible story! How had she missed the whole idea that Christ died for *all* men? Josiah certainly lectured her on it countless times, but she never really listened to her brother—or any other preacher, for that matter. The one that morning, coupled with the jolt of reality from the rally the night before, topped off with the spirited conversations with the Bells during luncheon, had finally forced the words to sink in. How freeing this was!

Fortunately, the snow had stopped by the time they were ready to head home. During the long ride in between their ordinary conversations, Ida began reading the book she had bought the night before. Quickly she got caught up in the drama of the fictional story, because it was so pertinent to the very things they heard at the rally. She shared a great deal of it with Nan, who peppered her with question after question.

"Here is a statement from one of the characters, Nan, that sounds like something you or I could have written. He says that for him, the conflict between slavery and abolition had never been real before, until he met suffering first-hand for the first time. He goes on to say that previously it had only been in the word *fugitive* and not that the person was actually a mother or child. No longer. That is precisely what has happened with me. That scene we witnessed on the street recently has opened the floodgates of my heart. There is no going back now."

"Now I *know* I must read this book of yours when you are done!" said Nan. "I will be praying over this situation while you read, but if you find more to share, please do!"

They rode on in silence for a time and then Ida spoke up again. "There is a preacher in here who actually justifies slavery from the Bible! Or tries to, for nothing could be further from the truth. Using the Scripture that 'everything is made beautiful in its season' he goes on to say some people are born to rule and some are born to serve. Poppycock! God is never on the side of those who traffic in human suffering, no matter how hard they may try to twist the Bible's words around to their position. At least the one we heard this morning knew God's heart in this thing. And was not afraid to proclaim it from the pulpit."

"That is incredible, Miss Ida, I agree. But I have heard such things many times as I have attended the various meetings over this past year. As I told you, I have prayed fervently for months that your heart would somehow be touched by the truth of this horrible malady on mankind. It breaks my heart that it took the deaths of that family to do so, but He has heard my pleas at last!"

By the time the two reached home that evening as the sun set against more clouds heavy with snow gathering in the western sky, two decisions had been reached by them. One was, Ida would offer the use of her home as a Depot on the Underground Railroad, if it was needed. *If? Certainly* it was needed! They had heard repeatedly at the rally that the use of established old homes in a community often reduced the suspicions that could arise, and Ida's house had been in Trenton for many long years now. Few would suspect an older woman like herself of being involved!

The second decision was that Nan would move in with Ida to help her with this endeavor. They would tell everyone that Ida needed more help now, and due to their close friendship and the lack of any family around, this arrangement should arouse no suspicions, either. It would be dangerous work, they knew, but well worth the risks.

"Nan," Ida asked as they took in their luggage and secured the house for the night, "do you know how we can get in touch with people organizing the depots? That one man on the program said to contact him."

"Yes, I have a friend who can make those arrangements for us. One thing I have already learned, however, is they operate in the strictest of confidence. It is far too dangerous to do anything less. So, let me get this part done and you focus on how we can get the house ready. There will be much to do before we can start accepting passengers. God will show us the way!"

"Nan, we will have to be very cautious from here on out, you know. I think I know what I'm getting us into but equally as certain that our enemy has many traps laid out before us. Are you sure you are all right with joining with me on this effort? You don't have to, you know. It is my house and my idea. And a dangerous one at that. I just want you to be *sure* before you commit to this. I am an old lady but you have your entire life in front of you. It is a little more solemn for you to make this decision."

"Definitely! I'm positive, thrilled to be offered the chance to join you, in fact. I'm afraid I wouldn't have the courage or resources to do this without you, which is why I haven't taken action before now."

"Nor I without you, my young friend. One thing I want you to know is that slave family's deaths will *not* be in vain if others can be helped. I pray it is so!"

The next day Nan gave notice at her job at the Emporium and also at her Boarding House. Within a couple of days the ladies had decided to build a false room in the cellar of the house, hidden by a massive wall of shelving that would camouflage the area, yet be easily moveable. After a couple of days of fervent prayer, Ida approached a carpenter in town whom she had known for a long time and felt he might be sympathetic to their cause and thus could be trusted. To their great relief, he readily agreed to do whatever he could to help them. They would stash all their jars and bottles of various foods down there, gathered from the gardens behind the house. In addition, they made hasty plans to expand the gardens that spring. That way, most of their vegetables needed for the meals for their passengers could come from there. It would not be necessary to go to the Emporium constantly to purchase large amounts, which would be conspicuous even to a casual observer. They bought a few chickens to they could have fresh eggs as well as the meat from time to time to add to the pot. In addition, it would all make great barter with neighbors, too, to secure an occasional ham or wild turkey for even more food.

The biggest blessing, however, came one day as Nan was making an apple pie when a friend from church, Callie Morgan, happened to drop by to see her.

"Nan," said Callie, "my mother's birthday is next week. Would it be possible for me to purchase a pie like that for her party? She asked for one but I never have mastered the art of pastries, nothing like yours at least!"

"Well, yes, of course, but I couldn't charge you for doing that. I'll be happy to make you one."

"You should start a business doing this. Everyone always wants your pies at the church socials, you know! You make the best apple butter in two counties, too. Folks who don't have apple trees on their property would be happy to pay you for your talents!"

That gave Nan and Ida something to consider, that if others already knew about their love for putting up apples in various forms, why couldn't they use that to help cover the extra mouths they would be feeding soon? They already had a good amount put up but made immediate plans to work feverishly through the fall of that year to fill the shelves downstairs with "all things apple" and people came from miles around to buy them. When the war finally broke out and times became very hard, they began giving them away to those who couldn't pay, believing that God would provide for their passengers somehow. The abundant harvest they had that year answered every concern they had voiced in their prayers for a more than adequate supply!

A few days later after the room was complete and they had hauled blankets and other necessary items down to the cellar for their expected guests, the two were sharing some quiet time together over a cup of tea before bedtime.

"We need to spend time in fervent prayer, now that our labor is finished," said Ida quietly to her friend. "For protection for us as well as for our passengers, provision of food and clothing that we might need to give to them, perhaps even a few medical supplies for those who arrive in need of those. I was reading last night a verse of Scripture that I feel will become my focal point as we begin this venture, Nan. It is Matthew 9:36, which records a summary of Jesus' feelings when He saw the multitudes gathered around Him. It says He was moved with compassion because they fainted and were spread abroad, as sheep having no shepherd. That is what these runaways are, sheep without a shepherd. We must step up to provide that same kindness and compassion to them in His Name. As they scatter to the far corners of the land in their efforts to escape the brutality of slavery, we must remember why we are doing this. Never for ourselves, not even for them, but for Jesus alone!"

"That is a beautiful thought, Miss Ida! We must remember to pray for our own courage and boldness as well," added Nan, "so we are prepared for whatever might come as a result of all this. We know He has established this work of our hands, and I believe His promise that He will bless it. May God alone be honored by our work for Him!"

"Amen!" Ida hesitated a moment, then continued. "I also have something else I need to get off my mind, Nan."

"What's that, Miss Ida?"

"I need you to know that God has moved in my heart these last few days, in no small part due to that book I bought at the rally. It all started of course the day we saw the slave family die on the street, but my confirmation has come from hearing the words of the two Harriets, along with the piercing question the preacher asked during his sermon on Sunday. The Lord has truly changed me!"

"In what way, Miss Ida?"

"All these long years of my life, as you know, I have carried a bitter resentment deep in my heart against all people of color, because of what happened to my family when I was a youngster. I wouldn't admit it was there for a very long time, even spent quite a few years justifying it and skirting around God's opinion of it. But no longer. The Lord has fully forgiven me now, and I cannot describe how freeing that has been! You see, I didn't know I was under any bondage at all until He removed it. For instance, I can see how my attitude unfairly affected my family all that time as they dreamed of sharing the Gospel with the red men in Indian Territory. I was terribly angry with them for this! It is to my everlasting shame that I didn't believe those folks even had souls, thus didn't deserve to be saved. How could I have been so blind?"

"You know, as I see it, we all have our own bondages to release to Him. Mine was resentments against my father, for forcing me to live with him and look after him as he was dying, when I had a chance to marry and move away from Trenton to start a whole new life."

"I had no idea! You were in love?"

"Yes, I was. Oh, we were both very young and God knew I had no business marrying this man, so *He* stopped me, not my father. Therefore, I was also furious with God. In the end, His way was best, of course. I had time with Pa to serve him and care for him when he needed me. If I had married and moved away, I shudder to think what would have become of him in his helpless state. From that time, I grew up in many ways, but especially in my trust of my Heavenly Father. All the resentments melted away as He set His love firmly in my heart through that difficult circumstance. You see, your bondage is not so different from mine, yet the answer came the exact same way, by His miraculous hand of mercy. I'm thrilled that He has set you free from all that and allowed you to have a new heart for those who have skin that is not white."

"Oh, He has set me free, indeed! If only—"

She stopped and chewed her lower lip a moment, as though trying to decide what to say from there.

"If only, what, Miss Ida?"

"If only I had the chance to tell Josiah and Amanda how deeply sorry I am for the way I acted all those years, all the unkind and stern things I said to them whenever they brought up their dream. If only I had the chance to give them money to support their mission off in Indian Territory. And now it is too late. If only they were still alive to know this happened to me! Oh, so many regrets!"

She wept for several moments as her friend tried to comfort her.

"Miss Ida, don't carry on like that. I'm sure they are with the Lord and know all this already. They both are happy now that you have a new heart."

"I knew Him," she sniffled, "from the time I was a young child, no question in my mind about that. But what I never really did was to allow Him to fully remove my bondage to sin and set me free, so He could be my Lord as well as my Savior. Call it what you like, I experienced it. And I am incredibly happy!"

As they prayed they offered all they possessed in time, talents, money, energy, and whatever else would be needed as they took a stand against slavery, right here in their own little town. The miracle was quiet but complete as His peace settled over them, and they felt the comfort of His wings surrounding them as they took refuge there. They worked through a few more details together before retiring. Each slept soundly, to awaken ready to begin their new adventure led by God along this dangerous pathway to freedom. Who would the Lord bring their way? How would He take care of needs, indeed, bring the victories? What they had to do was invite Him to use them, and then watch to see how He provided! With Him on their side, soon they would be able to rescue many from the evils of prejudice and depravity that had allowed this tragedy to take place in their beloved country!

April 21, 1867
Trenton, Ohio

"My aunt *said* that about her regrets in not supporting Papa's dream of ministering to the Kiowa?" asked Mandy, her eyes wide.

"Yes, she did, Amanda. I have longed to tell you this specific part of the story because you need to know how much she changed, how different she was in these last years as opposed to the way she apparently was long ago. I only wish she could have told you this herself. It would have meant a great deal to her to ask for your forgiveness face to face."

Mandy wiped away the tears, realizing that she could have come to Ohio as a Kiowa woman, proudly, and her aunt would have received her with joy. If only she had known! But wasn't that the point, in learning to trust God's ways as higher than ours? She had been forced to trust, without knowing the whole story. Of course, others might not have accepted her as readily as Ida Clark! And therein lay the problem. Could she have inherited the estate as a Kiowa? Never, not with the existing laws. Maybe someday soon, but not now. Therefore, God's way still was the best one, even with the deception. With white blood coursing through her veins, who's to say that Mandy was *not* white? Only the nuances of the law, and as long as it remains blind, then it doesn't matter!

"Of course I forgive her! How I wish, too, that I could have told her this. Life is hard to figure out sometimes, you know?"

"Yes, it is. I think the main point you need to remember right now is that your aunt left you the estate to give you money to minister to the Kiowa people out there in Indian Territory. She wanted you to share the Gospel however you desired or needed it to be done. She left no qualifiers on this, left it up to you alone. If she had not believed those people were capable of being saved, that they needed Christ, she would never have done this! If you want to buy meat with it, so be it. If you want to buy Bibles, great. If you want to build a new mission church, by all means do it!"

"How I wish I *could* buy Bibles written in Kiowa! They have no written language, though, so that is not possible. Again, maybe someday but not now. All our teaching is done orally. We also teach English so the people can read the English Bibles we have. It is important they learn how to do this, as the world is rapidly changing. More and more often the Kiowa will find themselves interacting with the white men out there, one way or the other. The more of them who know the English language, the better, and the more who know Christ, well, that can change everything for both races! Right now, of course the biggest need is for meat and for other healthy foods so the children can grow strong. That will also mean the people are not always having to scrounge to find good hunting grounds, which is when many conflicts arise between the whites and the Indians. When bellies are empty, it is difficult to teach about God's love! Nan, I'm not sure I can put into words what your having shared this with us means to me personally—more than anything in the world!"

April 21, 1867
Indian Territory

"God, tell me why Prayer Woman has not come home yet! It has been too long, am afraid she and Lily have great trouble. My spirit is not happy. Do You speak with me on this, to let me know they need my prayers?"

Ken-ai-te fell to his knees on the prairie but raised his arms up toward the stars overhead in surrender to his God. Would He speak that night? Would they be words of comfort or warning? Did his heart have the courage to listen, even if the message was not what he wanted to hear?

"Does she not return because she no longer wants to be Kiowa? Will color of my skin keep her away from here and with new white friends? You say there no difference in whites and Kiowa. Yet many of each fear, hate, and even kill because of the differences. How can You let it happen? War fought to stop this but yet, it still is. I cannot be with my family because of the color of my skin. I speak the wrong tongue. You caused many nations to start at the Place of Speaking, no that not right, maybe House of Talk? What is name Prayer Woman taught me? Oh, yes, that funny word, babble, I remember now. Tower of Babel—where many tongues started, to keep people from building big lodge up to the sky. Why this still happen now, to divide instead of unite people? Means some kill and hate without reason, just because of red skin or white skin. Evil *cannot* win but it always try! Want to fight those who believe this way, even Kiowa who do. But know I must trust You to see the heart and wash it from sin. Not for me to use force. I trust You with Prayer Woman and daughter as well. Lord, take away my fear!"

No answer came in the silence. A lone coyote howled off in the distance. A child whimpered back in the village behind Ken-ai-te in the darkness. He remained on his knees for some time, trying to listen for God's response.

"Will Prayer Woman ever lie beside me again in our tipi, care for our children, or advise me as chief over our people? Or does she choose this white place over the Kiowa? Has she forgotten the children here who starve to death every day because she does not come home? Even *her own sons?* I cannot go to her because of the color of my skin. But in this America my wife talks about so much, how can that be true? I fear what she learn now, maybe to hate me, too." A steely hardness formed around his heart in that moment. He clenched his fists at the stars. "This cannot be! I will find her, no matter the danger, and take her back!"

As soon as the words escaped his lips, Ken-ai-te knew they were not honoring of the God to whom he spoke that dark night. He was grateful there was no moon to shine light on his shame as he bowed his head. Prayer Woman was not his to take. He did it once and learned that bitter lesson well.

"Please forgive my wrong words, God. She is gift from You to me. Know that well. I cannot demand gift. Will wait for You to bring her home again. Keep her safe while I cannot! I sense something not right but know You are in charge, not me. My heart bursts with love for her, and for You, my Father. Protect my family from any who might hurt them. Help me understand and be patient! Amen and Amen!"

CHAPTER TWENTY-FOUR

"The eyes of the LORD preserve knowledge, and he overthroweth the words of the transgressor." Proverbs 22:12

April 23, 1867
Trenton, Ohio

"We have a small problem, Amanda," said Matthew, his face a somber mask, "and the effect may be tremendous on your case."

She sat in his office with her hands folded in her lap, hardly daring to breathe.

"What—what do you mean?" she stammered.

"Well, it seems that our response to the petition to block your aunt's will was never filed with the court over in Hamilton. That is our county seat, where all the paperwork ends up even when we hold court here. We—that is, the attorneys here in Trenton—have regular messengers who take these papers for us back and forth all the time. They are hand-picked men of integrity who can be trusted implicitly. In addition, we have a Bailiff who helps the judges when they come for court sessions here, and he manages it all for us as a rule. He has been doing this a long time without any complications or problems whatsoever. I really cannot for the life of me figure out what happened, but maybe it was just a fluke somehow."

"How will this affect my case? I mean, can't you go ahead and file the correct paperwork now?"

"There are strict legal limits on how long we have to do those things, and that deadline has now passed. I expected a confirmation back this morning from the messenger service of it having been filed but naturally did not anticipate the answer I got. They told me there was no such response on file! I have asked for a clarification as to how I should proceed.

Meanwhile, on the outside chance they will accept it late, I immediately sent it back over there earlier this morning. If you miss filing deadlines, it is possible the judge can simply dismiss the case."

"Dismiss it? You mean, as in it's over?"

"Well, over in that you would be out of luck, if that's what you mean. The judge would have no choice but to grant the original petition, then."

"Oh no! How could this happen?"

"As I said, I have never had something like this occur in all the years I have been practicing law here. It is awkward not being in the county seat but the system we set up has worked fine until now."

"I will be praying the next message will be good news, then! God knows the person behind this; however, I would bet anything I could guess who that is!"

"He's the only one who has anything to gain from creating this kind of confusion and havoc, sad to say. What baffles me is *how* he managed to interfere. But never fear, we will get past this. I should have an answer for you at our meeting tomorrow."

"Matthew," Mandy said with great hesitation, "I'm not sure how to tell you this, but Alex has been threatening me, and Lily as well. It has been quite unsettling and frightening to hear some of the awful things he says."

"What? When?" His eyes widened and his face flushed. *At least he is taking it seriously.*

"Well, several times in the last couple of days, to be honest."

"Why didn't you tell me before?"

"I, well, honestly, it embarrasses me to bring the complaint to you. It's really between Alex and myself. But Nan insisted I tell you, said it might have an impact on how the judge rules eventually, if he knows about this."

"She is correct, it certainly *will!* I'm glad you told me but only wish you had done so before now. I want you to stop going out alone, you or Lily. You cannot risk further encounters with this madman! And, I do not want you to even give him the time of day, do you hear me?"

"Well, I certainly do not intend to encourage him to talk to me, but when he stands in my way, I really have no other choice. As for going out alone, I cannot be held hostage by him! Although your suggestion is an excellent one, how can I let you know that I must go to the Emporium, for instance, so you can leave your important work to accompany me? No, that won't work and you know it. Thank you for your concern, but I will simply have to be more cautious about where I go and when."

Matthew growled, "How I wish we had a sheriff here in Trenton. People have said for years we don't need one but I disagree, perhaps because I often deal with those who have broken the law or experience havoc because of someone who has. This is yet another good example of *why* we need to change that and soon. And if Clark knows what's good for him, he better not try to follow through on any of his vicious threats!"

"I really don't think he will, but it is upsetting. Yes, having a sheriff would make many circumstances easier, all right. We have no law enforcement out in the Territory, either, and for the most part we don't need it. But as people move in there to settle, I'm sure this will become an issue there for us as well."

"Not to change the subject but I do need to brief you on something else while you are here. Our next strategy in this case is more complicated but is supported by what I told you that first day, that you must be seen out in public and frequently by the people of Trenton. The more often, the better."

"I was afraid you were going to say that. As you can tell I am not a fan of this idea, but there is a sewing circle at church and I suppose I could join that. I'm not really interested but it would give me something to do with my hands. Lily is great at needlework as well. Maybe she can go with me part of the time. I'm used to staying very busy at home, so all this leisure time I now have is not very welcome. Yesterday in particular was difficult as after our brief meeting in the morning, I was on my own most of the day. Not my best day the way it started, to say the least, but God redeemed it anyway. He and I had time alone that we usually do not have."

"Time with Him is never wasted, is it? The sewing circle is an excellent idea. Not only will you get to know more of the women in the group, but you might also find yourself having fun doing it. I hear they are very friendly. By the way, Frank and Sally Patton asked me at church Sunday if I could bring you and Lily over tonight for dinner. I'm sorry I almost forgot to tell you. I've been so preoccupied."

"That will be fine. I recall meeting them briefly but didn't get to visit very much. It will be good to get better acquainted with them."

"They own a fairly good-sized farm just outside Trenton, which of course keeps them busy and they don't often get into town to socialize.

Sally therefore tries to have frequent dinner parties to give them a chance to visit with their friends, and she was most eager to include the two of you in this one. Their four sons are fine young men who help around the farm now that they are almost grown. I believe the Mallorys might be there as well. Have you met them yet—Michael and Anna? They are delightful people, too, who also dearly loved your aunt."

"No, I haven't met them, I don't think. Do they have a family?"

"Yes, they have a daughter about Lily's age, I believe. Their son unfortunately drowned a few years back in a fishing accident, a devastating tragedy, to say the least. Michael is one of my best friends, and we served together in the war, until I was wounded. He came home unscathed, thank the Lord. Michael owns the leather shop in town and Anna owns the millinery store next to it."

"Oh, I have seen both of them. How interesting they are owned by a couple. It's exciting to me to get to know more of Aunt Ida's friends. One lady I spoke with at church said she remembered me from when I lived here before, but being so young, I honestly have no recollection of her. Of course, I didn't tell her that! Thank you for letting me know about these folks, as it will help me better know what to talk about and which topics to avoid. One of the drawbacks of new friendships is bringing up something that causes additional hurt unintentionally. I think this is one reason I'm a bit hesitant to step out and make friends with those I have met, for fear I might say the wrong thing." *Or, they may ask me questions that I cannot answer without more lies!*

"You will be fine, I'm sure. I will pick the two of you up at 6:45 then, if that's all right, as dinner is at 7:00."

The pair discussed a few more legal matters for a time and then Mandy left.

I wish I understood better everything Matthew told me. It was all over my head, I'm afraid. God, give me a brain that can absorb these technicalities. Thank You for bringing me to Matthew, whom I can trust in these matters when I do not have a clue.

Mandy did a little bit of laundry at the Boarding House and soon it was time to leave to pick up her daughter at the Cordons.

I wonder what she will be excited about today. Seems every day there is something new for her to share. It is a blessing she is getting to spend this time with a friend. I only wish she would be more focused on us going home instead of on what life is like here in Trenton.

Lily as usual bubbled over with joy when Mandy picked her up at Ginny's house. Mandy's mind still rolled with the legal details, but she tried to pay attention to what her daughter said about her new friend. Suddenly one statement definitely caught her ear!

"Ginny and I decided that I should stay here in Trenton when you go home, Mama, because each of us has always wanted a sister, and now we have one! You know I told you we had talked about this but today we promised each other that it was no longer a dream but a plan for our future together."

"What? What on earth are you babbling about? Staying here? You know you cannot do that. What are you thinking?"

"Why not?" Her big dark eyes glistened with tears. Mandy knew she would break her daughter's heart with her next words, but there was no other way to say it.

"Surely you jest! You *know* why! And, that I cannot talk about it out here on the street like this! Put that foolish notion away and don't bring it up again, do you hear me?"

"Mama!" Lily stopped, stomping her foot to emphasize her anger. "You cannot be serious to turn me down on this! I love the idea of living here in Trenton in a real French villa instead of out on the prairie in the middle of nowhere in a—"

"Lily! Stop that right now!" She jerked her daughter's arm, which caused her to stumble a couple of steps. Mandy's heart seized with a wave of instant regret. *Lily could have fallen! I must learn not to overreact like this and stay calm. All I wanted to do is stop her from saying too much!* Regaining her composure, Mandy loosened her grip slightly while hoping Lily would rethink completing that sentence she started. It could doom them both if the wrong person overheard!

Immediately, Lily pulled free of her mother's grasp and ran ahead of her toward the Boarding House, but not before Mandy caught a glimpse of reddened cheeks. Had she really come that close to slipping up, or was she just angry? Either way, there would be an even sharper reprimand coming for her daughter that evening! Mandy ground her teeth in frustration but outwardly tried to show no sign of how upset she really was.

Lily ran up the steps at the end of the street into the safety of the Boarding House. Mandy slowed her pace to give herself time to think as she walked that last block. What could she say to her to emphasize the danger of—

"Cannot even control your own brat now, huh?"

The sarcastic voice jolted Mandy back to the present very quickly. Her heart raced at the sickening recognition she had of its source, now standing right in front of her.

"Stay out of what you can never understand, do you hear me, Alex? Matthew says you are never to talk to me. And that includes right now." She brushed past him and raced the last few steps to the safety of the porch, hugging the nearest post for support. *I will not look back at him! No matter what!*

But she could not escape the sound of his cruel laughter nor close out the words he shouted at her as she pushed inside and slammed the door behind her.

"One of these days, I will silence both of you, do you hear me?" he screamed. "Get out of town now!"

"Good gracious, dear, whatever is all that noise out there?" Mrs. Wilson had been sitting at her desk in the foyer and rose with a frown. Seeing the stricken look on Mandy's face, she said, "Are you all right? Do you need to sit down?"

"No, thank you, I'm fine. Now I am, at least. It was my so-called *cousin* shouting at me. He is furious that he was left out of my aunt's will and now is taking every opportunity he can to frighten me."

"From what I heard, it sounds like he is making threats against you. You have good reason to be fearful, going against the likes of him. Perhaps I should guard my tongue better but it is not gossip if it is true, right? Such an unsavory character!"

"Yes, you are right about the threats. Every time I go out now, he seems to be wherever I am, as though he is following me."

"From the little I know about the man, you could be right. He is known for his persistence, which is a kind way of saying he tends to be a big bully to get what he wants. Perhaps you should be careful about being on the street unaccompanied for the time being."

"Well, I was with Lily, and I thought he wouldn't bother the two of us. But I was wrong. I cannot ask someone to go with me every time I step onto the porch! That is ludicrous. I suppose he knows that."

"All appears to be quiet for now so perhaps he went away. I'll check." She peeked out behind the curtain in the Parlor. "Yes, I can see him quite a way down the street now. You should relax a bit and take a deep breath before climbing those stairs."

"Did Lily go up to our room, or did you notice?"

"Yes, she did, and she seemed quite upset as well. I do hope that incident doesn't give her nightmares."

"She had already come inside when he accosted me. I'm afraid we quarreled about something personal, Mrs. Wilson. It is probably all forgotten by now. But I really must go up to check on her, nevertheless."

When Mandy slipped into the room, Lily had her back to the door but didn't turn around. Mandy waited to see if she would acknowledge her mother's presence, and when she failed to move, she softly said, "Lily, I'm sorry for the quarrel. I hope you can see the foolishness of what you proposed."

Lily whirled around and Mandy gasped. The fury on her daughter's face startled her.

"What, you don't think anyone would want me, Mama? Is that it?"

"Of course not, my dear. Please, let's sit down to talk about this calmly and rationally. It has nothing whatsoever to do with being wanted, but everything to do with where you live, where you belong, where God has placed you and intends for you to stay. It was never my intention to upset you like this. Please?"

Mandy indicated the chair next to the one she sank into in the small sitting area, but Lily did not move, just stood there glaring at her mother.

"One of the books I read from Ginny's bookshelves is about a girl who decides she wants to go live in Paris without her family. She runs away from home and takes off on her own, determined to get to the city without anyone's help. Along the way, she encounters several intriguing characters in that fascinating city and has some fantastic adventures. At least I'm not suggesting I do something like that, but living with Ginny and her parents could be quite exciting, you know. Traveling to France several times a year, wearing gorgeous French gowns, having private tutors, eating gourmet meals without having to cook them—that sounds like Heaven to me!"

"I have to admit, there might be a certain appeal about all that to younger people, Lily. But usually this type of lifestyle happens when one is older, not at twelve. Or have parents who travel frequently and take their children with them, as Ginny does. You do not."

"I know, and that is the problem! I live in a *tipi,* Mama!! On the prairie! I want to live in a French villa, have the finest clothing money can buy, and plenty of food. Please don't make me go back to Indian Territory! I beg you!"

Mandy held her tongue for a moment, praying for wisdom. "Are you unhappy being Kiowa, Lily?"

"No. Well, yes. I mean, maybe. I don't know, it's all so confusing. When I am there, I am happy. But when I am here, I see no point in ever going back again. Why am I so mixed up?"

Mandy reached out to hug her daughter and to her immense relief, Lily melted into her arms instead of pulling away, the tears flowing.

"Honey, life can be so confusing sometimes and occasionally we make unwise choices that can further complicate things. This is one of those times. You want both ways of life but cannot have both. I've already explained in great detail how impossible it is to reach for a dream that is possible for Ginny but is denied to you, by right of your birth. Anyway, at this point, you are way too young to have that kind of responsibility thrust on your shoulders, which is why God has given you parents who can see a wider picture than you can at your age. You must trust us to help guide you on this one."

"Papa is not here. How can I ask him his opinion?"

"By relying on how well you know him and remembering he would only want what is best for you. I can assure you, your father would say the same thing I am, that staying here in Trenton is simply not an option. Perhaps in a few years you can return for a visit. Or even to live, if that is important to you then. But not now. We have an essential task to do while here, and it does not involve French dolls or art tutors. I need your support in this, especially since we cannot go home as quickly as we had hoped."

"A few *years?*" she shrieked and pulled away from her mother's embrace. "I can't wait years, Mama! I will be an old woman by then. I want to live *now.* Can't you understand that? Papa would, I know he would."

Lord, help me! How can I help her comprehend this? Hmm, stay silent? What do You mean? I cannot—and bit off the retort before it formed in her mind. Silent.

Mandy sank back into the chair but never took her eyes off her daughter as she continued to rant, pacing about the room, each sentence growing louder than the one before, accusing her mother of not listening nor caring because she wouldn't respond. Finally, Mandy could take no more and felt the Lord releasing her tongue to speak once more.

"Do you know," she started, and Lily immediately stopped. Miraculously, she remained quiet and still for the moment. "I am only hearing words about you, none about anyone else. What about all our people at home who are starving, who sleep with empty stomachs and awaken to find nothing in their cooking pots? Who bury their children and elders because there is not enough food to stay alive? *That* is what brought us to this place, not the French villas or fancy dresses or dinner parties!"

She interrupted herself to add, "Oh my goodness! Dinner parties! I almost forgot to tell you that we are expected at one this evening, and Matthew will be coming to call for us at 6:45. What time is it now?" She reached into her pocket to check her watch, breathing a sigh of relief. "It's only 5:30. I lose track of time so easily because I had to learn to live without it for all those years. Remembering now is hard for me. I'm relieved we aren't late."

"A dinner party?" Lily's tone perked up. "At someone's home?" Eagerness returned to her voice instead of the anger of a moment before.

"Yes, I forget whose home. Matthew made it clear we must attend. It is part of his strategy to get people to accept me as Aunt Ida's heir. I'm not sure I'm entirely comfortable with this but I'm trying. Could we please agree not to argue any more? We will need to get ready in a bit, and I must go down to let Mrs. Wilson know we won't be dining here this evening. I forgot to tell her before I came upstairs."

"I promise, Mama, not to keep pushing this right now. But at some point, but you will have to listen, *really listen* to me. This is not a passing fancy. I'm serious and I want you to understand why. You asked if I have forgotten the people at home. The answer is no. I have not. But I think you might have forgotten a few things about living here, things that you pushed aside for a long time but need to pay attention to now. You cannot keep me in slavery all my life! I will be free one way or the other!"

Mandy shuddered. She had uttered those same words to Ken-ai-te long ago! And often! How could Lily throw them back at her now? Why was she losing touch with her daughter over something so trivial? *Of course* Lily could not stay here! What could she do to prevent this from happening? Yet, truthfully, she had a point. This would have to be further discussed after they got home when perhaps her father could help explain it to her.

Ken-ai-te, what must I do? What should I say to her that will shake her out of this fantasy? She must be made to understand how foolish she is being! Where are you when I need you?

She knew she would be writing a lengthy entry to him that night in her journal. Whenever she poured out her heart this way, she felt closer to him, and it brought her great comfort in her miserable loneliness, far from her beloved here in this white town. How she longed to feel his strong arms around her again!

A familiar voice sounded in the hall outside their door, then a gentle tap. Nan was home from work and as she usually did, had stopped to say hello.

Mandy rushed to throw open the door and invite her friend in. How she needed a friend and ally right now!

"Come on in here, Nan! How good to see you!" Mandy hugged her, quickly closing the door behind her.

"Well, I'm not sticking around for this," snapped Lily. "I'm getting out of here! How could *you* be on her side, Miss Nan? You of all people, I thought I could count on to see my side! Oooh, you two are so infuriating!"

"What do I have to do with whatever it is you're upset about?" asked Nan, a bit startled at this uncharacteristic outburst. "I don't even know what you're talking about. Who is taking whose side in what? I just got here!" Nan shrugged at Mandy, who did not even try to explain the unexplainable to her friend!

Without another word, Lily shoved past Nan, ran into the hall and down the steps. Mandy had to admit feeling relieved that there would be no more arguments for now. She shut the door and burst into tears.

"What is the matter with me? All I seem able to do these days is cry!"

"Lily is still stuck on that same idea of staying in Trenton, I assume? You told me yesterday how adamant she has been about it. I figured as much when I saw her face, filled with fury. She has always been very respectful of you, Amanda. What has caused her to suddenly become the opposite, do you suppose?"

"In a word, Ginny."

"As in, her friend Ginny?"

"Yes, none other. Oh, not that Ginny is urging her to be disrespectful, only that ever since she started spending time with her, Lily has turned into a different person. Life is very hard for us right now. I wish I could explain further but cannot. But I need you to pray I will find the right words to tell her the reason why she must go home to Indian Territory with me!"

"I will certainly do that, Amanda. It was my hope that after dinner this evening I could share with you more on the story about Bessie and her brother Samuel. That is why I stopped in here, to see if that would be agreeable."

"That would have been lovely but Lily and I have plans. Matthew wants to take us to visit some friends of his for a small dinner party. I'm not sure how late we will be out but not late. If you are still up, maybe we could visit then. I am most eager to hear more of this story."

Nan's face fell and Mandy felt sad to be the cause of it. The way her eyes narrowed, was that a trace of disapproval of where they were going? Or who they were going with? Or merely simple disappointment?

"Sure, let me know when you get back and we'll see. How did your day go? Other than the argument with Lily?"

"I met with Matthew this morning and found out some paperwork is missing. It has caused him quite a bit of frustration but apparently nothing he can't deal with. He cannot figure out how it happened is what is troubling him. It was all a bit over my head, frankly. I've never dealt with lawyers before!"

"They can be tricky, all right. Matthew is one of the best, though. I'm sure he will figure it out soon. And he is a very fine man of integrity, too. Helps that he's handsome, right?"

They both laughed. "Yes," Mandy replied, "he is that, even with the eye patch."

"I think he is more handsome because of it, personally!" said Nan with a giggle. "There aren't many men around here his age who don't have some kind of war wound. In my opinion, an eye patch is not too bad. Oh, and speaking of Matthew, did you tell him about Alex's threats?"

"Yes I did, and you were right. He said it would make a difference to the judge, so I'm glad I took your advice and talked to him about it." And then her smile faded as she recalled the newest encounter with the man. She continued. "A few blocks from the Boarding House, it happened again as we came home from the Cordons' home. He even shouted at me after I ran in here and slammed the door to shut him out. Mrs. Wilson was not happy over that!"

"She doesn't take too kindly to people threatening her guests! What is wrong with him?"

"I don't know but if he doesn't stop soon, I think I'll lose my mind! If he does it one more time, I'll—"

"You'll what, Amanda?"

"I—I don't know but I would love to remind him that I learned a trick or two from the Kiowa that I might use on him if he dares harm one hair on my daughter's head!"

CHAPTER TWENTY-FIVE

"And thine ears shall hear a word behind thee, saying, This is the way, walk ye in it, when ye turn to the right hand, and when ye turn to the left." Isaiah 30:21

April 26, 1867

"Do we have another dinner party tonight?" asked Lily. "I thought I might wear my blue dress to this one and tie my hair back with the matching ribbon. Would that be all right, do you think?"

"Yes, we do. The blue one would be fine. Didn't you wear it to church last week? I suppose it won't hurt to repeat it. We cannot afford for you to have a new dress every time we go out. Put the white shawl over your shoulders and perhaps it won't appear to be the same gown."

"Good idea!" Lily busied herself with the preparations with her hair, and Mandy mused about how much happier she had seemed the last day or two. Maybe she merely needed to get some of her emotions out. *A young girl has many twisted feelings. I well recall how I felt at that age. Aunt Ida was very strict with me which caused a great deal of friction between us. Later in the camp, I had the same reactions but because I was a slave instead of a rebellious youngster. God, help me be kind and understanding, as Your Word teaches I must be.*

The last days had been such a blur. One invitation after another, one for a fancy luncheon served at a beautiful home very similar to the Cordons' villa, and two dinner parties, plus the one this evening. Had Mandy lost count? Maybe it was more? Her daughter was ecstatic at all the attention, while Mandy cringed every time Matthew told her about another one.

In about an hour, she had to attend a hearing at the makeshift courthouse here in Trenton. The judge had come into town and was hearing some kind of motion that Matthew had filed. He explained it all to her that morning in their usual meeting but she had barely comprehended all the legal jargon, only knew she had to meet him that afternoon at 2:00. How she dreaded this because her attorney had warned her that Alex would be there. Her stomach turned over at the very thought of seeing him again up close, and the idea of having to sit in the same room with him for a time made her rather queasy. She would be depending on God's strength to get her through this. Fortunately, Lily had agreed to stay at the Boarding House to do some reading instead of going with her mother. No matter what, she *must* keep her daughter away from that madman!

As she entered the small building, accompanied by Matthew, Mandy breathed a sigh of relief because Alex was not present. Another man sat at the other table across the room from them, who turned out to be the opposing lawyer, Dave Harris. His clothing was slovenly, especially compared to the crisp look of Matthew, and it appeared he hadn't shaved in several days. Mandy found herself proud to be represented by someone who obviously knew how to dress before a judge at a hearing, even if it was only taking place in a large cabin in downtown Trenton and not in a fancy courtroom. A third table, larger than the other two, sat up front, maybe for the judge? It was surrounded by two small desks, one on each side. Matthew told her the man seated at one of those was Tommy Kendrick and he was the Bailiff. The other table was for stacking up paperwork as it was presented to the judge but for now it was empty.

"Most of the time, Amanda, you won't be required to attend these but for this first one, I wanted you present, so Judge Adams can see you in person. First impressions do count, even for the legal profession, you know." And he winked at her. The gesture troubled her but she dismissed it. He was only trying to put her at ease, she knew, but she wished he wouldn't be so familiar with her. *Ken-ai-te, I miss you terribly!*

After all the legal formalities were out of the way and they were once again seated after the judge entered, Alex suddenly breezed in, slipping into place next to Mr. Harris.

"About time, sir," the judge intoned, glancing over his eyeglasses, perched on the end of his nose. If he had attempted to be intimidating, in Mandy's opinion, it was working! She had to focus to keep her jaw from flying open in awe. How she wished fervently she could scold this horrid man so easily with a look like the judge's!

Alex mumbled an apology but the judge ignored it and continued leafing through the massive amount of paperwork he had on his desk. *Is all that only for this case? Oh my! I have only signed four or five papers so far, although Matthew warned me there would be many more before we were through.*

Mandy started to whisper a question to her attorney. He quickly shushed her, but not before the judge glanced up disapprovingly.

"I am sorry, Your Honor. My client has never been in a courtroom before. It won't happen again, sir."

Judge Adams went back to his reading. Mandy blushed and slid back into her chair, wishing she could just disappear. She should be back home tending to her two sons, gathering wood for the campfire, and tanning hides for clothing for next winter—not sitting in a courtroom in Trenton and feeling totally out of place.

Does a fish feel this way when he is caught as he flops about on the shore of the river, desperately trying to breathe again? Does he beg God to rescue him, to help him take just one more breath? Because that is exactly how I feel right now! God, help me! Please get me out of here!

After a brief exchange between the judge and both attorneys, using language she couldn't follow and saying things she couldn't begin to understand, the judge picked up his gavel, slamming it down hard. The sharp crack startled Mandy. She jumped and cried out.

"Oh!" And then clapped her hand over her mouth. Too late!

Judge Adams said in a loud voice while staring her down, "Court is adjourned until next Friday. When I hope the defendant will be in better control of herself!"

Had she jinxed the whole case with her behavior? But she had not expected that loud bang when the gavel met the wooden desk! Could she not be human but also deserving of the inheritance her aunt wanted her to have? Mandy was about to cry when Matthew turned to her and patted her on the shoulder.

"He liked you!"

"Who? The judge?"

"Yes, who else?"

"But he was not happy with me at all! What makes you think he liked me?"

"Because I know him well and if he had not liked you, he would have been much harsher when you violated the rules of court as you did. It isn't your fault, Amanda. I should have instructed you better before we came in here. Courtroom demeanor can be tricky. You cannot go into court and appear cocky or argumentative, bored or defensive, even. The judge will be immediately on his guard if you are any of those. But not understanding the need for silence until you are spoken to, that is a common mistake, and Judge Adams is not as harsh as some about this. Oh, he will let you know when you are in the wrong but at least he won't cite you for contempt as easily as several others do."

"Contempt? What is that? I mean I know what the word means but what does it mean to 'cite me' for it?"

"Tell you what, I'll explain it to you while I walk you back to the Boarding House. How does that sound?"

As she bade Matthew goodbye a short time later, she thanked him for his lessons in behavior while in court. But inside, she felt overwhelmed and deeply frustrated. All she really wanted to do was run away to hide in a certain warrior's tipi on the prairie out in Indian Territory!

My beloved, I miss you so much! But I do have a good attorney, even if I don't understand everything he tells me. I have to trust him with my life, with our lives and future. How I wish I could talk with you again, if only for a moment. Feel your arms around me. Hear your heartbeat as I lay my head against your chest. Know your love is truly forever. Can you hear me calling out to you right now? I pray you can.

After a delicious dinner that evening along with charming company from Matthew and his friends, Lily and Mandy returned to the Boarding House. She sent Lily to check with Nan to see if she was willing to come talk to them for a while. Quickly she returned with Nan in tow!

"I'm glad you are willing to share with us, even with the lateness of the hour," said Mandy as the two ladies settled into chairs and Lily plopped down on her bed, eager to hear what Nan had to say. Apparently, the bad mood from earlier had disappeared. Mandy was deeply grateful that her "other" daughter was back tonight!

"Thank you for inviting me. I had just started drinking a cup of tea so hope it's all right I brought it with me."

"Certainly. I think you wanted to tell us about how you and Aunt Ida met Bessie, is that right?"

"Yes, it is important yet heartbreaking to relate this to you, as it gives you vital information on how God changed your aunt's heart during that horrible time. Some of it you already know from the letters, but Miss Ida said she didn't have the strength to tell you all of it. The adventure started with a lantern signal off in the woods behind the house…"

September 1, 1860
Trenton, Ohio

"Nan, I believe we have some passengers this evening!"

Ida's voice was soft but filled with excitement. They were on the porch rocking and waiting in the dark, listening to the crickets while enjoying the cooler fall nighttime breeze. Earlier, they had been alerted to expect a delivery that night. The message had come through Claire Gates, a young lady who sold flower and vegetable seeds to many in these parts, but her real intention in calling at Wellington Oaks had been to let the ladies know a Conductor was due soon at their Depot. How she knew they never asked, simply paid for a few more seeds to keep things legitimate, in case anyone was watching. The seeds were always welcome, as they meant more food for the many mouths they had to feed, but they also provided the perfect cover for this purpose.

"You are correct, Miss Ida. I see the signal now and am headed for the cellar to unlock the door from inside. Be careful out there!" She silently disappeared into the house, leaving Ida alone on the porch.

Ida's heart skipped several beats as she ran to the cellar door to unlock it from the outside, using the key she always kept around her neck. Nan had hers on as well of course, because they had decided to have a lock on each side for safety purposes. An intruder might break one lock but perhaps couldn't reach the other. So far, their plan had worked well.

Lord, will I always be this nervous when we have arrivals? Protect all of us from the evil in the night, from its prying eyes as well as any wicked intentions for harm!

She pulled out the key as she heard soft steps behind her, then opened the door once she heard the click on the other side. Turning to her guests, she gestured toward the steps.

Whispering, she said, "Please go on down there but do hurry before anyone on the street spots you! My friend Miss Nan is inside to show you where to go from there."

The Conductor nodded as he watched his charges disappear one at a time into the darkness beneath the house. Ida opened her mouth to say something but he raced away without a word. There were seven passengers this time but one of them seemed unable to walk on his own. *I wonder what's wrong with him? What kind of a problem is that going to be?* Anxiety crept up Ida's throat until she thought she might be sick. One of the others helped the man maneuver the steps but the going was difficult and much slower than Ida would have liked. She glanced around frequently, to see if anyone on the street might have spotted them but fortunately no one seemed to be out tonight. *Thank You, Lord, for protecting us!*

When the last one passed through the doorway and she had locked the door's latch behind them securely, she felt a flood of relief. As she ran for the front door, she returned the key to its safe spot inside her dress, ensuring the ribbon around her neck that held it was hidden from sight as well. Once inside the foyer, she slammed the door shut and bolted it firmly behind her. She headed for the cellar without even stopping for a lantern. Ida knew the way through the house well even in the dark and saw no need to give any eyes outside a chance to see where she was going.

Tapping twice on the door before opening it, as she and Nan had arranged, she picked up the dimly lighted lantern sitting on the table beside the entrance to the lower floor of the house. After closing the cellar door behind her, she rushed down the steps. Nan was ushering the last person into the secret room and Ida joined her to speak to them a moment.

"Welcome to my home. My name is Miss Ida and this is my friend Miss Nan. Please listen carefully. I know the space is cramped but it's better than being outside in the open. There is a bucket in the corner for personal use. Miss Nan and I will return soon with provisions for each of you. We are going to close the opening now with some heavy shelving but since we have been unable to make this room secure from sounds, you can still hear what's going on here in the basement. That also means anyone out here can hear you if there is talking inside or even snoring or coughing. If you hear two taps on the door upstairs that means one of us is coming down, therefore you are safe. If you do not hear those, it means someone else is coming into the cellar, thus you are in danger so you must be absolutely silent. Do you understand?"

They all nodded, and Ida noticed that the one who had been stumbling on the steps was already lying down, with one of the passengers bending over him.

Nodding in his direction, she asked, "What is wrong with him? Has he been injured or is he ill?"

One of the men solemnly replied, "He got snake bit on his leg when we crossed the river earlier. Don't think he's doing so good after our long run here."

The one bending over him looked up and Ida gasped. It was a woman! They didn't get many female passengers and this one was dressed like a man, which is why she hadn't noticed earlier. Tears streamed down the brown cheeks.

"Can you he'p him? He be hurtin' so bad!"

"I will bring medicine and bandages when I come back and see what I can do for him. I'm sorry about your husband."

"He not my husband, he my brother. Samuel."

"Oh, your brother. What is your name?"

"Bessie. Bessie Langston. Please, he is all I have. Can you he'p him?" Fresh tears appeared but she gulped and continued without waiting for a reply. "And, well, thanks for not sending us away."

"Why, Bessie, I wouldn't dream of sending you away simply because he is hurt!" Ida was unsure what kind of treatment these folks had been exposed to, but in her household at least, they would be accorded kindness. And that most decidedly did not include rejecting them as passengers because of this!

One man scowled and grumbled as he plopped down on the floor.

"He gonna endanger all of us. You should make him leave."

"Nonsense, sir. I won't hear of such talk. There are blankets around the room if any of you need them so try to get some rest. There are a few deliberate cracks in the shelves that will allow air and light to seep in. It's not much but it's all we can risk. Now, we really must secure this room in case anyone noticed something suspicious when you came in. We will return directly." She smiled at Bessie, who nodded briefly in response, quickly turning back to attend to her brother once more.

With great effort, the two women pushed the heavy shelving piece in front of the opening to the small room built into the far corner of the cellar. Jars, packages of various kinds and sizes, along with other miscellaneous items filled its entire length and breadth. They quickly rearranged a few that had shifted out of place, then stepped back briefly to ensure all was in good order. Nan scuffed her shoe to cover the drag marks in the dirt floor so no one would notice that the shelf had been moved. All these precautions were in case anyone came down here unexpectedly, which was highly unlikely, but one never knew who might be spying on them.

Neither said a word until they were back upstairs and able to breathe a sigh of relief for the moment. They quickly went to work getting the simple meal together for their guests and also gathering a few medical supplies they thought might be needed to treat Samuel's leg.

"I cannot imagine how frightening that must have been for him and his sister," said Nan, "when he got bitten by a snake! In the dark, on the run from the slavers, afraid of endangering all the others if he cried out, shivering in the cold, soaked to the skin, in terrible pain, and afraid he would die if he didn't get a doctor's help right away. Yet, sadly, there could be none."

"Maybe what we have to offer will help, but if it was a venomous one, I'm not sure there is anything we can do. Poor Bessie!"

"Yes, I have been praying already for his healing," said Nan, "but also for her comfort. They have sacrificed so much for freedom!"

A short time later, they were met by the hungry and grateful passengers, who gobbled down the hot stew as quickly as they could, using the bread to sop up what they could not manage to get in the spoon. Each of them gulped down what seemed an enormous amount of water. After having survived what must have been a treacherous crossing over the river, yet here they were, thirsty. Whether out of fear or due to the long walk without provisions or rest, or both—whatever the reason, they all needed water.

While Ida worked she prayed fervently for each one. *God, how I do pray they will be as thirsty to hear about the Gospel! If You will give me an opening to share with them, I will certainly obey.*

The bucket had to be emptied already so Nan rushed off to do that. When she returned, the sad look on Ida's face told the tale about poor Samuel.

"Seems it must have been a venomous snake, indeed," she told her friend after pulling her aside, "as the wound is all swollen up horribly, even though the attack happened not long ago. I've put salve on it and a bandage but there is little I can do for his pain. I did give him some laudanum but he has to be ready to run again by tomorrow night so I cannot give him any more."

Bessie wept quietly. Nan noticed that the man who had complained earlier did not look happy about sharing this space with someone who was moaning in pain. *Well, too bad, sir! This could easily have been you and there would be no one to care!* Instantly she felt shame for her lack of compassion. What if this happened to her? Would there be anyone but Miss Ida who would even notice? As she gathered up the dishes and replaced them in the baskets for transport back upstairs, Bessie reached over to her, whispering almost in her ear.

"Thank you for your kindness. Why do you do this?"

"Because the Lord has commanded us to do what we can to help until slavery is destroyed. We both feel quite strong about it. I wish we could do far more than provide a couple of meals and a night's safety for all of you."

Samuel suddenly roused and opened his eyes. "I worry about my sister here, after, um, after God takes me Home."

"Hush, Samuel! You ain't gwanna die. That's all there is to it. Ain't that right, Miss Nan?"

"Only God knows the answer to that one, Bessie. For now, we must leave it all in His hands."

"God!" she scoffed. "What's He ever done for us slaves? 'Cept get us beaten and threatened and worked until we drop dead?"

"Bessie, don't talk like that!" her brother scolded. "He loves you and you need to get your heart right with him. Don't let what has happened in the past or what happens to me make you bitter. Please, sweet sister!"

"God told you we would be free. What about that?"

"Yes, He did. You know that's why I decided to run for it and take you with me. But please, whether I go on with you or not, you simply *must* listen for His voice. My whole life I've tried to teach you this. Don't let this end with me hearing you speak against our God. Please, I beg you!"

CHAPTER TWENTY-SIX

"A false witness shall not be unpunished, and he that speaketh lies shall perish." Proverbs 19:9

April 27, 1867
Indian Territory

"Father, I plead with You for word from my wife!" cried Ken-ai-te. "She was to be gone for only a few days but already it has been almost two—what does she call them?—yes, *weeks,* two weeks. What if she is sick or Lily is injured or, or, God I cannot even put the horror into words what my heart is thinking! You know, so please give me Your peace to reassure me that nothing has happened to either of them."

"What, Papa?" Red Hawk sat up and rubbed his eyes. He had been awakened by his father's prayer.

"I am sorry, son," he said to him in Kiowa. "Go back to sleep. I pray for your mother and sister." *I didn't even realize I had spoken out loud. My heart is poured out before You, Lord. Hear my cries!*

He smiled at the brave young man he saw before him, as the boy closed his eyes again. The last year had made a big difference in him, growing taller and stronger, not to mention wiser, by the day. Ken-ai-te found it hard to contain his pride at times when he looked at his oldest son, for Red Hawk looked exactly like his father. Everyone said it, even his wife saw the resemblance. Spotted Rabbit, sleeping peacefully next to his older brother, favored his mother more. But Ken-ai-te could see many things in both boys to show they were more Kiowa than white. Although he honored their white heritage openly, deep inside he felt somehow completed in his life's work, knowing he had sired two sons who would carry on their father's blood long after he went to sleep with his fathers.

I mustn't think that, though, as I know now I will sleep with Jesus instead. At times it is difficult to remember all the parts of my faith when I talk to You. Prayer Woman often tells me that You will sort it all out for me, though, because it is never intentional to remain in my ancient heritage. I only revisit it from time to time. I hope that is true because I would never offend Your holiness on purpose. It's just that these thoughts have been a part of me for many moons, too many to count, in fact, so it's hard to think differently at times. Thank You for forgiving me and being patient with me.

He rose and went out into the darkness, gazing up at the stars. Maybe it was the constant emptiness in his stomach that drove him to spend more time with his heavenly Father. Maybe it was the cold spot on the buffalo rug next to him, where his wife should be lying. Maybe it was the anxiety deep in his soul for the two who were absent from their tipi.

"God! I call on You right now to speak peace to me! I admit to You that I am weak and afraid for my family, for my people, for me as their leader. Strengthen me by Your victorious right hand. Your Word speaks to me over the noise of the grumbling of the restless young warriors and the growling of the empty stomachs of the children. Help me listen only to You!"

He closed his eyes but kept his head raised to the heavens for some time as he sought to listen to his Father instead of talking to Him, arms outstretched above him in worship. After a time he fell to his knees, folding his hands as he had often seen his beloved wife do whenever she would seek Him. And waited.

As the earliest streaks of dawn splashed across the horizon, Ken-ai-te finally opened his eyes, proclaiming in a loud voice, "Amen!"

He gave back his wife and daughter into the Lord's keeping for a while longer, now ready to face whatever this new day brought. Waiting had never been easy for him but with Jesus' help, he knew he could do it. Besides, there would be much to do getting ready for the search he would be leading that day for an honorable hunt for deer or antelope or even rabbit—anything to keep the children alive a few more days, until Prayer Woman returned with the money to buy food. This would distract him for a while at least. With God's blessing it might bring meat to cooking pots in the village that night.

"Thank You, God, for what You will provide! Please let my wife know she is in my prayers this day."

April 27, 1867
Trenton, Ohio

"Lily, do you promise me that you girls will not leave the Boarding House this morning while I am gone?"

"Yes, Mama. I'm excited that Ginny's parents allowed her to come over here for a short visit at least. Of course, I don't have a French doll house that is four stories tall to keep us entertained but she is bringing some books with her for us to read. Mrs. Wilson told us that we could use the Parlor as long as we were quiet. Don't worry, we'll be fine. You won't be gone all that long, will you?"

"No, dear, I won't. Matthew wanted to take me out into the countryside for a bit, to show me where his parents' farm used to be and a handful of other sights that I haven't seen before or at least in many years. Much has changed here in Trenton; I'm certain everything else around it has as well. I'm glad to get out of town for a while, to be honest. It's such a gorgeous day. That is one reason I hate to see you stuck inside, but with Alex out there, I don't feel comfortable for you and Ginny to leave the safety of the house. I do hope Mrs. Wilson realizes that your version of 'quiet' may not be the same as hers! Perhaps a few giggles won't disturb the other guests too much. You may always come up here to the room if you would prefer."

"Yes, there will be some of those, I'm sure. It's one of my favorite parts about being with Ginny. She makes me laugh! I haven't gotten to laugh like that in, well, I was going to say a long time but truthfully, as in *never*. What is there to laugh about in a Kiowa village?"

"Hush! Do you want someone to hear you? How many times must I warn you?"

"Sorry, Mama," she whispered, "but it's true."

The truth sliced deep into Mandy's heart, for her daughter was right. Lately, there had been very little laughter at home. *Lord, I lift up Ken-ai-te to You this morning. I pray that all is well with him and the boys, along with the rest of the people in our camp. Would it be too much to ask if they could find something to bring them joy today? How I wish I were there with them this day! I miss you, my love!*

During breakfast, Nan asked Mandy if she was still going riding with Matthew that day.

"Yes, I am. I know you don't approve but I need to get out of town for a while and it's such a gorgeous day. Too bad you have to work or you could go with us."

"I'm sure Matthew wouldn't be happy with that arrangement," she snapped sarcastically. Was Nan *jealous* of her time with her attorney? Or only because he was a handsome man and she would be unchaperoned with him? What was the root of this edge to her friend's voice?

"Oh, goodness! You act as though we are romantically involved. May I remind you, Nan, I am a married woman! And he is merely my attorney. Yes, he is trying to get me out in public more but not for any ulterior motive. Stop thinking that! It's not honoring of our friendship, for one thing, nor kind to him at all."

Nan clamped her lips shut and stared at her empty plate, but would not meet Mandy's stare.

"I have to get to work. Have a *nice* day," she said, not without sarcasm.

Mandy sighed. *Am I being too trusting? Is there something I am missing here, Father? Please show me if I am doing anything wrong, or wrong in the sight of others at least.*

"Don't let her get to you, Amanda," said Mrs. Wilson after Nan left the room. The other boarders had already departed from the dining room, along with Lily. "You do know that Nan and Matthew had quite a fling at one time, right? I think there might be a tad bit of jealousy still lingering."

"Really? No, I didn't realize that, though I had suspected it for a while, from a few little things each of them had said and how they act around each other. Was it long ago or more recent?"

"Well, I think about a year ago. Everyone expected them to marry but they were never even engaged, only courting rather seriously. I am not sure what happened, not my business to speculate, and she has never told me a word. But I know it was not a happy break-up, for either one of them. Poor Matthew, I had very much hoped he would end up with a nice girl like Nan. Bless her heart, Nan very much needed this to work out. She has been denied so much in her short life. I do hope this bequest your aunt left her will enable her to go somewhere else to get away from memories and start over. And maybe finally settle down with a family. She deserves it!"

"Yes, she does," said Mandy slowly. This certainly explained a great deal. Although bordering on gossip, she was grateful Mrs. Wilson had told her. She had not felt comfortable asking Nan herself and of course would not dream of bringing up something quite this personal with her attorney. But it helped her understand better why Nan may be a little uneasy with her going riding in a buggy with Matthew today. Now, she began to have grave misgivings about it herself. Should she cancel? She needed to pray about this before making a decision.

She excused herself and went out onto the porch to settle in a rocker for a bit, one of her favorite places to get away by herself and pray these days. Nothing like being out on the vast prairie, observing nature at its best, but a good second choice. How she missed her beloved home! When would she get to return? When would this eternal lie be done with?

At dinner, Mrs. Wilson asked how the buggy ride went that day. Mandy glanced at Nan but she wouldn't meet her gaze. She took a deep breath before answering her landlady.

"It was great fun! We drove quite a distance, actually, further than I thought we were going to go, and I saw many of the tiny villages around the area. Having grown up here, Matthew knew his way around which was a blessing, since I was lost much of the time. I can find my way around the prairie but not here! All the woods, rivers, and streams get me so mixed up, and all the farms look the same."

"Did you get to see Matthew's parents' farm? It's huge and so beautiful. The Fosters own it now. With the help of their five boys they have built it up even grander than when the Graysons owned it."

"Yes, I did, and you are right. Matthew told me the sheer size of it is why he decided to sell it after his parents passed away. There was no way he could manage it all properly and keep up his law practice. In addition, he showed me the two other small farms they also had owned, which he of course had sold along with the larger one. I, for one, am grateful he decided to focus on being an attorney instead of becoming a farmer like his father."

"In case you are wondering," Mrs. Wilson went on, "your daughter and her friend were perfect young ladies this morning while you were gone. They stayed in the Parlor like they promised to do, playing a couple of games, reading their books, and chatting quietly."

"Thank you for telling me that. I wondered how many giggles they shared, too!"

"Lots of them, Mama, in case you are interested in knowing!" said Lily. And they all laughed over that.

The topic of conversation switched several times from there during the rest of the meal, all without Nan opening her mouth. When they were finished, Mrs. Wilson asked who wanted a piece of her homemade apple pie. Everyone chimed in with an enthusiastic yes except for Nan, who quickly excused herself and ran from the room. Eyebrows went up but no one said anything. However, Mandy knew she must confront Nan about this issue between them. She was her only friend in Trenton and Mandy couldn't bear to have things unsettled with her.

After dessert, Lily began a game of checkers with Mrs. Wilson and Mandy excused herself and went upstairs to try to talk to Nan. If she would open the door to her, that is. She breathed a prayer for wisdom as she knocked.

"Nan, it's Amanda. Please let me in. We need to talk."

Silence. Nothing for several seconds. Slowly the door opened, revealing a red-eyed Nan standing there with tears still shining on her cheeks. She didn't say anything but did step back so Mandy could enter.

They talked for quite some time and Nan poured out her heart to Mandy about how miserable she had been over Matthew taking her friend out riding that morning. Mandy mostly listened because Nan seemed to need to talk more than be consoled.

"I realize how silly I have reacted, and I do apologize. This is not your fault. It's mine. I don't know if you knew about this or not, but Matthew and I were seeing each other for some time last year."

"Yes, but I only learned of this a few minutes ago."

"Mrs. Wilson?" she asked.

She nodded and Nan smiled, then continued.

"I had a difficult time accepting it when Matthew broke off our courting, really without much of an explanation. He is probably the most eligible bachelor left in Butler County! In fact, I felt such despair, thinking I would never get married now, unless I move away. But I couldn't leave Miss Ida and I had no money to go anywhere else. Now that problem is solved, or almost at least. And I have a new dream. But the old one keeps chewing pieces of my heart and I haven't been able to let it go. Everything lately has brought it all to the surface. Tonight I realized that I can no longer simply ignore it. What I need to do is face my feelings for him."

"Oh, Nan, I'm so sorry. I really didn't mean to rub salt in your wound, you know. I have gratefully accepted Matthew's friendship, along with his legal counsel of course, because I desperately need to win this case. I, well, I cannot explain it fully right now, but it's terribly important to me. And when Matthew told me I had to be seen out in public, I guess I fell a little too easily into that trap. I must confess, I was caught up in the whirl of activity for a while but now I am growing less and less comfortable with this myself. It's one reason I told Matthew that Lily and I would be walking to church in the morning, that we would see him there, but not sit with him, certainly not appear with him in his buggy. He was confused and perhaps a little hurt but I think he understood. I kept repeating that my husband wouldn't be happy with this, either. It's almost as though he doesn't believe I *have* a husband."

"Well, that is the popular rumor right now, you know."

"What is?"

"That you aren't really married at all. That Lily's father and you are, well, not married."

"What? Why didn't you tell me that earlier? I had no idea! What rubbish! My husband and I have been together for almost fifteen years now and we have three children. I love him desperately. *Desperately*. And miss him terribly. The only reason I am here is because he insisted I come."

"Why didn't you want to come without him urging you to do so, Amanda?"

"Um, I cannot explain fully because it's very complicated." Mandy pulled out her watch. "Oh, my, it's bedtime. I really must see that Lily gets enough sleep that she can get up in the morning on time for church. And that her mother can as well. I am sorry if I hurt you but it's over. The riding and being with Matthew, except in the office, I mean. He said there is a community picnic of some kind next Saturday and I did agree to go to it with him, but this coming week will be strictly business. So you can know your dream is safe as far as I am concerned. If you still wish to pursue it, that is. Or are free to follow that new one God is shaping for you now. You seem to have as much at stake in this inheritance being settled in my favor as I do."

"Thanks, Amanda. No, not nearly as much as you do, with starving people back home depending on you bringing that money to them. But yes, in a way, I guess you could say I have a lot riding on the decision. Not to mention, how much I care about you as a friend! You are so sweet to be concerned about me. Thank you, too, for coming up here to talk. I didn't have the courage to face you, feeling the way I do. You tell me how Lily is often confused about things, and I feel the same way! However, I am not a young girl who is trying to fit into a culture that is vastly different from the one she grew up in. I mean, living on the prairie has to be quite different from living here in a town."

Oh, if you only knew how *different!*

As Mandy drifted off to sleep that night, after writing furiously in her journal to her beloved Ken-ai-te for quite a while, she prayed fervently about something on her heart.

God, I want to tell Nan the truth about my heritage and why I am here. Is that within Your will for me, to at least let her know? I promised both Ken-ai-te and Jacob that I would not do this, but I feel if Nan and I are to remain friends, she deserves to know. Honestly, I cannot stand her not knowing, not having anyone to share this conflict and fear with. Besides You! I know I always have You to talk to. But it's just not the same. Does that make sense?

If You are giving me Your permission, please open a good opportunity for us to talk soon. Give me the right words and prepare her heart to receive this secret I carry. I cannot afford to lose the only friend I have right now! But yet, somehow the longer I know her, the more strongly I feel she will welcome the news, not reject me because of it. So, here's to tomorrow being another big day for me! Go before me to prepare the way that I might walk in it. By Your power and wisdom, I pray this. Amen.

Mandy slipped into a sound sleep, a smile on her lips.

"Let me go! You cannot keep me a prisoner like this forever, you know. I don't care if you are my husband!"

"You will never get away from me, *never*. I will kill you before I let you go. You are mine and mine alone. No one would ever want you after finding out what you are, you filthy *Indian!* Are you really wanting to starve to death on the street? Because you know that is what will happen to you if you leave my house and my protection."

"No! This is a nightmare! It cannot be real! You are not my husband. Ken-ai-te is my beloved. What have you done with him?"

"Done with him? I killed him, don't you remember? He is gone and you are mine now. And no one can stop me from using all your money as I see fit. It's mine, too, according to the law. Once we married, your fortune became mine. Now, get out of my way so I can go spend some of that delightful money!"

"Let me go! Alex, you are not my husband! What is going on here? Help me!"

"Mama, wake up! You are having a nightmare!" Lily shook her mother repeatedly, trying to rouse her from the troubled sleep she had been having. "Please, Mama!"

"Lily?" Mandy fought to focus her eyes in the dim light. "Is that you?"

"Yes, it is! I'm so relieved that you know who I am, finally."

"Finally? What is happening?"

"You were having some kind of awful nightmare, saying the most horrible things! Like Papa was dead and you were married to Alex!"

"What? How ridiculous!" She paused a second, eyes wide. "Your father is *not* dead, is he? Please tell me he is alive! He is my only hope to get out of this mess. I have to know that he is waiting for me back home!"

"No, Mama, he is quite alive. Or was when we left him. You have been tossing all night, then started crying out all these awful words that scared me terribly. Whatever possessed you to think you were married to your cousin?"

"Well, in the first place," Mandy said as she sat up in the bed and lighted the lantern next to her, "he is not my cousin. Not really. He is an imposter. But in the second place, even if your father *were* dead, I would never, ever marry such a cad as Alex Clark! Or whatever his real name is!"

"I can't tell you what a relief it is that you are all right. You had me really worried there for a moment."

"I apologize for scaring you, Lily. I'm quite all right now. Go on back to your bed so I can turn out the light. Although, I'm not sure I will get back to sleep tonight now. What if the dream comes back again?"

"Why don't you read some Scripture for a bit before you try to go back to sleep? You always tell my brothers and me that is the perfect solution when we cannot sleep! God will speak peace over you and I shall pray for that to happen, my dear mother. Start with Psalm 4:8. Do you want me to quote it for you?"

Mandy's heart warmed to her daughter counseling her with Scripture against the fear in her heart! How often she had done exactly this for her daughter over the years since she was born. To pray verses over her baby, her toddler, her little child, and now her almost-grown daughter, whose faith never seemed to waver, even when her own became wobbly at times. What a blessing!

"All right, I will let you do that. I think all I need right now is to hear you recite those words, and I'm sure I can sleep again."

She gazed into her mother's face. "I say this often when I face my own fears, Mama. 'I will both lay me down in peace, and sleep; for thou, LORD, only makest me dwell in safety.' Such good words to soothe the heart and mind. Now, lie down and do what the psalmist said! I will turn out the light. Good night! Sweet dreams!"

CHAPTER TWENTY-SEVEN

"For God sent not his Son into the world to condemn the world; but that the world through him might be saved." John 3:17

April 28, 1867

"Anyone other than me ready for that delicious meal of fried chicken and mashed potatoes, waiting on us back at the Boarding House?" Mandy's question was met with an enthusiastic response from both Lily and Nan as they walked back there from church. To top it off, Mrs. Wilson had made one of her famous apple pies. By the time they were through eating, everyone was stuffed and all declared it was time for a Sunday afternoon nap.

As the three went upstairs, Mandy asked Nan if she minded finishing the story about Bessie.

"Last time, you kind of left us hanging, you know! Lily and I want to know if Samuel survived and what happened to Bessie."

"I'm sorry, it's such a long story and I don't want to bore you, but it is an important one to share with others, for the truth to be known. Countless ones worked bravely behind the scenes to make the Underground Railroad a success as a whole, and many gave of themselves far more than I ever dreamed about doing. Not to mention the sacrifices of the runaway slaves who came as passengers through that system."

"Oh, you could never bore us with this, believe me!"

"I agree, Miss Nan," chimed in Lily. "After reading that book, I want to know the end of your story, too. This is a true one, whereas that one is fiction. But it seems to be very similar to what the real people who lived through it endured."

They all settled in for yet another part of this exciting tale!

"You are exactly right, Lily. I'm proud of you, wanting to hear the truth. Someday you can tell your grandchildren and great-grandchildren what really went on during this terrible time in our country's history. Indeed, you *must!* Let's see, I think I stopped after the night the passengers in Bessie's group arrived in the cellar."

September 2, 1860
Trenton, Ohio

"Miss Nan and I are here with your breakfast, folks!" said Ida. The two ladies quickly set their things down and rushed to shove the shelving out of the way so their guests could move about.

"Glory be!" one of the men exclaimed. I's a field hand and bein' cooped up in a tiny room like this is hard on me!" He pushed his way forward and out before anyone could stop him.

"My, you are an energetic man, aren't you, *sir?*" Nan asked with more than a little sarcasm, stepping out of his way before he mowed her down!

Ida continued. "All of you are welcome to come out into the cellar and move about if you would like while you eat. How I wish I could allow you into the gardens as it is a beautiful day out there. Unfortunately, this will have to do."

Nan went to retrieve the bucket and take it upstairs. She noticed Bessie had not moved away from her brother, where she cradled his head on her lap as she had been the night before. Gulping against the stench from the contents of what she carried, she briefly met eyes with Bessie.

"Why you do this?" she asked, nodding at the pail. "I should do it for you."

Nan smiled. "No, Bessie, that is my task here today. How is Samuel this morning?"

"Much weaker and the leg has turned very dark where the bite is. I know he has to be in pain, but he is asleep for now."

"Think you can get a bit of oatmeal in him? It would be nourishing for him if you can."

"I'll try." Tears slipped quietly down her cheeks, and she lovingly stroked his face.

Nan raced upstairs to get the bucket deposited on the back porch and grab an empty one. They kept those stored out there just for this purpose. Later in the day one of them would take it to the outhouse for emptying.

"Thank goodness the porch isn't visible from the street," she said quietly as she hurried through this unpleasant task. A small sacrifice, considering what their passengers were enduring below her feet.

By the time she returned, Ida had managed to get everyone served and they were sitting everywhere in the cellar eating and talking quietly. Bessie shook her head at Nan's unasked question about whether Samuel had been able to eat. Nan's heart sank. Without nourishment, even water, he wouldn't last long in this battle against the snake venom. In fact, she was shocked he had managed to live through the night.

Wonder what we will do if he is still alive tonight when the group is ready to leave? We cannot keep him here without help. And if his sister stays, what on earth will we do with her until the next group comes? She will have to stay out of sight the whole time, which could be a couple of days or a couple of weeks, who knows? God, please show us what to do!

"Bessie, here is some porridge and bread for you," Ida said. "You simply must eat, my dear." Ida set it down in front of her on the blanket. Bessie immediately burst into tears!

"There, there," Ida said consolingly. "It will be all right, you will see."

"I—I never had a whole piece of bread to myself until I come here. Least ways, not one that was not crawling with worms. When I saw the one last night, I was, was shocked. Now, here is another this morning. It's all too much. And shared with me by a white woman, too. We's told that white women are jealous of our brown bodies, will kill us if given the chance. The massas choose out the prettiest Negroes for their own and the ladies of the house, they be furious. Why you not try to kill us but instead feed us bread? I don't understand." She swiped at the moisture on her cheeks with the back of her hand, greedily chomped down on the bread, and took a big spoonful of the cereal.

Ida glanced over at Nan. The expression in her eyes said it all.

Father, this is why we do this work. Exactly this. Please forgive those who have so mistreated this precious soul, for I cannot. God, what makes such monsters out of human beings? Meeting suffering in this sweet and gentle person in the depths of her hurt has forced me to confront the truth—no longer words in a book but a flesh and blood real woman. I cannot stop her pain nor what lies ahead for her, but at least I can serve her a bowl of porridge to get through the next few hours, with her own piece of warm, fresh bread. How I take such a little thing like that for granted!

Ida swallowed hard against the pangs in her own heart and smiled at her friend across the room. They worked silently to gather up the dishes as each passenger finished the simple meal. How she wished it could be more! *And an end to this terrible conflict in our country and the curse of slavery that started it all.*

Ida and Nan picked up the two baskets of dishes to return them upstairs, amid many thanks from the passengers, promising to come back with more water in a short time.

"While we are gone," said Nan to the whole group, "you all might want to try to get some sleep. You are going to need your strength for tonight."

Suddenly, Ida stopped and put her load down a moment, patting Bessie on the shoulder with a smile, hoping to bolster her courage a bit. Earlier the woman had withdrawn when touched but this time she did not reject it. The pitiful tear-stained expression broke Ida's heart afresh and made her realize nothing would help her new friend except God's divine healing.

"Bessie, you ask why we share food and hide you, at great risk to ourselves," said Ida. "It is because of the love of Christ that lives in our hearts. No other reason. I can't answer for the sins of other women, but we have a reason for hope they apparently don't have. That hope brings us peace in the midst of the worst storms of life. Someday, somehow, I hope I have a chance to share more about this with you. You have nothing to fear from either of us. For now, we must get back upstairs, and you need to rest. I want you to know I'm praying for you."

Bessie nodded, tears glistening in her eyes, but she said nothing.

Some time later, after cleaning up all the dishes and eating their own morning meal, Ida and Nan sat down for a cup of tea together. It had been a stressful morning for them, made even more difficult by the tragedy of Samuel's suffering and pending death.

"Miss Ida, what are we going to do about Samuel if he cannot walk tonight when the Conductor comes?"

"I've been thinking about that. We will have to keep him here, that's all there is to it. I'm certain Bessie won't leave her brother when he is this ill, so I suppose we will have to keep her as well. After he is gone, perhaps she can help us a bit around the house, as long as we are extra cautious about anyone spotting her through the windows. I don't know how we will manage until the next group comes but we simply must. He cannot be turned out in his condition!"

"No, of course not. There *must* be something we can do to help Bessie, though. Poor soul, she will be quite lost when he dies. I cannot imagine what she has been through. Did you see her right hand? The fingers appear to be mangled."

"Oh my! I hadn't noticed. Wonder what happened?" said Ida.

"I hate to ask and tried hard not to stare but it appears the injury is not fresh. Whatever caused it, I found myself wincing every time I saw it. How can anyone treat these folks so harshly?"

"I asked myself that after the deaths of my family long ago. The Indians were not any more merciful to them than the masters of these slaves have been. Brutality breeds more of it, no matter the color of a man's skin."

"Yes, it is the evil in their hearts that makes the deeds so foul, not the way they were made on the outside."

"I pray I never have such a hard heart as those who prey on other people", said Ida. "I do not ever want to be that callous to the suffering around me, much less indifferent to it. There was a statement in the book that I cannot recall precisely at this moment. It refers to the thin line between those who profess Christian and political perfection because they loudly proclaim to have overcome every human weakness and prejudice—all while continuing to oppress others. Those with such hypocritical behavior seem to have the same heart beating in their chest as I. The difference is, they put the proper effort into cultivating it rather than gazing into pain-filled eyes as we did this morning, and then letting the Lord do His healing work in them."

"Why, Miss Ida, what a profound thought!"

"Not mine, the author of the book, but I do thank the Lord for the opportunity to try to change this horrific tragedy, one piece of bread at a time!"

"Miss Ida, I have this sudden urgency to go back downstairs to check on Samuel. If he does pass away, I don't want Bessie to be alone with that, when she has no hope of seeing him again someday in Heaven."

"I quite agree, Nan. God is putting that feeling in my heart as well."

As they descended the stairs, they were quiet, hoping for a miraculous turnaround for their patient. But it was not to be.

"Miss Nan, Miss Ida," said Bessie in a quiet voice. "Samuel be at peace now. No more pain. No more—" Her voice broke, and they knew. Samuel was with Jesus. And Bessie was truly alone for the first time.

"Oh, Bessie, I'm deeply sorry for your loss," said Ida, wrapping her arms around the grieving woman. Nan patted her on the shoulder and when Ida released her, she took her turn to embrace their new friend. Bessie received their condolences with obvious relief that they were true to their word, that no harm would befall her at their hands, that they genuinely cared for her.

"Because he was so grievously injured," said Ida, "this is best, that he can go on to his eternal rest. I really feared for how he would manage to continue the run to freedom with all of you tonight, as I knew you would not want to leave him."

"No, I don't want to leave him even now."

"What if I promise you that we will bury Samuel in our own family cemetery out in back of the house?" asked Ida. "It is consecrated ground, where others in our family are resting or will be someday. We will treat his body with great respect, I assure you. It is still daylight outside; therefore, we cannot take him out there now. But tonight, after you are gone, we will take care of him. Would you leave him, knowing that?"

"You would do that for a runaway slave?"

"Of course we will," said Nan. "What's more, we will put up a marker once it is safe to do so. If any of our neighbors see us doing that right now, they might be suspicious. But later, when we can add it safely, we will. I promise he will be buried with a cross over his grave, as befitting his faith in Christ."

Bessie began weeping copiously at that point but nodded through her tears.

"He, he would be proud to be laid to rest by you folks. You's the kindest ones I ever meet."

"Not *kind*, Bessie," said Ida, "filled with Christ's love. There is a difference. I know Samuel has told you about Him many times in the past. He was deeply worried that you would be alone when he died. But we want you to know, you will never be alone when you have us as friends. Nor as long as you have Christ filling that hole in your heart."

Bessie looked up at her, startled. "How you know about the hole?"

"Because all of us have a hole exactly that size before we come to know Jesus. He created us and made that hole there in each heart, just big enough for His Spirit to fill."

"Not sure I understand you but I like what you say about filling the hole. Samuel's love used to be there, but what I do now he be gone?"

"You turn to Christ. He will fill it, not only for now, for always. Forever."

The questions began then. Quietly, patiently, and carefully Ida answered each one as though speaking with a child instead of a grown woman. In truth, Bessie's spiritual understanding was that of a young child, who needed milk and not meat...yet. Nan sat in awe as she watched Ida take on all the burden of this young girl's fears and hurts of a lifetime. Without blinking an eye, she rapidly shot down every objection Bessie had while kindly steering her toward the love of the Savior, who stood ready to embrace her once she was ready.

"After hearing all this, Bessie, do you feel you might be ready to ask Him to fill your heart-hole with His love? To agree with Him that you have sinned and need a Savior because you cannot do that work yourself? Another thing, are you ready to go to Heaven this night, should that happen, as it has with your beloved brother? He was ready. But are you?"

"Do you think I'm ready? I don't know how to say the right words. He always talked about saying a prayer but I don't know how to pray. No one ever taught me, but I saw him pray lots of times."

"I think you are ready but I don't want to rush you. We've talked a long time, so if you want to think about it first, that's fine with us. But your brother had no idea he had a date with destiny when he met that snake last night. Who knows but that you have one this night, too? None of us knows when that moment comes, but we must each be ready. I can pray with you, if you'd like, or you can pray alone. Simply talk to God. He is already listening! And loves you very much!"

After only a few more questions, Bessie admitted she was finally ready. Right there in that dank cellar, Bessie Langston's chains fell off as she met her Savior Jesus Christ. In those moments, she came to realize that she truly would never again be alone! The joy in her voice was enough to bring smiles of happiness from all around them, in fact.

"Thank you, Miss Ida, and you, too, Miss Nan! I feel so light! Now, I am truly free, indeed! Soon my body will be free in Canada, but this day I am free from my sins, right here in Ohio. God be praised! I heared my brother say that one time but I never felt like praising Him before now. Oh, I wish Samuel could have lived long enough to hear what I just did. He would be so happy!"

"Yes, he would. The truth is, he knows it now, right now, up in Heaven. And he's singing with all the angels to rejoice in your decision. Welcome to the family, my sister in Christ!" Both ladies smiled at her incredulous look.

"Sister? We's be sisters?"

"You bet we are! Bound by Christ and His love for all men, no matter the color of their skin. For all eternity!"

April 28, 1867
Trenton, Ohio

"I cannot for the life of me," said Mandy, "understand anyone believing that Negroes have no souls or are not worth teaching to read and write. If I'm not mistaken, it was actually against the law in certain places to do that."

"Yes, it was," replied Nan. "The next day at luncheon, your aunt even discussed with me the possibility of adopting Bessie someday, that maybe in this way we could skirt the laws against Negroes learning to read as well as teach her all that she had missed growing up on that plantation under slavery. Your aunt desperately longed to be a mother, a blessing God denied her. But she took many under her wing—me, included—and treated us like her children. When you are used by God to bring a soul to Him, the link is even stronger."

"I know what you mean," Mandy said, smiling at her daughter. "There was a young cowboy on the train, Mr. Bart Conway, who accepted Christ after I shared with him for a couple of hours. It does bond you with that person all right! That has happened to me many times out in the territory over the years. I really never expected it while on a train crowded with people!"

"How wonderful!" Nan exclaimed. "Then you know what I'm talking about. It didn't take long for them to draw close. Bessie praying to receive Jesus was the best part of all, in fact it made every bit of the danger and risk worth it."

"That is what my husband and I have been doing in Indian Territory for years, sharing the Gospel and rejoicing as folks accept Him. Seeing their lives turn around as they experience peace in their hearts for the first time, especially in older age and drawing near to death, has been the most rewarding thing I have ever done."

Then Mandy decided to skip topics again to keep from saying too much about the mission work she and Ken-ai-te did. How she longed to share more but what if she said too much and aroused suspicion? Best to let it lie for now. Or should she follow her instincts to go ahead and tell Nan everything? She couldn't yet decide.

"Back to Bessie's story, though. Wouldn't adopting her have caused some problems?"

"Yes, it certainly would have, and I pointed out to your aunt that trying to explain Bessie's sudden appearance in our home would only serve to endanger all of us, the young girl included, and she knew I was right. In the midst of the preparations for leaving that night, she and your aunt had an emotional goodbye, as you can imagine. In fact, when they hugged that last time before the Conductor came, Miss Ida told her she had a gift for her."

"A gift?" asked Mandy.

"Yes," replied Nan, "a very special one. It was a small Bible, small enough to fit in one of the large patch pockets Bessie had on the loose jacket she wore. Miss Ida thought she could easily tuck it in there for safekeeping until she arrived in Canada. She had lovingly selected it from among her collection of Bibles. Then she told her to read the book of Ruth as soon as she could, although she recognized Bessie most likely could not read. But she hoped she would make it a point to learn once she reached freedom! Miss Ida said she felt about Bessie as Naomi felt about Ruth, but she would have to read the story to know what she was talking about. Even if they never saw each other again, Miss Ida told her when they were reunited in Heaven, she wanted a hug from her!"

Mandy laughed, imagining what that would be like, to see her aunt embrace a former slave. The very thought touched her heart deeply!

"You know what Bessie said in return? She replied, 'I can't believe how I have grown to love you this much in a few short hours. You are right, I cannot read but someday I gwanna learn. I will take the Bible with me and the first thing I read will be this book of Ruth you mentioned. I am going to make you another promise, one that nothing on earth can prevent me from a-keepin'. One of these days when this here war is over, I is comin' back here as a free woman. I want to live with you and Miss Nan, if you will have me, and I can take care of the house for you. I was a house slave and know how to keep house for white folks. I knows you will be proud to have me looking after you, as proud as I be in doing it for you. Thanks for all you did for my brother, too. That mean so much to me.' We were both in tears, although we truthfully never expected to hear from her again. But we did!"

"Did she really did come back?" asked Mandy.

"Oh, yes, she did. Your aunt bawled her eyes out for days over Bessie. We prayed for her faithfully, that she made it to freedom in Canada, and that someday we would see her again. But as I said, neither of us really expected that to happen. There were many passengers after that but none touched Miss Ida's heart quite like Bessie. However, one day shortly after the war ended, there was a knock on the front door. When I went to open it, there stood Bessie! Miss Ida and I couldn't stop hugging her, laughing and crying, and, well, you have to understand what a victory having her here with us was—one over slavery and oppression, even the war itself! Nothing short of Heaven could have pleased your aunt more than having Bessie here. One of the first things we did was take her out back to show her where her brother's grave was, and how we had erected a small cross to mark the spot, as we promised to do. It's still there, a silent reminder of the sorrow of slavery and yet the freedom in Christ many of them had, including Samuel."

Mandy had no response to this powerful statement but sat quietly trying to fully absorb all she was hearing. About her aunt. About Bessie. About the Underground Railroad. About the power of Christ to redeem and restore souls in His timing. About the freedom from bondage of all types that God does for any who turn to Him in repentance. It was a lot to take in!

"You know, your aunt was probably the most excited when she could teach Bessie about the Lord and about His Word while she lived here with us. Every day as we worked, our conversations were about these things. It was almost like going to church to worship Him, just coming over here and being with those two! I had gone back to the Boarding House by then as well as to my job at the Emporium because our days with the Underground Railroad were over, thankfully. But every chance I could squeeze out, I came here to be with them. Miss Ida taught her to read as well, using the Bible she had given her when she was here. Although she never mastered the art of writing her name, due to the injury to her hand, she often said that at least she could read it when she saw it written. And that made all the difference for her. One thing Bessie kept asking that was the hardest for Miss Ida to answer was one that has bothered me all my life. Perhaps you will have a good answer to it."

"What was the question?" asked Mandy.

"She wanted to know where God was, what He was doing when she was suffering so as a slave."

"Yes, that is a tough one. What was Aunt Ida's answer?"

"That He was in the same place He was the day His only Son was being tortured and killed on the Cross. In Heaven, sovereign over the universe, extending His mercy and grace to all who would believe, despite the pain and suffering. That is where He was and still is today."

Mandy laughed out loud. Then stopped to explain her response in the face of such a serious statement about life.

"I'm sorry, I'm not laughing at you or at my aunt. I'm laughing because that is precisely the same question I asked repeatedly after I was captured and cut off from my aunt and all semblance of life as a white woman, facing a bleak future without joy or hope. I simply couldn't believe God could be in such a place as that, could have planned for me to be there, could have any purpose whatsoever in allowing me to be dragged there and kept against my will. But He did!"

"Really? I have a great deal to learn from you, I can see that already. Because I'm asking that same question right now, seeing how Miss Ida suffered when she has done such great good in this town and for its people. Her heart was broken and God healed it, gave her new purpose, a reason to live. But how He could leave her broken and sick and dying in such pain—I have to tell you that I have struggled mightily with this."

"Of course you have. You had to watch a beloved friend, as Aunt Ida obviously has been to you for such a long time, as she slowly ended her life here on earth. And to see it happen with such a loss of dignity and strength as it took place. It must have, indeed, been very difficult for you personally. I'm eternally grateful God gave me the opportunity to come to see her before He took her Home, and to meet you and learn much that I had no way to know otherwise. But it's hard for me to understand, too, Nan. I don't have all the answers, by any stretch of the imagination. I have a few because of how God has led me faithfully through a great deal. However, I still have more to ask of Him. This is not a really good response for the question. But it's the only one He has ever given me that makes any sense at all."

Mandy got quiet for a moment, then continued.

"This I do know: He is a loving God, not a spiteful One. He could never sit by and watch one of His creations suffer without having a reason behind it. Even if we humans cannot possibly see it. But the good thing is, we can rest assured that He is in control and knows what He is doing. His timing is perfect, as is His Will. We must accept that and trust Him. Simple as that. Easy to say, not as easy to live! He had a reason for allowing Christ to die on the Cross and I'm very grateful He did! Even the Lord Himself couldn't see the why behind it all, as we learn about Him in the Garden the night He was betrayed. But He obeyed, even though He could have prevented it. He had the power and authority to, but He remained committed to His Father even unto death. That one fact has made all the difference in the world to many ever since that fateful time. And you know what, Him being in Heaven is exactly where we *want* him to be, with the promise on His lips that someday He will wipe away our tears and make all things right again. So, instead of railing against injustice and unfairness, I've tried to learn how to relax and let Him be God. I'm not very good at that sometimes, but I do try!"

"Very well said, my friend. My, what a serious discussion this all turned into!" said Nan as she yawned. "I think I would like to have a nap in my room for a while. See you both later," she called as she closed the door behind her.

"Mama, I think Miss Nan's idea is a perfect one. Do you mind if I sleep for a bit?"

"Not at all. I think I will go out to the front porch, though, so I won't disturb you. I want to read in my Bible for a little bit. If you need me, you know where I will be."

Nestled in the rocker, Mandy randomly leafed through the Scriptures and finally closed the book to speak directly to the Lord.

I have decided it is time to share the truth of my heritage with Nan. She deserves to know and keeping her in the dark about it any longer would be deceitful and might potentially harm our friendship. Is the peace I'm feeling because You agree with that? My promise to keep this a secret bothers me a little but I believe Ken-ai-te and Jacob would both readily agree that Nan is trustworthy, if they knew her as I do. Give me the right words and prepare her heart to hear what I have to say. Open the door for an opportunity for me to talk to her soon. I don't want to lose the only friend I have here in Trenton, but somehow, after hearing today about Bessie, I don't think I will!

CHAPTER TWENTY-EIGHT

"The secret things belong unto the LORD our God: but those things which are revealed belong unto us and to our children for ever..." Deuteronomy 29:29

April 28, 1867

"Ah, there you are, Amanda!" exclaimed Nan a few minutes later as she came out to the porch. "Mrs. Wilson said she thought you were here and she was right. I wasn't able to sleep very long, as it turns out, but I was wondering if you might like to go for a stroll around the park before dinner?"

"That would be perfect," replied Mandy. "Lily is taking a nap but I couldn't sleep, either. Let me go put my Bible inside and I'll be right with you. Even though we were in church this morning, I feel I have been cooped up so much today and am in need of a touch of Mother Nature for a while on this gorgeous afternoon!" *God, is this the opportunity already? Show me if it is, or keep my tongue quiet if not!*

A short time later Nan suggested they sit on a park bench for a while to enjoy watching the ducks swim on the pond. *Here is the perfect chance! Lord, help me!*

"Nan, I am grateful we had this time together as I have something to talk to you about that I cannot risk anyone overhearing." She glanced around briefly but saw that, in spite of the glorious weather, few were out today, at least in this part of the immense park. God had opened the door, now it was up to her to step through it!

"What's on your mind, Amanda?"

"I have been keeping a secret from you and it's time you knew about it. There is good reason I haven't said anything up to now, but you deserve to know the truth. Besides, I just have to share it with you, or I'll go mad!"

"Oh, my! Must be pretty important. By all means, I don't want you to go mad! Talk away, I'm listening."

"When I was captured by the Kiowa warrior long ago, he didn't let me go nor did I escape. After some time with his people, I realized I had nothing to go back to. No white culture would accept me, since I had been with the Kiowa for that long. Therefore, what was the point of risking my life in trying to escape? Besides, eventually, I, well, I fell in love with him, my captor, and miraculously, he did with me."

"Fell in love?" Nan was wide-eyed.

"Yes, I did. And I, um, I married him."

"Your husband is a Kiowa?"

"Yes, he is, full blood, and now the chief of our village. And we have three children. Together. Are you shocked?"

"No, not at all, not after hearing all this time about his kindness and gentle spirit as well as his faith in Christ. Just a little surprised is all. But how exciting for you! So, do you live, like in a tipi?"

"Yes, we do, all five of us."

"I take it that means the children are half Kiowa and half white, right? Lily's skin is as light as yours is. What about your boys?"

"Their skin is darker, like their father's. Because you see, the truth is, I'm half Kiowa myself."

"You are? Are you joking with me?"

"Are you upset at that thought?"

"Not at all! Quite charmed, actually!" Then she frowned.

"What is the problem? You have quite a scowl on your face."

"I don't think Miss Ida knew of your Kiowa heritage, did she?"

"No, she did not. I did not know, in fact, until I had been with the Kiowa for several months, as my husband and I were preparing for our wedding. We got word the US Army soldiers were searching the region for white captives of the various Indian tribes so they could return them to their families. I didn't want to go back by that point! After all those months of praying for rescue, I realized I wanted to stay with my beloved and with the people who had accepted me despite my being white. Yet, I felt compelled to follow the destiny God had ordained for me, thus how could I stay? I was, after all, born white. Not Kiowa."

"What happened? I mean, what changed your mind?"

"My adopted mother, Sleeping Bird, revealed to me that she had a journal written by my father. In it, I learned of my Kiowa mother."

"How on earth did your father's journal end up in a Kiowa village in the middle of nowhere, the exact spot where this warrior took you to live?"

"That, my dear Nan, is a pure miracle from God! No other explanation. Not a coincidence, I don't believe in those. But God-planned, all along! It's a long story and I'll tell you about it some other time, it's really quite interesting. In the journal, my father confessed that he had lied to me all my life about my heritage but now felt God was urging him to tell me the truth. Sadly, he was killed before he could come home and do that. And then I was taken. My husband had no idea what was in the journal, either, because he couldn't read English. Sleeping Bird was an elderly white woman, captured as a young child, but who had gone on to have a good life as a Kiowa as she grew up. She knew how to read English, knew the secret of the journal, and felt if I knew the truth, God would release me from that conflict I was feeling about whether to go back or stay. No one was left to go home to, except of course Aunt Ida. I knew how she felt about the red men. There was no way I would have even tried to explain all this to her. It was almost more than my own mind could handle, much less someone who hated Indians. The thought of telling her that her beloved brother married a Kiowa and had a child with her intimidated me to the point of silence."

"So, you read this journal, chose to stay, and married the warrior, right?"

"Yes, I did. By finding out I was half Kiowa, I felt that 'half of me' could easily stay and be his wife without feeling any conflict whatsoever. Plus, that half was much stronger after months of living as a Kiowa. Therefore, my children are in reality three-fourths Kiowa and only one-fourth white. Lily takes after me in skin color but the boys are darker, like their father, as I said."

"What is your husband's name, if I may ask?"

"His name is Ken-ai-te, and as I said, he is now the chief in our village. It falls to him how he will continue to feed our people, which is one reason this whole adventure carries such great meaning for us."

"What a unique name! With a story no less unique! Oh, my goodness, that's so exciting! Here, I've never even *met* an Indian before, and suddenly find out I'm best friends with one! Everything makes much more sense now. Like why you have chosen to come here as a white woman instead of as, well, yourself."

As she spoke her eyes dropped to Mandy's left hand and the gold band on her finger.

"Ah, yes, that," said Mandy. "I needed it to convince everyone I'm married."

"Do Kiowa women not wear a wedding ring?"

"No, they do not. Nor do they have wedding ceremonies like we do, that is, as is the white custom. Ken-ai-te and I did have one long ago because I insisted on it. We combined Kiowa traditions with white ones, to mark the beginning of our marriage. Prior to that of course, we had been living together in his tipi, but not as man and wife. In fact, he never touched me before we were married—another miracle from God. He certainly had the right under Kiowa tradition but God was already working on his heart by then. And he refused to take that privilege, even though he didn't understand why until much later. At any rate, I felt I needed something more than a nod of his head to celebrate that special time!"

"I quite agree. You two have such a beautiful love story! How special the ceremony to seal that love between you must have been."

"Eventually, it was. Our first attempt was interrupted by a brutal attack from our worst enemy. But that is a tale for another time! Point is, we did have the ceremony later. But no ring. However, I am every bit as married as any white woman!"

"Yes, I'm sure you are. The more I hear, the better I understand why you chose the lie or ruse or whatever you want to call it."

"I never believed Aunt Ida would want to have anything to do with me if she found out the truth. When she wrote and asked me to come, I refused. I was *terrified!* But my husband and Jacob insisted—"

"Wait a minute," Nan interrupted. "Who is this Jacob?"

"Oh, Jacob Murphy is our best friend and runs the nearby Trading Post. A real frontiersman, who loves living among the Kiowa out there in the territory. Anyway, Jacob is the one who made our trip here possible. Again, a long story that I will tell you more about later, but he and my husband brought Lily and me to Fort Smith where we could catch a train to come east to Trenton. What I was saying is they insisted that I consider how this vast fortune Aunt Ida said was mine could change the course of our people's lives for the better. We are starving out there, Nan. Every day, more children and elders die, because of a lack of sufficient food. Even my own boys are at risk. I'm scared to death they may have already died, in fact!"

"Oh, Amanda, how awful for you and for the Kiowa people! No wonder you need that money so badly. I hope you realize now, however, that you could have come as a Kiowa and your aunt still would have left everything to you. You do know that, right?"

"To my everlasting shame, I do now. If only I had stepped out in faith and come without worrying about this, things would have been much simpler. I would have the money by now and have been back home to save more of the children."

"Oh, but you are forgetting about Alex! *He* is the problem, you know, not your lie. If he is fighting this viciously to stop you as a white woman, can you imagine how much worse it would be for you if he knew the truth? Whatever happens, Amanda, you must *never* breathe a word of this to anyone else but me. I'm flattered and humbled you told me, and I would die before I let a soul know about it. But if Alex finds out, things will be incredibly difficult for you to prove your case. If Miss Ida were still alive, she would ignore all the objections, but she isn't. Believe me, they are real problems in the little minds and hearts of some folks hereabout. Too many have lost loved ones in Indian attacks, and the hatred, in case you haven't noticed that fact, is real and cruel. I honestly think many have more sympathies for the Negroes because of the runaway slave problem, than they do for the Indians out on the frontier. It's terribly unfair but true."

"Yes, I know you are right about having to hide this from Alex. I shudder to think what he would do to my reputation if he knew."

"It would be in tatters before sundown, and the fortune would go to him. And both of us would be without dreams."

"Oh, that's right, your dream coming true depends on mine!"

"It certainly does, and if someone else gets the fortune I would be sad but if Alex gets his hands on it, I would be devastated. And expect Miss Ida to haunt my dreams for every night to come!"

"Do you honestly think she would be fine with the truth about my heritage, if I had been able to tell her?"

"I'm positive she would have. I have already related to you more than one conversation she and I had on this subject, about how sad she was she couldn't tell you how God changed her. But don't beat up on yourself about it. You did what you felt was best at the time. What about your mother? Is she still living? Or is the part about her dying giving birth to you true?"

"She is not still alive, I'm sad to say, but she did not die in childbirth. From what Papa wrote, he said right after I was born, she needed to go take care of her folks who had become ill with a terrible fever, and they both agreed it was too dangerous to take a newborn into that. So, he stayed behind with me and she left. Something must have happened to her, Papa said, because she never came back. And when he began searching for her, there was no trace anywhere. The Kiowa back then would move their camps often, following the buffalo as they roamed across the prairie. Her parents' village was gone when he got there, with no way to know where they had ended up. Finally, he gave up looking, as he knew that she would never willingly abandon her new-born daughter and husband. With great reluctance he accepted the fact that she most likely had died, perhaps from the same fever her parents had."

"What a sad tale! I'm so sorry about your mother, Amanda. And you said your father died as well. How did that happen?"

"He was killed by a Comanche war party, on his way back to the mission. One of the warriors stole his coat as a trophy and later my husband ended up killing this man in a brief battle. The coat became his trophy at that point. Unknown to him, the journal was inside the pocket of it, and Sleeping Bird found it when he brought the coat back to the tipi. Now you know how that journal ended up with my husband. Crazy the way God works, isn't it?"

"It sure is! And that was all before you were captured, right?"

"Yes, it was. Isn't it amazing how God works things out for our good, often in rather creative ways, but always in good ones?"

"Truly, it is. I'm speechless!"

"Well, I'm vastly relieved to have the secrecy gone and the devil is defeated by that fact. Do you know, I had a horrible nightmare last night, that Alex and I were *married?* That he had killed my husband and stolen me for my fortune. In addition, I thought he was now going to kill me, too!"

"Oh, my! What did you have for dinner last night?"

"Same thing you did, fried fish! We live at the same Boarding House, remember?" And they both laughed. "I just don't want to ever again have that nightmare. When I awakened, I felt strongly that the shroud of lies and secrecy that I've been living with finally had begun stealing my sleep. And that is not to mention eroding my confidence in Matthew's ability to bring this case to a good and swift conclusion. God wanted me to tell you about it, not only so I would have someone to talk to when needed, but also to take away one of the devil's weapons against me. The relief I feel is enormous!"

"You cannot talk about this, Amanda, not to me, not to Lily, not to anyone, do you hear? If Alex or his cronies ever got wind of it by accident, all would be lost!"

"Yes, you are right about that. But at least now when I say something mysterious, you will know why. Instead of wondering what I'm hiding."

Nan blushed slightly.

"See, what did I say? You were wondering, now admit it!"

"Well, I have to say that at times I did have a couple of questions. But no more."

Nan grew quiet and Mandy noticed right off because where she had been jubilant and almost giddy a few moments ago, now she was almost sad.

"Nan, what is wrong? I sense something is amiss here but have no idea what."

"Well, I also have a secret to tell you. I've been praying about it for some time but wasn't sure if I should confide in you or not. Since you have done so in me, I feel the same trust in you and agree totally with your conclusion that when we hide behind lies and deception, our enemy uses it against us in multiple ways to rob us of our peace and joy. The Bible tells us that the truth sets us free, right?"

"Yes, it does, in many places and in many ways. Now it's my turn to listen and yours to talk!"

"Maybe it's because of retelling you and Lily the stories behind the Underground Railroad days and our participation in it, as well as how we met Bessie through it, but something has left me deeply troubled. As you said you were, I need to tell someone about it, even though nothing can be done about it now."

"My goodness, another mystery! Do go on."

"Remember how I told you about Bessie disappearing a short time back?" Mandy nodded and she continued. "She left a note saying she had decided to move on west, where many of the former slaves were finding more acceptance than here in the East. But in all the time we had known her, never once did she mention doing this. In fact, she hated living in Canada, where she escaped to after leaving our home, and said she would never leave Wellington Oaks again as long as she lived. The whole time, she seemed very content and happy living here with us. So right off, I was suspicious about this sudden departure of hers for the West. Plus, she had been beaten one time by her master for stealing a piece of bread. Out of spite he smashed her right hand with the butt of his rifle. She wanted very much to learn to write her name but no matter how hard she worked at it, she couldn't make her fingers cooperate. It was necessary for her to use her left hand in learning to write but she could barely scrawl the letters. The note was written by someone who could hold a quill, Amanda, not by Bessie!"

"Oh my! No wonder you were suspicious."

"Yes, I suspected it was Alex who wrote that note, from the way he said he found it on his desk, instead of on Miss Ida's, to whom it was addressed. The whole thing didn't make sense. A few days later I found out that my suspicions were, in fact, true."

"Really? Why did Alex write a fake note? What happened to Bessie?"

Nan cleared her throat and looked down at her fingers in her lap, where she wrung a handkerchief, over and over, obviously out of nervousness.

What on earth is going on with you, Nan? This is not like you at all!

"I'm getting to that. One day, about a week later, I was making an apple pie and needed some filling from the cellar. Alex was gone so I thought I could run downstairs to retrieve a jar without him knowing about it, since I couldn't very well wait to finish the pie until he came home and could fetch it himself. He had threatened me within an inch of my life if I ever went down there. Usually he would go get whatever I needed from the shelves if I nagged him long enough. But this was different, I told myself. He would never know."

"And let me guess, he came home and caught you down there."

"Yes, unfortunately. I had gotten the jar and was started back to the steps when I spotted something out of the corner of my eye, back in the shadows under the staircase. It was only a flash of red but it seemed oddly familiar somehow. I put the lantern down and stooped to pick it up. When I jerked it, it came loose—but with a bunch of dark curls, too!"

"Oh no! Not—"

"Yes, Bessie." The tears dripped down her cheeks. "It was the red bandana that she always wore, and I realized with a sickening lurch that her body was underneath it. I was so preoccupied with my horror of finding this that I failed to hear Alex creeping down the staircase, right above my head! Until he got to the last step and demanded to know what I was doing."

"Oh, my heart would have stopped at that point if that had been me!"

"I think mine did! I gasped and jumped back, still clutching the piece of red fabric with the hair attached to it. All I could think to do was wave it in his face. Over and over, I asked him, 'What is this?' He stood there with a smirk on his face and calmly asked me what I thought it was.

"I cried out, 'This is Bessie's headscarf, and the rest of her is lying in that shallow grave over there!' You know what he did? He laughed! *Laughed*. My dear sister in Christ, dumped in a grave in the floor of the cellar without even a cloth over her body or a funeral to mark her passing! I was horrified, to say the least, but he thought the whole thing was funny. That she was dead and that my fury, my outrage was *funny!*"

"Did he admit to killing her? But why? What about the fake note?"

"I asked him that, and he said she got to snooping down there. She found 'something that wasn't for her to know about' he said. And he caught her. She was going to tell his grandmother, but he couldn't have that. He, he, he choked her to death!"

"Oh, no! What did she find that was so horrible Aunt Ida couldn't be told?"

"He had some large barrels of whiskey hidden he apparently did not pay tax on and was trying to keep them out of sight. It would have been an enormous amount he owed on that much of it, plus the penalties, including a possible prison sentence for evading the tax. But was that worth killing the gentlest soul God ever created on earth? *No!*"

Nan collapsed into Mandy's arms, weeping.

"I, I simply cannot, can, can *not* understand the depths of that man's depravity!" she blubbered. "How can he murder a woman so easily because she stumbled upon a secret? That monster has no conscience at all! He never even asked her to keep it to herself. They never liked each other, but out of respect for Miss Ida, Bessie kept her objections and suspicions about Alex to herself. But if she wasn't around, Bessie could lay into him good! Oooh, she could have whipped a horse with that tongue of hers when she got started. She used to tell me that was her ole enemy at work, because since she found Jesus, it was much tamer than before. I would hate to have seen it back then! But honestly, as a rule, she was soft-spoken and gentle to everyone else, except for Alex. I guess he knew his goose was cooked when she said she was going straight to Miss Ida. Her orders to him to never bring spirits into any part of the house except his study had obviously been violated and she would have been furious! I can see where he felt he had no choice but to silence her. But to end her life by strangling her like he did, over such a relatively petty thing, it makes me sick to my stomach!"

"How could he make up that lie, casually pretending she had left of her own free will, without any real explanation at all or even a goodbye? That must have broken my aunt's heart for sure."

"Yes, to say the least. It infuriated me yet again, to think Alex was the source of even more hurt for this lady whom I loved and admired so much."

"But why didn't you report the murder to the authorities?"

"You forget, there are no real 'authorities' as you put it, to report it to. And who would have cared if a former slave died? Not too many around here. They lost too many of their menfolk in that war, to care much about what happened to the ones they blamed for their loss. So what if a slave dies or disappears or is hurt? What would they have done to Alex, if I *had* reported it to someone?"

Mandy sat in stony silence, in shock at this last question. She was right, they would never have taken Nan's word over Alex's! And if they had, what would Alex have faced for Bessie's death? Maybe a slap on the wrist? But no formal charges, no prison time, no hangman's noose. The reality was sickening.

"The truth is, Amanda, I cannot lie to you. I was terrified of him. He had intimidated me many times, until I had taken to avoiding his presence whenever I could in order to keep the peace and keep my heart rate down. Now I was face to face with the evidence of exactly how ruthless he could be, and I was scared. Any anger quickly disappeared, eaten up in the fog of the fear I had looking him in the eye. All I wanted right then was to get safely upstairs and out of that house! However, I knew I could not turn

Miss Ida over to him! I had to stay to protect her. But he knew that. So, he took it one step further."

"What? What do you mean?"

"He told me if I said one word to anyone about Bessie, he would kill Miss Ida! He would *kill* her! I couldn't be responsible for her death, too! I felt in a small way it was my fault that Bessie had died, because I knew in my heart how horrible he was and failed to speak up to get him out of the house. He not only threatened me, but he also threatened your aunt. I realized with a shock that I couldn't tell *anyone* about this. Ever. But now I see how wrong I was about holding this back. And especially in not telling you sooner."

"You know what just occurred to me? That cellar is where Bessie was reborn into new life with Christ, right?"

"Yes, it is."

"Well, it is also where she got to meet her Maker. So while she was not ready to leave yet and it was grossly unfair for her life to end the way it did, especially after all she had been through, it is somehow fitting that she took both these steps in the same place. I am going to focus on that more than on the sadness of her death."

"That's a great point, Amanda. Thank you for sharing that insight. I had never thought about it that way. It does ease the pain a bit."

"It seems we both had deep secrets to confess today. Where does this leave us, then? How do we get justice for Bessie? Maybe Alex did cause Aunt Ida's death in some way, or at least contribute to weakening her so she had nothing to fight with. How can we find out? This man is brutal and cunning with, as you said, absolutely no conscience whatsoever!"

"The plain truth is, we can do nothing about him. Not one thing."

"To the contrary, we need to devise a scheme to bring about God's vengeance for this evil man. The hardest part will be to wait for His timing to enact it. What we cannot do, God *can!* Be praying, Nan, *hard*. We must see him brought down, however we can. Before anyone else gets hurt!"

CHAPTER TWENTY-NINE

"In the fear of the LORD is strong confidence: and his children shall have a place of refuge." Proverbs 14:26

April 29, 1867

"Amanda," whispered Nan as she grabbed her friend's arm in the hallway outside her room, "I know I told you that we were never to speak of this again, even between us. But I have a ton of questions I'm dying to ask you! About you-know-what." Although a serious topic, Mandy had to hold in her laughter at the way she was acting!

"You know I'm happy to answer them but do understand the reason for great caution. Now that most folks are in bed, this would be a good time for me to come to your room and we can talk more freely. Lily has already turned in but is not yet asleep and is, of course, reading."

"What else?" And they laughed.

A few minutes later, they settled in Nan's sitting room, adjoining her bed chamber.

"This is the first time I've seen your room, Nan. This is very nice! You have far more room than we have."

"But of course, only one bed. Since you required two of those, that room was the only one Mrs. Wilson had available."

"Now, what questions are you dying to ask me?"

"Well, for one thing, what is your real name? Is it Amanda? Or do you have a Kiowa name?"

"My Kiowa name is Prayer Woman. My—"

"I love that! Prayer Woman, yes, it suits you perfectly."

"My English name is Mandy. I never cared much for Amanda, although Aunt Ida insisted on using it at all times when I was growing up.

You probably noticed that is what she called me when she first greeted me. When I wrote to Aunt Ida, I made up a 'white sounding name' for my husband so as not to offend her when she read the letter. I couldn't very well tell her his name was Ken-ai-te, now could I?"

"Absolutely not!"

"Thus, he became Ken Alton, as that was as close as I could come to his name. Therefore, I was Mrs. Ken Alton, or Amanda."

"Ahh, that explains quite a bit, then. So, tell me what Ken-ai-te is really like, and how it is to live with a Kiowa warrior in his tipi. Oh, do I sound insufferable? I don't mean to at all, certainly didn't mean to insult you or him. I'm just dying of curiosity. When can I come visit? Do you have beds or what in this tipi? I have *so* many questions!"

Mandy laughed. "Yes, I can see that you do. Well, we don't have beds or sheets or any of those kinds of modern inventions. We live very simply, sleep on buffalo rugs which, once you get used to the smell and feel of one, they are really very comfortable, also incredibly warm in the winter! Our meals we cook over an open fire in a pot of sorts made from the stomach of a buffalo."

Nan turned up her nose at this and Mandy laughed. "Yes, it all takes some getting used to, but believe me, I think you will find it interesting! A few of our delicacies you might want to skip on your first meal there but later you should get used to them—perhaps even grow to love them, as I do. Most likely when you come, you will stay at Jacob's home. Before you raise any eyebrows on this, hear me out. His is the only place in our tiny settlement with enough room for you! He lives in the back of the Trading Post that he runs with his daughter Hannah, not a big home but quite comfortable. He drives his wagon to the nearest fort for most of his supplies about once a month or so, since we have no stagecoaches or freight lines nearby. As a rule he brings back the latest news for us and sometimes even a newspaper or two for all of us to pour over, about the world outside the territory. While he is gone, Hannah runs the store for him. Incidentally, she has become quite an excellent cook! She hasn't been there for long, having gone to school back East. That is a story for another time, however! Of course, you could always stay in the tipi with us but it would be a bit crowded, I'm afraid, without any privacy whatsoever."

"Sounds absolutely charming to me. Quite an adventure, I'd say!"

"It is a whole other world, all right. One that I love, as I said, and genuinely hope you will as well. It is my prayer you can fall in love with the people and the land as much as I have done. But it didn't happen to me overnight. It took some time to get used to a new culture, I have to admit. When you come, I would suggest you plan on staying a while, to justify the long journey out there, as well as giving the place and way of life a chance to grow on you."

"You know, I have another question, too, but I am not sure how to ask this one. I know you said that you came with the lie because you didn't want to risk offending or upsetting your aunt. But there must be something more to this story than merely protecting her from being hurt."

"One reason I never tried to contact my aunt, Nan, once I was married and settled into my Kiowa way of life, is that I honestly didn't believe she would ever have accepted me as anything other than white. I've already told you about that, but it bears repeating. In fact, I dare say, she would not even have responded to my letters, had I had a way to send them. In my head, I wrote a dozen or more of them. But of course never even bothered to write them down. What was the point?"

"Perhaps at one time that was true of Miss Ida, but I have already told you several times, and indeed, she told you herself: she changed! So dramatically, at times I wondered that she was the same woman I had loved and cared for all those years. But of course, she was. God transformed her heart, in fact, as she took incredible steps forward in that growth during the war years. I had worried about her for some time, thinking that surely some day she would see the wisdom of God's heart as she shared His Word with me repeatedly. You see, she knew the words but had missed the point. Christ did die for *all* men. What a joy it was to see this fully blossom in her once she embraced the truth of that simple sentence."

"I am still in awe myself of how He does that, Nan! I have seen it many times back home, as I have shared with folks about His love. I wrestled with this for such a long time about Aunt Ida before my husband gently pointed out that perhaps the long years since I had seen her had brought about changes in her of which I was unaware. He was right! After that soaked in, I knew I had to find some way to get a letter to her, to at least let her know I was alive—but even more, that I was happy. I never dared to dream I might actually see her again. I'm very grateful I got here in time.

However, I do regret having waited this long to come see her, and under these circumstances."

"I take it she was truly not happy when you and your father left for Indian Territory?"

"Not at all! It was bad enough that Papa insisted on going back. But to take me with him? She was mortified at the thought. And told him so. Repeatedly. But he didn't care. God had commanded him to go, that's all there was to it. I mean, I had always known she didn't like the topic of Indians but had no idea it was so deep-seated until that time. This had been my dream, too, ever since I could remember, to someday see the land my parents were deeply passionate about. Of course, I had no idea that my mother was Kiowa! But to hear Papa's stories about the place captured my heart completely long before I ever set eyes on the prairie where they lived and worked together."

"And where she died. It's all so romantic, except the part that you lost a mother you never knew, not to mention your father lost his beloved wife. Life is harsh at times, isn't it?"

"Yes, it can be. Not only on the frontier, everywhere."

"You have told me so much about the territory, I feel as though I know it already. But I am quite certain I have much to learn about it. Seeing it for myself is the best way to do that. I cannot wait for this court case to be settled. That way, I can get my money and finally afford to go out there to visit once you are back home. I'm excited about this dream of mine finally coming true! Can you tell?"

Mandy laughed and nodded. "You know, I never really answered your question completely, the one about how I knew the way Aunt Ida felt about Indians. It was a conversation I overheard between her and my father once when I was maybe about nine. I was supposed to be asleep, but I heard them arguing. Their angry words frightened me so I got up to see what was wrong, opening the door a crack. Something told my heart not to go any further. Standing quietly there, I peeked in at the two of them as they disagreed about this very thing."

March 24, 1844
Trenton, Ohio

"I just don't understand why you are being this unpleasant about the idea of my going back to Indian Territory someday, Ida. I know the dangers. But God keeps tugging on my heart and I need to listen to Him."

"My point is, you can spread the Gospel even better here in Trenton! At least these people can hear it and respond and believe in Christ. Those savages out there cannot."

"What do you mean, they cannot believe in Christ? I'm shocked that you would say something like that. And to me, of all people, knowing how I feel about them."

"It's because of that fact that I dare say it out loud. I mean, someone has to talk sense into you! They are like animals, dear brother. They cannot believe in the Gospel or reject it, either one. I'm surprised that you don't see that clearly spelled out in the Holy Scriptures."

"What on earth are you saying? That the Bible teaches only whites can be saved and go to Heaven? Are you serious?"

"Of course I'm serious! The Messiah came to white people and thus only whites can be saved. It is a concept which is very easy to understand. Those without souls do not have a chance, thus preaching to them is a waste of time. Especially when there are countless multitudes who do have a chance and who need a Savior so badly. Why not spend your time trying to reach them instead? I simply do not understand you at all, dear brother."

"I could say the same about you, sister. I'm truly floored that you would honestly say that out loud to me, a preacher of the Gospel. Do you honestly believe that Jesus was white? I know some pictures we have of Him in Bibles portray Him that way, but He was from the part of the world where their skin is much darker than ours. And don't forget, He was a Jew as well. They are not black there but certainly are not white, either. When Jesus said He came to bring salvation to all men, he meant exactly that, no matter the race or color of skin. What an insult to our Lord, to contradict one of the central themes of His ministry! I truly thought you knew better. I mean, you led me to Christ when I was a young boy and have nurtured my faith ever since. You are the reason I felt so readily the call to evangelize others, in fact. Without your faithfulness to me, I shudder to think where I would be. Dead, I am certain. But to say such a ridiculous thing to my face is deeply hurtful."

Very quietly she said, "You don't remember, do you, Josiah? The massacre, I mean?"

"No, Ida, I do not. You have briefly told me a couple of times about it but you rarely ever speak of its gruesome details. I realize that while I was too young to know what was about to happen to our family, you were fully aware of the horrors coming any moment."

"Yes, I was. I huddled with you there in that hidey hole where Mama shoved us both in the last few seconds before they burst through the front door. And I heard it all. The screams, the pleas for mercy, the—the…" She couldn't finish.

"Oh, Ida, please, don't torture yourself like that. It must have been a ghastly nightmare, feeling so helpless as you did, terrified that at any moment they would find the trapdoor in the floor to discover us hiding there."

"Mama had warned me to get you out through the escape tunnel and I did, just as they set fire to the cabin, finishing their horrible task. When we came out the other end, we ran and ran until both of us dropped from exhaustion. Do you remember that first night?"

"No, I'm sorry, Ida, I don't remember it, either. All I recall is Mama kissing me goodbye, telling me to be a good boy, to love Jesus, and obey my older sister. I recall feeling terrified, but not really why. After that, it is all a blank until we got off the stagecoach here in Trenton. How on earth you managed those long months of caring for me by yourself out in the wilderness without even a roof over our heads is beyond me. You told me that some neighbors finally took us in and helped you figure out where we could go that was safer than out there on the frontier. I'm grateful that you chose Trenton."

"Well, there wasn't much here back then but it was fortified, and folks assured me that they rarely experienced Indian attacks here. That was good enough for me. I didn't want to ever see another red man as long as I lived!"

"I can't blame you. How difficult it must have been, then, to see your brother go off to Indian Territory, of all places! That must have been a deep disappointment to you."

"Yes, it was, frankly. I felt I had been betrayed for a time. But I dutifully prayed for your protection while you were gone. And never took a deep breath until you returned home to me with sweet baby Amanda. How sad that she never knew her mother, either."

Josiah stared at the floor and finally cleared his throat, glancing back up at his sister.

"Yes, it was such a tragedy. But when you agreed to take us in and help me rear Amanda, I knew I had done the right thing in coming back here. I thought—"

"You thought what?"

"Never mind, not even sure what I was going to say. But back to the statement you made earlier, about the red men not being capable of salvation spiritually. I really take issue with that, Ida. In Romans, Chapter 10, Paul asks how people will know to call on Christ for salvation if no one goes to tell them. That is precisely what He has called me to do with the Kiowa. This is the foundation stone of my calling to Indian Territory, and I am going back one of these days. However, I do hope you will reread the Scriptures and earnestly seek God's heart in this matter."

Ida pursed her lips as she did when determined to have her way. If bitterness had a face, hers was it! "It absolutely won't do any good to pray for my enlightenment for a position that goes against Scripture. You are the one who needs to pray for a new heart in this."

"Never! Ida, I cannot *believe* you would say such a thing to me. And keep saying it! I just told you the verse in which He spoke. Would you deny that very thing which you have requested of me, to re-examine the truths in the Bible?" Then he closed his eyes and took a deep breath. "I apologize, Ida. I should never have said that to you. It is obvious we need to keep our opinions on this to ourselves. I love you, no matter what."

"Even when you are wrong?"

"Ida, I believe it is time I went to bed. I refuse to prolong this argument any further by responding to that. Good night."

And he stalked away. Ida covered her face with her hands. At first Mandy thought her aunt was weeping. But when she looked up at last, her eyes were dry, her face set, her lips pinched together in a thin line as they always were when she was furious about something.

April 29, 1867

"I never heard them speak another word on this subject. Even when Papa announced God had finally called him back to Indian Territory, he never mentioned this argument. To my knowledge, I don't think either one knew I overheard them because they simply didn't talk about this topic. Papa, however, did address it briefly in one of his journal entries.

"All he said was that he prayed often for his sister to change her mind about those of color not being capable of salvation. For you see, Nan, he based his whole ministry on the truth of that fact, that Christ died for all men regardless of the color of their skin. So, when I contemplated writing to Aunt Ida, I was certain that she would not want to hear about my life as a Kiowa. How did I know that the war would change her mind and help her see that Papa was right?"

"You couldn't have known, Amanda. Don't berate yourself for choosing a lie to protect both yourself and Lily."

"And I was trying to protect Aunt Ida, too, Nan. I didn't want to hurt her." She paused a moment and Nan glanced at her friend. "Well, the truth is, I was also afraid of being hurt myself, I must admit that."

"Certainly you were! No harm in that. How would you have felt if you and Lily arrived on Miss Ida's doorstep, only to be turned away because you are half Kiowa and married to a full blood warrior? I would have done the same as you did, in fact, I think any sane person would. What we cannot have happen, though, is for Alex to get wind of this. He must believe this lie, as must all others in this town. Do you understand that? You cannot let Matthew or anyone else know. That would be disastrous!"

"I know, you are right. As unhappy as I am about living this lie, for now I have no other choice. I want so much to ask Matthew what the truth would do to my chances of winning this case, but I don't dare! What if he would be under a legal obligation at that point to report this fact to the judge? No, it would be a disaster, one I cannot risk. At least my being a woman isn't going to be an obstacle. But a Kiowa woman? I doubt that any judge around here would take kindly to that news."

"Thank you, Amanda, for trusting me with this. We must continue to exercise the greatest of caution about this topic and discuss it only when we are alone like this. Even then, be aware that sometimes walls have ears, too!"

"One of my fears has been that Lily would tell Ginny, thinking in innocence that a child would never betray her. She considers her like a sister, even after this short time. But I have told her repeatedly that she cannot, under any circumstances, reveal to her that she is three quarters Indian! Perhaps you could reinforce that if you can catch her alone sometime, without others around."

"Certainly. Although I doubt she would listen to me, if she doesn't listen to her own mother."

"The truth is, I believe she would listen to you *before* she would listen to me, on any topic! But that is the nature of life when a woman begins to emerge from a child, right?"

"Have the arguments not eased any, then?" asked Nan.

"Not really. I did share with her about your secret. I hope that was okay to tell her."

Nan nodded and Mandy continued.

"I felt she needed to fully understand the danger we are all in from Alex. Words failed me at times as I tried to explain to her how the man could be so bloodthirsty, yet appear so 'normal' at other times. Perhaps her knowing the truth will re-emphasize to her why I urge caution so often, without filling her with constant fear. Only time will tell."

I will pray she will listen to you," said Nan quietly.

"She did not take kindly to the news that there would be no further dinner parties this week, either. I didn't realize how much she looked forward to dressing up and going out in Matthew's buggy. I'm relieved not to be going but guess it really isn't in our best interests to stay home all the time, either. Lily seems genuinely happy about the Community Picnic coming up in a few days, but I grow increasingly nervous about it."

"Why is that?"

"Being with Matthew that day, for one thing. And basically being 'on display' before everyone in town all day long, for another."

"It's usually a great event every year. Just go and enjoy it, don't worry so much!"

"Oh, I did join the sewing circle at church, did I tell you?" Nan shook her head and Mandy continued. "Matthew seemed to feel that would be a good thing. At least it keeps my hands busy! It's easy to lose the skill with a needle and thread if you don't do it all the time. Even in the last couple of weeks, I can see a difference. I hardly know what to say to the ladies but I am trying. Lily went with me one day, too, but was not happy. I told her we won't try that again! She is good as a rule with sewing but is deliberately rejecting anything that I suggest right now."

"I assume she knows that I am aware of your heritage?"

"Yes, she is. That will make things much easier when we are together, not having to dance around those details."

That night as she lay in her bed waiting for sleep, Mandy considered the enormity of what her life had become in the last week or so. Without her beloved husband by her side, she felt half-empty somehow, as though something had been ripped from her body. What would it be like if he died? She imagined the pain would be far greater than anything she had ever experienced thus far.

Please, Lord, don't make me walk down that path! At least not for many more years yet. I have been obedient in all things—well in most things. And I think You would have to agree. But oh, not that horror! Ken-ai-te, where are you when I need you so much? Do you ache with longing for me as I do for you? Or have you already forgotten my touch, our love, our life together?

April 29, 1867
Indian Territory

"Why, Father? Why no word? Is she hurt or sick? Has something happened to Lily and she feels she cannot come home again? I ask these same questions often but You are silent. Oh, Great Spirit, help me understand!"

Ken-ai-te fell on his knees, feeling the crunch of the dry, rough grasses of his beloved prairie under them, and gazed upward into the vast canopy of stars overhead, grateful the darkness hid his tears should anyone see him out here. But a glance over toward the tipis in the distance told him all were asleep, as they should be. Still, he could hear drifting his way on the gentle breeze soft whimpers from some of the babies and younger children whose stomachs, he was certain, rumbled with emptiness even in the depths of the night.

"Do they all have to die, Lord? How can I help them? It is my responsibility, yet there is no more game to be had. No, that is wrong. There is game, there *must* be, but I don't know where. I need your wisdom, Great Spirit. Help me!"

Ken-ai-te covered his head with his hands, bowed his face to the earth, inhaling the rich scent of the red dirt he cherished so much. How could he say he loved dirt? Because of Who made it! His very existence was named after it, *red man*, and now He honored the Creator of the Universe with all his heart as he worshipped Him. His lips moved in silent prayer and then ceased as he continued to listen for some time, hoping to hear His voice in the stillness around him.

"Lord, I feel You urging me to go to Prayer Woman, but how? I don't fear the danger but must think of my boys and my people, along with my beloved and the daughter of my heart. How would I find her in this Trenton place? Long ago I was without her in my life and there was an emptiness I failed to understand. The very first moment I ever saw her she captured my heart, in fact even before I took her body captive. For a while, I was not sure of my feelings for her, until I could no longer deny it was love. You worked slowly on my heart to feel sadness for how I treated her from first day she was mine. As she talked to me of Your forgiveness, I knew I had been wrong. Yes, desire was there but also pride. Both reminded me often of my rights as a Kiowa warrior. But You kept me from doing something I might regret later. I will forever remember the day I asked her to forgive me for all that."

He stopped and listened intently, thinking he heard something from the direction of the camp. *Only another child whimpering from hunger. God, fill him or her with Your love right this moment!* He remained silent, prayerful, waiting—but for what? An answer that never would come?

"Great Spirit of Jesus, even more than the forgiveness Prayer Woman gave to me, was my memory of the day I foolishly told her I had killed her father. The hatred and fear in her eyes cut my heart deeply. Somehow, she was able to forgive me for what she thought I had done. When I confessed my lie to her, the relief that filled her face clutched at my heart. That was all it took for me to recognize that You were the One who had truly captured my heart, Father, through this beautiful creature standing before me. I didn't admit it to her until much later, but I knew. Right then. As if I had been struck by a bolt of lightning. So how can I now live without her? The fact that You are pushing me to go to the far-away place called O-hi-o must mean You do not wish me to live without Prayer Woman."

He spent another moment in silence, and slowly got to his feet.

"You must show me the answer to my cries, Lord, in Your time. Please send Your Prayer Angel to bring comfort and protection wherever my wife is, whatever is happening to her. I can sleep now in confidence, knowing You are watching over her. But please make the return by her to our tipi happen soon!"

CHAPTER THIRTY

"So that we may boldly say, The LORD is my helper, and I will not fear what man shall do unto me." Hebrews 13:6

April 30, 1867

"Nan, I think I will lose my mind if these constant arguments with Lily don't stop soon!"

Mandy had just witnessed one of the worst so far, where her daughter stormed out of their room and slammed the door, hard, jarring a picture off the wall! She ran into the hall to try to catch her, but Lily had already raced down and out the front door. Nan, hearing the commotion, had emerged from her room down the hall and frowned at the anguish her friend was experiencing.

"Perhaps the time has come for you to either limit her exposure to Ginny or stop it altogether. Can you talk to Ginny's mother about this? Maybe she has an idea of the root of this abrupt change in your sweet daughter?"

"I think you may be right about that. I hate to cut off her only friend but that might become necessary if I cannot get control of her. Now she is insisting that she and Ginny are going to be sisters for real, that Ginny's parents have agreed to adopt her!"

"What? And she would stay here instead of returning home with you once this legal mess is finished?"

"Presumably. I cannot imagine a worst scenario for my daughter. Can you believe what would happen if the Cordons got wind of the truth?"

"Oh, my, it is definitely time to talk to Mrs. Cordon, even though she is not exactly a chatty kind of friend. Do you need me to go with you?"

"No, you need to get on to work. I must get to Matthew's office. I assume Lily has gone over to the Cordons. When I finish at the law office, I will go on over to Ginny's home and see if I can talk to Lily at least. How can I talk sense into her when she won't stop screaming at me long enough to hear what I have to say?"

A short time later Mandy stood in front of Matthew's office. *Lord, please let today have some good news for me. I really need it! I don't think I can take one more problem about anything right now!*

When Mandy entered, she noticed that Abigail was decidedly cooler in her attentions to Mandy than usual. *Maybe she is having a bad day herself. God, help her!*

"Hello, Miss Lawson. I am here to see Mr. Grayson as usual. Is he in?"

"No, he has not come into the office yet this morning, Mrs. Alton. Won't you have a seat to wait on him? I am not permitted to knock on his private entrance to the residence so I must also wait for him to officially arrive."

"Yes, I will wait. He said he would be here by 10:00 but perhaps he got delayed somehow."

She pulled out her watch to double check the time, to see if she was early or he was late. He was definitely the one not on time.

A few minutes later Matthew entered the office area from his residence, his face a grim mask. *Uh oh, not a good sign for the answer to my prayer about good news today!*

After greeting Miss Lawson, he said, "Amanda, I'm glad you are here. Come on back to the conference room, please. We have to talk." He stopped at his desk briefly, glanced over the top of it but didn't touch anything, then proceeded into the conference room and Mandy followed.

"Matthew, what is the problem? You seem quite upset this morning." He closed the door behind them and pulled a chair up close to hers.

"Papers. Lots of them. Missing. Out of my files, out of my documents sent to Hamilton, out of my desk, even! Between you and me," he whispered, scooting his chair even closer to hers, "I'm beginning to suspect Abigail is the culprit in all this mess."

"Miss Lawson? She seems so nice! What does she have against me?"

"Nothing, that is the point. Something funny is going on here, and I intend to find out what it is. I planted a paper on top of my desk late last night, in the 'urgent' stack. It will be interesting to see if it got sent out by messenger already. That is the reason I was late, on purpose. If I had been here, she would have waited for me to hand her the stack, but if I'm not here when time for the messenger approaches, she is to take the stack herself and put them in a large envelope, to have ready for him when he arrives. It is missing but I happen to know the messenger has not yet arrived!" He caught himself, as his voice had risen with each sentence until he feared his secretary might hear him through the door.

A little calmer, he continued. "You know why I know he hasn't gotten here? Because I intercepted him down the street and asked that he skip my office this morning! Even if she is guilty of this act, it won't explain all the missing documents and misfiled paperwork, but it's a good start. I trusted her so much, gave her the job to help her get on her feet. And this is how she repays me?"

"Matthew, perhaps there is a simple explanation, one we don't know anything about. Wouldn't it be best to question her before you get upset? And see what she has to say for herself?"

He opened his mouth to make a comment, but instead closed it and remained silent for several moments. Mandy had about decided to ask him another question when he finally spoke up.

"I think the real test will be on Friday at the hearing. Or more properly, what happens between now and then. Will all get filed as needed or will something else go missing? Judge Adams is getting a bit fed up with the incompetence and I don't blame him. But it's not *my* fault, yet my reputation is at stake here! Someone is trying to make it *seem* I am doing all this myself. When I am not. Clearly."

Mandy was unsure how to respond to all that. She did hear the part about the judge getting upset, and that alone was cause to raise her anxiety levels!

"Amanda, you might as well go on home. Nothing is going to happen today. I will keep you advised if I hear more from the judge about anything else that is missing. Right now, I've got to compose a document for the case and get it to the messenger service in a hurry, so Judge Adams will see it before the hearing on Friday."

"Do I have to attend that, Matthew?"

"No, not this one. But the next hearing, which I hope will take place a week from Friday, that one I pray will be our final one and you will be required to come to it. Only a little more than one remaining week, in other words, and you should be on your way home with the money in hand! All this other stuff is simply that, *stuff*. Don't worry yourself too much about it."

"Really? Only another week? And no more social gatherings to worry about?"

"Well, not counting the Community Picnic on Saturday, of course. You will need to put a box in the annual Box Supper auction. It's to pay for a new roof for the school this year."

"Box Supper? What is that?"

"Get Nan to explain it to you, could you? Now, you scoot on out of here and I will see you on Saturday. Remember, I'm picking you and Lily up at 10:00 that morning, and it lasts all day, with fireworks that night. Almost as much fun as the Fourth of July but with a purpose of community interest. Who doesn't want our school children to have a new roof?"

"Well, let me know how the hearing goes. And I will eagerly look forward to the picnic on Saturday. Lily and I both will."

As Mandy emerged from the office into the bright sun, she was blinded for a moment by the light. But out of the haze, before her eyes had time to adjust sufficiently, a fuzzy figure appeared. She froze in place.

"Why don't you give up on this futile attempt to stop me?" Alex snarled. "I can chop you and that brat of yours into pieces, with or without your lawyer, you know! And they will never even find all the parts!"

"Stop! Please, Alex, stop this insanity! Because you truly *are* insane, to say such horrid things to anyone, let alone a woman you are related to!" She had to gulp back the bile in her throat to keep her breakfast down. Would this man ever give up threatening her?

She tried to walk past him but misjudged the distance due to the lingering effects of the sunlight in her eyes, and instead bumped right into him!

"Sorry, Alex, the sun temporarily blinded me."

"Well, I could make it permanent, if you like. If you don't leave town, I just might decide to do that!"

The years of training as a Kiowa woman came through for her in the instant of rage and revulsion she felt inside. Without one whit of evidence on the outside as to how upset she really was with him, she pushed past and kept on walking, head erect, back straight.

Mere words cannot inflict harm, only arrows and bullets can do that! Thank You, Lord, for Your calmness being in control right now. I do honor to my husband, to our people and to the tremendous harm they have been done by the white man over the centuries, that has taught us how to react by not reacting!

She continued walking without ever once looking back. Perhaps Alex was truly stunned at her lack of a response, but she felt sure the Lord had struck him dumb, to match his lack of brains! At least, she hoped so!

It was only later that she wondered why she didn't go back inside the office to alert Matthew to the threat. Perhaps an indicator of how shaken she was by the confrontation with her enemy, but in any case, he didn't follow her as she walked away. Had she told her attorney, she was certain, in the mood he was in at that time, he would have torn into him without restraint! It was a good thing her mind never thought of that action she could have taken.

April 30, 1867
Indian Territory

"Does she know? Does she care? Does she hear my heart calling to her?"

Ken-ai-te's own heart filled with despair this morning as he watched his young sons struggle to gather firewood for the campfire and use the prairie chicken, shot early that morning, to now make a stew for their midday meal. Before long, he knew he would have to restrict their eating to morning and evening only, a drastic yet necessary action he dreaded with all his being. There would be little choice if something did not happen soon for all the Kiowa!

"Women's work!" Red Hawk muttered as he stirred the embers of the fire into flames hot enough for cooking.

And he was right. But what could they do, three men alone like this? They were doing the best they could, but it failed to be enough most of the time, it seemed. Ken-ai-te's prayers were a mix of Kiowa and English these days because he couldn't always think fast enough in his wife's language. He still tried to speak it to his sons but without Prayer Woman here, he fell back into his native tongue more and more. Who knew it would be such a struggle without his beloved wife at his side? They had always taken every stand against their enemies together, as God intended. *But how do we do that now, separated by such a great distance, especially when neither of us knows what the other is facing that day?*

The chief walked around the camp some more, prayers on his heart, but mostly his thoughts were focused on his family, so far away. As he neared the edge of the camp, he sank to his knees once more, but without much hope of any more of an answer than he had been hearing. Yet he longed for one and believed with all his heart he was heard. Why leave him like this, with only silence to meet his pleas for wisdom and help?

"Father, I call to You for understanding of why Prayer Woman has been long gone from us. It was only to be a few days, yet the message has never come for me to bring her home from that fort. Should I go after her? But what of the danger? Jacob says it grows every day. So does my heart's loneliness. I can talk to You about this but could never tell another person, not even my friend Jacob. Although the boys miss their mother deeply, they are too young to understand why she is not here. Especially because even I cannot answer that question!"

He rose and knew he must get the day started with the morning tasks. For a time he busied himself in the tipi but his mind was not on what he was doing. Inside he seethed. The anger grew until finally he snapped at Spotted Rabbit over something trivial. The pain on his son's face cut deep. After apologizing, he excused himself from the boys' presence, telling them he needed to read his Bible to get his heart calmed.

As he settled outside on a log to open this special book, the words seemed to all run together. *My comprehension of this language is still not strong enough, even after all these years, to fully know what many of these words mean. Prayer Woman usually explains them to me. But You can show me, I know. Untangle them and help me!*

God comforted him in the Psalms, until he felt stronger and more confident that He truly was at work, although out of sight right now. Somehow, he must get that across to his boys, to help them see that the growling of their stomachs was not punishment from God but a blessing that they had had food provided in the past. The hope their mother would return soon with money to buy what they could no longer hunt would sustain them until that time.

"Don't let them grow to resent their mother for leaving, Lord. It was not her doing. If anyone is responsible, if anyone is to blame, it is my own fault she is gone. I am helpless to change that now. What have I done?" He choked back his emotion that for a moment almost broke through.

"No! I keep my heart on His words, not on this evil thought that is not from Him. You directed us in this plan and we obeyed. Now, continue to keep my love safe as well as our beloved daughter. Bring them home to us soon. If possible, with money for food. While we wait, give me wisdom to know how to feed my people, especially my boys. They grow thinner by the day. Another baby in the village left us this morning, to lie in Your arms now. Too many empty arms and empty food pots, too many angry and broken hearts. Give me the words to share with my people during this difficult time."

Suddenly a shriek came from the tipi next to theirs, followed by the death wail. Little ones crying broke Ken-ai-te's heart but were sounds that had become all too familiar recently.

"Oh, God, not Blue Water!" Ken-ai-te called out, his heart heavy with grief. "She held that family together when their son died last moon. And now her? I knew she grew weaker all the time but did not realize she was that close to eternity."

He bowed his head to ask for God's comfort to envelop that tipi and surround the hearts there, now grieving the loss of a young wife and mother. He thanked the Lord she knew Christ well. How would he ever tell Prayer Woman about this loss? *She will be devastated to lose her young friend. Prepare her heart for this sorrow, Father. And help me as I go to console these dear ones.*

After emerging from the tipi of the family that had suffered such a deep loss, he spotted his sons with some of their friends at the fire circle.

"Boys, why don't we all take the rest of the day to go hunt, perhaps find a fox or a rabbit? Then maybe we will have something special for our pots tomorrow. Bring your bows and arrows and come with me. God will provide!"

April 30, 1867
Trenton, Ohio

Mandy's turmoil reached its limit late that afternoon. She sat in the Parlor meditating while leafing through her Bible, as she waited on Nan to arrive home from work. *Whenever Nan is around, life seems infinitely much brighter and easier to manage, even more optimistic and hopeful. Have we really only known each other a few short days?* Their bond was strong and with their faith tying them together as well, they truly had found in each other the sister neither had ever had before.

She reflected over the disastrous encounter she had had earlier with Mrs. Cordon, when she went to talk to her about Lily's attitude and insistence on the dream she had decided was a reality. The woman was horrified at the thought of an adoption or even a permanent living arrangement for Lily with their family. In fact, she accused Lily of being the one who instigated any childish schemes the girls had concocted together, because her daughter would certainly never have come up with such an outlandish plan! It was what Mandy had expected to hear, of course, but it was the *manner* in which she said it that had gravely offended her heart. Very condescending and unpleasant about it, as though Lily had become ungrateful for the many tremendous opportunities that a friendship with Ginny—oh, excuse me, *Genevieve*—afforded Lily in this small town. When Mandy tried to laugh it off as a silly prank, saying the girls must have each exaggerated what the other said, Mrs. Cordon became enraged and basically threw her out! So much for being nice. But it left a decidedly bad taste in Mandy's mouth. She fervently hoped that she would not have to encounter this woman again while here in Trenton.

However, the reality was that the girls had made some elaborate plans for the Community Picnic on Saturday, and Mandy hoped those would not be dashed. In spite of her misgivings about the girls continuing their friendship, she knew Lily needed a friend right now, not rejection and further isolation. If her daughter could keep Ginny busy, especially if she kept her away from her mother, perhaps the day would be a good one for all concerned. It seemed that even Ginny herself strained against the many rules and restrictions under which she was forced to live.

Only last night Lily told me about yet another instance where Ginny rebelled against all that and dreamed of the day when she would be old enough to leave the whole thing behind. Lily called it 'tyranny' but while I feel that may be a little strong, after the way her mother treated me earlier, I would tend to agree!

Softly she prayed out loud, "Lord, I feel Mrs. Cordon has pushed her daughter into much of this attitude with her refusal to allow Ginny some freedom in choices and activities, not to mention friends. Sadly, this seems to have rubbed off on Lily. How can I avoid doing the same with my daughter? I want my sweet girl back!"

Understanding a bit better what Ginny lived with softened Mandy's heart toward the child, yet she must keep uppermost in her mind the overall effect this was having on Lily. After several more minutes of sitting in silence in the hopes God would direct her in this situation, she finally came to a conclusion.

"All right, Father, I believe it would be best not to take steps to limit the girls' time together, at least not yet. I will let them have Saturday's festivities as they have planned and hope that freedom will ease some of the tension in my daughter's mind. You have the event fully in Your hands, and I will try my best to stay out of whatever it is You are doing. After that, I will figure out how to address Lily's attitude toward me in the remaining days we are here. Right now, my own tension is high enough as it is! Please let the day be fun for all of us and not a disaster!"

Nan had explained about the Box Lunch Auction, so Mandy had planned out her order with Mrs. Wilson. The kindly landlady had taken charge of putting those together for any who did not have a kitchen in their home where the meals could be made. The small charge for Mandy's selection would be added to her final bill at the Boarding House, along with the lesser amount for her own meal that day. Mrs. Wilson was keeping a small portion of the profit from each one she prepared but most of the money would be donated to the community project. Mandy liked the feel of a town pulling together to ensure that vital services could be provided when needed, such as re-roofing the school. Although she did not have children there, she didn't mind donations for the betterment of the minds of children, and a safe, sturdy building was important, too.

"My dear, are you all right?" asked an anxious Mrs. Wilson as she breezed through the room. Today was her pastry day, when she was making those for all the tasty items she had promised for the Box Lunches and the pie auction itself at the picnic. The dusting of flour on her apron and forehead told Mandy she was up to her eyebrows, literally, in pie crusts!

"Oh, yes, Mrs. Wilson, I am fine. I just wanted to sit here quietly while I wait for Nan to arrive from work. Busy with pies today?"

"Yes, I certainly am. I didn't want you to be ill or something and I became too busy to notice. Have a pleasant afternoon, then!" And she raced out as quickly as she had entered.

Why did Mandy feel so nervous every time she thought about the picnic? It sounded like a marvelous way for the whole town to get together to celebrate their community and its people, in fact it should be grand fun for everyone! Did the uncertainty seem to be smothering her because she had agreed, after a significant break, to allow Matthew to accompany her to it? Surely no harm could come from such a venture, since they would be in full view the entire time of dozens of families and individuals attending the town-wide festivities.

Lily wanted to go with Ginny and insisted on being allowed to walk to the park with her friend, where the picnic would be held. Could Mandy's emotions be due to the danger that simple act might put her child in from the monster who kept following close behind, everywhere they went? She prayed for protection for both of them to get through this. Only one more week of this nonsense, before the two of them could go home at last! Focusing on that helped some—but quickly the loneliness and misery crushed in on her once more.

My life is spinning out of control and I cannot seem to do one thing to stop it! All I want is to go home! Please, God, let me go back to Ken-ai-te and my boys. I promise to never again be restless with my life as a Kiowa! I don't fit in here, wasn't made for here, and the last fifteen years have been plenty of proof of that. The root of the evil spreading over Lily and over me for these last few days has been here all along, I couldn't see it until I moved away. Now that I'm back, the prejudice and ignorance is plain to see on every side! If you had made me for this life, I never would have left, or would have come right back. Instead, you showed me my destiny and it is not in this place. It is in the red soil of Indian Territory. In the arms of my beloved. In the warm tipi I share with those I love most in this world. It is there I am most content, most useful to Your kingdom.

Mandy searched through the pages of her Bible for consolation, in desperate need of encouragement in the wake of these bitter feelings. Suddenly her eye fell on a passage in Matthew 13 that caught her attention. She began softly reading out loud these words from Jesus Himself, verses 31-32.

"The kingdom of heaven is like to a grain of mustard seed, which a man took, and sowed in his field: which indeed is the least of all seeds; but when it is grown, it is the greatest among herbs, and becometh a tree, so that the birds of the air come and lodge in the branches thereof."

Father, are You trying to tell me that Lily's seed has already been planted, and that I must wait on You to bring forth the fruit You have planned for her life? Even Aunt Ida contributed to her nurturing, by writing all those notes in the book Lily started reading that first day here. As You were changing Ida's life, she passed that wisdom down to my daughter years later. That is fruit from Aunt Ida, enjoyed by Lily. What a blessing!

And the same with my own maturing, for that matter. This money is part of that fruit, is it not? I can see much good coming from it, least of which is saving the lives of many Kiowa, including my own sons and husband. Forgive me for being petty, even demanding, and for trying to rush ahead of Your perfect plans. Thank You for speaking to me through these verses, reminding me that the least shall be greatest in Your kingdom!

She had regained a great deal of her sense of peace and calm as she prayed on these words from Jesus, smiling now as the anxiety receded. Without warning, Nan burst through the door, flinging the door wide! With a panic-stricken expression on her face, she grabbed it and slammed it shut behind her. Leaning against it, her face bright red, she panted as if she had been running and couldn't get her breath.

"Nan!" Mandy cried as she rushed to her side. "Are you all right? Why, you are trembling! Do you want to sit down?"

"No, Amanda, I am *not* all right! Alex just *slapped* me twice, very hard, and in broad daylight in front of plenty of witnesses. I think the man has gone quite mad!"

"That is horrible!" cried Mandy. "What on earth caused him to hurt you like that?"

Nan plunked down on the settee and Mandy scrambled to get her a drink of water from the sideboard where it was always kept for guests as needed. She also grabbed a napkin lying nearby and poured a little of the water onto it.

"Here, put this cloth on your cheek. It has already turned reddish-blue, but maybe this will keep it from bruising too much."

"Thanks. It does sting. I, I was walking home from work is all, and I happened to pass by the millinery shop. Spotting Anna Mallory inside, I thought I'd run in to see her newest hat. We chatted several minutes before I left. As I came out of the store, I saw Alex down the street and deliberately crossed over to the other side to avoid him. It didn't work, as he saw me and followed me over there. For no reason at all, he started yelling at me."

"Yelling? Saying what?"

"Some terrible things, I don't know, the usual accusations. I was in a bit of a shock to be honest. Every time I tried to walk around him, he stepped in my way and wouldn't let me pass. Finally, he jerked me by the arm, pulling me up close, and slapped me! The blow caused me to stumble backward a step—and he did it again, before I could react! Then he calmly walked off as though nothing had happened. Several people witnessed it but were too far away to be of any help."

"Truly, we are dealing with a crazy man!"

"As well as a drunkard. Here it was, early evening, and his breath was already rotten from the liquor that I'm sure emboldened him to pull such a stunt as he did."

"Oh, my word. I'm speechless. How could he drag you into this mess, when it is *me* he is trying to harm? I'm so sorry, Nan."

"You forget, he had a head start with me, even before you arrived in Trenton. He knows well how much I despise him, especially now. I'm just grateful your aunt is gone, because I wouldn't wish her to have to witness this brute's behavior any longer than she did. *When* is God going to deliver us out of this evil hole we have fallen into, thanks to this wicked man?"

CHAPTER THIRTY-ONE

"For the arms of the wicked shall be broken: but the LORD upholdeth the righteous." Psalm 37:17

May 2, 1867
Trenton, Ohio

"What are you doing here? I told you to never come near this place. What if someone saw you, are you crazy?"

"Oh, hold onto your britches, honey. No one saw me coming to your fine, old house. My presence isn't going to stain your 'pristine' reputation, sir!"

"Well, get in here before you are spotted," he growled. And he jerked her arm roughly, pulling her in off the threshold. He slammed the heavy oak door behind her and threw the lock. Then he stomped into the study without so much as a backward glance.

She followed, weaving as she walked.

Once inside the room, he started to pour himself a drink but stopped when he saw how drunk she was. No, he wanted to keep his mind clear for this discussion. There had to be some way he could use her being here to his advantage and he would need all his faculties to figure that one out.

He laughed but without mirth as he took a seat behind the desk and studied her stumbling about the room.

"You must have had quite a party tonight."

"Yes, I did. Drowning my woes, as the saying goes. Oh, look at me, a poet! My goodness, aren't we getting culture all of a sudden!"

"Quit babbling, woman. Tell me why you've come."

"Party."

"I don't understand, what do you mean?"

"I mean, sir, that I don't party alone but tonight I got stood up. You failed to grace me with your presence. What else could I do but drown my broken heart in a bottle?"

"You're disgusting, you know that? Why did you come here, of all places?"

"Because you were the one who stood me up! Or don't you remember making the date? We can never go out in case someone sees us—might reveal a scheme or two that you wanted to remain hidden, along with me. We were to meet in the hotel late tonight, to make our plans, but guess who never showed?"

"Oh, that. I got busy is all, had somewhere more important to be. I figured you wouldn't mind as long as you had the booze you needed."

"Nice girls don't drink alone. That's what my daddy always taught me. And he was a gentleman, you see. Raising a proper lady. Which is more than you are used to, I suspect."

"Look, it's late. I'm tired and not in the mood for whatever kind of sick game you are playing. Just say what you came to say and get out."

She pulled herself up straight and smoothed down her dress, a snarl on her lips.

"I'm tired of staying in the shadows and slipping from hotel room to back room to whatever place you designate, all to keep anyone from seeing us together. Do you know what it feels like to do another's dirty work, only to be discarded like a used towel? That's how I feel now! I want what you promised me when this whole thing started."

"What's that?"

"Marriage. Proper and legal. No more hiding from all the folks in town. I want to live in this grand house, have servants who do my bidding, and wear the finest in clothes. All of it. You owe it to me and I'm here to collect."

"Marriage? Are you kidding me? Why would I ever marry the likes of you?"

"Because you promised, you scoundrel! You said if I did what you asked and behaved myself, there would be a future in it for me with you."

"I meant more jobs to do. What do you take me for? A fool? I would never marry you! It took a bottle of whiskey for you to be able to come here and tell me this? You really are pathetic, you know that?"

He put his head back and roared. She stood there staring, trying to comprehend the scene and his meaning through liquor-glazed eyes, to pull it deep into her brain, muddled though it was. Then she snapped as his meaning soaked in.

"How dare you make fun of me! This is not the whiskey talking, bud. I may not be the brightest person in the world, but I'm no one's fool! You told me—you said—I thought you meant—"

"It's obvious what you thought I meant but you only heard what you wanted to hear, not what I said. Never, in any of my wildest passionate moments, did I promise you marriage. Now, get out of here. And keep your mouth shut or I will shut it for you."

"Is that a threat?" she demanded, holding onto the nearest chair for support to stop the rocking motion of the room.

"No, not at all. It's a promise. One you know that I can and will keep, if you get in my way!"

"Well, Mr. High and Mighty, what if I told you that if you do carry out that threat against me, you would be killing your own baby as well?"

Now it was his turn to be stunned.

"Baby? Whatever in the world are you talking about? I don't have a baby!"

"Not yet but you are going to! Yep, I am 'with child' as they say! And it is yours, *dear sir*. So, you better stop hedging on your promise and step up and be a man before you become a daddy!"

She grinned at him, expecting him to at least show some sense of propriety with this news. What man wouldn't? Only a cad, for sure.

He didn't say a word, just rose and stalked over to her, grabbing hold of her elbow once again, intending to escort her out of the study, moreover out of his house. But she was having none of his brush-off tactics now. She had had enough of the liquor and enough of his antics to embolden her when she probably should have had better sense. Retreat is sometimes the better part of valor but not a word in her vocabulary right now! She pulled free and took a couple of steps backward, shaking her finger in his face.

"No! Don't you lay a hand on me! I have it all written down, you know. And hidden away where you will never find it. Every single word that I've passed on to you, just in case something happened to me. And now the news about the baby—your baby—as well. If you pull one of your grim so-called jokes, the news will be all over town before you can blink! As I said,

I may have made a few mistakes in character judgment in the past, but I'm no fool! If anything happens to me, my murder is one you will not get away with, trust me. You have used me for the last time, do you hear me?"

Alex numbly stared as she turned on her heel and stormed out of the room. He winced with the sound of the front door slamming.

What am I going to do about her now? I must find some way to shut her up for good or she could ruin me! Whatever possessed me to use such a weak, silly girl as that? Not having her help with confusing the paperwork on this case will be troublesome but not impossible to overcome. But her mouth? Worse yet, the fact she seems to have a kind of backup for her blackmail—that could absolutely destroy me. I have to find that paper. A baby, are you kidding? Blast it all! I have to think fast and act even faster! As in right now!

May 3, 1867
Trenton, Ohio

"Lily, we need to talk before you leave for Ginny's. There are several things you don't know about but need to."

"If you mean that you talked to her mother, I've heard all about it. From Ginny. And I don't need to hear any more of your lies. How could you embarrass me like that? No, on second thought, don't answer that. With every day that passes, my determination to stay here grows stronger."

"But that's the point! They aren't going to adopt you, no matter what Ginny has dreamed up! It was only a childish fantasy, that's all. It's not a lie, it's the truth. One way or the other, you are going to have to face it. And no amount of your hateful attitude or cruel words are going to change that. This is not like you to behave like this, but it has to stop. When I leave here in a few days to go home to Indian Territory, you are going with me. And that's *final*."

"We'll just see about that. Perhaps I will run away first! Or join the circus. Or go to Paris. Somewhere, *anywhere* that you cannot find me! Now, leave me alone! I'm going over to Ginny's house and I don't know when I will return. And if you see me at the picnic tomorrow, don't try to talk to me! Because I won't answer, no matter what you say. Leave me to live my life the way I see fit and make both of us happy." She turned and whirled out the door before Mandy could stop her.

Run away? Join the circus? Go to Paris? Where does she get these ideas? How does she think she is going to survive? *Oooh, I give up!*

Mandy glanced down and spotted her pocket watch on the table. With a sinking feeling, the realization struck that she would be late for her meeting at Matthew's office if she didn't hurry. They were to discuss in more detail that day's hearing. Although she didn't have to attend, she needed to allow plenty of time this morning to go over everything with Matthew before he had to leave for it, and she didn't know when that was. Her biggest concern of course was whether or not the paperwork for today had been properly filed.

"Matthew, are you here?" she called as she entered the unlocked front door of his office area. Mandy noted that Miss Lawson's desk was empty, but every drawer was open and papers were strewn all over the top of it. Normally she kept a neat and tidy desk. *Perhaps she is ill today. This is so odd. But the door was unlocked; therefore, Matthew must be here. But who on earth has thrown those papers every which way?*

"Hello!" She walked back toward the conference room, then heard a sound inside. Mandy knocked on the door. "Matthew? Is that you in there? May I come in?"

The door suddenly jerked open, startling Mandy for a moment, and there stood her attorney, appearing to be a little frazzled but all in one piece. With his free hand he held up to his chest a pile of papers that threatened at any moment to explode from his grip.

"Oh, Amanda, hello. I'm glad you are here. Everything is in a bit of disarray this morning with Abigail missing." He walked to his desk and plopped the documents down before he dropped them.

"Missing? Miss Lawson is missing? Maybe she is ill today and was unable to let you know."

"No, she is not ill. I sent a messenger to her home to check on her. He came racing back saying her cat is inside meowing up a storm, begging to go out. But Abigail is nowhere to be found. We've sent for her landlady to come and check on the house, to at least let the cat out."

"Oh, that is dreadful! What could have happened to her?"

"I think I may have found the answer, or at least part of it. The *what*, if not the *who*. As you can tell, I have been going through her desk and I found a whole packet of papers in there, ones that should have been filed in your case but never were. Why she kept them all together like that is beyond me. They are incriminating evidence of the devilish work she has been doing to stop our case from moving forward. This could result in her going to prison once the judge finds out she had them!"

"Oh, my word. That is horrible. You said the other day you were beginning to suspect her of being involved. Now I guess you have your answer. She always seemed so nice to me."

"Yes, she had me fooled as well. I think I told you already that I gave her this job to help her get her life back in order. And this is the way she repays me—by betraying that trust? Well, at least we know who the rat is now. Since she is no longer here to interfere, perhaps we can move forward with your case without further delays. This cost us a whole week at least, and as you can tell, I'm furious about it!"

"Don't you have a hearing to attend this morning? Perhaps I can help you in some way."

"Yes, you are right, in fact the hearing is in about half an hour. I could use some extra hands, all right, if you have time. Hopefully I can show the judge what has been going on, instead of merely telling him that it was not my incompetence to blame for the delays. Let's see, although I had hoped to organize everything, it's clear I don't have that kind of time. So if you can look through all these," and he gestured toward the pile on his desk, "I'll get that file I told you about and then we can work through all of them together."

"Certainly." Matthew went over to Abigail's desk and rifled through several items on top and in one of the drawers while Mandy worked.

She quickly began sorting the papers as best she could. Not knowing what any of them were complicated things a bit but she figured if she could just present him with a tidy stack, it had to be better than what they started with. How could Abigail do this to Matthew? And why would she create such havoc to stop Mandy from getting the inheritance she deserved?

"Do you have those done?" Matthew asked as he walked toward the conference room.

"Yes, I think so, maybe not in the right order but at least easier to look through now."

"Let's go in here and lay it all out. We are running out of time to do this properly but at least some semblance of order will be helpful."

They worked quickly and within minutes had the task completed.

"I've got to get to the hearing here in a couple of minutes," he said, after consulting his watch. "Thanks for your help. What we have found is nothing short of unbelievable. She tried to frame me for incompetence and destroy any chance of you getting the inheritance from your aunt that you deserve. Well, I'm onto her now! She better not dare to show her wicked little face around here ever again. I say 'good riddance'!"

"Surely she wouldn't come back after her plot was discovered!"

"You would think not. Thing is, I really don't see how she could ever have figured out this elaborate of a scheme on her own. She had to have help. While I may not yet have the proof of who hired her, I vow I will before I'm through. In fact, I promise you, Amanda, that I won't give up until I do!"

"That's reassuring, but I'm sad it came to this. I hope the judge will listen to you."

"I'm sure of it, with this to show him," and he indicated the file they had just put together.

"Do you think, then, that this will all be done by next Friday?"

"I feel more confident now than I have since we started, frankly. Between all the threats against you and this evidence, I believe the judge will issue a quick ruling now. A great deal depends on today—which reminds me, I need to get going so I'm not late. The biggest thing that concerns me, still, is the fact that there may be others involved. Abigail couldn't possibly have done all this by herself. Perhaps today I can uncover some new rat holes!"

"I hope you will get back in touch with me when you finish with the hearing. It would be interesting to know the judge's reaction to all this news."

Matthew raced out the door, waving his hand behind him. *God, go with him!*

May 3, 1867
Indian Territory

"Jacob, we must talk." Ken-ai-te's manner was solemn, not jovial as it usually was when he came to visit. In addition, his voice had a hard edge on it that troubled the frontiersman. Immediately he was on the alert.

"Certainly, my friend." He stopped his task of stacking several small boxes of ammunition on a counter. "Is there trouble in the camp?"

"More starvation than I have seen in my lifetime. That enough to hurt my heart, know God's heart must be hurt more than mine."

"Yes, I'm sure you're right about that. He does care when we are hurting. I am getting very low on food supplies here in the store, but I want to you to take some items back to the camp. Your people need it far more than any strangers who may come."

"But I have no more money to pay you. Cannot take what I have nothing to trade for or buy with."

"I understand. But you must take it as a gift from me to the Kiowa—for the children, if nothing else. You can bring me a rabbit skin the next time you kill one, as I am out of those here at the store. Mothers love those to wrap their babies in them because the fur is very soft. I try to keep at least one in stock all the time."

"Why she not send word?"

"What?" The abrupt change in the conversation threw Jacob for a moment. "Oh, you mean Prayer Woman, don't you?"

Ken-ai-te nodded, a miserable expression on his rugged face.

"If she hurt, or Lily maybe, she cannot leave O-hi-o, cannot send word to us. Could she be in fort already but army soldier won't help her as promised?"

"I doubt it, Ken-ai-te. Most likely, the process of getting the estate settled has taken much longer than she thought. Legal business can often stretch out into weeks or months unexpectedly."

"Months? As in many moons?"

"Yes, sometimes, I'm sad to say."

"Not wait much longer. Need Prayer Woman home. Not know how to sneak into this place, though, to take her so others not see me. I go and figure it out, though. Cannot leave her there. *Cannot!*"

Jacob paused as though carefully measuring his next words. Ken-ai-te glanced up at his friend to see why he had not replied. Why did anxiety twist his stomach?

"My friend, I hate to bring this up but what if she doesn't want to come home, after all this time? Have you thought about that? Didn't she say that was one of her fears, that she would get there and not want to leave?"

"Then I take her back by force. Did it once before, can do it again."

"Yes, you did. But I don't think you want to try that now. However, I do understand how you feel and I'm sure the boys miss their mother deeply, too. To be honest, I seriously doubt that is the problem. Maybe what we need to do is pray. God knows the reason for the delay. Before you risk your boys losing both their parents and a sister, why don't we see what He has to say? Let me get these last few tins of food I have left packed up so you can take them back to the village with you. After that, you and I, my friend, need to get on our knees together. God has the answer! Of that I am confident."

Ken-ai-te nodded, relieved that he could share such deep feelings with his friend. He hadn't believed he could get the words out, but Jacob knew. *He knew.* The warrior had forgotten for the moment that he went through this when his own wife left him years before and took their daughter away because she didn't like living out here on the frontier as he did. Yes, he *knows.*

"You right. God listens to prayers. We talk about this but no prayers together. Need to pray now!"

May 4, 1867
Trenton, Ohio

"I am having a great time, Nan, how about you?" Mandy had been laughing at a children's puppet show that one of the churches had put on. Now she was resting under a tree at a table that had been set up there when Nan walked by, so her spirits were high.

"Oh, me, too! The Box Lunch Auction is about to start. I'll bet I can pick yours out from all those lined up there on the back of the wagon!"

"Bet you can't!" Mandy giggled.

"Um, maybe the one with the big pink bow on it? That looks like you."

"Are you kidding? I really don't much care for pink, thank you very much. So, nope, keep guessing!"

"Then it has to be the one with the big yellow bow. Yes, that's yours for sure."

"Keep going!"

"You really did this right, Amanda! Well, I give. Which one is yours?"

"It's the one with the four red bows on it, for each person in my family and for the red soil of Indian Territory! Oh, how I do miss it!"

"Of course, I should have known that right off! Can you guess which is mine?"

"I would say the blue bow, since that is your favorite color?"

"And you would be right, first time!"

"I wonder who will bid on our boxes? They get to have lunch with us, isn't that right?" asked Mandy.

She nodded. "A good thing that ole Alex is such a skinflint that he wouldn't part with the money for a bid. Wouldn't that be terrible to have to eat with him?"

"Oh, Nan, you are awful! But yes, it would be. Fortunately, I haven't seen any sign of him all morning. My, I do believe I'm getting hungry. I'm used to Mrs. Wilson's fine cooking, and she has outdone herself on my auction lunch. The other one, that I will be eating, is much smaller, not nearly so grand! But still very delicious and I can't wait to eat it."

"Yes, same here. Let's go on over there by the wagon, as they will want us to line up next to it while the bidding is going on."

A short time later, the excitement of the bidding on the Box Lunches was in high gear, with plenty of cheers and teasing from the audience along the way. Nan's was bought by a handsome older man who had a wooden leg but a very nice smile. She seemed pleased so Mandy was happy for her. He had been at church the couple of times Mandy and Lily had gone. Presumably he knew her from there. Mandy's was one of the last to come up for the auction. Immediately Matthew bid on it! *Oh, please don't let him get it! I really don't want to encourage him that way!*

But sure enough, when all the bids were in, the top one was Matthew's. She smiled sweetly as he came to claim his prize and she identified whose it was, to loud applause. He beamed and she tried to be polite. *Maybe Nan would like to trade?*

Matthew suggested they eat down by the duck pond, a location that at least Mandy felt comfortable with, since there was a public path and several benches in the area. As a rule, there were plenty of folks around there, not as isolated as some other parts of the park were. Mandy had brought a large blanket with her to set the food out on. Once they were settled on it, she asked Matthew if he would pray over their meal before they began, which he did.

"You have been avoiding me today, Amanda, ever since we arrived. Have I done anything inappropriate to cause you to be uncomfortable?"

"Completely to the contrary, sir," she replied, successfully dodging a direct response to his statement. "You have been quite the gentleman, and I do sincerely appreciate that. In fact, I wanted to ask how the hearing went yesterday."

"Oh, very predictable, as I figured it would be. The Judge chewed me out for the lost papers, but I explained what happened and he settled down and gave me another chance to get them all filed by Monday. He was duly impressed, too, with the packet of documents we put together that were hidden by Abigail. I am facing a long day tomorrow of trying to reconstruct in detail what all Abigail did to hamper your case, using those papers. Normally I would never work on Sunday but this cannot be helped. It all has to be completed by the new filing deadline."

"Speaking of her, is there any sign of her yet?"

"Not a hair. Her landlady said she didn't pack anything so it appears as though she left for the evening, expecting to be back in time to let the poor cat out. The woman is looking after the animal until Abigail returns. This is just highly unlike her, at least the Abigail I thought I knew. I am deeply concerned that something might have happened to her. Whoever was paying her to misfile and lose papers might have gotten tired of it and, well, sad to say, since she has no family nearby, there is honestly no one except me to even miss her. And her cat!"

"That is very sad! I cannot imagine such a lonely lifestyle as that. Oh, one other question about the hearing—did the judge say anything about next week being the final one?"

"Yes, he did indicate that if everything is caught up by that time, there should be no further delays. I will be sure to let you know."

"Thanks, that is so sweet of you. More cake?"

"Yes, I would love another small slice. Mrs. Wilson is an excellent cook. I can see why everyone loves living at her place!"

"Well, if I cannot live at home, it is a good second choice."

Matthew shifted positions slightly, leaning down on his elbow which brought his face a little closer to Mandy than she liked. As she tried to straighten up, however, her hand slipped, causing her to fall almost directly onto him!

Pushing away, she cried, "Oh, I'm so sorry, Matthew! I didn't mean for that to happen."

"Don't apologize. I found it rather nice!" And without warning he leaned over before she could move too far. And tried to kiss her! She deftly moved out of the way at the last second, which allowed his lips to lightly brush her cheek instead of her mouth. Like a shot, she jumped up and moved back from him.

"Matthew! What has gotten into you?" she demanded, her eyes flashing.

He rose to face her, his face flushed.

"Now it is my turn. I sincerely do apologize, Amanda. I don't know whatever possessed me to be that rude. I feel terrible about it and do promise nothing like this will ever happen again, I swear it."

"It better not! Or I will be forced to find another lawyer to handle my case. We are so far into this now, I hesitate to slow things even more by starting over with someone else, but if I ever sense anything inappropriate again, believe me, I shall do it!"

She began hastily picking up the remains of their lunches, slamming everything from plates to napkins to leftover food into the boxes and pushing down the lids. He hurried to help her, but she jerked her box out of his hand.

"I can do this myself. After all, I am technically the hostess here and you the guest. Many thanks for purchasing my box and the lunch was enjoyable until, well, we are done now and I want to go home." He opened his mouth, she assumed to offer to take her in his buggy, but she quickly added, "I will walk, thank you. It will do me good after all that rich food. Good day, sir."

She turned to go, juggling the boxes and trash from their meal and dragging the blanket behind her. Tears stung her eyes. All she wanted to do was get away from him before she started crying. A mixture of disappointment, fear, and anger had swelled up inside her until she was afraid she might break down in front of him despite her best efforts to put on a stoic Kiowa face.

"Amanda," he called out, but she refused to turn and face him again, instead kept on walking. At least until she dropped a couple of the things she was carrying and the breeze blew them everywhere before she could grab them again. Of course, she had to stop briefly at that point, giving him a chance to catch up to her and help retrieve a few of the items.

"Please, let me take you home. It's the least I can do."

The tears came in spite of her best efforts, and she looked up into his handsome face which by now was a miserable mask to match her own.

"Why, Matthew? Why did you ever think for one moment doing that was all right? I'm a married woman! Can you not get that through your head?"

"Yes, I know. But, well, I guess I succumbed to a mix of your charms topped off with the romantic moment and—and the stupid gossip. Just for a moment, but then it was too late. Can you ever forgive me?"

"Of course, but I shall have to give myself some time to put it in the past. God may do this instantaneously, but it takes me a little longer. I can easily forgive but it's the forgetting that is hard."

"Thank—"

"Wait," she interrupted, "what did you say about 'stupid gossip'?"

"Many in Trenton believe that you have no husband, that you only made him up to explain the presence of your child. I never accepted that. But when you hear it over and over, I suppose it seeps in anyway."

"Not married at all? They think Lily is, is *illegitimate?*"

"Yes. This is why it has been so very important for you to get to know people and for them to know you. I wanted to be delicate about it in the beginning, but now need to try to explain my unforgiveable behavior. The only way to do that at this point is with the truth."

"*Truth?* How about having faith in me and my integrity and the heritage I have from Aunt Ida, to know that I would never behave in such a manner as that? It's insulting!"

"I deeply regret that I had to tell you, in fact, had hoped it would never come to that."

"For your information, I had already heard about this from someone else but really didn't believe it. Now, I can no longer deny its existence in the small minds of this town. But in *you?* I honestly thought you knew me better than that by now."

"Again, I apologize with everything in me. What I did was utterly inexcusable. Perhaps I should get you home now. It will be very much noticed if I don't escort you out of here since the whole town saw us arrive this morning in my buggy and walk away together after the Auction! So, grit your teeth if you must, but we have to leave together."

Mandy nodded but said nothing further. In truth, she was grateful she didn't have to walk back on her own. Her knees were a bit wobbly from the incident. Nan had been right, Matthew was a cad, after all!

God, get me out of here soon and back to my beloved! Oh, Ken-ai-te, how on earth will I ever explain this to you? When we are back together again, it won't matter so much. Since you will never meet Matthew, I think I can tell you the truth but gently. And later. Much later! After we have the money firmly in hand and Matthew is out of our lives for good!

CHAPTER THIRTY-TWO

"But God hath revealed them unto us by his Spirit: for the Spirit searcheth all things, yea, the deep things of God." I Corinthians 2:10

May 4, 1867
Indian Territory

God, be with my wife Prayer Woman this night. Provide for her whatever she needs, as I know not what those are. But You do. Do not let her desire the white men's ways so much that she forgets the ways of her father and all who came before us. Protect her from all harm, also our daughter Lily. Let this time be one of joy between them but bring them home soon. Ease the hearts of our sons who miss their mother but help them learn to be strong because of Your love. Fill our empty bellies with You when we have no food in our pot. I beg for their lives, as so many die each day from not enough to eat. Give me wisdom to find new game each day that dawns. Forgive me for being impatient with Prayer Woman for not coming home sooner. Thank You for hearing my prayers this night. Show me how to walk close to Your path in the new day tomorrow. For Name of Jesus, Amen."

Ken-ai-te opened his eyes and gazed up into the night sky above. Wonder filled his heart once more for the stars that appeared close enough he could reach up to touch them. There was no moon but he knew that is why the countless pinpoints of light overhead appeared so vivid. He closed his eyes once again, breathing in the smell of the prairie at rest. The call of the coyotes that seemed to encircle the village brought a sense of normalcy as they cried out to each other in the absence of the moon. This was home. He was happiest when here with his family.

But for now, things were not complete for him. Although he had not the words to state all his deep feelings, nevertheless they were there in his heart, calling out to be expressed. As a rule, Prayer Woman did that for him with her chatter in the evenings that filled their tipi with the warmth of love and laughter. Now, it was cold, dark, silent without her presence. How could he explain all that to the boys? They were old enough to not cry over missing her but he knew inside they wanted to. Because he wanted to. His arms longed to hold her, to smell the sweet perfume of her hair under his chin, to feel the warmth of her skin beneath his fingers as he kept her close to his heart. Everything was wrong this night. When would it be right again? He wished he knew.

Slowly he made his way back inside the tipi to check on the sleeping forms on the small cots in front of the fire pit. Even breathing reassured him they were fine. But how could he ever be "fine" again until his wife was by his side once more?

Sleep evaded him for some time. When it did come, it was fitful as he tossed first one way and then the other on the massive buffalo robe, too large for only one person. The darkness seemed to slide away from him for no reason, replaced by a dim light that soon burned bright enough to light up the entire tipi.

Ken-ai-te sat up abruptly and rubbed his eyes at the sight. *Am I dreaming or is this real? What is happening?*

He hardly dared to breathe as the light seemed to hover right over the cold fire pit. Softly, the sound of a single flute came out of the light but Ken-ai-te had never heard the tune before.

God, are You here with me? Can You tell me what this is?

"Ken-ai-te," a gentle voice called to him out of the ball of fire in front of him. Suddenly he could see the form of the Prayer Angel who had come to them before, her long white wings curving downward, fluttering softly as she hung there in the air, almost in the very flames themselves yet not consumed. The buckskin dress was as he remembered, with the light blue feathers in her long silky black hair. Her hands formed in prayer as they always were when she appeared. Why was she here tonight? The thought caused cold chills to scamper up his bare arms. He shivered slightly, staring intently as he sat up to face her.

"Listen carefully," she continued. "You must go to Prayer Woman. She and Lily are in grave danger. Only you can protect them. At first light you must go by horseback as quickly as you can."

"Danger?" he whispered. "What kind? But how can I go when the risk is so great for me to be in that far-off place? Do you speak to me on behalf of the Lord? Please tell me, I must know!"

"Yes, brave Kiowa warrior Ken-ai-te, I come to you from the Father, as I have done before. He will go with you but if you do not obey, they will die. Go find them, now!"

With that, the ball of fire receded rapidly until it was a tiny dot of light, quickly swallowed up in the darkness. The warrior gasped slightly at what had just happened. Had he heard a message from God? Surely he had! Now he must obey. He jumped up and stalked outside, pacing around the campfire pit.

"But how? How can I do this thing, leave my boys and go far away into a white man's city? My heart says I can do it, that I must do it, but my head is not certain of it. How can I know?"

As soon as the words slipped out of his lips, Ken-ai-te had his answer: Jacob! His friend could help him, of that he was certain in that moment. But, again, how? In his heart the Kiowa felt confidence Jacob would know, and how to tell if this message truly came from God. If so, he would know how they could make it happen. The warrior knew if given a task in the territory, no one could achieve it faster or better than he could. But in this far off O-hi-o? A very different matter. The advice of his friend and fellow servant of God was what the warrior knew he needed at that moment.

Without further thought, he slipped inside the tipi to check on the boys before racing back outside. Within moments he had asked another brave to look after his sons, should they awaken before Ken-ai-te could return. With God's blessing, that should be quickly, for he would need the night's sleep if he were to accomplish this fearsome command.

All the way to the Trading Post, Ken-ai-te prayed for wisdom, pleading for the right words to gain his friend's assistance. God speaking in a dream? How could he be certain? Would Jacob laugh at him for this? What if he was wrong?

With every pounding step the pony took to bring him closer to the store, Ken-ai-te became more certain that Jesus had, indeed, spoken to Him that night. He recalled another anxious father who was awakened in the middle of the night by a dream and told to immediately take his wife and young son away into a strange land, or the child would be killed. History proved this to be true. Due to the father's obedient heart, God protected His own Son from being killed that horrible night. If Prayer Woman and Lily were truly in danger, He obviously had chosen to use Ken-ai-te to protect them, even far away in Ohio. Regardless of the danger. A sobering thought but one he was willing to face as well as all potential risks in order to save his family!

Racing up to the door of the living quarters behind the Trading Post, Ken-ai-te pounded hard, calling out his friend's name.

"Jacob, my friend, open up! It is Ken-ai-te. God has spoken to me. I need your help. Now!"

Moments later, the latch slowly slipped open and the door swung away just a crack, revealing a sleepy man scratching his head and squinting into the darkness.

"Ken-ai-te? What on earth are you doing here at this time of night? Has something happened to one of the boys?"

The Kiowa did not wait to be invited in but pushed past his friend into his living area. Whirling around to see him as Jacob closed the door and lighted the lamp on the table between them, Ken-ai-te blurted out the story of the dream. He carefully related every word of what the Prayer Angel had said. Jacob had been told of this heavenly messenger who had appeared to them when the baby died as well as at a handful of other important times, but his friend had never seen her himself. Would he believe him?

"Prayer Woman and Lily are in danger! I have to get to them, now."

"I am sure they are lonely and perhaps confused over certain aspects of the white society they are in, but in *danger*? You said the other day that you were concerned you had not heard any message from your wife. Could your concern have created this danger in your mind? I mean, did the Prayer Angel say what kind of danger they are in?"

"I not know. Only know what she say God told her to say to me. I must go to this O-hi-o place as fast as I can. Please, can you help me? Should I wear white man's clothing for this? And hope no one asks about the color of my skin?" A string of Kiowa words followed.

Jacob put his hand up. "Oh, hold on, slow down a moment here. You are speaking in Kiowa rather than English but way too fast for me. Sit with me while we talk calmly of this dream. That is a serious decision to make in the middle of the night like this." He gestured for his friend to sit with him in front of the cold fireplace.

"No sit. No time. Must go now. Prayer Angel say—God say—they *die* if I not go!"

"They will, um, die? Are you sure?"

"Yes. No time for talk. Told to ride at daybreak, much to do before sun rises."

"But what about the boys?"

"I leave with Yellow Eagle. They will be, um, how you say?"

"Fine?" Ken-ai-te nodded eagerly. "Yes, I'm sure they would be in good hands with him and his wife. They would do anything possible to help you, I know, including looking after your boys if you leave the village, as they did when we took your family to meet the train. But shouldn't you think this through, perhaps pray about it first?"

"I pray all way here. Now need help. Wisdom on how to get there."

"You need wisdom about a great many things, Ken-ai-te. If God has decided, He knows how you can do it without endangering yourself before you even get there. Maybe if I went with you?"

Ken-ai-te's eyes lit up. "You do for me? Long journey. Many days from store."

"Yes, I agree, I need to think this through. But first let's pray about it and see what God has to say to us. Then we will plan. Please sit with me."

At this, the Kiowa finally agreed to rein in his flurry of energy a bit. Prayer was the best first step, he knew. After that, go to save his family.

Some time later the two men concluded their prayer time and rose from the floor. They often were on their knees before the Father for many things, whether together or separately, but this was cloaked with far more than their usual pleas for wisdom or courage or protection. All that and much more had passed between them, petitioning the Lord for His assurance they both keenly needed. For two men not easily persuaded to share the most intimate thoughts of their hearts, they had poured out their hearts together that night. They embraced briefly.

As Jacob stepped back, he looked intently at his friend.

"Ken-ai-te, I am convinced now that you are right. God does want you there to protect your family, even if it doesn't make much sense to us. But I also believe he is calling me to go with you. If you agree, my friend, I would like to suggest you go as my servant, if it would not offend you too deeply to pose as that. I mean, a great chief does not serve others, I know, people listen to him. But in this situation, the white people along the way and once we arrive will pay attention to us far more quickly if you are silent, allowing me to seek your advice only in private. That will allow me to appear to be the one in charge. It is for your protection as well as my own—ultimately that of Prayer Woman and Lily, too."

"Yes, much trust in you. Prayer Angel tell me to go by horseback but long ride for that. Take many days. Maybe we take spare ponies, ride hard, changing ponies as needed, without rest? Or buy or trade for more if needed. Not take so many days that way."

"Good idea. If we use your ponies instead of my horses, they should be able to make the trip much better. We need to avoid roads and towns as much as possible, taking off through the countryside instead, as we did a few weeks ago with your wife and daughter. There is greater risk of your presence being challenged if we encounter people along the way. You will need to help us find the right routes, even though it will be unfamiliar territory to you for the most part. I trust your ability to do that."

Ken-ai-te nodded and smiled grimly. They would both be needed if this were to work. God must have known that!

"Somewhere around here I have a map that shows Ohio on it and the eastern part of Indian Territory, the one we used when planning how to get Prayer Woman and Lily there safely. Give me a moment to think where I put that." He rifled through a number of charts and maps, muttering as he tossed several aside, one by one. Finally, he found what he sought.

"Here it is! I figured this might come in handy one of these days when I bought it but had no idea how much it would be needed." He spread it out on the table before them, pulling the lantern close enough they could make out the markings on the parchment.

"This is Ohio, where we need to go, specifically, here is Trenton," he said, tapping the map. "This area over here is where we are, only further west. Right in the middle, this is Ft. Smith, where we took Prayer Woman and Lily to the train a few weeks ago. Of course we already know that route. After Fort Smith, it is all new territory, with many more people and towns. We can ride overland, only stopping for water, perhaps to buy food once or twice. That way, I believe we could make it within a few days all the way to Cincinnati and then on up to Trenton. Riding the train would help make it a shorter journey but last I heard they don't allow Indians on the trains so that's out. We can't risk a delay we aren't prepared for. Hopefully this plan will give us enough time for what God would have us do."

The Kiowa nodded. "God's plan protect wife and daughter, trust God for that."

"Yes, I think God's plan will also protect Prayer Woman if no one is told she is your wife at first. You would need to go as a close family friend, as I am. No one must know your real identity. Not knowing what we will face when we get there is going to make it a bit difficult. But I'm afraid the whole ruse of Prayer Woman and Lily going as whites will be revealed if you show up as her husband. We must let her make the decision of when to tell people, not us."

Ken-ai-te seemed a bit reluctant at that and Jacob could certainly understand why. What could he say to convince him this was the best way?

"Prayer Woman never told her aunt your real identity. Therefore, you can be of far more help as a friend than as her husband when we first arrive. Using your real name without fear of exposing your family's lies should make it a little easier to endure. I'm sure the truth can be told very soon once we are there to protect your family. By the way, we should be able to discover upon arriving why it has taken this long without any word. Not to mention what danger they are facing, too. Keeping your secret will make this possible without other problems arising."

Finally, Ken-ai-te nodded. "Agree to this plan. Keep secret of my wife and child. I pretend to serve you, my friend. Not a real lie."

"No, you are right, that part is not a lie. You have been a good friend to me for a long time. God will take care of us this way, I'm sure. I am sad that it is necessary but glad you understand and agree."

"God's plan," he said simply as though that explained everything. "Must go back to village now to rest and prepare for journey. Will be back at first light with four ponies."

"Oh, one other thing. You must leave your weapons at home. Being armed would be a most grievous offense. I will have my rifle and pistol, that should be enough for both of us."

Frowning, he asked, "What about knife?" His hand went to the sheath at his waist.

"Yes, you should be able to take your knife with you. Depending on where we go while there, you may have to leave it in the hotel room, but it will be most helpful on the trip there and back."

"Can daughter Hannah run store for you?"

"With help from a couple of your braves, as they usually do when I am gone, yes, I know she can manage. And not only *can* but *will*. When I tell her we are obeying a command from God, she will cooperate. Can you speak with the men you trust in the village to help her?"

"Yes, will awaken them and they will come with me, at first light."

"You had best get on your way. We both need more rest before we leave as well as time to pack, but we will leave as soon as possible in the morning. Bring whatever food you can spare and we will take the rest of what we need from the store as well. I of course must leave some for Hannah but maybe your men can hunt for her, too. Remember to pack light for this trip, my friend." He stopped and chuckled. "What am I saying? I'm talking to a Kiowa chief! You already know better than I do how to pack for a long ride across the prairie by horseback!"

Ken-ai-te nodded and smiled. "I go now. Much we not know about going, but God know all answers, we only obey Him. Thank you for going with me, Jacob, my true friend. See you soon!"

May 6, 1867
Trenton, Ohio

"Matthew, there simply *has* to be a way for this to end this week! I cannot take much more of this uncertainty!"

"I understand, Amanda. It has been a difficult time for you and Lily, I know. Truly, I am doing my best to bring this to a close. The hearing on Friday should be our final one. Keep praying I can continue to ferret out the ones responsible for the delays. It's maddening to know we cannot prove the source of this evil, but at least God will have the final say. Of that we can be confident!"

"I need to go the Emporium for a couple of items and get back home. I will leave you to your work. Let me know if you find out more, Matthew."

"I certainly will, Amanda. Be careful out there!"

As she stepped out into the morning sunlight, Mandy breathed a sigh of relief. *That went well. I wasn't sure we could discuss things calmly and without emotion, but he is a professional and with God guiding our tongues, we did it.* She shuddered as she recalled the awful episode between them on Saturday. Doing all in her power to control the situation, she nevertheless knew the

Lord was ultimately in charge. The same was true for her relationship with her daughter. It was all in His hands now. But was she willing to leave it there and trust Him to work it all out?

By the time she had made her selections at the store and arrived back at the Boarding House, Lily was gone. Presumably, she had gone on to Ginny's. Mandy wasn't happy at the thought she was out there alone on the streets but she supposed no further than she had to go, it would be all right. Relief washed over her that there would be no more arguments for now. They had started their day with one that made her skin crawl with the memory of Lily's harsh words, saying she would rather die than live in the territory as a Kiowa. *Die?* She tried to shake off the cloud that hovered nearby. Her eyes fell on her Bible, sitting on her bedside table. Therein lay the answers she needed!

Taking that sacred book out to the front porch with a cup of tea, Mandy sat in a rocker to let God's love wash over her to calm her frantic heart.

"How can I face even one more day of arguments with Lily? I have no strength left, Father. Please do *something* and do it *now*. You work best when I am at my weakest. As empty as I feel this morning, even broken, there is plenty of opportunity ahead for You to be glorified. Attempting to keep my daughter happy while holding high my hope in a quick resolution to this legal case is wearing me down. Give me wisdom and courage to get through this day, one step at a time! I simply must get back home to Indian Territory the first *second* I can get my hands on that money. I am trying to be Your servant, willingly obey Your commands, not my own heart. Please do whatever is necessary to save my people, not to mention my family. I miss them so much! Comfort my heart as I wait on You to act. Always guard my steps from the danger all around me. Protect my child, Lord, I beg You! The forces of evil are doing battle for her heart. I ask that this child for whom I have prayed all her life and who knows You well might this day make the right choices in Your sight."

When she picked up her Bible, it fell open to I Samuel. She began reading randomly through the first chapter. In the story of Hannah, she read of a mother's love, so strong she promised to give her child back to God's service if He would only bless her with a baby. Very much like her own love for Lily! The passion and desire that was evident in this woman's every word to honor God above all else, even when being tormented and ridiculed, touched Mandy with the struggles she was enduring.

Slowly, moment by difficult moment, peace filled her heart and mind. Her focus on doing the Lord's will more than on her own increased, bringing comfort and strength. She let it all go, again—the chaos, turmoil, anxiety, anger. Released it to Him. None of it was hers to carry any longer.

This had been her pattern all her life but never had it been more real than when she was living in the Kiowa village long ago, without her Bible and with fear surrounding her. To her surprise, here in Trenton she had encountered the same misery! Yet in both places, God surrounded her with His Word, His people, His truth. That was all she needed, ever. Joy bubbled over, in spite of her circumstances, astonishing her at first.

"Hold on there! *Joy*, a mere emotion? Hardly! I must remember always that it is not an emotion but a Fruit of the Holy Spirit! I seek *Him* and He blesses me with joy, as He is doing right now. I seek Him and He gives me peace. I seek *Him* and He reveals His love. Thank You, Almighty God!"

Mandy knew she could endure whatever lay ahead of her because it was all in God's capable hands. They were the same ones that had been pierced for her on Calvary and now held her close to His heart out here on this porch, right this very minute! For quite some time she sat in solitude and silence, drinking in the chirping of the birds around her and breathing in the fragrance of the flowers in the garden.

Finally, she could hold it all in no longer. Out loud she declared her victory to the Creator of all the beauty and power, that had brought her back from the brink of the sadness which had been plaguing her for days.

"I feel as light as a feather, no longer downcast and lonely. What a glorious spring day this is, after all!"

CHAPTER THIRTY-THREE

"...My grace is sufficient for thee: for my strength is made perfect in weakness." II Corinthians 12:9

May 7, 1867
Trenton, Ohio

"Mrs. Wilson, have you seen Lily? She is not up in our room. I expected to find her there when I got home from the sewing circle meeting. I've looked out in the gardens and on the front porch but do not see her, and I wondered if you have."

"No, Miss Amanda, I haven't seen her, either. Did she go to her friend's house today?"

"Yes, she did, this morning. I expected her to stay over for luncheon, but I thought she would be home by now. It's almost dinner time."

"Hmm, I am not sure what to suggest then. Perhaps you could go to her friend's house to see if the girls lost track of the time."

"That must be what happened. I will do that, be right back. If she happens to return home while I am gone, tell her to stay here, will you?"

"Sure thing, dearie. Don't stay gone long or you will miss my pot roast tonight!"

"It smells heavenly! Be right back."

Knocking on the door of the Cordons' home gave Mandy the jitters. The last time she did this it was quite unpleasant. She fervently hoped today would not be a repeat of that.

"May I help you?" asked the servant.

"Yes, I came to get my daughter, Lily Alton. Is she still here with Miss Genevieve?"

"No, she was here for a time this morning but left before luncheon today. I haven't seen her this afternoon at all."

"What? May I see Miss Genevieve, please? I need to talk to her right away!"

"Well, she is—"

"Don't say it, *indisposed!* Well, she can just get *unindisposed* because I *am* going to speak with her and immediately!"

The maid started to close the door but Mandy pushed on past her into the foyer.

"Genevieve!" she called loudly in the direction of the long, winding staircase. "Where are you? It's Mrs. Alton. Please come down here right now so I can talk to you. I'm trying to find Lily."

"What's the meaning of this loud intrusion, Louise?" roared a man's voice as he entered the foyer. This formidable man must be Mr. Cordon himself. He did not appear to be happy about Mandy's intrusion. *Too bad!*

"Sir, this lady pushed her way in here, saying she is looking for her daughter who is not here. And now she is demanding that Miss Genevieve come downstairs right away to talk to her."

"May I ask who you are?" he snapped as he turned toward Mandy.

"Sir, my name is Mrs. Amanda Alton. We haven't met but my daughter Lily has been spending a great deal of time here with Genevieve. I cannot find Lily this afternoon. I have reason to believe your daughter knows where she is."

"Don't be ridiculous. How could she know where your child is, if you don't keep up with her any better than this? Are you in the habit of allowing her to run all over town by herself?"

"Of course not, sir. Please, get Ginny, that is Genevieve, down here so I can find out when she last saw her. I wouldn't ask if it weren't important. What if it were your little girl who was missing? Wouldn't you be checking out every clue you could?"

At that he seemed to soften and instructed the maid to go up to fetch his daughter down immediately. Mandy's relief was vast, but the question still remained, *where was Lily?*

When the young girl appeared at the foot of the stairs, Mandy asked her anxiously, "Genevieve, when was the last time you saw Lily? I expected her home quite some time ago but she never showed up and I am quite concerned. When did she leave here?"

"Mrs. Alton, she left this morning, shortly after she arrived. She and I were talking when all of a sudden she became quite upset. Before I could ask what was wrong, she raced down the stairs and out the door, right in the middle of our art lesson. I haven't seen her since that moment."

"This *morning?* What? I thought she was supposed to stay through luncheon with you and your family, then come home later this afternoon. What caused her to become that upset this morning?"

"Well, she and I, we were talking about, well," and she licked her lips nervously, glancing at her father as his scowl deepened, "about—a doll that came from Paris. Yes, that was it. My doll. She remarked how pretty her real eyelashes were. That's all. I have no idea why she left so suddenly."

"Did she say anything that might help me know where she went from here?"

"No, ma'am, not to me. As I said, she left without a word."

"But she was upset? As in crying? Or as in angry?"

"Um, as in crying."

"Over a *doll?* There has to be more! What are you not telling me? Tell me the truth. Now!"

Ginny backed away a couple of steps and wouldn't meet Mandy's eyes. Instantly she knew the child was lying. But why? What was going on here?

"Mrs. Alton, my daughter has answered your questions," Mr. Cordon intervened. "Please stop scaring her and disrupting our home. I'm going to ask you to leave now. Genevieve, go on upstairs and finish your homework."

She scampered up the stairs much faster than she had come down, leaving Mandy stunned. *Did this man honestly say the peace in his home was more important than finding out where my child is? Unbelievable!*

Mandy called out to her, "Genevieve, if you think of anything further, please let me know!" But she had already closed the door of her room firmly behind her, giving no indication that she had even heard the plea.

Near tears yet determined not to cry in front of this horrid man, Mandy stood there a bit numb for several moments before she moved toward the door.

"I am sorry to have bothered you, Mr. Cordon, and to have 'disrupted' your peaceful home. I will honor your request and leave now. But I am frantic to find my lost child. Regardless of what you think, I'm a good mother but had to take care of important business today and *thought* my daughter would be safe in your home for the day. Apparently not. She came at your daughter's invitation. Something happened here, that much is clear. I will be back later to find out precisely what!"

Mandy turned on her heels and walked out the door as it slammed shut behind her.

Lily! Where are you? What has happened to you? Did you really make good on your threat and run away? Or are you lying somewhere hurt, perhaps dying, and cannot get home? God, please! Tell me what to do!

For the next couple of hours, Mandy frantically searched everywhere she could think of, and most places twice. Just as she was about to give up in despair, standing on a street corner wringing her hands and on the verge of tears, she spotted the familiar sight of Matthew's cabin at the end of the street.

Matthew! Perhaps he can help me find her. He knows this town better than I do, certainly. I don't know where to turn next but maybe he has a better idea of where to look!

Pounding on the door and breathless from running all the way down the street, Mandy began sobbing. "Help me! Matthew, please! I need your help! Lily is gone!"

Within moments the door opened. Concern lined his handsome face.

"What did you say, Amanda? Lily is *gone*? But how, when? Please, come in."

She collapsed in his arms, not even caring if anyone was watching nor how her response would be interpreted by others or even by him. Her life was falling apart and she needed another person to care!

"Amanda," he said a short time later after she had poured out her terror to him. "Drink this cup of tea, it will help soothe your nerves. I'm not very good at this, I must admit. But I can be a good listener when I need to be. Tell me what has happened to Lily."

"Thank you, Matthew. First off, I want to tell you that I rather overreacted the other day at the picnic. You startled me is all, and hurt my feelings. But it was, after all, only a kiss, and nothing more."

"Yes, nothing more and nothing more was intended."

"So, let's forgive and forget, shall we? I didn't come here to discuss this, however. I came here because I simply had no other place to go for help. Lily has disappeared and I have no idea where to look for her."

"Do you think that she ran away, as you told me she had threatened to do? Or perhaps she is at her friend's house and stayed longer than expected with her."

"Oh, I already questioned Ginny. She has been gone since this morning, apparently, while I was here with you. The details aren't important, but I don't know what to do." She stopped a moment. "Interesting that I turned to you before Nan, even. Don't read more into it than that; this is merely a desperate act of reaching out for help. Nan was at work and I knew I couldn't expect her to leave to help me search. I hoped you weren't in an important meeting with a client. The truth is, however, since leaving the Cordons' home, I have been searching everywhere I can think of, more than once in most cases. I don't know where else to look for her. She has no other friends here besides the Cordons' daughter, and she hasn't seen her since early this morning. I'm terribly frightened!"

"Of course you are! These are the times when I wish we had a formal law enforcement body here in town. It probably won't be long before we do, but that does not help us this afternoon. Do you suppose she might show up for dinner at the Boarding House? Maybe she went somewhere to think or pout or whatever it is that young girls do when they are upset. You can tell I'm not a father, can't you?"

That brought a hint of a smile to Mandy's lips. "At home sometimes she will go for a long hike into the hill country by our um, town, but she always comes home in time to help me prepare our evening meal. Perhaps you are right. But if she is not in our room, would you go with me to the Cordons and see if they will let us talk to Ginny alone? I think she knows more but was afraid to say much in front of her father. He intimidates *me*, so I am quite certain he does her. If I knew what made Lily abruptly change her plans for the day and leave there, what they were talking about, if she said where she might go, then maybe I would know where to start looking for her. I have a multitude of questions but no answers!"

"All right. Just stay calm—well, as calm as you can be under these awful circumstances. We have to think this through carefully, not in a panic. Let me get my coat. First, let's hurry to the Boarding House to see if she has come home yet. If not, we will head over to the Cordons' home. How's that?"

"Thank you, Matthew. I'm deeply grateful."

No Lily at the house and when the two got to Ginny's, the lanterns were already lit outside in their drive. Mandy's heart sank at the prospect of getting to talk to Ginny further, especially without her father present. She knew the servants lighted those only after the family had retired for the night, and even though it was still twilight, it was a signal they were not to be disturbed.

Surprisingly, Mrs. Cordon answered the door herself! She muttered something about a sick maid and graciously invited both of them inside. Mandy was nervous after their last conversation which turned into quite a scene, but she needn't have been. The woman was very kind when told that Lily was missing. And, she knew nothing about it! Apparently, her husband didn't take the situation seriously enough to even mention it to his wife. Shocked to learn Mandy had been there earlier, Mrs. Cordon immediately ushered them up to the nursery to visit her daughter. She was ready for bed, sitting on the floor playing with one of her dolls.

"Genevieve," Mandy began calmly, "I'm sorry to disturb you again, but I want to ask you one more time what you and Lily were talking about when she became upset. Can you remember?"

"Yes, Mrs. Alton. I remember very well. I do apologize but I couldn't say anything about it in front of my father earlier."

Precisely as Mandy had suspected!

"So, what happened?"

"We were talking about her coming to live with us, and I told her that it wasn't possible for us to adopt her, after all. Something about the international laws or whatever, but in any case, she needed to go home to her own family, not live with us. I was very sad to have to tell her that our idea would not work, but she was devastated. She began crying and begging me to reconsider. I told her my father wouldn't back down and it was no use. I have tried to convince him for some time how much I wanted a sister. Mama understood. But at times he is so mean!"

"Genevieve!" her mother said sharply. "That is enough."

"I'm sorry, Mama. But he really can be, you know that. He doesn't intend to be, not at all. But—"

"Genevieve, our guests have no interest in our family business. However, they do need to hear from you about the incident that upset your guest this morning."

"Genevieve," Mandy persisted, her panic mounting by the second, "did Lily say anything about where she might go when she left here? She never came home and I cannot find her no matter where I have searched. Do you have any idea at all where she might be?"

"Well, that awful man who follows us everywhere was in the park trailing around behind us yesterday again. Maybe he took her."

"Awful man? *Took* her? Who is he? Why would you think such a thing?"

"He said he would, if he ever caught her there by herself!"

"What? Who *was* this man? Can you identify him?"

"I don't know him, but I think Lily called him 'Alex'."

Mandy gasped as her knees buckled. Matthew sensed her reaction and caught her in the nick of time to prevent an embarrassing fall to the floor, easing her into a nearby chair.

"How often did you see this man?" he demanded.

"All the time. Lily was very frightened of him and said she was not supposed to talk to him. So anytime he came close to where we were, she needed us to run away from him. I thought it was just a game. So—" she stopped, the color draining from her little face, "she was *serious*? He really wanted to, to *harm* her? I had no idea!" And Ginny began to cry softly.

Her mother reached out to pat her shoulder to console her and Ginny melted into her arms. The misery and pain on her mother's face touched Mandy's heart.

Mrs. Cordon said, "I had no idea about all this, Mrs. Alton, or I would have informed you immediately myself! I told Genevieve that of course their harmless childish fantasy of becoming sisters was ridiculous but the idea of having a sister like your daughter was sweet and charming and they loved to pretend anytime Lily was here. My husband was not happy when he heard about it, but I saw no harm in letting them indulge in it from time to time, and I even encouraged it as a game between them. If I had known someone might try to harm your daughter, I would never have allowed her to leave here alone."

"If Alex has touched one hair on Lily's head, so help me..." sniffled Mandy. A stern look from Mrs. Cordon reminded her that Ginny did not need to hear any plans for revenge over what might happen to her friend.

"Amanda," said Matthew solemnly, "I believe we got our answers. Why don't we leave and allow Genevieve to go on to bed? I think we are through here, don't you agree? With the sun going down, perhaps Lily has returned home by now and is wondering where you are."

Mandy walked so fast to the Boarding House, Matthew had a difficult time keeping up! She prayed fervently that the whole kidnapping idea was not true and that her daughter would be waiting in their room. But, as happened earlier, she was nowhere to be found when they arrived, had not been there all afternoon, either, insofar as any of the guests knew. Mrs. Wilson kindly allowed Matthew to help search the grounds and house thoroughly, but no Lily.

Nan rushed in as this was going on, having heard the news shortly after leaving work. The two of them filled her in with the meager information they had discovered thus far.

"I got here as quickly as I could. Why didn't you come tell me at the Emporium? I would have left and helped the two of you search for her."

"I didn't want to put you in a difficult bind, Nan. You have had to miss a great deal of work lately and I knew there was little you could do. I thought Matthew's presence might melt the Cordons' block of ice hearts, but as it turned out, Mrs. Cordon was very kind. How on earth did you find out?"

"No one can hide something like this for long around here. I ran into a friend who had talked to you earlier when you were looking for her, and she said Lily might be missing so I raced right home. How are *you* doing, Amanda?" She squeezed her friend's hand and Mandy fought back her panic.

"I honestly think I'm in a state of shock. It hasn't really sunk in yet that she's gone. The information Ginny gave us about a man who followed them, one Lily called Alex, scared me and infuriated me, all at the same time! How could he take an innocent child like that? And why? What on earth does he expect to gain with such a horrific and cruel act? If my husband were here, he would beat him until he confessed but I'm a lady and I can't resort to such tactics!"

"If he gets in my way," answered Nan, "I can guarantee that I will do that to him! In fact, I think we should march over there right now and confront him. Maybe he will admit what he has done so we can rescue her."

"As much as I would like to get my hands around his throat right now," said Matthew, his face a grim mask, "I do not believe that would be a good idea. It might cause him to do something rash. No one can fathom the mind of a madman! We need to stay calm and positive here for the time being.

Besides, we cannot prove she has been kidnapped nor by whom. Until we learn more, all we can do is guess why she is absent. It could be disastrous if we start throwing around unsubstantiated accusations about Alex while we are in the midst of this lawsuit. So, let's not jump to any conclusions just yet."

He stopped for a moment, deep in thought. "You know what, I have a friend who might be able to help us. The only problem is, he has been on an extended business trip out of town and I'm not sure if he is home yet. He is what is called a Private Investigator. During the war, these men were used often by the government to root out those involved in espionage. Since that time their unique talents and connections have proven repeatedly to be useful to uncover many other criminal activities as well. I have been amazed at what all he can learn in a very short time, with his vast experience, as well as that of his team. If he is back, I know he will be most eager to help us. Alex has never been one of his favorite people, anyway."

"I've never heard of such a thing," said Mandy. "But it sounds like he would be most helpful to have on our side. It appears Alex has quite a few enemies in town."

"Yes," replied Matthew, "he certainly wouldn't win an award for being an outstanding citizen, would he?"

"I'm sorry to interrupt you folks, "said Mrs. Wilson, "but it is time for dinner to be served. Due to the unusual circumstances, I will be happy to serve you as well, Mr. Grayson, if you would like to stay and eat with us."

"Thank you, no, but that is very kind of you. I really need to go try to talk to my friend as soon as possible. Amanda, you should eat something." He looked at Nan, worry lining his face.

"Yes," she quickly responded, taking his hint. "Let's go eat and let Matthew get along on his errand. I'm sure Lily is fine and will be here soon. She wouldn't want to miss the delicious pot roast we always have on Tuesday nights."

Mandy smiled and nodded. "Thank you, Matthew, for your kindness. Nan is right, Lily is well known already for never missing a meal prepared by Mrs. Wilson, especially not this particular one. She will be here anytime, I'm sure."

"That's the spirit, to stay positive!" he said. "One last thing, I hate to push business into the middle of this difficult moment, but in the morning, I need to get your signature on one more document that must be filed tomorrow. Please don't miss our appointment, all right? I am hopeful it will be the last, in preparation for the final hearing on Friday. And you know, if Lily shows up tonight, my friend's help won't even be needed. Nan, try to get her to eat and rest this evening, will you? She has had quite a shock this afternoon."

"We will look after her now, Matthew, don't you worry," said Nan. "Thanks for doing so much to help."

"I will of course be praying, and if you hear anything further, don't hesitate to let me know tonight. Otherwise, I will see you, Amanda, in the morning."

"Thank you, Matthew. These last couple of hours would have been a nightmare, had it not been for you. See you tomorrow."

After eying the empty chair at the table which Lily usually occupied for meals, it was all Mandy could do to pick over her dinner while her stomach did flips inside. Finally, Mandy excused herself and went out on the porch to watch for her daughter, hoping against hope that as the day wound down, she would surely come home. Nan joined her after a time and they sat out there in silence, together.

When the moon rose over town, Mandy sighed and with a heavy heart went inside and up to her room. Nan wanted to go with her but she politely declined, saying she would be fine. Besides, since Nan had to be up early for work, she didn't want to impose on her further.

Once inside, Mandy lighted the lantern and listlessly dressed for bed, although she doubted she could sleep a wink. The in-depth time she had experienced with the Lord early that morning had helped sustain her through this terrible crisis so far, but she needed even more of His presence now that she was alone with all her thoughts and fears.

Father, how can I face bedtime when I don't know where Lily is tonight? Does she have a comfortable bed with plenty of food to eat? Or is she cold and alone and maybe even in danger from that monster Alex? How I need Your peace right now!

"God, I shall go *mad* if I keep thinking about this!" she cried. "Help me! Give me a sign that You are in control and are with my little girl! Oh, Ken-ai-te, I need you by my side tonight to hold me and tell me everything will be all right!"

She curled up on her bed, clutching her Bible, but when she tried to read its comforting words, the pages swam before her eyes as the tears overflowed and she dissolved into sobs.

Writhing on the bed in anguish, feeling alone, abandoned, terrified, Mandy called out repeatedly to her Savior for His compassion to fall fresh on her desperate heart. Memories of long ago intruded, causing her to shudder with the heaviness of them. Of another time when she felt the same way, but for a vastly different reason. Yet, God had been faithful back then. Could He do it again? *Would* He do it again?

Suddenly, her eyes fell on a single white glove on the floor beside Lily's bed across the room. Grabbing it up, she held it up to her cheek and continued to weep.

"Oh, Lily, will you ever wear this again?" A wave of irritation flooded over her for a moment as another thought took over. "Why is it that I cannot seem to teach you better responsibility, in particular, how to keep your gloves together? We have only been here a few weeks and this is the third pair of gloves I have had to buy you. How I wish they would sell just one alone instead of only in pairs. I keep telling you that you absolutely cannot go without gloves in proper society but you won't listen. Not having grown up wearing them, I know they are a bit of a nuisance to you. If you want to be accepted here, though, you have no choice, you simply must learn to wear gloves!"

Hearing the words spoken out loud, they seemed rather foolish now. *Why didn't I let her go without them? What difference does that oft-repeated lecture mean now? It only served to make her more miserable. I would give anything to take the words back, if she could just be in my arms once again. We will soon be back home where gloves are unheard of, a white invention to torture young girls! We* must *be home soon! Please...*

Her tears overflowed, dribbling down onto the smooth white glove in her hand. She pushed it into her eyes, as though doing this might help her be closer to her little girl once more. Using it to dab at the flow of moisture coming from them until it was damp and twisted into a knot, she gazed at the moist clump of fabric in her fist, somehow feeling strangely comforted by it. It was a connection of sorts with her child in a moment when she desperately needed to feel that. Finding it at this precise time was no accident. Can God's Spirit inhabit a mere glove, she wondered? And the answer came back as a gentle whisper.

Of course He can! He is the Creator of the universe. *Nothing* is impossible to Him. No Prayer Angel was there to speak on His behalf, ministering peace to her troubled heart, but this lone glove was a symbol somehow of His presence. And in a strange way, her courage was bolstered by its feel in her hand. God was still in control, knew where Lily was at that precise moment, was watching out for her. In addition, He cared about Mandy's broken and fearful heart, enough to show in a physical way that He was there for her, no matter what. She sat up, dried her tears, and stared down at the glove nestled in her fingers.

"Thank You, Lord, for this unusual gift and for Your peace that defies understanding. You calm me even at such a horrible time when by all rights, I should be falling apart. With Your help, I know now, I *can* get through this. It breaks my heart that I cannot even let Ken-ai-te know I have lost his beloved daughter—which may actually be a blessing since I think the shock might kill him on the spot. How I do hate this town and all it represents! I want more than ever now to go home to my family, as well as to my beloved prairie. But I certainly cannot leave now, without my little girl.

"Therefore, I claim Your promises in Isaiah, to give my daughter Your words right this moment, to be bold in her witness to those who hold her captive, to cover her in the shadow of Your hand, those precious hands upon which her name is engraved—*Lily*. This day I praise You for allowing me to be her mother and for the wonderful plan for her life which You created long before You formed her body. You have heard the prayers of many mothers in the past, such as those of Hannah and of our Lord's mother, Mary, for their sons yet to be born. Hear mine, dear God, for my child who is in such peril this night! Return her to me quickly. Until that moment, help me trust in Your protection which is far greater than my deepest fears!"

CHAPTER THIRTY-FOUR

"As cold waters to a thirsty soul, so is good news from a far country." Proverbs 25:25

May 8, 1867

Matthew, I do apologize for being a little late this morning, but I slept rather fitfully for most of the night. Then I managed to oversleep once I did doze off. I hope it's all right that I brought Nan with me. She said she wouldn't let me out of her sight this morning. Her boss wasn't as enthusiastic but somehow she managed to get off at least half a day, more if needed. I'm very grateful for her sacrifice."

"It's fine, Amanda, I am glad you are here now. How nice to see you again, Nan. I was about to go to the Boarding House and collect this signature from you there, as I figured you might not be up to a public appearance this morning. Sleep certainly evaded me, so I can imagine how your night went. Sign here, will you?" He pointed to the paper on his desk as Mandy dutifully signed it.

"Is this truly the last of the lot?"

"It certainly ought to be. I cannot possibly conceive of any further documents the judge might require."

"That's a relief to know. By the way, God's Word is a wonderful aid to sleep. You should try it sometime."

"I'm amazed at your peace of mind," he said. "Many prayers have gone up for Lily's safety during the night as well as for your encouragement. It's good to know God brought you the peace you needed at least."

"Mrs. Wilson is making sure that all of us at the Boarding House have ample opportunity to pray fervently as well," added Nan.

"That is very kind of her, Nan, and I do appreciate it, also your prayers as well, Matthew. I have every assurance that He will act this day to protect my daughter. Truth be told, I waver between that confidence and my anxieties that do threaten to overwhelm at times. The prayers I know are what makes the difference for me. Now, to the business at hand. Did you get to talk to your friend who is the, umm, what did you call him?"

"Private Investigator. His name is Paul Owens, and unfortunately, he is still out of town but due back late this evening. However, I did talk to his wife. She assured me he would be here in the morning to help us search for Lily. Meanwhile, she has alerted his team. When he returns, things will move swiftly, I'm sure. Some of them are already scouting around, seeking information and clues as to her whereabouts. And Alex's."

"So we have to wait another whole day before we can look for her again?" Mandy's voice was losing its calm around the edges. She swallowed hard against the fear that constantly battered her heart and mind. This was not what she had hoped to hear! Nan patted her hand lovingly and squeezed it tight.

"I'm afraid that is correct. I honestly have no idea how to proceed without his expertise. Although, with Paul's men out there working on this, it's not like nothing is being done all day. Their work takes time. We simply have to be patient and let them do their job. I'm convinced they can do what we cannot."

Mandy opened her mouth to say something, but Matthew held up his hand to stop her. He could sense her rising panic and rushed to finish.

"Look, I know this is difficult, but please, let's see what they can dig up. In the meantime, this evening I will be attending a, well, a type of dinner party I guess you would call it. There should be present certain, shall we say, 'elements' of society that seldom see the light of day. It's a strange situation, hard to explain, but the purpose of this gathering is not entirely for entertainment. Before you start wondering how I could go have fun in the midst of all this, hear me out. It really is not what it may seem. While checking around discreetly for information earlier this morning, I discovered that the one I believe who can help us the most is to be a fellow guest at this event. The best way to talk to him without arousing his suspicions is in a relaxed social setting where he will be drinking. If I can catch him off guard with enough liquor in him, I believe he should be able to point us in the right direction—provided I can apply exactly the right amount and type of pressure that will make him sing."

"Sing?"

"Sorry, it's an expression. To give us information that he otherwise would be hesitant to produce. Anyway, if you can hang on for one more day, I feel sure we should know where to find her by morning. Otherwise, we would be scrambling to discover the proverbial needle hidden in a haystack, without his help."

"I think the bigger question is," replied Mandy, "can *Lily* survive one more day? The thought of what she is going through right now is more than I can, or want to, imagine."

"Please, Amanda, don't torture yourself with that thought," said Nan. "Keep positive, remember? This Private Investigator idea sounds quite intriguing. I've heard of Mr. Owens but have never met him. Wasn't he the one, Matthew, who found the man who robbed the Emporium last year? I seem to recall that's where I heard of him."

"Yes, he was. How clever of you to remember! Anyway, how about I treat you two ladies to a nice luncheon over at the hotel? It would be good for all of us, to help perk us up a bit. They have their famous chocolate layer cake for dessert today! I saw the sign as I came to work this morning."

"Ordinarily, I would jump at that," said Mandy. "Today, I'm afraid I really am not hungry. However, I do suppose I ought to eat, as Mrs. Wilson and dear Nan kept pounding into me last night at dinner." And she smiled at her friend.

"Excellent, it's all set then. I must attend to a couple of matters here and afterward we can go on over there. It shouldn't take more than a few minutes. This afternoon I will be attending a business meeting on a complicated matter unrelated to this situation that requires more preparation on my part, so I need to work on that for a while before we go."

The first thing, however, that required his attention was to notify the messenger service he needed them. Nan volunteered to go across the street to their office for him. Matthew was eager to get the paperwork Mandy had signed earlier sent on its way to Hamilton to be filed as quickly as possible. Within a few minutes, the man showed up and quickly departed. Mandy breathed a sigh of relief knowing that fateful paper in his saddlebag would arrive safely and on time. *God, please, let this be the end of it!*

Mandy and Nan sat in the waiting area while Matthew worked intensely for about half an hour longer. They hardly spoke, not wanting to disturb Matthew, thus further delaying him. Mandy filled the time with silent prayer for her daughter. Every time her confidence waned, Nan's smiles bolstered her up, and she knew her friend was doing the same thing. Mandy was touched that Nan had boldly asked for time off work to remain with her through this ordeal. It never would have occurred to her to ask for this. But oh, how God was providing before she could even request His help through others in the midst of this terrible storm!

As they walked out of the door a short time later and Matthew turned to lock the door, Mandy heard a familiar voice behind them.

"Amanda, is that you?"

She turned to see her beloved husband and their dear friend Jacob, standing there on the path leading up to the cabin! In person!

"Jacob!" she cried, racing the few steps to hug him. "How wonderful to see you! But how—why?"

With great restraint she more calmly greeted the one she *really* wanted to hug.

"Chief Ken-ai-te, how delightful to see you again as well!" She stuck out her hand to shake with him, then felt a bit foolish. Oh, how she wanted to grab him instead, never letting go again as long as she breathed!

He stared at her while shaking her hand, his black eyes sparkling. Drinking in every second of the feel of her husband's fingers on her own after such a long absence, Mandy dreaded the moment when, for propriety's sake, she would need to release his hand, preferring to hang onto it as though for dear life. How she had missed that warmth and strength!

"Good to see you, Miss Amanda. "How are you?"

Perfect grammar. The basics and not one bit more. Disappointment swept through Mandy's whole being. *Is he not happy to see me? Not as much as I am to see him again, or...*

"We decided to come see what was taking you longer than you anticipated. Your husband is gravely worried about you," said Jacob.

"My husband?" she repeated without understanding.

"He asked us to come in his place. He could not leave your little one as he is ill."

"Is S—uh, *Sam*, is he all right?" It was the only name she could think of quickly. They had never given any thought or preparation for what the boys' names would be! Her heart jumped into her throat. *Has Spotted Rabbit been injured or—oh please no—perhaps is starving?*

"Oh, yes, your son should recover soon, but your husband *Ken* felt he needed at least one parent there when he was sick. His brother was relieved as well, to keep his father close."

This was getting way out of hand here, with one lie after another being told!

"That's a relief to know my husband is taking care of him. I have missed both him and the two boys deeply."

"Amanda, I take it you know these gentlemen?" Matthew's eyes were wide as he looked Ken-ai-te up and down, taking in the full sight of an Indian in his native clothing, standing in broad daylight right here in his hometown, in front of his cabin no less.

"Oh, I'm sorry, Matthew, and you, too, Nan! Yes, I certainly do know them! These are dear friends from Indian Territory. My husband has been worried, sending them to ensure that Lily and I are all right."

At the mention of her daughter's name, Mandy's façade fell apart, along with her shallow sense of confidence. She caught a sob in her throat but managed to quickly swallow it.

"Jacob, I take it?" and Matthew extended his hand. "I am Matthew Grayson, Amanda's attorney here in Trenton." Jacob warmly shook hands with the man.

"Jacob Murphy. And this is Chief Ken-ai-te, of the Kiowa people. He is my best friend and a close friend of Amanda's *husband.*"

Nan choked a moment, then her eyes widened, but she said nothing.

She knows he is my husband! Oh, please don't say a word, Nan! She did not, but the two exchanged glances and Mandy saw her eyes were sparkling bright!

Ken-ai-te extended his hand to the attorney, who hesitated only a moment before taking it. In that lone second in time, Mandy's heart almost stopped! He mustn't offend the chief! Let alone, her husband! Finally, as they greeted one another, Mandy let out her breath with great relief, unaware until that moment she had been holding it.

And then she winced as he mangled his name!

"It's Ken-ai-te," she said slowly for his benefit.

"Thanks, Amanda. Obviously, I have never met a Kiowa before. I apologize, sir, for not getting your name right the first time. I hope you won't hold it against me!"

They smiled at each other, although Mandy could see there was no warmth in her husband's expression. At least Matthew said he was sorry. What more could he be expected to do?

"And I am Nan Brewster," interjected the forgotten one standing there. "I am a friend of Amanda's. It is my great pleasure to meet you both at last. She has talked a great deal about you to me, and I'm dying to hear more about Indian Territory and the Kiowa people!"

She quickly shook both men's hands, not waiting for them to initiate it. While her obvious fascination with Ken-ai-te amused Mandy, she could see that her friend's attention was fixed principally on Jacob! Mandy smiled at her brazenness but it endeared her to this dear lady even more! Not to mention her discretion. Without a moment's hesitation, she chatted with the two guests, but Mandy could see the twinkle in her eye when she glanced at Ken-ai-te, for of course she knew!

"Good to meet you, Miss Brewster," said Jacob, smiling broadly. One would have to be a toad on the ground to miss the pleasure in his face at the sight of this young woman!

"Nan, please. We are all on a first name basis around here in Trenton."

Ken-ai-te smiled at her as well, obviously also taken with her energy and beauty. A tiny spark of jealousy burned in Mandy's heart. *Why doesn't he look at me like that? We've been apart almost a month now, and you would think his smiles would be only for me!* Immediately, Mandy felt deep shame for her silly reaction and begged the Lord's forgiveness. *I'm so mixed up today, a complete bundle of nerves. Where is the peace I was bragging about a short time ago? Seeing my beloved has wiped it all out. I just want his arms around me and my baby back and to go home! Help me, Father!*

"My goodness, gentlemen, I take it you have had a long, hard ride to get here." Matthew glanced down at the dusty boots and moccasins of his guests. "Why don't we go back inside here to my office for a few minutes? There have been some developments in the case and you should be told all the news, but not while we stand in the hot sun."

Matthew ushered them all into the conference room, where there was plenty of seating for all five of them. In the confusion, Mandy thought she saw a frown from Ken-ai-te but it was fleeting and she couldn't be sure.

What is he upset about? He knows I cannot greet him as I would like! Neither of us can!

She fought back her irritation and smiled broadly at the new arrivals as they all sat down, still shocked to see them after so long. Mandy sat next to Nan and Matthew took the seat on her other side. The other two men sat across from them but Ken-ai-te kept his eyes off Mandy, which unnerved her. Brushing it to one side, however, she braced herself for having to share the news about Lily in a moment.

"Please tell me," she said, "why you two have come all this way? It must have been such a dangerous journey for you both, but especially for you, Ken-ai-te." He nodded but still would not look at her.

"Yes," Jacob replied, "it was. We have been riding day and night for three days, in fact. The horses are tethered just out of town, but we need to get back to them soon to feed and water them. I felt it was important for us to find you before we took the time to tend to them. All we had was the name of your attorney. I intended to inquire about where to find him, but we actually found the office quite easily. Is there a livery stable in town that can take care of the four ponies?"

"You rode all that distance without stopping to rest?" asked Matthew in amazement as Jacob nodded. "Oh, to answer your question, we do have a livery here. They can go out and round up the ponies for you, if you'd like. When we leave here, I'll send word to the owner. I'm sure if you can tell him where they are hidden, they will be able to take care of them for you."

Jacob nodded. "Thank you. That would be most helpful. Back to Amanda's question, I don't know if you are a man of faith or not, sir, but we are. It's a bit complicated to explain but God commanded us to come, saying that Amanda and her daughter Lily were in danger here in Trenton. In short, we came, regardless of the risks. They were to have been home weeks ago. All of us have been gravely concerned that something unexpected might have happened. Without any way to communicate with them, it has been agonizing, waiting for them to return." And he looked directly at Mandy. "So, are both of you all right?"

Mandy's eyes filled with tears. How could she ever hope to explain this horrible tragedy to her husband?

"No, Jacob, we are not," she replied, her voice breaking as she fought for control. "God was right, we have been in peril ever since we arrived.

Without Matthew's help, I fear we would have perished for sure. As it is, Lily is, well, she has gone missing."

"*Missing?*" cried Jacob. "What do you mean?"

Ken-ai-te stiffened in his chair and Mandy saw his copper fingers grip the chair arm so tightly the knuckles instantly turned white. But he said nothing.

"When? How?" demanded Jacob.

"She, she has simply disappeared." Her voice broke into sobs, and she was unable to speak further. Nan patted her hand to encourage her friend in her misery.

"Gentlemen," continued Matthew for her, "she disappeared on her way home yesterday from a friend's house, a few blocks from the Boarding House where she and her mother live. We didn't find out about it until several hours later. After that, it took another couple of hours to search for her the best we could as well as to question the young friend she was visiting to get more details. At first we thought she might have run away, but as we finally discovered late last night, apparently that is not the case. As you can see, it has all been quite upsetting to Amanda, and I have been doing my best to help her figure out what happened, in order to determine how to proceed from here to look for her."

Mandy wiped her eyes and tried again. "Lily's friend Ginny said that my *cousin* had been following the girls and expressed several threats against Lily, even saying he would take her captive if given the chance. I knew nothing about this at all until she was gone. He has been harassing me for a couple of weeks, even against Nan because we are friends. Although he had expressed threats against Lily it was always because she was with me. I had no idea that there was more to this until last night. Matthew finally got Ginny to admit to us that he had continued to do it even when the girls were together walking around town. If I had known, I would *never* have allowed her to go and come from her friend's home without me to accompany her. It never occurred to me that she might be in any real danger. How could I have been so blind?"

Nan spoke up. "Amanda, please don't blame yourself. You are not responsible for that madman's actions. The point is, gentlemen, that Amanda's so-called Cousin Alex apparently has taken her but why we are not sure. He has made no demands thus far, which has made the whole thing quite puzzling."

"Wait," said Jacob, did you say this was your *cousin?* Wasn't he the one who is living in your aunt's home?"

"Yes, he is," replied Mandy. "Only it turns out, he is not related to me, after all. He is an imposter, a liar, a thief—and a murderer!" Another sob caught in her throat at hearing the words stated out loud like that. Cold chills swam up and down her arms and she shivered. Nan put her arm around her shoulder to try to calm her, but it helped only a little.

"Now, Amanda," said Matthew, "we are not sure about that last one, but it seems apparent that he did try to kill Miss Ida but fortunately did not succeed. Not quite the same as murder."

Mandy licked her lips. *Should I reveal Nan's secret now? I must defend my attack!* She glanced at her friend sideways, but Nan wouldn't meet her gaze. Mandy felt her stiffen next to her.

"Well," she said slowly, trying desperately to form the words in such a way as to keep Nan's name out of it. But how? "I know he has killed at least once."

"What?" Matthew's face reflected the level of how stunned he was at this news. "Who?"

"I'm not at liberty to say right now, the whole awful mess was told to me in confidence, but it is a highly reliable source. He killed a woman, then threatened to kill the one who found the body if she told anyone. To help protect her, I've kept quiet. Until now. But yes, he is a horrid man, and that is the one who may have my little girl!"

She felt Nan relax slightly but knew she had put her in a miserable situation by blurting this out like she did. Later, she would owe her a profound apology, but for now she was grateful the Lord helped her think quickly to step gingerly around the mess she almost made. Yet, Mandy also felt relieved that finally Matthew knew exactly what kind of person they were dealing with. And that went double for the other two.

"Yet you live in the house with this man?" Jacob was incredulous and Ken-ai-te's face flushed. It was difficult to see that on his copper skin but she knew him so well, she could tell. He was barely reining in his anger and she saw the struggle to remain silent.

"No, Jacob, I do not live there. I live at the Boarding House, as Matthew said a moment ago. We all three moved out of the home when my aunt passed away a couple of days after we arrived. The reason I have not been able to come back to the territory is that Alex filed a lawsuit to stop me from getting the inheritance. Matthew has been working frantically ever since to get this to come to a conclusion legally. Until it does and the judge rules in my favor, I cannot get my hands on the money. Thus, I could not return home. The thought of leaving here empty-handed after all we have been through is difficult to explain in a few sentences, but it was simply not something I could do in all good conscience. I guess this is my punishment for wanting the money so badly!" And the tears came again.

"There, there, Amanda," said Nan comfortingly. "You know God is not punishing you for any imagined greed. The inheritance is rightfully yours and soon will be yours legally as well." Nan again patted her on the arm as she spoke, and Matthew covered her hand with his own. Quickly Mandy withdrew it but not before it was noticed by the others. *Oh, Matthew! Why can't you leave me alone, especially in the presence of these two? How will I ever explain this to Jacob, much less Ken-ai-te?*

Mandy shook off her tears, knowing that Ken-ai-te would never respect her for showing emotion in front of others. It was one thing in the privacy of their tipi. He tolerated it at those times without a reprimand, but here? Never, in a million years. Oh, yes, she knew he would have plenty of words to fire at her when they were alone, whenever that was. Well, too bad. She lived *here* now, not back on the prairie in their tipi! And the tears were entirely appropriate, even expected. In fact, had she not shed them, she was certain Nan and Matthew would find that an odd reaction. And they would be right.

"Indeed, gentlemen," said Matthew, "it has been a difficult few weeks, and this last day has been the worst for all of us. We feel so helpless, but I'm working on a solution to that."

"For your information," added Mandy, "Matthew helped me search the town as much as we could, along with Nan. But frankly this is beyond our ability to track her down."

When she said the word "track" she saw Ken-ai-te's expression change to one of eagerness, even hunger. Again, she knew him well!

"Mr. Grayson," said Jacob, "Speaking of tracking Lily down, Ken-ai-te is the best tracker in the whole territory. He can find her, believe me, given the chance."

"I wouldn't doubt that," he replied, looking straight at the warrior, "if you were still back home. But here in civilization, I'm afraid it is a different sort of tracking that must be done. The hard dirt of our streets don't leave traditional footprints, for instance, and we have no idea where to start looking, to be honest. But I have a friend of mine who I'm confident can help us tomorrow. He is out of town now but will return tonight, and his wife has assured me he will be here in the office at 9:00 in the morning to meet with us. He is what is called a Private Investigator."

"I have never heard of such a thing," said Jacob. Ken-ai-te's face now paled.

Mandy couldn't take her eyes off her husband, although he still had never looked directly at her. She could imagine the anger he felt at being rejected for his skill as a tracker and realized that his pale face was more dangerous than a flushed one! *My, he is sure going through every single emotion in these few minutes, as I have been. How is he restraining himself? Heaven help Alex if my husband ever gets his hands on him!*

"It's all a rather new specialty in law enforcement that developed during the war and has continued to grow since then. He has done this with excellent success for the last few years and has a large team of trained men working under him. In fact, they have already been alerted, even in his absence. As we speak, they are searching for clues ordinary folks like us could never find. I know it's asking a great deal to expect all of you to be patient a little longer, but I am confident that if anyone can find Lily, it will be this man."

"Tracking still might be needed, so please keep the chief's skills in mind," said Jacob.

"That I will, sir," answered Matthew. "And now, you gentlemen must be exhausted and hungry, right?" Matthew's question caught Mandy off guard. But she knew it to be true, after their long journey.

"Yes, we could use a bed and some proper food," answered Jacob. "Our only food has been to nibble on pemmican while riding."

"Pemmican?" Matthew's eyebrows shot up.

"It's a type of dried buffalo jerky," said Mandy. "Very nourishing, if not tasty, but it can be eaten while walking or riding. Yes, I'm sure you two do need a good meal."

"I have a friend," said Matthew, "who runs the hotel here in town. Let's go get you two settled in a room over there. I'm afraid you will have to share, because while the owner most likely will be willing to take in an Indian who is a friend of mine, he won't rent a room to him, only to Jacob here with the understanding that Ken-ai-te—see, I got it right this time—

will be staying with him. There is an excellent dining room attached to the hotel where we can all go to eat. Does that sound good to everyone? The three of us were about to go over there ourselves, in fact."

Both men nodded and they all walked over to the hotel to secure a room for the men for the night. The owner, Cade Redding, was quite accommodating to having both as his guests, as friends of Matthew's, and had a room with two beds available.

"Tomorrow, Cade, we will figure out how much longer the room might be needed," said Matthew, "but for now one night is sufficient. And charge it to me, please."

Jacob said, "I have money to pay for the room, sir, but that is very kind of you."

"It's the least I can do, considering how far you both have come. Any friend of Amanda's is automatically a friend of mine." *He's simply being friendly, Ken-ai-te, please don't read anything more into what he said! White people do that!*

Once all that was taken care of, Matthew asked his friend Cade to contact Peter Gordon at the livery stable and request that he go find their guests' four ponies to see they were taken care of as well. Jacob informed him where to find them, and Cade said he would make sure that was done for them. Next came food!

They walked into the elegant dining room and sat down at a table over by the window. The waitress told them the menu items and took their orders. Matthew made it clear he was paying for everyone's meal. Ken-ai-te intently observed the entire room, Mandy noticed, keeping a wary eye on the only way in or out of the large room. But, as before in the office, his gaze never once was in her direction. *Perhaps he is afraid of unleashing his emotions if he does. Oh, how I wish I could talk to him alone!*

Suddenly, a loud voice sounded from behind a door that apparently led to the kitchen. It was slightly muffled but could easily be heard by all of them.

"What is an Injun doing in my restaurant?" he thundered. "Get that scum out of here or you are fired! Oh, never mind, I'll do it myself!"

Matthew sat up straight in his chair, alarm painted all over his pale face. He glanced in that direction just as the man behind the voice came barreling out of the door of the kitchen into the almost empty dining room. Mandy flinched, dreading to hear the words to come.

"Get out of here! Did you hear me? I don't allow no thievin' Injuns in my place, and them that brung him can go, too! Out of here *now,* all of you! Or I will personally string him up right in front of you!"

CHAPTER THIRTY-FIVE

"Let them be confounded and put to shame that seek after my soul: let them be turned back and brought to confusion that devise my hurt." Psalm 35:4

May 8, 1867

Amanda, I'm sorry to leave you after all that has happened, but I feel I need to get back to work this afternoon. And you, my friend, need to rest. I can see from the dark circles under your eyes that without that, you won't be any good to your daughter or to anyone else."

"But—"

"Now, no 'buts' at all, I won't hear of them! If you don't go up to your room right now and promise me not to leave there until I get home from work this evening, I refuse to leave you. My boss will simply have to understand!"

"Nan, I do not need someone to sit with me. Of course you should go back to work. I'll be fine."

"Promise me, Amanda! You will stay put and let your body and mind rest?"

"All right, I promise."

"Good. Now, Mrs. Wilson will be here to watch out for you if you should need anything of course. And she will ensure that you do not slip out to go search for Lily, either!"

Mandy sighed. How she deserved such kind friends was beyond her! But how she would manage to sleep with all on her mind also escaped her understanding. She promised to *try* at least. And she would. Try. Whether or not it worked, remained to be seen. First, she decided to offer to help her landlady with the dishes. That should take her mind off her troubles, right? At the least, she would stay busy and take a little of the load off her friend. Of course, her generosity was well received, and Mandy was surprised how many dishes this sweet lady had to do after each meal! *I need to do this more often. Keeping my hands busy as we work and getting to chat with her are definitely helping to numb my mind at least. That nap I promised to take becomes more appealing with each moment I stand here drying these pots!*

A short time later, she followed through on her promise to Nan. She stretched out on the bed and…no sleep came. Pondering all that had gone on in the past few hours, the one thing that stood out of course was that her husband was here! In Trenton! How she longed to talk to him and hold him, however briefly.

"Well, I mustn't dwell on the impossible. If anyone saw us embrace, they would know we were not merely friends! That is one secret that absolutely *must* be kept. Perhaps this is God's protection, to keep me from being with him. That way, I cannot with one careless kiss accidentally endanger this whole structure of fabrication I have built up over the past few weeks. How have I turned into one who depends on lies to get me out of difficult situations instead of relying solely on what is true? I am absolutely miserable here in Trenton and want to go home where life is simpler and—"

She stopped because she had intended to say "easier" but nothing could be further from the truth!

"Have I forgotten so quickly what my life there is really like? Here, things *are* easier, but not happier. There, I am with my family and we can face anything together, with our faith in Christ to stand with us!" Saying all this out loud made her feel much better, knowing there would be an end to this farce soon, and a return to the beloved place where she was destined to live out her days.

After they were thrown out of the dining room, Nan had suggested they come back to the Boarding House to see if Mrs. Wilson happened to have some leftovers they could put together into a meal, and it proved to be a brilliant solution to their dilemma. She of course did have and was thrilled to accommodate them, equally as outraged as they were over how they were treated at the restaurant. Being pretty much the only one in town, there were few other options available. Mrs. Wilson was pleased to offer her hospitality to friends of Mandy's, especially ones who had come all the way from Indian Territory.

"She is truly a good-hearted woman," Mandy muttered to herself, "and I can never thank her enough for welcoming us the way she has, not to mention Ken-ai-te, especially. Taking pity on us the way she did, her kindness went a long way toward making up for the earlier fiasco. It didn't seem to bother her one whit that she had a Kiowa warrior eating at her table! We may not have eaten much but the impromptu meal not only was nourishing, it seemed to put us all in better spirits for a time. But what about *now*, Lord? I feel so empty and alone! Hold me close in Your arms, Father. I want my baby back! Is that such a wrong request?"

Mandy lay there crying for a time, until all her tears were spent. Would she ever see her beloved daughter again? Finally, she grew drowsy and had almost drifted off when a thought intruded.

"Oh!" she cried, sitting up in the bed. "I just remembered something. While we were eating, Matthew got a message from one of Owens' men saying he found a witness who thought he saw Lily being abducted. Now, what did he say? At the time, my misery had absorbed me completely and I failed to pay careful attention. I think he said the man believed he saw Lily being shoved into the back of a wagon and driven off in the direction of the warehouses down by the river. Is that right?" She frowned with the effort to recall the words exactly. "Yes, that's right, he said he couldn't identify the driver for certain but said it might have been Alex Clark! If this is accurate, then Alex himself kidnapped Lily and has taken her down to the docks. And that is where I will find my little girl! Why that wasn't more obvious earlier is beyond me. But it is now!"

She straightened her clothing and hair and splashed water on her face to remove the puffiness around her eyes from the weeping, eager to make herself presentable at least. The good news is that Lily did not run away but was taken from her mother's arms. The bad news is that she, indeed, was kidnapped, now in the hands of vicious criminals. Why did this realization not make her feel much better? Matthew's concern earlier about the warehouse area weighed heavily, but only for a moment, then she shook it off. He told her it had long ago been abandoned when the river routes changed, bypassing Trenton. It had become a harbor for many criminals to hang out and plan their mischief. Few residents ever went there any longer, fearing for their lives.

"God, I don't care about all that! I just know You can lead me to where she is. *Now!* The trick is going to be escaping the watchful eye of my landlady." She checked her pocket watch for the time and smiled. "She will be in the kitchen preparing tonight's dessert and rolls, too busy to pay attention if one lone boarder slips out the door!" Something nudged at her heart, even dancing around in her head, but she dismissed it. This wasn't the time to entertain doubts or questions. This was time for action!

Within minutes, Mandy was walking quickly away from the Boarding House, relieved to have managed to get out unseen by anyone living there. She recalled where the docks were but had not seen them in many years. Would she remember the way through the woods behind the town?

"It's a good thing that on one of my rides around the area with Matthew in his buggy, he pointed out the new bridge that leads down there. The old one, he said, had washed out years ago and for a long time no one could get to the river on a direct route. A few years ago, however, the new one was built, thus removing the problem of having to go the long way around. Trouble is, no one used it now. I think I can find it once I get close enough. It is a quite a walk but I have been cooped up too much lately. I am eager to get out and stretch my legs a bit!"

Before long, she had crossed the bridge and arrived at the edge of the heavily wooded forest behind the main part of town. But where was the pathway through there, to the river?

"There! I think that's it!" She scampered down the path and disappeared into the woods, a little nervous about being in a secluded area like this. "God, don't let me get lost!"

After several minutes along the winding pathway, she emerged from the trees and spotted the banks of the river right ahead.

"This has all changed from when I was a child and Papa used to bring me down here to teach me to swim. For many years it was a busy area for wagons carrying merchandise to store in the warehouses, awaiting transport by riverboats. Now, the buildings all appear to be abandoned and empty, as Matthew warned me they were. Many even seem ready to fall down with a strong wind! Hidden from view of anyone in town, small wonder it has become a haven for criminals. Yet, if that is where Lily is being held, somehow I must get closer than this if I'm going to find her. I'm afraid if I leave the safety of the trees, I will stand out to anyone watching, as an elephant would on the prairie!"

She shivered with uncertainty. And more. Was God warning her of danger? He had done so before and she failed to heed His Spirit. Should she turn back? Or go on?

"Matthew was right about something else, about the number of these warehouses. There are many more of them than I expected, plus, they all look alike. It would really take a great deal of time and manpower to search through each one. How will we ever discover where she is being hidden, assuming this is where they took her? What if our information is incorrect and she is not even here? Only with Your wisdom, Lord!"

Before she could take another step, a shadowy figure emerged from behind a stand of thicket next to the roadway and startled her. Instinctively, she backed up a couple of steps.

"Whatcha lookin' for, little lady?"

"Who, who says I'm l-l-looking for anything?" she stammered in fear.

"No one comes down here from town unless they are lookin' for trouble. Is that it? You lookin' for trouble?" He squinted at her and she frowned. The man looked slightly familiar to her. Where had she seen him?

"I am not here to harm you," she said in as confident a voice as she could muster. "Please go away and leave me alone. I'm merely on an afternoon stroll."

"Not anymore you ain't!" He lunged at her and grabbed her around the throat with both hands before she could react to defend herself. She tugged at his fingers with all her might, but it was no use. His strength was far beyond her own and he had used the element of surprise to catch her off guard. As he cut off her air and his face swam before her eyes, she felt her knees buckle under her. He was choking her to death, leaving her helpless to stop him!

At the very moment she felt her life was over, he released her, pushing her backward with a hard shove, and she fell into the grass.

"That's just a little warning, honey, that if you don't give up and go home right now, you won't live long enough to spend that money you are so keen to steal! Neither will that brat of yours! If messing with the paperwork wasn't enough for you to get the message to go home, maybe this will get your attention!"

Mandy rubbed her throat, trying to ease the pain in it, taking in great gulps of air.

"I'm not going home without my daughter!" she rasped, coughing to clear her throat. "You tell whoever you work for to return her to me immediately—and unharmed!"

"Fat chance he will release her! You are never going to find her in time, I can you tell you that!" he called over his shoulder as he raced away into the trees. Mandy sat there on the ground, weeping in pain and fear. The anger roared up inside, the longer she sat there.

Her daughter *had* been kidnapped! Their suspicions were correct. How she wished they were not. What had the man said about "he" would never release Lily? Not only this cockroach who attacked her was involved, but at least one other person higher up giving the orders. Could it really be Alex? And if not him, then who?

I know, Lord, it might be a bit unfair for me to condemn Alex for this heinous crime without any real evidence. But he deserves all Your wrath, plus mine, for what he has done in the past and for the threats he leveled against all of us. Every one of my motherly instincts are screaming at me that he is the one who has taken her! I never believed she would run away, no matter what she said in anger during our arguments. Now I know she did not. Please keep Your hands around her, right now! If I am wrong in my assumptions, forgive me. But I know I'm not!

She rose slowly and ran all the way back into town, glancing over her shoulder several times to ensure no one had followed her. Who could she tell about this? Matthew or Nan, for sure, but what could either of them do? Her heart longed to tell her husband but she knew the danger that would put him in, as he would feel obligated to hunt this man down and force him to reveal where his daughter was. Both her friends would be furious that she went down to the river on her own, plus she would have to admit she had broken her promise to Nan. Yet, she knew every single clue could help in catching Alex—or whoever—and doing so before Lily could be hurt. What did that thug mean by not finding her "in time"? The sense of urgency grew with every step she took, along with the awareness that she could not keep this to herself.

"I have to tell someone, Lord! Direct my steps."

Within minutes she stood in front of Matthew's office door. But it was locked! Where was he? What had he said about where he was going this afternoon?

"Oh, that's right, to meet with a client about another case. But where? He must still be in his meeting. Didn't he say he expected it to last all afternoon? I'll have to wait to tell him in the morning, I guess. Her heart clenched at the thought of another delay. Regardless, she must get back to the Boarding House before she was missed.

Up in her room, Mandy fell on the bed and quite literally cried herself to sleep.

A gentle knock awakened her, and she could immediately see by the shadows in the room that it must be close to dinnertime.

"Amanda? It's Nan. May I come in? Are you all right?"

Not waiting for a reply, she slowly opened the door. Mandy sat up and stretched, pretending she had been there all afternoon. Her throat felt swollen and sore. Her fingers went to the top of her bodice, to ensure it was high enough to cover any bruising that may have formed there from the choking episode. Had she dreamed the whole nightmare? No, the discomfort was real!

"I'm fine, Nan. I took a nap is all, and I'm a little groggy."

"That's to be expected, after all the excitement you had earlier. It's time for dinner and I told Mrs. Wilson that I would check on you. Do you want me to wait on you to freshen up or go on down?"

"You go ahead. I'll be along directly." *I need to get my story straight and figure out what to say to everyone.* She was dismayed to discover while freshening up that there were bruises on her throat but was relieved to see that the lace at the top of her neckline covered them completely. At least there would be no uncomfortable questions about them at dinner.

After again picking over her dinner, Mandy's energy remained sapped from the frightening experience that afternoon. *Should I tell Nan about it?* Later, when her head cleared a little and they were alone. Or not. For now, her heart brimmed with all the questions and unknowns that plagued her, not to mention the fact the desire to see Ken-ai-te alone grew by the second.

Mandy excused herself when dessert was brought in, saying she was retiring early. Her legs were restless and she jumped at every little sound as she slowly headed for the staircase. How could she sleep like this? The need for sleep paled against the need to be with her husband. But the Lord reminded her she also needed time to pray, something she hadn't been doing much of this long day. She winced at the thought. *How could I have endangered myself without asking You first?*

Nan's voice jerked her out of these thoughts. She called after Mandy before she left the room, "I had hoped to hear more about Jacob and how he lives back in the territory. I am very excited I got to meet him this morning!"

"I'll tell you tomorrow, is that all right? I'm really tired tonight."

"Sure, I understand. He's so handsome! And he's a widower, right?"

Mandy nodded and left the room without another word. The last thing she needed tonight was to jabber with Nan about a handsome man, when all she wanted was to feel her own handsome man's arms around her, shutting out the whole, crazy world right now!

As soon as Mandy closed the door behind her, she knew she *had* to get out of there! Unexpectedly running into Ken-ai-te that morning had been such a shock! Delight had shivered down her spine as it always did in his presence, even after all these years. It had taken a great deal of her energy to mask her true feelings at seeing him. Over the course of this long day, those had only grown until now she felt about to explode if she didn't feel his embrace once more, and soon. Seeing him had only served to heighten her longing for him and deepen her loneliness this evening without him.

"How many more nights, Father, will You expect me to sleep alone in this place? I want to go home! Help me! I beg You to do that so often, You must get tired of hearing it! But feeling weak and helpless as I do right now, I know I cannot do this on my own! Is it such an evil thing to want to be with my husband, especially when Lily has been taken from me? How much more do you expect me to take?"

She sat in her rocker for a time, not really praying or even thinking, remaining there in silence as though waiting for something. But what? A flash of lightning or voice from Heaven telling her everything was going to be all right?

"What I *need* is to talk to Ken-ai-te! If I don't get to do that tonight, and soon, I believe I shall burst! There won't be a chance for us to talk in the morning at Matthew's office, only living more lies in front of others. However, if I go out now, alone on the street after dark, I run a great risk of encountering the wrong people, namely Alex. Not only him but also every kind of criminal who might be wandering around at night, like the one who tried to choke me earlier."

Mandy abruptly sat straight up. "Wait a minute! I know where I have seen that creature before! He was with Alex one time when I spotted them standing on the street talking. He slinked away down an alley and out of sight, but I know it is the same man. I thought he looked familiar. So, he *is* one of his cohorts! That monster does not have the courage to do evil deeds himself, therefore must hire people to do them for him. Well, at least I can let Mr. Owens know about this man's comments tomorrow. For now, however, I have to figure out a way to see my husband!"

Slowly an idea began forming in her mind. Not perfect by any means, but possibly a way to see her beloved alone for a few minutes. She figured she could slip out of the Boarding House fairly easily; getting back in was another matter, but she would solve that problem later. The risks she might encounter were worth it all, if it allowed her time with Ken-ai-te. By keeping to the shadows, she might make it to the hotel without being seen. Getting in there, however, posed ominous questions such as how to find the right room as well as how to get up the stairs, all without being spotted.

Imagine the scandal that would erupt if she were caught—a married woman sneaking into the hotel room of two men! Would people be more understanding if the truth got out, knowing that one of them, an Indian no less, was her husband? She doubted it. Not here. Again, something she would figure out once she arrived at her destination. There was too much at stake for her to get caught, that was all there was to it! A nagging thought nibbled at the corner of her mind but she ignored it. The desire to see the Kiowa warrior whom she loved more than life itself overwhelmed all her fears and even her common sense.

Holding her breath, she snuck down the stairs and crept toward the front door. No one was in the Parlor, fortunately. All was quiet. Using her best Kiowa skills, she scampered the last few feet and unlatched the lock as silently as possible. Then she slid through the opening, gently closing the door behind her, and raced out into the darkness.

"Whew! I made it!" Heart pounding loudly enough she feared someone might hear it, Mandy felt confident she knew the way well, even without a lantern to light her path. As before, she used all her skills as a Kiowa to run as silently as possible. What would she do when she got there? Maybe this wasn't such a great idea after all!

Please keep Alex away from me, Lord. He won't expect me to be out this time of night. I pray I won't have to deal with him. I'm not sure I can handle that tonight. Maybe he's out of town, at least I can always hope so. It will take a major miracle for all this to work. I'm grateful You are a God of miracles!

She did her part and trusted God would do His, no matter how hard it might be. The distance seemed much greater tonight for some odd reason. Had they moved the hotel further away?

Rounding a corner, she breathed a sigh of relief. No, there it was, a mere handful of buildings away, silhouetted against the night sky by the lights from its many windows. Only a couple more alleys to cross. Now would be a good time for that miracle because—

Suddenly someone grabbed her from behind, one hand clamped firmly over her mouth, his other arm around her middle. Terror sliced into her heart as the man roughly jerked her up close with her back to him, pinning her arms tight. If she could utter a sound, which was impossible, would she *want* to scream for help? How would she ever explain what she was doing out like this? *God, help me! What does this man mean to do to me?*

CHAPTER THIRTY-SIX

"When thou passest through the waters, I will be with thee; and through the rivers, they shall not overflow thee: when thou walkest through the fire, thou shalt not be burned; neither shall the flame kindle upon thee." Isaiah 43:2

May 8, 1867

Help me, Lord Jesus! I have to get away from this maniac!
Mandy struggled a moment to get loose, but it was no use. A hoarse whisper sounded in her ear. "No scream!" Pure joy exploded in her heart as her assailant whirled her around and released her. It was Ken-ai-te!

"My love!" She melted into his arms as he swept her into a tender embrace, kissing her deeply, even as she returned the kiss eagerly. Her tears mixed with her soft laughter as she kissed him over and over while he held her close. Ken-ai-te, ever on the alert, stiffened as a cowboy sauntered by on the street, too drunk to walk straight, and he pulled her deeper into the shadows of the alley to avoid being seen.

"Why you out after dark alone?" he demanded in a soft voice, a fake frown on his face. Then he burst into a smile and hugged her tight again. "Not care, glad you here."

"You scared me to death! I know it was risky but I just had to see you tonight. And alone. Oh, how I have missed you! Did you think of me while we were apart?" Not waiting for his reply, words tumbled out that she had been thinking all day, in the hopes she might get to see him somehow, someway.

"How foolish you were to come here to Trenton! What if harm befell you? I couldn't bear to live without you. How did you know we were in trouble? As you have seen for yourself earlier today, there are many here who have a great deal of anger against Indians. They would as soon hang you as talk to you! My beloved, you are in terrible danger!"

He held his hand up at the torrent of questions and laughed softly. "Too many questions. Cannot think in English that fast. Prayer Angel tell me to come in dream. Jacob say we come but with another lie—he my master, I his servant. Do whites not ever tell the truth?"

"Yes, they do, and as a rule they do. But this one lie of mine has brought on many more. How I despise that! By the way, Nan knows the truth, thus knows who you are, but she is the only one who does. Believe me, she is absolutely trustworthy. Somehow, God will untangle it soon, I hope in a couple of days at the final court hearing. At that point the case will be over and I will have the money we so desperately need. Until then, we must do as Jacob says—keep pretending a little longer that you are his servant and that I am not your wife. Oh, that hurts my heart to say that, but it cannot be helped. I'm afraid this ridiculous ruse we are living is about to get far more complicated, now that you are here, especially with, with Lily gone."

He nodded solemnly and said, "We find. No cry," caressing her cheek gently as he wiped away a tear with his thumb.

"Where you go tonight?"

"You won't believe this, but I was on my way to find you! I had no idea how I would get into the hotel unseen, much less up to your room, just knew I had to try. Were you coming to see me?"

"Yes, think I can find house you stay in but not sure. You save me trouble to find it in dark. You good Kiowa, quiet and in shadows."

"Thanks, I had a great teacher! How funny that we both had the same idea. Wait, why did Jacob let you leave the safety of the room without him?"

"He did not. Had to per-suade him, think that is the word."

"As in... did you harm him?"

"Small bump on the head, he be fine. He tell me no, I tell him yes, must see Prayer Woman now. He not be happy when he wake up, come look for me."

"I'm sure you are right. If I am missed, they will be searching for me as well. Although we must make this short, I already don't want it to end."

"Your question, yes, I think of you while apart. Boys do, too."

"How are my sons? In all the concern over Lily, I haven't had a chance to ask you about them. They are also constantly in my heart and prayers, as you have been. Do they have enough to eat?"

"No one have enough to eat. But sons o-kay. Many in village not, many deaths and time grows short. Must have money."

"Oh, I am vastly relieved to hear the boys are all right. I am sad that no one has enough to eat, however. Who is watching over them while you are gone?"

"Yellow Eagle. He take good care of them."

"Yes, he will. My heart can rest easy, then. Soon our eating pots will be full once more when we return with the money for meat, for us and for everyone in the village."

"When that happen?"

"The case has to be finalized first. Matthew is confident we will win, but the law says we have to defend the ridiculous accusations that my so-called cousin has made against me. I grow weary of the effort but know it is for a good cause. In fact, my aunt's fortune was far greater than I ever dreamed. The amount is staggering, considering she was unmarried and living in a small Ohio town. I simply cannot give up when victory is in sight. Now, with Lily gone, I have a new reason to stay put, until we can find her. This afternoon I went searching on my own and discovered a new clue."

Ken-ai-te frowned. "On own? Too dangerous! Why not with me?"

"We have to keep you hidden as much as we can, remember? And never with me unless we are with others, too. I did it on the spur of the moment, without giving it a lot of thought. There wasn't time to figure out how to find people to help me. Do you remember the message Matthew got at luncheon, about a possible witness? He thought he might have seen Alex put a young girl into a wagon and drive down to the docks."

He nodded but still frowned. "Not know where this 'docks' is, what it is."

"There is a large river that runs through Trenton which used to be well traveled for commerce. The docks are wooden platforms built over the water, so the boats could pull up and unload the supplies they carried. Large buildings were created to house all of it, called warehouses, but it is all abandoned now. I went down there thinking I might find our daughter. But all I found was a man who tried to choke me!"

"Hurt?" he demanded, the frown deepening.

"No, I'm fine, but it was very scary, I have to admit. He said there was no way we would ever find Lily in time, even admitted that Alex had masterminded her kidnapping. At least she didn't run away, but that is small comfort when I think of the monster who has her!"

"Tell Matthew?"

"No, I haven't seen him. He had a business meeting this afternoon and a commitment this evening as well. I was supposed to remain in my room in the Boarding House but I simply *had* to get out to look for our daughter. And this evening, to see you alone!"

She pulled away enough to gaze into his dark eyes and study his handsome copper face. How she had missed that sight! But she must keep her head about her because if her conclusion was correct, they didn't have much time before one or both would be missed. Thunder rumbled in the distance, startling Mandy as a flash of lightning lit up the sky overhead.

"Rain comes," her husband said quietly.

"Yes, it does appear to be imminent. I really don't want to get caught out in it as it will be harder to hide the fact I was outside this evening if I come in soaking wet."

"Why you call this Matthew by first name? Thought whites did not do that except for family." *No sympathy whatsoever for how I might get caught in this storm!* She tried to shrug it off but the irritation dug its talons deep into her heart.

"Often, that is true. Given all the time we have had to spend together in working on the legal case as well as—oh, how do I put this? Well, let me say, building that case up, it made better sense to be less formal. Besides, he was a dear friend of my aunt, almost like a son to her, and he is a war hero too."

"Reason lost eye, in war?"

"Yes, as a matter of fact. He also was wounded in one leg rather severely. My aunt set him up in his law practice after his parents died. But you know what, I don't want to talk about Matthew! I want to talk about us, our children, our people, and why you came all this way!"

"Told you, Prayer Angel came in dream, said you in danger, would die if I not come to rescue."

"That I would *die?*" And she shivered at the thought. "I'm grateful you listened and came, Ken-ai-te." The enormity of the miracle of him coming was a bit overwhelming. Did he sense it?

"I've written down so many thoughts all these weeks we've been apart, and often begged you on paper to come. But I never believed it would really happen. To think how close to disaster I have been leaves me, well, shaken. And now our daughter *is* in danger, grave danger, in fact. This man who has her is so evil, I wish I had time to tell you what all he has done! But the important thing is, we simply *have* to find her before she is harmed! How I pray that she will not be the one to die!"

"I find. Not need white men to track her. Not understand why we sit and wait."

"It's hard to explain, I agree. And regardless of what Matthew said, I believe with all my heart you can track Lily, even here. It won't be easy but it can be done with your skills. As for the waiting, that is also difficult to understand. But we have no choice. One more day and with God's blessing, our daughter will be back in our arms!"

"Not trust these white men. You trust?"

"Yes, Ken-ai-te, I do. Over time, I have come to realize how reliable Matthew is in his job, and if he says this new man can find her, then I trust him. What else can we do?"

"Go find, tonight."

"As exhausted as you are and without any idea where to look? No, I believe we must be patient a little longer, my love. With all I have been through since coming here, I'm so relieved to have you by my side again. Well, kind of at any rate—at least nearby. I thought I knew what I was getting into by coming to this place, but it wasn't anything like I expected. From the start, Alex was hostile and hateful. Had it not been for Matthew's help and Nan's kindness, I honestly do not know what I would have done. Little by little I have made some good friends here, in spite of my loneliness and frustration. However, Lily grew more mesmerized every day with the white culture around us. Nothing I said or did helped. She only pulled further away from me and her Kiowa heritage. In fact, the night before she disappeared, we had a terrible argument in which she told me she wouldn't be returning to Indian Territory with me when my business was complete. She had decided to live here in Ohio instead!"

Ken-ai-te scowled in fury at this.

"She not white! She Kiowa. Why she say this?"

"It's all very complicated, my beloved, but this is the very fear I had when we first discussed the idea of me returning to Ohio, that perhaps I would find I loved it too much to go home."

"Do you?"

"No!" she shouted, then clapped her hand over her mouth, remembering the urgency of being unseen and unheard in this alley. She continued but in a lower voice. "Not in any way do I want to stay here. I have been tempted to give up several times, due to how miserable I have been without you here with me."

"Yet you turn to this Matthew, he give you comfort, like best friend. You my woman. He know you have man, but not act like it."

"Oh for pity's sake! You can't mean you are jealous of him!" She stared at his face. "You *are!* How could you think I might look on another man when we are apart? Do you think my love is that shallow?"

"You not come home."

"I *told* you why! Because Alex filed the suit against me and I cannot leave until I can get the money I came for. It is not my fault it has taken far longer than we thought it would, definitely not my choice. You expect me to go home empty-handed because I got lonely? Good grief! This has not been a Sunday School picnic for me, you know! Matthew is fully aware that I am a happily married woman with three children. He is not a threat to you, in any way. Incidentally, I am not 'your woman' as I've told you over and over through the years. I am your *wife,* not your woman. And not your property! Stop treating me like a prized horse instead of the woman you love!"

He said nothing, which disturbed her even more. Her anger rose.

"Not only have I been putting up with the threats from Alex, I also have had to deal with my grief over losing Aunt Ida. You haven't shown me any sympathy at all because of her death."

"You say she die, no need to talk further of her."

"No need? For the Kiowa, that is true, but not for white people!"

"But you Kiowa, no longer white!"

"I know that, more than you can imagine, in fact. I have embraced my Kiowa heritage freely back home, but while I am here, I am white. Well, at least I must think and act like one. Oh, I'm so confused! All I care about right now is getting Lily back! And here we are arguing about, well, about silly things like this!"

"Talk no help. Act, find daughter is all that matters."

"Why is it that your Kiowa brain cannot comprehend how my grief is cluttering my brain? I agree, we must find Lily. Being angry with each other is not going to help anything, least of all our daughter. You can be so infuriating when you want to!" And without thinking, she stomped her foot for emphasis.

As soon as she did, she regretted doing so. He *hated* it when she did that! She had learned long ago that the best way to rile him was to behave so childishly. Oh, when would she learn? Inwardly she winced with regret, but even in the shadows she could see the anger on his face, his dark eyes flashing, and the clenching of his jaw that indicated anger seething inside. How had things gone so wrong between them like this?

"Not happy for you to speak to me that way," the warrior said gruffly.

"Well, I am sorry you are not happy, *sir!* I'm not happy, either! You owe Matthew a huge debt of gratitude for all his extra efforts on my behalf, for that is why I still even have a chance to challenge Alex. You should treat him with more respect. I've never met anyone with as brilliant a mind for the law as he has. Not to mention a deep passion for justice, too. Even when I've been tempted to give up, he won't let me. He refuses to do that and keeps on fighting, pushing me to do the same."

"Not sound like he just a friend, seem like more. This why you not come home?"

"Don't be ridiculous! It's insulting for you to even ask me that. *Of course* he is only a friend. What if I asked you whether your eye had fallen on a maiden in the village while I was gone? Wouldn't you be hurt that I even asked?"

"Maybe has. You gone long time."

"What? Are you saying that you have fallen in love with someone else while I've been away? How *could* you? And in front of our sons? And then you have the audacity to turn around and question my loyalty to you?"

Mandy took a couple of steps back and glared at him. He pinched his lips together, a classic sign of his fury rising inside with every breath.

"Answer me! Before you tell me to be quiet, let me tell you that at this moment, I don't care if someone hears us or not! Who do you think they would believe if I said you had dragged me off the street and into this alley? A white woman or a Kiowa brave?"

"You not white. You Kiowa. Lie cannot stop that truth. Come home now."

She swallowed another sharp response as the veracity of his statement hit hard. But no one here in Trenton knew this version of the "truth" so she was safe. Right? *This gets more confusing by the minute! I didn't mean to say that, why did it pop out of my mouth? Stop talking, Mandy!* But she ignored her own warning.

"Are you serious? I will not leave without Lily! And I don't believe you will, either. In two days we have the final hearing. Assuming we find her before then, we can leave right after it is over. If I win, great. If I lose, fine. Either way, we can leave at that point, but not before."

"You tell truth now?"

"I can't. If anyone finds out I'm half Kiowa, they will not allow me to inherit my aunt's estate. And all will be lost, not only for us but also for our people. I must see this through without revealing that I am half Kiowa. Please, if you cannot understand, then you will have to trust me without it, Ken-ai-te. Do all these years of marriage and trust built up between us suddenly mean nothing now? I love you, Ken-ai-te, with all my heart. You are truly my beloved one, a gift from God. But honestly, I sometimes wonder how we have been able to live together, even having three children, without ever really knowing each other. I understand you don't know Matthew like I do, but I trust him implicitly, have had to. I had no choice. When Aunt Ida died and the suit was filed, he stepped in to help us find somewhere to live, to get us away from Alex and protect us from the danger he represented."

"Why not come home and he do um, case, without you here?"

"Because I had to be present to sign papers constantly. And attend a couple of hearings, too. Some I did not but several I did. He is fighting for justice for my aunt, as well as for me. Why can't you just believe me? Oh, look, we don't have time for this argument! I wanted to see you but not for this reason. You are making it so complicated with your jealousy!"

"Very simple. Lily gone. I track and find her, bring both home to tipi."

"I see. So, it was for Lily that you came, not for me. Yet, you are making this all about me somehow. And Matthew. I tell you, we don't have time for this!"

"Make time!" he shouted, grabbing her wrist.

"Hush! Do you want someone to hear you? Are you crazy? You are hurting me, Ken-ai-te. Please let go of my arm."

"No. Come home. Now."

"Not until we find Lily and get the money which is all that stands between our family and starvation this winter."

"You not willing to come, go back to lawyer. Not wife any longer," he growled, releasing his grip on her arm.

"What? How can you say that, Ken-ai-te? We have been married for almost fifteen years. You can't just throw me away like a useless piece of garbage. How can you let your jealousy blind you to our love like this?"

"Belong with him, not with me. You break God's laws and that of the Kiowa. You not worthy."

Suddenly all the anger and frustration and disappointment of the past few weeks exploded in Mandy's heart. She slapped him, hard. In all their years together, neither of them had ever struck the other one before. What had she done? Could their marriage truly be *over* because of one silly argument?

He stared at her in silence for a moment and then abruptly turned and stalked away into the shadows, leaving her alone in that stinking alley. Surrounded by piles of smelly refuse of all types, it was the perfect setting for a marriage in shambles. Her whole body trembled and the tears came. How could God allow this to happen, after all they had been through together?

Mandy raced through the streets back to the safety of the Boarding House, not caring who saw her now. She had to get back there before she completely fell apart! Ever since the shock of seeing her husband that morning after all these weeks of misery, she had been reeling from the reality of their strange situation, to see him but not be able to touch him and proclaim him as hers. By the time she arrived and thankfully was able to get in the front door before it was locked for the night, she was breathless with anxiety and fear as well as from the frantic run. Fortunately, again no one was in the Parlor so she was able to slip in and up the stairs unseen.

Breathless and shaking, she fumbled with the key at her door. She fervently hoped Nan wouldn't hear her and discover what she had done. Her legs trembled with fatigue and anxiety and she knew she didn't have the strength to explain to her friend where she had been. As she closed the door quietly behind her, the reality of the argument with Ken-ai-te and its implications hit her as though she had been struck by a stack of firewood logs. The anguish crushed the breath out of her and almost bent her double.

"Why didn't You stop this disaster, God?" she gasped through the sobs.

A not too gentle reminder nearly knocked her off her feet—the nagging thought she had ignored earlier.

I didn't pray about going to see Ken-ai-te before I left! Did You not want me to go and You were trying to stop me? I mean, I assumed you would want me to see my husband, it never occurred to me to ask first. But that's the point, isn't it? To ask first, before I act! That's twice in one day, in fact! Why do I keep getting this wrong? Help me!

Mandy dropped to her knees in front of her bed and poured out her heartache before the One who would truly understand her regret and fear.

"I thought I learned this lesson the hard way that horrible night long ago when, in a desperate attempt to protect Ken-ai-te's life, I offered myself to my enemy without asking You before I did it. The mess I made of things almost destroyed all of us before You intervened. How could I accuse my husband of being stubborn, when I was the one who was being stubborn against You? What if even You cannot fix this newest fiasco, Lord? What if he leaves here and won't take me back with him? What am I going to do?"

CHAPTER THIRTY-SEVEN

"Wait on the LORD, and keep his way, and he shall exalt thee to inherit the land: when the wicked are cut off, thou shalt see it."
Psalm 37:34

May 9, 1867

"Lord, maybe this is the day when You will deliver my little girl, as You did Daniel out of the lion's den!"

Mandy jumped out of bed and grabbed her Bible, settling into her rocker in the silence, to finally *really* listen to her Father speak to her heart. Yesterday had been such a disaster! Had it really been without any sincere prayer or attempts to discern His will in this whole mess? Sadly, Mandy had to admit it had. The darkness with which the day had ended threatened to drag her down again but she shrugged it off. She must trust Him to work to save her marriage, for there was nothing further she could do herself.

"How much easier it is for me to hear Your voice in my tipi, surrounded by the vast prairie, than here in this tiny room. Perhaps the red dirt reflects Your heart more or maybe the breath-taking sunsets and sunrises do. Whatever the reason, civilization is not where I can easily seek Your presence, I have discovered. Yet, You are everywhere. My attitude is what prevents me from being in union with You, not a lack of Your presence."

As she leafed through the Scriptures, asking for His Word for that day to be shown to her, she listened to the birds outside the window, chirping away in the early morning light.

"You care for them, so why not Lily, who is named after the very flowers You chose to illustrate the Father's loving care! Envelope her this day with Your protection, peace, and comfort. Let her know that her father and I both are searching for her in our own ways. We await Your direction to know where to find her. I don't wait easily! But help me wait on You, as You remind me here in Psalm 27:14: 'Wait on the LORD: be of good courage, and he shall strengthen thine heart: wait, I say, wait on the LORD.'"

A short time later of meditation and prayer, Mandy was ready to meet her day, filled with peace and hope for the many events she anticipated over these next hours. From the restoration of her daughter to the completion of the legal case in her favor; to the reunion with her boys and with her people very soon; to securing the money for the food they so desperately needed; to the healing of the deep hurts that threatened to rip away the very foundation upon which Mandy had stood at her husband's side for all these years—it all lay on her heart for His hand to bring it about. Besides the horrific fear for her daughter's safety, the biggest shadow that remained was the uncertainty now of whether her relationship with Ken-ai-te would ever be the same, indeed, would even survive this terrible crisis. Convinced it would *if* they could ever be together without the tension that happened last night, she prayed for his attitude toward her to soften.

"Of course, it wouldn't hurt if I could feel an ounce of forgiveness for him, I suppose, but right now, I do not. He behaved horribly during our argument, stomping off like he did at the end. That was no way to show his love, for sure! Why, he didn't even wait to ensure that I made it back to the Boarding House safely. How's that for a caring husband? Oooh, even thinking about it all has me all riled up again. That is not how I wanted to start today. Therefore, I will leave him in Your capable hands, Lord. Thank You that I don't have to deal with him this morning." As soon as she uttered the words, she realized her mistake.

"Actually, I *do* have to see him today. He and Jacob are coming to Matthew's office in a little while, to meet with Mr. Owens and figure out what we do next to find Lily. Lord, I will have to use all my strength to resist lashing out at him!"

Again, a thought flitted around her mind but she did not stop long enough to give it full credence, her attention elsewhere. She must hurry to get ready for the busy day ahead.

After everyone else had left the table following the morning meal, Mandy decided to reveal to Mrs. Wilson and Nan what she had done with her afternoon the day before.

The one thing I won't be telling either of them is what I did last night! Nan knows about Ken-ai-te but I don't think this is the time to share about our argument, when I wouldn't talk to her about Jacob because I said I was going to bed. One step at a time...

"In conclusion, it was a foolish thing to do, I know, but at least we got yet another clue to this whole mystery of what happened to Lily." Both ladies were stunned to hear about this incident, and she sensed deep disapproval, especially by Nan. "There is, indeed, someone behind all the threats and problems we have been facing, including the legal ones. I'm even more convinced now than before, it must be Alex. Who else would have anything to gain?"

"But what a dangerous way to go about it!" declared Nan, irritation lacing her words. "No matter how many times people try to protect you, you simply won't let us. You go right ahead and do what you think is best, ignoring all the warnings and offers of help. Well, fine. You do what you must, Amanda. As for me, I have to get to work. See you tonight."

She marched straight upstairs to her room without giving her friend another look. The door slamming spoke volumes.

After a moment Mrs. Wilson said quietly, "Amanda, I have to agree with Nan on this. I get why you are so frantic to find Lily, really I do. You are an excellent mother and you have tried hard to protect her, only to have that madman snatch her away. Please forgive me, but I feel I must speak frankly to you, as a mother would. There comes a time when you must learn that selfishness and stubbornness are not qualities that honor God. They glorify only yourself. *Your* intentions. *Your* goals. *Your* desires. I think you need to take a hard look at your heart, to see how you might soften it toward those who love you and care about you, instead of constantly defying them or riling them up."

Mandy sat speechless. She had never thought of it that way before. Mrs. Wilson was right, and she didn't know half the story. How rebellious and unkind she had been toward all those she loved! Instead of praying for her husband's attitude to change, she should be praying for her own. His was not in her control, anyway, up to God alone. Slapping him was a terrible way to show her love and compassion. He was every bit as frantic inside to find his daughter as she was. Nan deserved more consideration as well. Her new friend had poured herself unselfishly into Mandy's life. How could she repay this special lady by treating her with such callous disregard, in fact, to everyone who cared about her—all while claiming God's guidance? Her Father would never condone this behavior, no matter the justification behind it. Tears coursed down Mandy's cheeks but she made not a sound. Mrs. Wilson sat there a few moments, toying with her coffee cup, then rose and took a load of dishes into the kitchen, leaving Mandy alone.

Several minutes went by before Mandy picked up a few things left on the table, following her landlady into the kitchen.

"I'm sorry, Mrs. Wilson, I truly never meant to hurt anyone's feelings."

The front door slamming was another stark reminder of the depth of Nan's pain, as she left for work without saying anything further to her friend. Mandy's shoulders sagged with the weight of her conviction and shame. How could she undo all this damage?

"She'll be all right, dearie, just give her a little time. Tonight, though, you two need to sit down and talk, even if it's not for long. I think you have to say this to her as well. I hope you can hear the message from God's heart that pride is every bit as much of a trap as the stubbornness and self-focus become when not controlled by the love of Christ. Now, that's enough of my sermon for today!"

"You are right," Mandy said as she helped her with the chores in the kitchen. "How do I thank you for your advice and patience with me? You have been most kind, even when I don't deserve it."

"It's called grace, remember? I tend to get attached to all my boarders in various ways, but with you and Lily, it has been more personal than with most. Same with Nan. I like to think if I had ever had daughters—and a granddaughter—they would have been like the three of you!"

"What a sweet thought! Please know I will try harder to seek God's heart above my own. I do, but obviously not as much as I ought to, not really deep down. Reining in my selfish thoughts is harder than it ought to be, if I truly am living for my Savior. Right now, I'm a bit mixed up anyway, and that is a not a good combination."

"All of us understand that. And I shall have to pray even harder for you!" she said.

"I certainly need it," said Mandy. "And for Lily."

"Yes, I definitely will be doing plenty of that while I work today."

"Now, I must get ready to go to Matthew's office for the meeting with the Private Investigator."

"You go on, I can finish up here. Will Mr. Murphy and the Kiowa be there?"

Mandy smiled. Mrs. Wilson had trouble with his name, as Matthew did at first! Frankly, she did as well, long ago!

"Yes, they will be there, too. I doubt if I will be back for luncheon today. Unless we find Lily that soon!"

"That would be lovely! If not, I guess we will see you tonight."

At the appointed time of 9:00, the group met at Matthew's office and they sat down together in the conference room. Mr. Owens was conspicuously absent. Ken-ai-te focused on everyone else except Mandy. *How I wish I could apologize to you! If you'd only look at me, perhaps you could see the remorse in my eyes. Lord, this day is not starting out well!*

"Miss Brewster will not be joining us this morning?" asked Jacob. Mandy smiled. These two were really taken with each other and didn't seem to care who knew!

"No, she had to work today. She has been so involved in all this, I hate for her not to be here, though. Perhaps she can get off part of the day, later on." She did not add that Nan wasn't even speaking to her at the moment. The heaviness of regret pulled at her heart.

Jacob's expression lightened considerably at this news. Mandy noticed he kept rubbing the back of his head and wincing. *Guess Ken-ai-te hit him harder than he meant to!*

Too late, Mandy saw the warrior's glower deepen when she took a seat next to Matthew. *I couldn't very well sit next to my husband, now could I? I certainly cannot get up and move at this point. Please try to be a little kind right now. And I shall do the same.*

"Where is Mr. Owens?" she asked of her attorney.

"I spoke with him briefly earlier this morning, and he said he might be a little late to our meeting. He has to round up his men to get their reports first. Do you know he has ten men on his team? It shocked me to find he has that many on the job here in our little town!"

"Ten?" Mandy replied. "That's amazing. I hope one of them knows where Lily is."

"We'll have to wait until Paul gets here to find out what the men have dug up and listen to his conclusions before we can determine that. But I agree wholeheartedly."

A few minutes later, Mr. Owens walked in the door, accompanied by three men. Perhaps members of his team?

"Paul," said Matthew, "so good to have you here. All of you please take a seat," and he pulled up some more chairs to the table. He gestured toward Mandy while they all got settled. "This is Mrs. Amanda Alton, the mother of the missing girl. Over here is Mr. Jacob Murphy, who is a good friend of hers from Indian Territory. May I also present to you Ken-ai-te, a Kiowa chief who came with Mr. Murphy on the long journey from out West, because he is a close family friend as well. I believe I told you that Mrs. Alton and her husband minister to the Kiowa out there."

"Yes, you did. Happy to meet you." He nodded at each in turn, shaking their hands. "Please call me Paul, and I hope it is all right if I call you by your first names as well." They all nodded in agreement. *He didn't seem surprised to meet a Kiowa warrior. I assume Matthew must have already warned him ahead of time.*

"These are some of my operatives, folks," and he nodded toward his companions. "They are the ones who have been doing a great deal of checking into the disappearance of Lily even before I could get back in town. The others are still hard at work, even as we speak. I apologize that I have been away, but this team of men have done an incredible job of digging up quite a few leads in the last twenty-four hours. What I would like to do now is to compare any information you all may have, and compile all of it into a whole list of clues. Next, we will figure out where the holes still are in order to determine how we should proceed from there. My goal is to get us quickly to the last step, which is to locate and rescue your daughter, Amanda."

"Thank you, sir," she said. "It is my hope you can as well. She has been gone for three days now and I'm frantic to find her!"

"Of course you are. Matthew has filled me in on some of what happened, but I'm going to ask you, Matthew, to please list all the details on paper as we discuss them, to ensure we haven't missed anything. Small things overlooked often add up to big clues. Feel free, all of you, to add to it as we go through this."

"One important item before we begin," said Matthew, "is that my secretary, Abigail Lawson, disappeared without a trace two days ago."

"Seems to be happening a lot around here," said Paul without humor.

"Yes, more than usual, for sure. Well, anyway, while searching her desk for a particular document that should have been in her files, I found something I wasn't expecting. She had a secret file hidden in the back of one of the drawers, and I found a lengthy letter in it detailing some alarming information that I had suspected but could not prove until now. I'm hoping it will lead to the arrest of the one who has been behind all the mayhem going on lately."

"I'm betting I could venture a guess as to who that is!" exclaimed Mandy.

"Intriguing," said Paul, "but what does that have to do with this current problem of finding the missing girl?"

"Actually, it has everything to do with it," Matthew interjected. "Apparently, she was hired by Alex Clark to spy on us and 'lose' files here and there on purpose, to delay Amanda's legal case."

"So you were right, Matthew!" said Mandy.

"Yes, sad to say I was. Of course, I had no idea this was going on behind my back. I kept wondering about her but dismissed my suspicions as being unfair until I had something concrete to prove her involvement. I really wish I had been wrong about her. But as I told you the other day, nothing else made any sense. However, I'm not convinced that Abigail is the only one involved. A few details just aren't quite adding up, that she did all of it by herself."

"Knowing Clark the way I do," said Paul, "you are probably correct. He is quite cunning and uses manipulation and bullying to get what he wants. And apparently is not above blackmail, either."

Matthew nodded in agreement, his lips pressed in a thin line. Then he turned to his client.

"All this is why, Amanda, that it has taken far longer for me than I expected to get this legal case resolved in your favor. And thus, Jacob and Ken-ai-te," he said as he looked at the two of them, "for her to be able to return home with her inheritance, as her aunt intended. I know you both have been anxious for word from Amanda, but not any more anxious than she has been to leave Trenton, I assure you."

"He also is not above murder, Matthew," said Mandy. "I told you that the other day as well and I stand by my word, even though it was told to me in confidence and I cannot share who he killed nor why. But God's justice will be served and soon, I pray."

"I knew he was evil," Paul said as he shook his head in disbelief at this piece of news, "but had no idea he was capable of this, too. Although I should have known."

"He isn't your favorite person, Paul," said Matthew. "But don't feel bad. He fooled a great many of us for quite some time with his lies. Starting with coming here as an imposter."

"In case anyone is wondering, he wasn't the real Alex, after all," said Mandy. "It's a long story and I'll tell you all about it later. For now, we need to find Lily and I suspect that means we need to start by questioning Alex. Is that your first step, Paul?"

"Actually, no it isn't. If we spook him too soon by questioning him directly, we may never find your daughter. He could order her to be moved elsewhere and then we would have no idea where to search for her. And that is our number one goal, right? Justice for this man will come in time, as you said. For now, we need to figure out any clues that might lead us to Lily."

"I do have one last piece of information Abigail put in her letter that might help us all focus on how desperate and despicable this man really is, though I suspect all of us here know that already. It seems she was pregnant and—"

"Pregnant?" Mandy burst out and clapped her hand over her mouth in horror.

"Yes. And the child is Clark's. She said she was going to confront him later that evening and demand he marry her, as he had promised. The hidden letter was her protection, just in case. Her point was that if anything happened to her, surely her desk would be searched at some point and the letter found, throwing suspicion onto Alex. Abigail went on to say that if he refused, she would threaten to tell everyone in town what all she did at his direction. Plus, she was clear that he would be told about the letter. Apparently, she thought that was sufficient to force him to do what she wanted, and thus to avoid a scandal."

"What a mess!" Paul said.

"It certainly is. All this came from her own hand, so sharing it with you all in confidence is not gossip, but no one else needs to know for the time being. She is not here to defend herself and even if it is all a lie, this could ruin her reputation. Or, what is left of it after she faces charges for the crimes she committed, that is. Another thought in all this is that since she vanished that same day, once Lily is found we will need to investigate what has become of her and ensure that she has not come to any harm. Perhaps Clark is responsible for her disappearance as well. Who knows? I do hope she is found safe, but if so, I will promptly fire her!"

"I don't blame you for that sentiment one iota, Matthew," said Paul, "and I agree that she will be the next one we search for. This young lady is owed a modicum of privacy and respect, one way or the other, no matter how much criminal activity she engaged in nor the circumstances of her present state."

"The only reason I revealed it at this point is to, as I said, emphasize that we are dealing with a monster in Clark. I'm certainly relieved that you are no longer living in the house with him, Amanda."

"You and me, both! I shudder to think—" And she stopped herself in mid-sentence. "Well, never mind that dark thought. I want us to get back to Lily. Where on earth do you suppose she might be hidden in this town? Did you find any clues as to her whereabouts, Paul, or rather, did any of your men discover anything helpful?"

"Yes, they certainly did."

"Before you start, let me get that paper," said Matthew. "I will be right back."

Within moments he was settled back at the table, ink and pen in hand, ready to write as Paul began.

"First, we know Lily was at her friend's house, what is her name?"

"Ginny. Ginny Cordon," Mandy said. "They live on Castle Street, in that big house down at the end."

He whistled and his eyebrows shot up. "And these thugs didn't touch her? Seems like she would have brought them a hefty ransom, if they had taken her as well."

"She's not involved in the legal case, Paul," said Mandy. "I believe Alex is only concerned with stopping my inheritance."

"Well, that may be true all right, but one interesting thing my men found out yesterday is that several girls have gone missing from Trenton over the past three or four days. In fact, so far, we have found *six* of them have disappeared, including Lily! That would indicate to me this goes far wider than simply stopping your legal case, Amanda."

"Oh my!" she cried. "Six? But why? And who? I don't understand all this."

Paul continued. "I have a list of the girls here but we don't have all the details yet on how each was taken. What I do know is that, as with your daughter, Amanda, their parents don't believe they ran away. They simply vanished into thin air, without a word as to ransom or anything to lead us to the brutes who have done this. They are all twelve to fifteen years old. How old is Lily?"

"She twelve," Ken-ai-te spoke up for the first time.

"Okay, fits our pattern then. One question that occurred to me when I first heard this earlier is, what would a group of thugs want with six girls that age?"

He glanced over at Matthew, who nodded.

Why the grim look on their faces? What on earth is going on? Mandy's stomach clenched and she grabbed her middle instinctively.

"The answer to that question, Amanda," Paul continued slowly, "is not pretty to consider. Brace yourself; there is no easy way to say this."

"What? Now you are scaring me! Matthew, what is he trying to tell me?"

Paul cleared his throat. "We believe that Lily may have been taken to be sold to a slave trader, along with the other girls."

"*Slave trader?* Here? In Ohio? God, deliver my baby from this horror!"

CHAPTER THIRTY-EIGHT

"Fear them not therefore: for there is nothing covered, that shall not be revealed; and hid, that shall not be known." Matthew 10:26

May 9, 1867

"Not understand this 'slave trade'," growled Ken-ai-te. Mandy saw his knuckles go white on the arm of the chair nearest to her, as he gripped it tight.

This can't be happening! God, where is Lily? Please protect her! Her mouth dry, no further words would come out. With a mind numbed from this pain, she remained silent at first. Suddenly, she exploded with questions.

"I agree with Ken-ai-te," Mandy cried out as tears sprang into her eyes. "What do you mean by a *slave trader* took Lily and the other girls? I thought Alex was the culprit, not someone else."

"There is a lucrative slave trade that has grown up in place of the one that was active before and during the War Between the States. But their target now has become young white girls. As to Clark's involvement, I still firmly believe he is behind Lily's abduction. And he might be the one who took the other girls as well, or at least ordered it, in order to mask the taking of your daughter. His purpose, however, is clear to me: to sell all of them to the slave trader for a handsome profit. That is why no ransom demand has been received by any of you parents. They have no intentions of returning them to their families."

"If I may ask," Jacob said, "do you have any idea where the girls are going to be taken by this trader?"

"Most likely to Mexico. Some end up in Canada but most are taken south. And that is where we believe Lily and the others are headed, possibly as early as this evening."

"This evening?" Mandy almost shrieked. "Then we have to rescue her *now!* No more talking, we have to find her today!"

"Exactly, Amanda," Matthew said, handing her his handkerchief, which she gratefully accepted. Then he patted her other hand gently. *Oh, please, not in front of Ken-ai-te! Not even for this!* And she jerked her fingers out from under his and busied herself with wiping away her tears. Out of the corner of her eye, she spotted her husband's scowl and the fact he had not released his fingers from the grip he had on the chair arm. His fury was barely contained but she knew it would not stay there long.

"I still am a bit confused," Jacob said. "What kind of animal steals children from their homes and sells them in another country, like they were horses or cattle? In the Territory I could believe this—*perhaps*—but not here in a civilized place like Trenton!"

"Unfortunately, Jacob," said Paul, "there is a market for young girls in many places. While those in polite society don't talk about it, same as they didn't about the Negroes being bought and sold for decades, it is there, nevertheless, even here in our small town. One of my men is out running down a lead right now, interrogating a source to find out which place these girls are going to. I expect him to join us any moment. Meantime, if we assume for the time being that this is the case, the good news is the girls won't be harmed before reaching their intended destination."

"*Good* news?" Mandy gasped between sobs. "How is that good news?"

Again, Matthew and Paul exchanged odd looks that chilled Mandy's heart.

"Frankly," Paul said as gently as he could, "they are worth more if they haven't been harmed. Maybe not receiving top-notch care, of course, but at least they aren't starving or being harmed in any other way. *Yet.*"

Mandy gulped. She could have gone all day without that last word being spoken out loud. Goose bumps slithered down her spine and she shivered in spite of the warm room.

"As I said a moment ago, the time for talking about what is happening to my baby is over. I want action and I want it *now!*" She glared at the two men, as though daring them to continue this discussion any longer instead of starting the active search.

"That is our goal, of course, but where would you suggest we start looking for her, for instance? That is the point of my investigation, Amanda, and the information that Matthew is writing down for us will help us figure this out once we are done. One step at a time here."

"I think I maybe got too close when I went down to the docks yesterday. Otherwise, that man who accosted me wouldn't have been hanging around there. Isn't that obvious? So if I can figure that out, why aren't you combing the place right now, looking for her?"

"*Accosted?* What are you talking about, Amanda?" demanded Matthew. "Who was it? And for heaven's sake, what were you doing alone down by the docks? I would have thought you would know better than to go there by yourself, as dangerous as the place is! I warned you, remember, and did not think I needed to spell it out for you. Perhaps I assumed too much."

"I—I know, Matthew, I shouldn't have gone. And certainly not by myself. But I was restless yesterday afternoon after Nan went back to work, so I sneaked out of the Boarding House and took a walk out of curiosity. I figured if someone saw Lily being pushed into a wagon which then headed in that direction, why not check it out? It used to be a very pleasant area to visit but I quickly discovered that is no longer true, as you tried to tell me. Although I saw the man, I didn't know him. But he came out of nowhere and tried to choke me. I have to admit, I was terrified, but then he suddenly released me and threw me down to the ground. It was not the fact that he assaulted me that I wanted to tell you about, however. What he *said* is what upset me more than my sore neck and hurt pride. He indicated that someone else was involved besides himself, admitted numerous attempts had been made to slow down the legal case, and then he warned me we would never find Lily in time. So that makes more sense now that we know about the suspected slave trader business being involved. Right?"

"Yes," the lawyer said. "I have to agree with you on that point. But I am relieved that you are all right after such a terrible scare."

"Thank you for your concern, but I'm fine," and she turned to the Private Investigator. "What about searching the docks for her? Can we go do that right away?"

"A little easier said than done," said Paul. "When I get my whole team back together, we certainly will start there. But as I am sure you observed yesterday, it is a rather large area. I hope to find a clue as to where to start, rather than wasting precious time searching dozens of empty warehouses. Many of them are all but falling down, too, so we need to be cautious about moving around inside the buildings. It will be easier if we know where to start and have more men to help us search. Another point to consider is the kidnappers may move the girls if they find out we are getting close. So rattling around those warehouses without a clue where to look could give them time to escape with their hostages. That, we do not want."

"Since we now know that Alex hired Abigail," added Mandy, "I even more strongly believe that he has planned the whole sordid affair. But why on earth would he sink that low as to be involved in anything so despicable? It just doesn't make sense. Decent people don't do things like this! But what am I saying? Who ever said he was among those?"

Matthew nodded and asked, "Did the man explain what he meant by finding her 'in time'?"

"No, I wondered about that, too. I wasn't exactly in a chatty mood at that point, and he ran away before I had a chance to recover enough to ask."

"I think I know," Paul said. "One of my men found out there is a rumor floating around that the girls are to be moved from Trenton sometime tonight. Coupled with this information you shared, I believe it is accurate."

"Tonight? That means we truly *are* out of time!" said Mandy. "Moved where?"

"As I said earlier, my guess is Mexico," said Paul. "That's a long way from here, I know. Canada is a great deal closer, but the market is not as lucrative there."

"Go find, now," growled Ken-ai-te. It was obvious he was also tiring of all this talk and no action!

"Oh, we shall, believe me, sir. Only a little more fact gathering before we leave. Matthew, what did your informant have to say, the one you contacted last night?"

Before he could answer, there was a knock on the door. Matthew rose and opened it to find one of Paul's men standing there. Ushering him in, Paul immediately asked him what he had discovered.

"The rumor has been confirmed by two different sources, so now is fact and no longer an assumption. The girls are to be moved tonight and they are headed to Mexico."

"Excellent work," Paul said as the man pulled up a chair and sat with the others. Then he turned back to Matthew and waited for him to answer his earlier question.

"My informant's name is Hank Ellison and he absolutely identified Clark as the one behind the abduction of Lily. I had no idea until now there were other girls involved but it's logical he took them as well, perhaps to throw us off the track. At any rate, Ellison gave me the name of the man he claims took her and where we might find him. I think we need to go talk to him right away, before he has time to disappear as well. According to Ellison, if he can be believed which I think he can, this Colt Barnes character is willing to confess, if we can find him."

"That is, indeed, good news. We have been tracking these brutes for some time for several reasons, and this is the closest we have gotten to identifying who any of these smugglers are and where they hang out."

"I didn't know you were looking for them, Paul," said Matthew.

"No, you wouldn't, if we were doing our jobs right, my friend! But yes, we have. That is why I took this as seriously as I did after you contacted me, figuring it probably was part of this whole mess. Therefore, we need to rescue at least six girls, not merely one. Where did he say we could find this Barnes character?"

"At a well-known den of thieves in town called the Jolly Roger, basically a saloon, but with rooms in back for those running from the law."

"Oh! I saw that when I was racing back into town yesterday," cried Mandy. It's over on State Street but at the far west end. Let's go!"

"Whoa, hold on there, Amanda," Paul said. "You aren't going anywhere near that place. It's not fit for a lady like you."

Jacob spoke up, "Ken-ai-te and I are going with you, but Amanda, why don't you wait on us at the Boarding House? You'll be safe there."

"Not on your life! I have seen one of the men and none of you have. If I describe him, perhaps this Barnes fellow can identify him, too. I'm going, and that's final."

"This could get pretty rough, you know that, right? I really wish you'd rethink this and stay away." Paul glared at Matthew, as though he could stop her. But the attorney held up his hands in defeat.

"If she is this determined, nothing is going to keep her away. Let her come."

Ken-ai-te's frown caused Mandy to shiver again. But she didn't back down. He wasn't in charge of what she did right now, she was. She wouldn't be denied. The promise she made Mrs. Wilson earlier flashed through her mind but she pushed it aside. This had to be God's will! He wouldn't deny a mother being involved in finding her own daughter, right?

A short time later, several of Paul's men had gathered with the others in front of the Jolly Roger. They were eyed suspiciously by all those entering and leaving the place, which seemed to Mandy to be very busy for a weekday afternoon. She tried to ignore the looks and started to go in.

"Amanda, now I'm drawing the line right here," said Paul. "You are not to enter until I say you can, do you hear me? This is what Matthew has hired me for, to know things like this. What you need to do is listen to me, will you? You could jeopardize your daughter's life inadvertently if you spook the wrong fellow in there. I'll go first, the rest of you stay here. You men, keep a sharp eye out for anything or anyone suspicious. And keep her here. I will be right back."

They all paced around outside for several minutes, impatient to get in there and question the one who might lead them to Lily. Mandy kept having to lift her skirts to step over mudholes that were everywhere. The street, if you could call it that, was a mess, and she wondered how the hard rain last night would affect their efforts to find Lily. One of the men had a long rope and he kept winding it up into a tight coil, then whipping it out again and starting over. How she longed to see that tied around Alex's neck! Suddenly, Paul reappeared, as promised.

"Colt Barnes is here and is willing to cooperate, as your informant indicated, Matthew. The trick will be to see how far we can push him. We are all going in, but slowly, Amanda in the middle, surrounded by us men. Once we are in the back room, we can relax a bit, but let me do the talking. This is the type of people I deal with for a living, and I do know what I'm doing. There won't be an opportunity for me to stop at each point along the way to explain things to everyone. Trust me, keep a sharp eye out, and follow my lead."

They walked through the saloon itself with several unsavory characters sitting around tables drinking and gambling. The way they eyed Mandy made her skin crawl. She was grateful for the protection around her and focused on getting away from their stares as quickly as possible. When the group entered the back room, Mandy gasped. Barnes was the one who had choked her the day before! Her eyes widened but wisely she didn't say anything. However, Jacob saw her reaction, as did Ken-ai-te.

Paul immediately lit into the man, asking him point blank about an effort he was involved in to kidnap several girls and sell them as slaves in Mexico. Since much of that was conjecture, Mandy figured he was trying to gauge the man's reaction to all this, to figure out what was true and what wasn't. His wisdom fascinated her, how he worked this questioning!

After several moments of denial and stalling, the man finally admitted under intense pressure that he had, indeed, been involved. Mandy's knees went weak. He had just confirmed their whole strategy! Barnes rambled on for several minutes, sharing names and dates previously unknown to them. Now all that remained was to find out where the girls were being held. Yet, Paul kept drilling him about several things that seemed to have no relevance to the situation at hand. Finally, Mandy's impatience got the best of her. She couldn't remain silent one moment longer!

"Tell us—" she started when Paul interrupted, glaring at her.

"Barnes, I asked you a question. Again, when was that?"

The thug whirled around to look at Mandy standing behind him, as though only now seeing her huddled in the shadows. His eyes went wide. Without warning, he balked at the grilling, became surly and defiant again, and finally refused to reveal anything further. He snarled his warning to her from the day before.

"Not sayin' nothin' else. Besides, there ain't no way you are going to find them girls in time. You might as well give up and go home."

"Where are you holding them, Barnes?" demanded Paul, getting right in front of him, planting himself directly between the man and Mandy. *"Where*, I said?"

"Where the sun don't shine! Get away from me! I said, I ain't tellin' you nothin' more. Can you not hear or somethin'? Now, get out of my face!"

"You were sure singing a different tune a few minutes ago. What changed?"

He remained silent, arms folded across his chest, staring at the floor. Mandy's heart sank. Had she, in her eagerness to hear where her daughter was behind held, somehow soured the interrogation?

Jacob stepped forward. "Paul, may I try something? I have an idea."

"Sure, if you think you can break this man, be my guest."

"Sir, my name is Jacob and I'm from Indian Territory. I have come all this way because my Goddaughter is one of the girls you and your cohorts are keeping prisoner." His voice was calm and measured. Mandy was amazed at his control. "You can imagine how angry I am right now. But in the Territory, we have a method for extracting information from people that I'll bet you've never heard of here in Ohio. It isn't common among more civilized folks, but it sure works among the Indians."

The man sat up a little straighter in his seat but the expression on his face didn't change.

"Ken-ai-te, my friend, do you have your knife with you?" He nodded. Jacob continued, never taking his eyes off the man's face. Mandy's heart pounded in her ears. What was Jacob up to?

"I want you to know, you are a monster and you are going to be treated like one. Chief Ken-ai-te of the Kiowas is an expert at skinning a man alive, did you know that?"

Mandy gasped! What on earth was Jacob talking about? Skinning a man? *Alive?* Her husband could do that to another human being?

The face that moments before had been defiant drained of its color and Barnes licked his lips nervously.

"You, you can't do that, not here! Maybe where you come from, but we are civilized here. They won't let you do that! Owens, tell him! Stop him!"

Ken-ai-te whipped his knife out of its sheath at his side and advanced toward him, a menacing look on his face. Then he *smiled* at the man. Well, maybe more of a smirk!

"Owens cannot help you," said Jacob. "You belong to me now, Barnes, and I don't care about civilization. That's why I live far from it, where we can do whatever we like. When Chief Ken-ai-te here is through with you, you will be beyond caring, too. What is left of you we will feed to the buzzards and what they won't eat, we will dump in the river. Now, one last time, *where is Lily?* Or he goes to work, I promise you!"

Barnes jumped up out of his chair but Paul shoved him back down.

"Shall I hold him still for you, Ken-ai-te?" he asked. "I can hold one arm and Jacob the other, if you like."

"Yes, good idea," he replied, and they complied. "Will start with chest, one strip at a time, until he scream like woman! He tell us soon." He laid the knife down long enough to rip the helpless man's shirt open, baring his entire chest, causing Barnes to scream obscenities at him. Ken-ai-te calmly picked up the weapon again, brandishing the large blade before his terrified eyes.

Mandy's stomach lurched. She swallowed hard against the bile rising in her throat as she dug her fingernails into the palms of her hands. How could her husband be this barbaric? Had he ever skinned anyone? He had never said a word to that effect, in the entire time she had known him. Other warriors in the village might have done so in the past but not since she had lived there. But Ken-ai-te? She stared at the wicked looking knife in his copper fist and closed her eyes. She couldn't bear to watch. Perhaps she shouldn't have insisted on coming. Wild horses couldn't have kept her away, however. *God, we must know where Lily is. Whatever You have to do, please!*

The man screamed in terror and jerked against the two men's firm grasp on his arms, whipping his head around, trying hard to get loose. It was no use.

Ken-ai-te laughed! "I not even touch him and already he scream! This going to bring me much pleasure."

Paul said, "You had better cough it up now, Barnes, or believe me, you are going to regret holding your tongue! One way or the other, we will get what we want. How, is up to you."

"All right, all right, I'll tell you! He's going to kill me, but I'll tell you. Just call off that Injun there! Please, for the love of mercy, stop him!"

The two men eased their hold on him but did not let go. Ken-ai-te stopped right in front of him, leaned close to his face, and snarled, "Where Lily?"

"At the wharf, in one of the buildings there."

Paul asked, "Which one? There are many of them and they all look alike."

"I don't know. All I know is the girls are there, waiting to be taken by wagon later tonight to Mexico."

Paul sighed and Mandy gulped, on the verge of tears. So, Paul's operative was correct, they were going to Mexico. *God, please not my baby!*

"We figured that much out, you piece of scum," Owens snarled at him. "What we want to know is which building. We aren't settling for an 'I don't know' from you! That won't save you. You *do* know! You took her there, now tell us where she is."

"They have moved them several times. You have to believe me, I don't know. He's going to *kill* me, I tell you!"

"*Who* is going to kill you? Who hired you? Maybe that is a simpler question than the other one. But you need to answer both. I'm warning you, I'm running out of patience!" Paul got right in his face this time, anger exploding from every word. "Seems that either way, you are dead meat. If I were you, I would do anything I could to avoid the skinning, but hey, that's me. How about it? You better start talking and fast!"

"I, I can't tell you who hired me, *either*. Oh, *please!*" he begged as he eyed the knife. "All right, all right! Uh, I, I think it might be a, a blue one, maybe. There are several of them, and honest, I don't know for sure!" He squeaked in fear, never taking his eyes off the warrior and his weapon.

"We go find blue one. If not there, I come back for you, a piece at a time!" Ken-ai-te growled at him.

"And I will help you, Ken-ai-te," said Paul, "if this snake has lied to us! Men, tie him up and bring him on down to the river as soon as you can. I have a feeling we are going to need every single hand to search the blue buildings until we find Lily!"

CHAPTER THIRTY-NINE

"Say to them that are of a fearful heart, Be strong, fear not: behold, your God will come with vengeance...he will come and save you."
Isaiah 35:4

May 9, 1867
Warehouse District

"Which one?" Paul demanded of their prisoner as they stood on the waterfront staring at the large number of dilapidated buildings in front of them. "There are four blue ones that I can see, or what I think used to be blue. It's difficult to tell at this point."

"Barnes, you'd best speak up and answer Mr. Owens," said Matthew with a grim expression, "unless you want another round with Ken-ai-te and his knife." But the man remained sullen, refusing to answer.

"There *must* be some way to figure this out!" Mandy said. She turned to the warrior. "Chief Ken-ai-te, what do you think? Can you help?" With all her heart, she *really* didn't want her husband to follow through on his threat against Barnes. But what other hope did they have to find Lily in time, if this man didn't help them further? The answer, of course, rested in her beloved's ability in tracking. And in God's direction! *Lord, help him!*

Ken-ai-te stalked around each of the blue ones, staring at the ground intently. Occasionally he would kneel to examine something more closely, then rise and move on.

"Thought you said he could track her," said Paul. Jacob nodded.

"He is. It takes time, it cannot be rushed. As you said, not the same as back home, but he will find her. After all she's his—" He stopped himself abruptly. After a moment he continued. "He cares for Lily a great deal, we all do. You will see, he can track anything, anywhere, long after white men have given up."

The rest of Paul's men had joined them by this time, so they had a good group waiting to complete the rescue. All eyes were now on the Kiowa. The tension mounted by the moment.

Finally, Ken-ai-te stretched out prone on the ground, despite the mud, his face turned sideways.

"What on earth is he doing now? Odd time to take a nap," one of the men said.

"Believe me, he is not taking a nap!" said Jacob. "He is checking out the soil levels. Observing them from that angle can tell him if the top layer has been disturbed, even slightly, and how long ago."

"But the rain has washed away all traces of that. What a waste of time," he muttered. "You've got to be kidding me!" another one snapped, not kindly.

"Nope, I don't kid about serious stuff like this," said Jacob. "I have seen him do it many times, both when hunting for game and for men, over all kinds of terrain, in all types of weather conditions. I never tire of watching this as it progresses." He glared at the man who was being derisive in his tone of voice. "I only tire of stupid questions and those who ask them." He walked off, to move closer to his friend as he worked.

Mandy overheard this exchange, bristled inside, and gritted her teeth to bite back the sharp words forming on her tongue for the man's ignorance. *He could track in the dark, blindfolded! How dare you insult him like that! He's a Kiowa chief and the best tracker in our tribe. Everything you know, as smart as you think you are, could fit in his little finger!*

She edged over to where Ken-ai-te had hopped up, brushing as much of the mud and dirt off as possible. Then he picked up a trampled plant of some kind, holding it up to his nose. He looked all around the area and walked toward one of the blue buildings on the end. Kneeling, he examined the ground intently again, all else forgotten for the moment. It never ceased to fascinate Mandy how such tiny clues could be so important. *Please, Lord, show him the right pieces today to lead us to Lily! Without Your wisdom, none of this will make sense, even to him.*

Mandy could hear the waves from the river lap at the wooden piles nearby and she shivered. Even in the late afternoon sunlight, she felt chilled to the bone. But she was grateful to be here, maybe within a few feet of her daughter, watching her husband use all his skills to find their child. They always stood together against all enemies, and this was no exception. A herd of stampeding buffalos could not have kept her from this moment with her beloved!

Finally, he spoke. "Rain last night wash away much but older wagon tracks still there with new ones. Fresh marks from one man start here by wagon, lead over there, back to wagon, then it go in there." He pointed away from the one blue building they had been focused on, toward a faded grey one that looked as though it might fall down any moment. With several obvious holes in the roof and part of one windowpane missing, it screamed hopelessness at them.

"But didn't Barnes say it was a blue one?" asked Matthew. "How do you know that is the right one, from among all of these?" He gestured widely to indicate their many choices.

"Man lie. Tracks do not." Ken-ai-te rose and loped over that way while the others quickly followed. When he stopped, he put his finger up to his lips to caution silence, in case someone inside might hear them.

Once again the warrior got down with his nose almost at the threshold and stared for several moments. Mandy held her breath. What would he see there in the dirt and grime? Aware that her eyes were untrained for this, nevertheless she sadly could see nothing of any value. Nothing, in fact, that would indicate anyone had entered there in the past year or so. Dust heavily coated the two dingy windows, despite the recent rains, making it impossible to see inside, and the building appeared to be abandoned. Her heart begged for any clue, any hint as to her daughter's whereabouts, without success. Nevertheless, Mandy continued to plead for divine intervention.

Softly, so softly Mandy had to strain to hear the words, Ken-ai-te said, "Man came in short time ago. Wagon—"

Without warning he jumped up and pulled a tiny scrap of fabric loose from a wood chip in the door frame, holding it out to Mandy. "Hers?"

"Yes!" Mandy cried in a whisper. "It is from the dress she was wearing when she disappeared!" She clutched it to her heart and for the first time held great hope they might find her in time, after all.

"Good girl, Lily," said Jacob quietly.

"She leave clue, no accident," Ken-ai-te said in a low voice with pride. "What taught."

He looked deep into his wife's eyes for the first time that day and once more their hearts were connected without further words, as they usually were. What a refreshing moment of joy that was for her! They were back on the prairie, together again where they belonged, far from this horrid place with fear in their hearts for their child. Hope filled her and pushed out the despair.

Suddenly the prisoner began struggling with all his might against the ropes holding him fast, and the two men guarding him took hold of his shoulders to prevent him from escaping.

Jacob strode over to him, getting right in his face.

"This is the place, isn't it? Tell me! You knew all along!"

"Yes! Okay," he said from between gritted teeth. "Just keep that savage away from me!"

"Get him out of here!" Paul ordered the ones guarding him. "The sight of him makes me sick to my stomach. Take him back to the office and guard him well there until I come get him. I'm not taking any chances that he might call out a warning or in the confusion to come with this rescue that he might get away. He will pay for his crimes, on my life!"

Every nerve in Mandy's body was taut. In a short time she would either be reunited with Lily or—well, that alternative horrified her but had to be accepted. How she prayed for a rescue and quickly!

In a hushed tone but with firmness Matthew said to Mandy, "I think it would be a good idea if you stayed out of the main fracas here. I'm sure your husband would not be happy with us if we allowed you to come to harm while rescuing your daughter. Why don't you go over there behind that stack of old crates to wait until this is over? I will stay with you, because I want to make sure you remain safely out of sight where you won't be in any danger during the rescue effort. Once it is safe, I will escort you in to be reunited with Lily."

She opened her mouth to protest but a quick frown from Ken-ai-te, who obviously had overheard the statement, caused her to stop the sharp retort she was about to give. "Perhaps you are right, Matthew. Thank you for thinking of my safety. I will agree to wait over there with you until I can go into the building to get Lily."

A brief nod from her husband told Mandy she had done the right thing. At least he wouldn't have to worry about her getting hurt while he was busy routing the kidnappers. She wasn't happy about the arrangement but didn't see she had a choice. The one glance she had shared with Ken-ai-te had refreshed her hopes that perhaps he wasn't as angry with her as she thought. No need to jeopardize that with another foolish action. No, she would wait to one side for a little longer as God worked His miracle—but not idly. Someone needed to be praying!

"Paul," said Jacob, in a quiet voice, "how about having several of your men surround the building and in particular watch the back of it, to ensure no one tries to sneak out that way? Perhaps if we catch them by surprise, we will be able to arrest most of them before they can regroup and defend themselves. Or worse yet, harm the girls they have in there with Lily. Doesn't look like it will take much to break through any of this rotting carcass of a building. At that point you, Ken-ai-te, and I can come in from the front, along with a couple others."

Paul said, "All right, sounds like a good plan to me—"

Ken-ai-te interrupted. "I go in there." He pointed overhead to the highest eave on the building. A huge hole in the roof extended down onto the wall itself, leaving a gape which a man could easily slip through. *If* one could get up there!

"Great idea," answered Jacob. "If anyone can do that to surprise them from up above, it will be you. I swear, you are part mountain lion and part mountain goat when it comes to climbing impossible places! Since you will be the only one with eyes on the thugs we are after as well as the girls, we will wait for your signal to start. Be careful, my friend."

Mandy heard this and smiled. She had witnessed countless times back home when he had accessed all sorts of nooks and crannies in what few mountains they had, in order to squeeze into tight spots or jump high enough to get to the unreachable ones. He had never tried it on a building before but she knew instinctively that he could do it easily. Her beloved was about to demonstrate how he could reach a rooftop the same way a spider goes up a wall, without ropes or any help at all! She only hoped the roof would hold him so he wouldn't fall through on the first step, as she didn't want to entertain the thought of possibly losing her husband in the effort to save their daughter.

Paul said, "Good idea to let Ken-ai-te give us the signal. No more talk now, just follow the plan, fellows, and we will have this done before you know it." His men scattered silently around to the back and sides of the warehouse out of sight, while Paul joined Jacob at the front door, their guns drawn.

Mandy held her breath and watched Ken-ai-te begin the slow climb by jumping up onto the windowsill, and from there hoisted himself onto a rafter. After that he swung himself over the ledge and onto the tin roof overhead without a sound, where he flattened his body in the late afternoon shadows. He made it look quite easy, yet she knew it was not. After a moment he stuck his head inside, popped back out and waved at the others, again disappearing into the building through the hole.

As soon as Jacob and Paul saw the signal, they both slammed themselves against the front door, splintering it into pieces all at once, and rushed inside. Meanwhile, the others did the same from each direction, some coming through windows and others through other doorways.

Paul hollered loudly, "Come out, you are surrounded! Put down your weapons and let's do this peacefully, with your hands held high so no one gets hurt! We just want the girls released unharmed. Do as we say and do it *now!*"

No shots came in response but neither did anyone come out where they could be seen. Could Ken-ai-te have been wrong? Where were the girls and their captors?

Pulling away from Matthew's protective grasp, Mandy could wait no longer and raced through the splintered remains of the front door. Keeping to the shadows as much as she could to avoid being seen, she spotted the men standing there at the outer edges, weapons at the ready. No sign of Ken-ai-te, even when she gazed up into the rafters overhead. How she wished she had on moccasins instead of these clunky shoes! They made too much noise as she walked and left her with little flexibility as well. Whatever made white people think that these were superior to a buckskin shoe that made no sound?

As her eyes adjusted to the dimmer light inside what was left of the building, she spotted what appeared to be a walled-off area in one back corner of the gigantic space inside. From there, came a muffled commotion of some kind, followed by a couple of screams! Mandy's heart leapt. *Was that Lily? Please keep her safe, God!*

Paul's voice again boomed out, startling her.

"This is your last warning! Come out now and it will go easier on you." He gestured to the men to head that direction, as they slowly moved forward. "You aren't walking away from this, regardless. Come out with your hands up high where we can see them!"

A few seconds later the whole wall in the corner shattered with a crash as a large buckboard wagon came banging through the opening, which she could now see had actually been a large hidden doorway. The two horses pulling the wagon rushed right by everyone at first in a frantic effort to escape, urged on by the driver. But two of Paul's men quickly recovered enough to grab the reins of the horses on each side to stop them. The driver kept whipping their backs to force them forward, but they could go nowhere with their lines being held fast.

In that split second, Ken-ai-te swung down from above where he had been hiding and slammed into the man driving the rig, feet first, knocking him off his perch and onto the floor. He and the warrior rolled over several times, finally coming to a stop. Mandy saw her husband whip his knife up to the man's throat, speaking something harshly to him that she couldn't hear. She knew he wouldn't plunge the knife into his throat unless he had to. Only a lunatic would argue with that knife! She had her hands clamped over her mouth to prevent her from screaming and drawing attention to herself until this nightmare was over. All she wanted to do was hold Lily again!

Three other men scurried in various directions from behind the wagon, one leaping through what used to be a window and racing away into the shadows. Another was quickly apprehended by Paul himself, and the second by one of his men. Mandy overheard Paul tell Ken-ai-te as he took custody of the driver that his men would track down those who had managed to escape. But where was her daughter?

The rescuers began picking their way around the numerous crates stacked everywhere as well as over the rubble on the floor, making for the gaping hole in the back of the building. Whimpering could be heard, then one voice distinct from the others.

"I think we are about to be freed!"

Mandy's heart stopped. It was Lily! She raced toward the source, calling out her name. In a couple of moments she found her, crouched down in the room, huddled with the others, and they hugged amid many tears of rejoicing!

"Thank the Lord that you are all right, my child!" Mandy winced as she said that "forbidden" word but Lily said nothing, simply smiled even broader. "Did they hurt you?" her mother asked as she held her close.

"No, they, they threatened to and scared all of us half, half to death. We were cold and hungry most of the time but they never laid a hand on any of us. Right now, I'm most grateful to be your child, Mama! I'm so relieved that you found us at last. They were getting ready to take us away from Trenton tonight, to be *sold,* if you can believe! What if you hadn't come when you did? Oh, Mama!" and she collapsed into a torrent of tears.

A couple of moments later, Lily said, "Did my eyes deceive me or did I see um, Ken-ai-te and Jacob?"

"Yes, honey, it's a long story but they came in answer to God's command and are largely responsible for your rescue. Matthew and his friend Paul Owens plus his men all played a vital role as well. There are a great many to thank, as a matter of fact, but the important thing is we have you back, safe and sound!"

"Oh, Mama, I don't want to ever leave your arms again, as long as I live!"

"You might change your mind before long, but for now, I'm happy to accommodate you!" As she hugged her, she whispered so no others could hear, "When you see your father, please remember he came as a family friend!" Lily nodded as she ran to embrace him when he headed her way.

Meanwhile, the rest of the rescue party comforted the other girls, assuring them they were now safe and would be returned to their parents very soon. Each was asked about any injuries but none reported anything except being hungry and tired from their ordeal. Not to mention, vastly relieved to have been rescued! The grim future they knew awaited them would haunt their dreams for some time to come, but at least they were safe now.

Matthew walked up and shook hands with Paul, thanking him for all he had done to help them locate and rescue the girls.

"My men will deliver the others to their families," he told the attorney. "I didn't have time to even notify the parents this was happening, so we will have a great surprise for them when we get the girls home!"

"I know they will be most grateful, as we all are for your invaluable help in this effort!"

"The real hero of the moment, in my humble opinion," said Paul graciously, "is definitely Chief Ken-ai-te. Without his help at the end there, the driver would have gotten away, and we believe him to be one of the major ringleaders of this group."

"How exactly does Alex Clark fit in with all this?" Matthew asked.

"Well, we will have to interview each of these prisoners plus all the girls to be able to determine who actually planned this atrocity on our city and her youngest citizens. However, my guess is that Clark *is* the one behind it all. There must have been someone far smarter than these rogues to plan such a devilish scheme as this one has been. Our suspicions, however, won't stand up in court until we have more evidence. By the time we have finished this investigation, we should have more than enough to convict him, if he was involved. We'd best get to it."

Several of the rescuers offered to escort the other girls back to town and the eager arms of their parents, amid many hugs from Lily for each one. Apparently, she had been responsible for keeping them calm and encouraged during their ordeal, and they were openly grateful to her. She accepted their kindnesses with humility, giving God the praise instead of keeping it for herself. Her mother beamed with pride as she heard this exchange before they left.

One of the girls said with tears glistening in her eyes, "I don't know what we would have done without Lily to help us through this! We didn't know each other until three days ago but her courage kept us going. Not to mention the prayers of our parents, I know. I'm quite sure we will all be the best of friends from now on!"

Paul and the remaining ones secured their prisoners in handcuffs and ropes and also headed away from the docks, promising to be in touch over the next couple of days. Matthew suggested to the others that they go back to his house for dinner. At the mention of food, Mandy realized they had been so busy, they never stopped for luncheon! Perhaps it was the relief of seeing her daughter again, but suddenly her mouth watered at the thought of getting to eat. Sadly, it was probably too late for one of Mrs. Wilson's meals.

"On second thought, perhaps I should take Lily home to rest," she said. "Are you hungry, my dear, or would you prefer to go back to the Boarding House instead?"

"Oh, yes I would like to eat first, Mama! They didn't feed us much while we were here, and I'm starving! We were all very much afraid they were going to kill us any minute. One man said they wouldn't do that, because we had been captured to sell us in Mexico as slaves. Isn't that terrible? No one told them, I suppose, that slavery has been outlawed! I guess not in Mexico, however. Anyway, one man in particular said repeatedly he would take great pleasure in slitting my throat. I was terrified he would keep his word and prayed every Scripture I could think of whenever I heard him spitting his hateful words." She shuddered at the memory. "They blindfolded us when he arrived every time, but I will never forget his voice! I honestly don't know whether slavery or death would have been worse. That bed of mine is going to feel very nice, compared to the stinking and rough blankets we have slept on the last two nights. I prayed very hard for you to come, Mama! Why did it take you so long?"

"We all thought you had run away at first, to be honest. Ginny didn't tell us until late that first night about the threats from Alex. It was only then we realized that you had been kidnapped instead. However, by then it was too late to start the search in earnest. The next day Jacob and your—um, our friend Ken-ai-te arrived and things got crazy because Paul was out of town and we had to wait on him to return before we could pull all the clues together, to know where to look for you. Even after an extensive search in town, none of us had any idea where else to search. Then we finally were told you might be down here. My goodness, what an ordeal this has been for all of us. As you can see, we really did come as soon as we could!"

"How did the man who took you convince you to go with him?" asked Matthew.

"He came from behind and put a cloth over my mouth. It must have had something on it that knocked me out. I never even saw him."

"That would be rather convincing, all right!" replied Matthew.

"When I came to, I was in a building with the other girls. I was quite dizzy, as they all were. I think they were putting a drug of some kind in what little bit of food they gave us, to keep us quiet. On top of that they kept moving us, always with blindfolds on, so I was never quite certain where we were. That one thing frightened me the most, that you would never find me!"

Mandy's stomach churned with the thought of how her daughter had been treated. *Thank You, Lord, for getting her away from those horrible men!*

"Our *friend*," said Jacob, "tracked you when no one believed he could do it. He saved you, almost entirely on his own, in fact!"

"With other help," the warrior said quietly. Mandy winced, seeing the pain on his face at not being able to acknowledge his daughter, having to settle for only a quick hug. *This lie has got to stop!*

As they all gathered at Matthew's home a short time later, Mandy scurried around to try to help Matthew figure out how to feed everyone. Suddenly Nan arrived on the scene, bearing two huge baskets of food!

"About an hour ago I heard that this rescue was being done, and I couldn't stay at the store another minute. In case you are wondering, there are few secrets in this town! All I knew was that I simply had to come try to help. But by the time I got down to the docks, everyone was gone except one of Mr. Owen's men, who told me what had happened and where all of you were. I figured Matthew wouldn't have enough to feed everyone, so I raced to talk to Mrs. Wilson, and she graciously consented to hastily raid her larder to scrape together enough for everyone. I hope this is all right, but at least I can guarantee it is good food!"

They all laughed, appreciating Nan's resourcefulness more than words could say. Mandy filled Nan in on what all happened that day and Nan couldn't stop hugging her friend. There would be time enough later for the two to talk in order for Mandy to offer her profound apologies for their earlier disagreement. For now, joy overflowed on every side as they basked in its warmth with their dearest friends. Besides, Jacob was there, and Nan's smiles were as much for him as for anyone else! Especially when she discovered how much danger they had faced at the warehouse. She told him repeatedly that she was vastly relieved that he hadn't been harmed. Watching them together warmed Mandy's heart and filled her with even more joy for her two friends.

As they were finishing up the impromptu meal, a knock was heard at the door. Matthew went to answer it and came back with a broad smile on his face.

"I just now got word that the final hearing has, indeed, been scheduled for tomorrow morning at 10:00 with Judge Adams. Amanda, I believe you are about to inherit your aunt's estate, at long last!"

CHAPTER FORTY

"...Fear ye not, stand still, and see the salvation of the LORD, which he will shew to you today..." Exodus 14:13

May 10, 1867

"Good morning, Matthew. Is this really going to happen today, after all these weeks of delays and disappointment?"

"Hello, Amanda. And yes, it is! We are finally on the docket, which is the list of cases to be heard. In fact, ours is the only one today. I believe all my paperwork is in good order and that when the judge hears everything we have to present to him, he will make a quick and favorable ruling. Good to see you, too, Lily. I trust you got some rest last night."

"Yes, sir, I did. Mama did not want to leave me alone this morning so is it all right if I read during this—what do you call it?"

"It's called a hearing, and of course you may read all you want. Please remember you must be quiet, however. That means no whispering or speaking out loud at any point, or the judge can have you thrown out. We certainly wouldn't want that," he said with a smile.

"I promise! What is the saying I read in a book once, 'quiet as a church mouse'?"

"Jacob," said Matthew, "it is good to see you this morning, and you as well, Ken-ai-te. I really enjoyed visiting with you both last night. It is my fervent prayer and expectation that, after this hearing today, you gentlemen will be able to start for home very soon, along with Amanda and Lily of course. We shall be sorry to see them leave but I know you all are anxious to get home with the money to purchase meat for your people out there in Indian Territory. Let me show you where you may sit. Amanda will be up here with me at this table. The three of you may choose seats in the first row here in the gallery area, which is a fancy word for audience. That way, you will be right behind us."

"I'm surprised," said Mandy as they were seated, "to see this many people come today! There are the Mallorys, both of them! And Callie Gordon is here as well. Also, a few other familiar faces from church and the picnic but I don't know their names."

"Yes," replied Matthew, glancing around. "Folks are curious of course but have come to support you in this as well. I told you our strategy would work. Now you are seeing the payoff from all the dinner parties, your sewing circle, and so forth. This is impressive to the judge, you know? Of course, he isn't aware why they are all here, only that people are interested in the outcome. That alone can make an impact on his ruling. He still goes solely by the law and the documents presented to him outlining each point of it for the two sides, but he is human. I doubt if any are present for Alex. Sorry, maybe I shouldn't say that, perhaps some of them are. I'm grateful they are all taking time out of their lives to come today, regardless of the reason."

"Nan is supposed to be here, too," Mandy said, "if she can get off work for the morning. May I save her a seat, or will she be allowed to enter the courtroom after the hearing has started?" Mandy felt sad her friend might miss this, after all they had been through together. She had much at stake in this ruling as well. In addition, she had expressed disappointment at not being present when Lily was rescued the day before, although there would have been little she could have done to help. Except pray, and she admitted she had done plenty of that while working!

"She may slip in as long as she does it quietly, no problem. By all means, save her a seat. I do hope she gets to be here, but it is a rather boring procedure, to be honest. The judge will likely ask some questions of you, Amanda, but probably not any others. To do that, he will have you sworn in by his Bailiff over there, Mr. Tommy Kendrick. He basically runs the hearing for the judge, also to ensure all the paperwork from today gets filed properly in Hamilton. Mostly, the judge reviews the documents and asks the two attorneys various questions here and there, nothing too exciting. I expect us to start very soon, as Judge Adams is quite punctual. He has already met you, Amanda, so nothing to be nervous about. Remember, I told you last time that he likes you!"

But Mandy *did* have butterflies flitting through her stomach. The importance of today couldn't be emphasized enough, but the fluttering kept reminding her how much she had at stake. *I'm grateful I had a good morning meal or I might be getting weak-kneed about now!*

As they all took their seats, Matthew flipped out his pocket watch, glanced at it, and frowned.

"What is it, Matthew? Is something wrong?" asked Mandy.

He replied softly. "Nothing is wrong exactly, just odd. Clark is not here yet. He had better hurry up as this judge is a stickler for punctuality, unless he wants to start out behind in the game, as it were. I wonder where he is?"

Mandy realized that she hadn't given the man a thought since entering the room. *Of course* he should be here! The empty chair that Matthew indicated should be occupied by the man spoke volumes.

"That's his attorney, isn't it, over there by himself?"

"Yes, it is. I'm going to go talk to him quickly before this gets started."

After speaking quietly with the man for a few moments, he returned to the table and plopped down in his chair next to Mandy.

"Well, we are in a bit of luck here because Mr. Harris has no idea where his client is at the moment. Perhaps he has changed his mind and will forfeit the case by not showing up at all."

"Forfeit?" asked Mandy. "Meaning, he loses?"

"And you win! God has a real sense of humor, wouldn't you say? We have spent all this time trying to figure out a way to stop the man and God apparently did it for us!"

Mandy's heart soared and she turned to look at her loved ones behind her. They had overheard the comment and were smiling as broadly as she was!

"So, what happens now?"

"Well, the judge will be coming in here within a few moments. Once he discovers Alex's absence, he will probably issue his ruling immediately in your favor. He might ask a question or two of you but it's highly doubtful."

"And I can go home?"

"Yes, Amanda, you can go home. Of course, you will need to wait another couple of days while the paperwork clears before the money is finally yours, but after that, the entire estate will be yours alone. Well, minus the two bequests, to the church and to Nan. Unfortunately, since this is

Friday, nothing can be filed until Monday, of course. At that point, however, it will be over and the money will be in your hands."

"Amanda!" called out a breathless voice. It was Nan!

"Oh, I'm thrilled you made it!" cried Mandy as they hugged. Mandy's heart flooded with relief to have her here.

"At first my boss wasn't too keen on my leaving. After he finally said all right, then I was afraid I would be late. I apologize if I'm panting but I ran all the way here. Trouble is, I only have an hour. Do you think, Matthew, that the hearing will conclude by that time?"

Matthew said, "Most likely. In any case, don't worry. No telling exactly how long it will take but it should be well within an hour. If not, you may slip out as long as you do so without any disruptions. I'm glad you are here to support Amanda."

As Nan walked back to speak to the others, her eyes were solely focused on Jacob. Before Mandy had a chance to indicate where she should sit, Jacob pointed to the chair next to him and rose to help her into it. Mandy's heart fluttered. The love on both faces sparkled from their eyes like sunlight on a river early in the morning!

How on earth did they go from perfect strangers yesterday to having moved past friendship to this already? God, only with You behind it would that be possible. Please bless their hearts, as they will soon have to separate, with thousands of miles between them. But for now, I am thrilled for two of my favorite people in the whole world. Thank You, Lord!

Nan leaned over to speak to Lily, but a booming voice sounded in the courtroom.

"Attention, please. All rise! The court of the Honorable Horace Adams is now in session." Everyone present did as requested, and the judge entered from a side door, dressed impressively in a stately black robe. He took his seat before them at the large desk at the front of the room. "You may be seated," the Bailiff announced.

Mandy gulped and breathed a silent prayer for the judge, once again pleading for God's mercy in these proceedings. *I've sacrificed much for this and my people are in deep need, Lord. Hear our cry!*

"As this is not our first hearing, I'm aware of each of the attorneys, for the plaintiff and for the defendant. Mrs. Alton, I see you are here with Mr. Grayson, and—"

He stopped in mid-sentence, glaring at the empty chair beside Mr. Harris and frowning over the glasses perched on the end of his nose.

"Mr. Harris, where is your client?" he growled, clearly displeased.

"I—I am not sure, Your Honor. That is to say, I really don't know, sir. He was told what time to be here but perhaps he overslept." And he shrugged his shoulders.

Mandy's thoughts were less kind. *Or he is passed out drunk somewhere after hearing about the disastrous end to his evil plans last night. Oh, Lord, that was wrong for me to make such a hateful assumption. Please forgive my rude attitude. But so much rides on this hearing today! To think he doesn't have the common courtesy to show up for it. After all, he is the one who caused all these weeks of misery and separation, thus requiring this hearing to have to be held!*

"Come again?"

"He hasn't gotten here yet, Your Honor. If we might have a short delay, perhaps he will yet arrive before time for your ruling."

"The paperwork is in shambles, you have a missing client, and you have the audacity to ask for a continuance?"

Harris didn't say a word but instead studied his shoes.

"No, sir," he finally muttered, "When you look at it that way, I would like to withdraw that request, if it please the court." He looked up, a sour expression on his face.

"It most certainly does please the court to grant the withdrawal of your request, sir, since I have no intention of dragging these proceedings out any longer than absolutely necessary. Oversleeping is not an acceptable excuse for his absence. Especially since he was the one who filed this suit in the first place, to object to the disposition of this inheritance as set forth in a perfectly valid and legal will. By not showing up today, he stands to forfeit the entire case. In addition, I have the legal right—no, far more—the *responsibility* to find him in contempt for such a blatant insult to the integrity of this court as well as to me personally. Do you understand all this? Moreover, does your client?

"Yes, Your Honor, I believe he does know all that. I am most apologetic to the court for this, sir."

"Once I get through all these formalities, I will issue my ruling, based on the testimony included in all these briefs and other legal documents I have before me. If your client is not here by that time, I will assume he is no longer interested in challenging this will. He will receive not one more second of my valuable time, wasted in waiting on him. Do I make myself clear, Mr. Harris?"

"Yes, sir, most abundantly clear, Your Honor. Hopefully he will be here momentarily."

Harris flopped back into his chair but from the weary look on his face, he didn't appear to Mandy to be confident his client would show up anytime soon.

Mandy prayed with a hopeful heart. *Father, that would be such a blessing if I never had to see him again and all this would be done without further delay or problems!*

"We have a few preliminaries to go through but if he is not in that seat by the time those are completed, he will forfeit his rights to challenge this legal will. Now, Bailiff, please read the formal statement of the case for all to hear."

"Yes, Your Honor. This is the case of Alex Clark versus Amanda Clark Alton, in the matter of the Last Will and Testament of Ida Clark, deceased. Plaintiff has filed stating that the disposition of the estate in this matter should be set aside, and he be declared as the only true legal heir. In support of this, he—"

A loud choking gasp from behind Mandy caught her attention as the Bailiff continued to read the information. It had come from her daughter! What was wrong with Lily? She whirled to look at her. Her face had drained of its color. Her eyes stared wide and straight ahead, focused on the man who was speaking before the court. Mandy started to run to her side but steeled herself not to. Ken-ai-te was there, next to his beloved daughter. Whatever the problem was, it needed to be addressed by him, not by her. Not now. However, she couldn't tear her eyes off her stricken daughter. *What on earth is wrong with her? God, help her!*

Lily's whole body stiffened as she rubbed her hands repeatedly on her skirt. Tears now streamed down her face, but she hadn't made another sound. Ken-ai-te felt the change in his daughter's demeanor and turned to look at her. He appeared puzzled and touched her hand, then drew back with a look of shock. Mouthing the word 'cold' to Mandy, she could see his concern etched into the deep frowns on his face. Her stomach lurched but she felt helpless to ease Lily's anxiety. Something had obviously frightened their daughter terribly. But what?

Matthew pulled on Mandy's arm to remind her she was to face the judge, not look back at the audience. She reluctantly obeyed. Praying fervently for the drama going on behind her, she found it almost impossible to focus on what the man was saying as he continued his work of announcing the case before the court. *How I want to turn and take her into my arms! God, hold her for me!*

"That's him, Mama!" Lily suddenly shrieked as every eye trained on her. She stood to face the Bailiff, pointing a shaky finger at the man with one hand while wiping away her tears with the other. "He's the one who wanted me dead!"

Mandy's heart stopped. *He* wanted Lily *dead?* But why? Alex was behind the abduction, not this man! Right?

"What's the meaning of this interruption?" the judge demanded as he slammed down his gavel. "Who are you, young lady, and what on earth are you talking about?" Before she could respond he continued in a loud voice that almost shook the windows. "Interruptions will not be tolerated! Bailiff, please remove this girl immediately!"

"But he is the one, I swear it, Mama! I would know that voice anywhere! I was blindfolded but I heard his voice several times threatening to kill me!"

"Your Honor," Matthew stood and addressed the judge, "please, may I make an effort to get to the bottom of this before you have Miss Alton removed from the court? If I might have a moment, I think I can answer your questions. I suspect you are removing the wrong person, and I think you really need to hear me out, if you will, sir."

Judge Adams stared at him intently for a moment, then relaxed slightly.

"Mr. Grayson, continue, please. This is highly irregular but I trust you will be brief. Bailiff, you will remain where you are and young lady, maybe you should have a seat before you fall down."

Lily was shaking badly by this time and her father gently guided her back into her seat and put his arms around her shoulders to comfort her. How Mandy wished she could also feel those strong arms bringing her security! But right now, they were needed elsewhere. She was grateful he was with their daughter in these moments when she could not be there, even though they were only a few feet apart. Her heart was breaking but her attention was drawn back to Matthew. Shocked at the unexpected glowering expression of pure hatred on the face of the Bailiff, staring at both her and her daughter, a growing suspicion replaced her curiosity. Was he the man responsible for all their suffering, and not Alex? How had she been so wrong?

"This is Lily Alton, sir," Matthew said, pointing at her, "and she is the daughter of the defendant. A couple of days ago she was kidnapped and—"

"Kidnapped, you say?" roared the judge.

"Yes, sir, taken away from her mother. Only late last night Lily was finally rescued by the combined efforts of a number of family and friends who managed to find where she had been hidden." Then he added, gesturing toward Ken-ai-te, "Including miraculously being tracked by this incredible Kiowa warrior here who is a close family friend. Fortunately, she was set free without harm. Several men were arrested and five other girls besides Miss Alton were also freed from a vicious slave ring operating right here in Trenton. These criminals were stealing young girls off our streets and hauling them to Mexico to sell them in the slave trade there. Through an intensive investigation, we knew the primary one behind this heinous crime as well as the others involved. Unfortunately, a couple of them managed to escape during the chaos that followed setting the girls free. This man, Tommy Kendrick," he said as he now pointed to the Bailiff, "was apparently one of those who escaped. It all makes perfect sense now, finding out he was a part of the whole wicked scheme."

The judge glowered at his Bailiff but said nothing, so Matthew continued.

"His brutality obviously has terrified this young girl, who never saw his face but did hear his voice repeatedly. Each time, he threatened to kill her instead of selling her in Mexico. Just pure meanness, Your Honor, no other reason. She kept trying to tell us about this man whose cruelty frightened her deeply, how he treated her as though the abduction was a matter of personal vengeance against her. None of us, sad to say, quite understood how ruthless he really was nor how traumatized she was by his threats. Until now."

"Oh, for heaven's sake, Judge! Surely you aren't buying any of this malarky Grayson is spinning here! I'm—"

"You're *done* is what you are, Kendrick," snapped the judge. "Now be quiet. Mr. Grayson, you may continue."

"At any rate, as you can see, simply hearing his voice this morning has triggered all that fear to once again overwhelm this poor, defenseless young girl right here in front of all of us. Your Honor, I respectfully request that we need to have this man, Tommy Kendrick, arrested on a charge of accessory to kidnapping and also for attempted murder!"

"What? That is an outrage, Your Honor! I've never been this slandered in my life! He is the one who should be arrested, not me!"

"Hold on, Mr. Grayson, and you, too, Mr. Kendrick. Calm down. No one is being arrested right now, at least until I can untangle this mess a bit more. What does all this have to do with the case before this court today, Mr. Grayson, other than the coincidental relationship between Mrs. Alton and her daughter?"

"It is a separate matter, Your Honor, granted, but we believe we can prove the kidnapping of Miss Alton was precipitated by the lawsuit filed by Mr. Clark. Therefore, it was not at all a coincidence but a vital part of the plot stopping Mrs. Alton from inheriting the estate from her aunt. While more investigation does need to be done about various details, the case remains that Miss Alton has recognized Mr. Kendrick's voice. Her entire demeanor bespeaks the truth of her charge, sir. She has no reason on earth to lie and make this accusation against him, except stating the facts as they exist. I have solid evidence, including the word of an informant who helped us determine the area last night where Miss Alton was being held, that several men from Trenton were involved in this crime. Those we have in custody will, I'm certain, reveal the names of their accomplices soon enough. None of us had any idea Kendrick was one of these, let alone the one who viciously threatened my client's daughter. Now it appears he might have even played a major role in this tragedy. It is my contention, sir, that he shouldn't be allowed to further traumatize this young girl and her family by taking part in this hearing as the Bailiff. That is why I respectfully request that he be locked up until he can be transported to Hamilton, pending further investigation into the matter. After today, I feel we have sufficient evidence to warrant such an extreme action. I hope Your Honor will agree with me."

"My goodness! That is a mouthful, sir. Mr. Kendrick, what do you have to say for yourself?"

"It's all lies! I never touched a hair on that girl, don't even know who she is."

"That's not true!" Lily jumped up again. This time her voice was no longer weak but instead strong and forceful. "You *were* there, don't you dare pretend otherwise! I would know your voice anywhere, from the awful things you said you would do to me and to the other girls as well. Your friends wanted to sell us in Mexico but not you. You were far too evil for that. None of us believed we would see another day if you had your way!"

CHAPTER FORTY-ONE

"No weapon that is formed against thee shall prosper; and every tongue that shall rise against thee in judgment thou shalt condemn..." Isaiah 54:17

May 10, 1867

How could he have done that to Lily? Mandy was on the verge of tears but fought them back. She must remain strong!

"Young lady, um, Miss Alton," said the judge grimly, "if what you say is true—and I have no reason to believe otherwise—then Mr. Grayson's charge is enough for me. I would normally ask the Bailiff at this point to remove the person in question from the court. Instead, I'm going to ask those two gentlemen on the front row over there behind Mrs. Alton to do the honors for me. They look like strong enough fellows to get the job done."

Matthew turned to look at Jacob and Ken-ai-te, nodding. They rose while Nan hopped over into Jacob's empty seat to hold Lily's hand. Mandy sighed from relief. *Again, God, You have provided someone else besides me to comfort my Lily! Thank You she is not alone!* Her heart swelled with pride as she watched her tall husband walk forward to assist in taking the man into custody. *I wonder if this Kendrick guy has seen the knife at his waist yet? Maybe that will convince him to go quietly! It sure would me. If he knew how skilled Ken-ai-te is at using the weapon, he would be begging to go peacefully!*

As the two got closer to Kendrick, he suddenly turned from angry to whiny.

"Your Honor!" he cried. "You can't be serious! I didn't do anything wrong. This girl must be mistaken, is all. I wouldn't harm her or any other girl. I'm as lost as can be with all this, honestly!"

"Mr. Kendrick," said Judge Adams, "If you are innocent, it will all come out in the investigation. We will leave that to the professionals rather than making any predispositions at this point. However, I am taking Mr. Grayson's statement to heart, that if you are the one Miss Alton heard, you should not be in this courtroom today. Therefore, I'm asking that you cooperate and go quietly with these two gentlemen. Mr. Grayson, would you show them where to confine him? Here is my key to the storeroom, off my office. You are familiar enough with it, and it will have to do since we have no jail here in Trenton. We will resume the hearing as soon as all of you can get back in here."

He tapped his gavel on the desk.

"Court is in recess for five minutes."

Jacob reached out to take the man's elbow to escort him as requested, but Kendrick jerked his arm out of his grasp and jumped back a couple of steps, fury obvious on his face.

"Let go of me, you, you *frontiersman!* How dare you pretend to be in charge of me? Judge, I'm not about to go anywhere with these two or anyone else, certainly not going to cooperate while you lock me up like a stray animal! I haven't done anything wrong. Everyone in town knows what that girl is, what her mother is, and if given the chance, I would have no qualms about killing either of them. They deserve it! That woman has no right to this inheritance, by the way, being what she is." He stared right at Ken-ai-te and added, "Besides, no filthy *Injun* is going to touch me!" Mandy's heart trembled with fear for the anger in the man's eyes, directed at her beloved!

"What do you mean by saying that given the chance you would kill both of them?" Matthew's words were full of anger. But it was more a righteous fury, not that fueled by hatred the way Kendrick's were. His spirited defense had startled Mandy. She was grateful Matthew was on their side, not having witnessed this side of him before. Had the man Kendrick really said he would kill both her and Lily? But why?

"Mr. Grayson, I will ask the questions here, thank you," said Judge Adams. "But I also want an answer to that!"

Matthew mouthed the word 'sorry' to the judge but did not back down a bit. Mandy noted that he clenched and unclenched his fists repeatedly, as though battling with himself over what he wanted to do physically to this man. The brute seemed to have forgotten he was in a court of law here!

The judge had the authority to do whatever he deemed necessary, including adding to the charges pending against him. Matthew obviously had no intentions of allowing Kendrick to wiggle out of them.

"She's not, well, she's not white! The kid, I mean. It's obvious to anyone who looks at her that she had a Negro slave daddy! At least, that's the rumor running around town and I believe it. Just look at her darker skin and hair. Even an idiot could tell that! I believe that kind should be put down, like you would do to a rabid dog. They don't have souls, you know, so what's the harm? If I had been there, which I am absolutely denying I was, I would have—"

His cheeks flushed and he clamped his lips shut. But he had already said too much.

"Would have what, Mr. Kendrick?" Matthew said. "With apologies to the court, Your Honor, but I simply cannot remain silent in the face of this outrage!" The judge nodded and Matthew continued.

"*Kill* her or at least threaten to? Is that what you were about to say, sir? Because that is what you were accused of doing by Miss Alton. Thank God you didn't succeed. Before you sell this *Injun*, as you put it, short too quickly, you might want to consider that when questioning of an informant broke down yesterday, it was his quick action that dragged the information out of him—thanks to the threat he would skin him alive if he didn't tell us where Lily was being held!"

"You *are* kidding, right, Mr. Grayson?" asked the judge, his jaw dropping open at this. He glanced over at Ken-ai-te with an expression of shock, who met his stare without emotion.

"Not in the least, Your Honor. When we got to the area, it was his skill in tracking that led us to the correct building down at the docks, to rescue the girls, including Lily. In other words, this *Injun* helped us find her in time, to set her free before you could carry out your diabolical plan, Kendrick, to enslave her for life. These facts are ones, Your Honor, you couldn't possibly have known about yet need to in order to understand the depth of the depravity we are dealing with in Mr. Kendrick."

He paused briefly, as if to give the judge a chance to step in if he chose but continued when he gestured for him to go on.

"As for the rumors, I say hogwash! I've heard them, too, but dismissed them as idle gossip that doesn't deserve a response. And certainly not a standing before this court. After all, isn't that what this great nation recently fought a vicious and bloody civil war over—whether people have the right to be whatever God made them? I sacrificed a great deal to preserve this union with that right intact and to see the Negroes set free. With all due respect, Your Honor, I have no intentions of standing here silent while this man," dramatically pointing again to Kendrick, "willfully ignores, even defies that right! Not while I am an American, *sir!* Whether this girl is half Negro or not, she does not deserve to be killed because of the color of her skin. The war decided that for everyone in this country, both North and South. This madman must be shut up for his rantings against common decency, not to mention the law!"

Now it was Mandy's turn to drop her jaw. She wanted to stand and applaud but sensed that would be most inappropriate. Would the judge feel the same?

"Well said, Mr. Grayson," commented the judge. "Mr. Kendrick, first you state you don't know the girl, then you admit you would willingly kill her, given the chance. So, which is it? And no, you don't have to answer that, because the law protects you against self-incrimination. What you *will* do is go quietly with these two gentlemen, without further denigrating comments before my bench, or I will have you bound and gagged and dragged out of this courtroom! Do you hear me?"

"Well, if I am to be arrested, I am not going to take all the blame for this myself. I didn't do this alone, not by a long shot. You say you found several of the people involved? Well, you didn't get the top dog—Alex Clark! He is the one who is behind all this misery. Every bit of it. He blackmailed me into helping him. I must admit, it didn't take much because of the rumors. I was glad to get rid of this half-breed. One way or the other. You need to talk to Clark. He is the one who hired me and all the others! I'm just a victim here myself."

"Oh, spare me the drama, Kendrick!" Judge Adams looked as though he was about to throttle the man himself! "Believe me, we will be questioning Mr. Clark about this, should he ever show up. Meantime, get this man out of here, whatever way you have to. I want him out of my sight, now!"

Matthew picked up the key to lead the trio from the room. The two men each grabbed an arm roughly but firmly and escorted him away without further protest. Until he reached the door. At the last moment he shouted over his shoulder.

"You have to get Clark! He is a ruthless liar and a thief who will stop at nothing to get what he wants!"

Everyone in the courtroom sat in stunned silence, including the judge. Mandy took advantage of the break to rush to her daughter's side and cradled her in her arms while she cried.

"Why did he want me dead, Mama? I don't understand. What did I ever do to him?"

"Hush, my dear, don't fret over it now. He cannot hurt you further. You are absolutely positive in your identification of Kendrick's voice, is that correct, Lily?"

"Yes, Mama, I am. I shall never forget it. I wish I could! Don't you believe me?"

"Of course I do, dear. Those are very serious charges the man is facing now, and I wanted to ensure that your testimony against him is accurate, with no room for error. Your ear is sharp at home, no reason it is anything less than that here."

"Another thing, the lie about my father is ridiculous. Why would people believe such nonsense? We don't even have Negroes in Indian Territory. Don't they know that? My father—" Mandy squeezed her daughter gently to warn her against finishing the statement. "I was going to say, my father is an honorable and brave man and I'm proud to be his daughter!"

"Your father is proud of you as well," said her mother.

The three men returned and Mandy hurried back to her seat. After all this drama, the remainder of the hearing should be fairly calm! Considering that Clark still had not shown up, plus was implicated now by Kendrick in the kidnapping which of course confirmed their informant's statement, perhaps this next part would be quick and easy. Nan kept looking at the watch in her pocket and Mandy knew she was anxious to not overstay her absence from the store. The hour must be about up.

The judge rapped his gavel and brought the court to order once again.

"Now that that unpleasantness has been taken care of, we can get back to the business before us today. The case has already been announced and court called into session. I need only to remind everyone that even though this is an informal hearing, I do require strict discipline in my courtroom and will tolerate no further nonsense. Is that understood?"

He glanced up over his glasses at the end of his nose, stared intently at those gathered before him, and both attorneys nodded their heads in agreement. As he gathered up all the documents and studied them briefly, he shook his head.

"Looking over this paperwork that was submitted to me in this matter, I find part of it in excellent form but the rest of it most certainly is not. Mr. Harris, some of your required information is missing. In fact, this is one of the sloppiest presentations of legal facts that I have ever seen. We have discussed this once before in a hearing, yet your incompetence or negligence or both make it necessary for me to mention it again. How long have you been practicing law, young man?"

"For about ten years, Your Honor. I thought I had it all in order. I do apologize, sir. Working with my client has been quite difficult, to say the least."

"I don't want to hear your excuses. They don't fly with me, is that clear?"

"Yes, Your Honor," he replied grimly.

The judge spent a few minutes shuffling papers around on his desk until he appeared to be satisfied and stacked them in two piles on the small table to his right.

"That, Mr. Harris," and he nodded toward one of the stacks, "is your job, not mine. On the other hand, the documents that the attorney for the defendant has presented," tapping the other one, "are all in order as far as I can tell. The biggest question before us at the moment, however, is where is your client, Mr. Harris? If he cannot be bothered to show up for court in his own suit, I see no reason why I should not go ahead and rule for the defendant in this matter."

Mandy's eyes popped wide. Was it truly all over? *God, thank You!*

Before the judge could continue, however, the door at the back of the room burst open. Alex appeared and staggered down the aisle to the front, waving a pistol wildly in his hand!

"Judge," he slurred as he charged right up to the desk of Judge Adams, "I got shomethin' to shay..."

"Sir, you are drunk!" proclaimed the judge with a disgusted sneer. The man's bloodshot eyes and disheveled clothing confirmed the suspicion but they all could now smell that he reeked of alcohol, even this early in the morning. "How dare you come storming into my courtroom in this condition, and even armed! I will see you in jail with the key thrown away for this outrage!"

Alex stood there with his jaw hanging open, as though he couldn't comprehend for a moment the judge's intent. Slowly his face reddened and he slammed a fist down on the judge's desk.

"Stop with the threats! You need to award this estate to me and get rid of this imposter here, do you hear me? Or you are going to be sorry!"

The judge flinched a moment, then recovered.

"I've already thrown my Bailiff out of this courtroom today and if you don't want to find yourself taken into custody as well, I suggest you apologize immediately to the court for the disruption as well as for that threat against me. Sit down right this moment and be quiet until you are asked to testify. Mr. Harris, restrain your client this minute!"

"Alex, please, have a seat here and—"

"Shut up, you useless piece of scum! All you have done is tell me how I can *not* do this case." He turned back to the judge.

"This woman," he shouted, pointing at Mandy, "is a fraud and not who she says she is. I'm not too drunk to take matters in my own hands if I have to, in order to stop her. But it is your job to do that and I expect you to do it. My grandmother would never have agreed to this will if she had been in her right mind."

"If you utter one more word, Clark," said the judge, his voice barely concealing the anger under the surface of the words, "you are going to be hit with far worse than charges for contempt of court. Put the gun down right now or I'll have you removed and confined. I've warned you, so sit down and allow your attorney to do his job to argue the case. *Now!*"

Alex stood his ground, the gun still in his hand but now at his side. Glaring at Mandy with eyes flared wide, he glanced back and forth from the judge to his attorney and back at Mandy. His jaw worked hard with the anger he was barely suppressing.

Without warning, he strode over two steps, grabbed Mandy by the arm, and jerked her up out of the chair. In one swift movement, he roughly pinned both arms to her sides, and she let out a yelp of pain. Then he whipped the pistol up to her temple, dragging her backward a couple of steps away from Matthew and the others, almost to the door leading to the judge's office.

Gasps could be heard from everyone. Mandy glanced over at Ken-ai-te, whose face reflected shock but also deep anger. No one moved a muscle, not wishing to rile this madman holding Mandy hostage.

"Now, I'm ready to talk, and no one else gets to, you hear me? Or I blow this lady's head off!"

She remained still for the moment but continued to search Ken-ai-te's face for a clue as to what she should do, or shouldn't do. *God, please don't let him harm me, especially in front of Lily! This maniac has got to be stopped, though! Help me!*

"Alex," she began, "you don't want to do this, you know you don't. I understand—"

"Shut your mouth! You understand *nothin'!* And my name isn't Alex! It's Ford, Benjamin Ford, and it's time folks around here got used to calling me by my real name."

Mandy turned her head slightly to look into his eyes and saw he was telling the truth, this time. Maybe one of the only times he had done so in years!

"Why did you impersonate Alex Clark?" asked Matthew. "Why go to all that trouble?"

"Money, you lout! What do you think? I said none of you understand anything about me. I met the real Alex in the Army and he told me all about his fabulously wealthy grandmother, loved to talk about her. Funny thing is, I really didn't pay much attention until he got to the money part. After he was badly wounded, I got this brilliant idea to pretend to be him once he died. My plan was to come here and somehow get my hands on this vast fortune he kept going on about. When the doc said he might survive after all, I had to take matters in my own hands with the simpleton, which was easy given that he was confined to his bed. I sure couldn't leave him alive if I was going to assume his identity."

Nan gasped and clamped her hand over her mouth.

Dearest Nan, how your heart must be broken to hear about sweet Alex's murder like this! I'm very glad my aunt never knew the truth.

"Turns out," he rattled on, "it was much easier than I thought to fool the old biddy, but as time went on it got tiresome putting up with her. So, I had to kinda 'accelerate' my plan a little because she got to be too much of a snoop, her and the others, too. They wouldn't stay out of the cellar."

"What's in the cellar?" asked Dave Harris. "You never told me about anything being down there."

"Well, for starters, there are several large vats of whiskey. Yeah, kinda proud of myshelf for, for that. Uhh," he stammered as he appeared to be having trouble keeping his train of thought.

He closed his eyes for a moment and swayed slightly, moving Mandy with him. She rooted her feet out of a momentary panic to stop the motion. What if he fell, taking her down with him? Would he shoot her before they reached the floor? In a few seconds, he regained his balance and reopened his eyes, squeezing her tighter and she winced.

"What did you ask? Oh, yeah, about the whiskey. Great stuff. Without taxes to pay on it, fun to drink and know I'm getting around the law on that one."

"You have untaxed whiskey in the cellar?" asked Matthew. "What's so great about that?"

"Because I cheated the government! Boy, you are one dumb lawyer. It's always a good day when you can do that."

"Alex, I mean Benjamin, sorry," said Nan all of a sudden, boldly speaking up. "Wasn't the whiskey what Bessie discovered? That led to her death? *At your hands,* right? Over *whiskey?* A really poor excuse for killing such a kind soul as she was!"

"What?" exclaimed Matthew. "You killed Bessie, the servant who lived with Miss Ida for a couple of years?"

"Yeah, what of it? No one cares about a Negro woman, and a slave at that! She got in the way is all, so I stopped her."

"You seem to forget, I know about that," snapped Nan. "Remember what you told me when I found Bessie's body? What you said you would do if I told anyone? Well, I'm telling now because you can no longer hurt Miss Ida or me!"

When he didn't answer her, she went on.

"You told me you would *kill* Miss Ida if I told anyone about Bessie! Is that what you did, *kill* your grandmother? Did you poison her?"

"This gets more ludicrous by the minute!" said Dave Harris, clearly disturbed to hear all this coming out about his client. "I had no idea, Your Honor, none at all. Alex, please stop this madness!"

"Shut up, Harris! Not stopping now or ever. I am in charge now, don't you get that yet? You will listen to me, all of you. If you think I'm crazy now, wait until you see what I have planned for this busy-body here." He jerked Mandy tighter again, and she gasped in pain. "When I get through with her, even her own mother won't recognize her!" *God, You alone can deliver me from this monster!*

"You haven't answered my question," said Nan, standing up from her chair and taking a step toward him. Mandy's eyes widened. She held her breath.

Nan, what are you doing? I'm screaming at you, pleading with you here! He will kill me if you don't stop! They know now, that is all that matters. I'm afraid he will kill you, too, if you don't stop aggravating him!

"Did you poison Miss Ida, Benjamin?" she pressed. "To get her estate and thus protect your secret, your precious whiskey in the cellar? You said you had to 'accelerate' your plan, was that how you did it?"

"Maybe I did and maybe I didn't, ain't sayin' one way or the other. But my 'secret' as you put it is not whiskey alone. Not by a long shot! Hah, there is a funny joke, get it? A shot of whiskey?" He chuckled at his poor humor. "People in this hick town would be shocked to find out what else I have hidden down there!"

"You mean other than dear Bessie's body?"

He didn't answer, just stared at her. Mandy glanced at him and could see the hatred splayed across his face, feel his panting breath, the alcohol smell almost overpowering her this close up, and she shivered.

"Mr. Ford," said Judge Adams quietly, "You do know there is no way you will ever get your hands on this inheritance now, right? You have just confessed to several crimes while committing another felony! Why not give up and stop adding to your charges?"

"Don't you want to know what else is in the cellar, judge? Bet the rest of these here folks would like to know. I mean besides the rotting carcass of a Negro slave."

Nan cried out and took a step forward in her rage.

"How *could* you?" Suddenly she caught herself and stopped, panting with the effort it took her to swallow her angry words in the face of this latest insult.

"All right, since you are in the mood to share with us your secrets," said Judge Adams in a calm voice obviously meant to placate him, "go ahead and talk. We're here and are all listening. But first, why not put the gun down and release Mrs. Alton?"

"Hah! *Mrs. Alton?* That's a nice way to say it, right, *Cousin* Amanda? Bet they would love to hear how your child was conceived, wouldn't they?"

"Alex, uh, Benjamin," Mandy pleaded, "what on earth are you talking about? Something that private and personal has nothing to do with this case. Please let me go and we'll work this all out. You're scaring me with that gun pointed at my head. Since you have admitted you are not Alex Clark, after all, you are *not* my cousin, in any sense of the word. So drop the charade!" *If Nan can be bold, I can as well! Seems all he understands is brute force!*

"Of course I'm your cousin, you little runt! What are you talking about?"

You could hear a pin drop in the courtroom.

What is wrong with him? He truly has gone mad! God, help us all!

"We are here to find out," he sneered, "what the judge has to say about the inheritance. I have made my demands clear, that it will all be mine and mine alone, or I will cheerfully blow your head off, *cousin*. So, what do you say, judge? It will be my honor to keep my word if you don't speak up right now!"

Mandy noticed with a quick sideways glance that while everyone's attention had been focused on Judge Adams and on the insane ramblings of Alex/Benjamin for the last few minutes, Ken-ai-te had managed to slip out of his chair unnoticed by the man. He had an idea, she knew, of how to set her free! The warrior disappeared behind the office wall off to the side of the room, but she figured he was slowly making his way around to the back while ducking down to hide behind the spectators in the full courtroom. His silent moccasin steps couldn't be heard and as long as he could remain out of sight of Alex, he could position himself to strike when the time was right. The knife at his side would already be out of its sheath, she knew. This tactic had worked in battle many times. Would it work here? Could the knife find its target in time to prevent this madman from pulling the trigger?

Her only concern was how to know when he was ready since she could not see him, in order to duck her head out of the way. *God, You will have to let me know when that time comes. Ken-ai-te and I can often communicate without words but will it work now, without eye contact? This seems to be my only hope of rescue. Please help me have the courage to do this! And may my beloved's aim be straight!*

For now, her attention needed to be off her husband or Alex might sense something was amiss. She scarcely breathed and steeled herself not to make any overt glances toward the back of the room, for fear of alerting Alex to the plan to stop him. *My confidence is in You, Lord! May Your hand be upon that knife as my husband uses all his skill as a Kiowa brave to throw it any moment!*

She needn't have worried. Alex/Benjamin was too busy with his drunken rage to pay attention to one missing Indian in the room. Mandy fought to keep her breathing even to prevent her captor from suspecting a thing until it was too late.

"Sir," tried Matthew again, "have you no respect for your grandmother? She made out her will legally and left the estate to Amanda. You can't just charge in here to change what she has done according to the law. Can't we talk about this, calmly and rationally?"

"Are you nuts? Talk about what? What I'm about to do to *dear* Amanda? Who her child's daddy is, or more properly, what *race* he is? What else I must protect in the cellar of *my* house? These are things not negotiable, already explained. This lady," and he jerked her body tighter against him again, causing her to further cry out, "is not getting one red cent. Not one penny! Not one bar of gold!"

"Gold?" asked Matthew, his jaw dropping. "You have hidden gold in the house, or rather in the cellar?"

"Yep, sure have, about a hundred bars of it, or thereabouts."

Gasps could be heard across the room at this news and Mandy's eyes widened. *Gold? In the cellar?*

He continued, "It would have stayed that way, too, if not for the snooping. I told all of them not to go down there but they didn't listen. Not my fault they wouldn't. I went to great lengths to steal all those shiny bars a little at a time, from both the Union forces and the Confederate Army. I switched sides so often, I lost track of who I took it all from, frankly. Started my little freight business while I waited for the old lady to kick off, to haul it all from a cave down in Kentucky as respectable goods in order to keep anyone from becoming suspicious. But the only place I could find to hide it was in the cellar of the house. Right under the old woman's nose! Kinda hard to spend it around here but I'm working on that. On my life, I swear there is no way you, lady, are going to get one single bar. You hear me, *dear cousin?* You get nothing! Except a bullet in your brain. After we have a little party together, that is."

Mandy's stomach heaved. She struggled valiantly for a moment, but it was no use. Her arms were pinned tight, and the pain increased with any movement. There seemed to be little she could do to get loose without risking him shooting her, or others. *God, help me! Only You can rescue me this time!*

CHAPTER FORTY-TWO

"Some trust in chariots, and some in horses: but we will remember the name of the LORD our God." Psalm 20:7

May 10, 1867

"Did you say have some respect for my grandmother?" Alex/Benjamin sneered. "Are you crazy? Where was her respect for me? She pretended all the time to be so *religious* but yet she disinherited her only grandson. How is that living your religion? How is that for being holy? She didn't know the meaning of the word, to treat me like she did. I've about had a gutful of her sermons and Bible verses and lectures on common decency and love. *Love!* Are you kidding me, *love?* She never loved me, nor my mother or brothers. But I showed her a thing or two before she died!"

"What did you do to your grandmother?" asked Matthew, measuring his words carefully. "Did you poison her, as Nan asked? What did you do?"

"Of course I poisoned her! The cancer wasn't working fast enough and I got tired of waiting for her to die."

Hearing this, Mandy let out a soft cry, followed by one from Nan. The monster actually *smiled.* Mandy's stomach clenched and she fought her urge to scream. *My poor, poor aunt!*

"She was too much trouble," he went on, "to feed and give her medicine and all. I'm not a nurse! I didn't want Nan around to mess things up. So, I kicked her out. I was going to use a pillow on the old lady to end it faster than the poison was doing, but then Nan moved back in. On top of it all you, lady, showed up to steal it all away from me! If it wasn't one whiner, it was another one. I finally washed my hands of her and let the two of you do all the dirty work. Why wouldn't she just *die?"*

Matthew asked quietly, "What about Lily? Did you kidnap her in an effort to stop Amanda? Is that what happened? Did you hire all those thugs to threaten them and when that didn't work you—"

"Yeah, yeah, I did that, too. Figured if the brat disappeared, she would give up and go home. But that didn't work either. I have no idea how they found her, thought she was well hidden, her and the other girls. Could have made a pretty penny with that one in Mexico, believe me, as innocent as—"

"I think we all get the picture," snapped Matthew, "no need to keep talking about it. You engineered a clever plan that almost worked. One thing you forgot about was the power of a mother's love."

"Huh? Oh, yeah, guess I did misjudge that. Why couldn't you have gone home where you belong? I only wanted you to leave me alone. But no more! I am glad you are here now, my little half breed."

"Half breed?" exclaimed Matthew. "What on earth are you talking about? You insulted her daughter's parentage and now you are doing the same with Amanda. How dare you!"

"I dare because it's true. Her daddy, and her daughter's daddy, were Negroes. Did you not know that? Which makes her a half breed, along with her brat."

"Sir, Amanda's father was a minister and respected member of this community and a brother to Miss Ida. Where did you get the idea he wasn't white? You know, it doesn't matter where you heard that nonsense, it simply isn't true."

"Well, it is about her kid, then. I know it is because, because I started that rumor." And he cackled at his own sick joke.

"Not funny at all," growled Matthew. "So do you admit the gossip is untrue? For your information, Lily's father is white, lives in Indian Territory, and is a missionary to the Kiowa people. If you had bothered to get to know Amanda when she first arrived, instead of threatening her every move, even her very existence, you could have learned that, as I did."

"I don't admit to nothin'! Or did I just do that? Can't remember," and he shook his head. This is going from bad to worse! *Please, Ken-ai-te, kill him before he says too much!*

"One more time, sir," said the judge, "I'm going to ask you to put the gun down and release Mrs. Alton. You don't need to hold her hostage to get what you want—you already have an audience for your cleverness in committing all these crimes."

He glared in response but said nothing.

However, Matthew wasn't finished and kept at him. "Alex, uh, Benjamin, I mean, didn't you pay several people to delay the legal case you filed, to force Amanda into giving up and leaving town before it was finalized?"

"Yeah, I guess I did."

"As in who? Perhaps Tommy Kendrick, the Bailiff for this court?"

"Yeah, good ole Tommy. He's my drinking buddy. We have had some good times together. Where is he? Thought he would be here today."

"The judge has confined him, pending an investigation into his role in Lily's kidnapping. But I need to hear it from you, that you engineered that and paid Kendrick for his part in it."

"Yeah, yes, I did. Good enough for you?"

"What about Abigail Lawson, my secretary? Did you enlist her help doing the same thing, to misfile papers and lose them, in order to delay this hearing?"

"Ah, sweet Abigail! Yeah, I did that, too. She did a good job, only she got greedy. And pregnant."

"Pregnant?" Matthew asked calmly, not at all surprised of course. Once more gasps could be heard from all over the room. Talk about juicy gossip coming out. Mandy's insides squirmed at hearing this news made public. She knew Matthew wouldn't have pushed him about Abigail unless it was a piece of the puzzle that had to be revealed, to take this monster down permanently. It was sad that Abigail's reputation would have to be tarnished, but part of the price to be paid for consorting with a criminal like Alex.

"Yeah, she was going to have a little—"

"Yes, yes, we get the picture." Again, Matthew had interrupted him to avoid hearing unpleasantness that need not be spoken out loud. "She has disappeared, did you know that? Do you have any personal knowledge of what happened to her? Her poor kitty would love to know where her owner is, if she is still alive."

"Stupid cat. Hated that thing. Wouldn't go over there because of its constant noise."

"Back to Abigail. What happened to her?"

"Huh?" he said, as though he hadn't a clue.

"Did you kill Abigail to keep her quiet when she became pregnant with your child and demanded marriage? Is her body also hidden in that despicable cellar?"

Mandy's eyes widened. *What? With Bessie?*

"Oh, all right, yeah, I strangled her to keep her from telling everyone about my scheme to stop Amanda, and to shut her up about the marriage thing. And about the baby. Someone had to silence her! The cellar seemed the perfect place to dump her. You know, out of sight, out of mind, and all that."

The silence in the courtroom was profound for a couple of moments. Matthew's grilling had led to several secrets being revealed, most of which they already knew or had suspected. However, the confession of the various schemes and evil actions needed to come from Alex himself, in order to provide the evidence needed to convict him of each crime. And the cad walked right into his own trap! Disaster still lurked around the corner since the vicious gossip was closer to the truth than anyone imagined. *Thank You, God, for keeping that one hidden, just a little longer!*

"Should have done the same to this here lady long ago. My life would have been much simpler if I had. She is a liar and a fraud, and that is what she accused me of."

"How has Amanda lied? I don't understand. Enlighten me, please." Mandy realized he was pulling him in deeper and deeper and without the man even realizing how twisted everything had become, and from his own lips. How clever Matthew was at this!

I suppose that is why he is considered such a shrewd lawyer! Paul did the same thing with his questioning of the informant yesterday, and now Matthew is. I'm amazed! But please, please don't push this. I don't think he knows the truth and I don't want him to, or to share it if he does! If only you knew the truth...another consequence of all the lies!

"How has she lied to you or to the court?"

"She wants to own the property and she can't, because she is a woman! My grandmother told me that she was forced to keep everything she had in her brother's name, because legally she couldn't have it in her own."

"You are right, sir, in saying that used to be the case. However, Ohio has recently passed a law, the first in the nation I might add, to allow women to own and inherit property in their own name. Once Miss Ida knew about this, she immediately changed everything into her name, instead of keeping it in Josiah's. That is how she discovered she could also write her will to allow Amanda to inherit the estate, after she found out she was alive and living in Indian Territory. Or, maybe you didn't know about this part?"

"What? But she's a *woman!* I don't believe you, not one word!" His grip on Mandy had slipped slightly due to the profuse sweating he was doing at this point, and now he gripped her tighter to regain his firm hold. She bit her lip to keep from crying out. A drop of his sweat dripped onto her hand. Inside, she cringed, wanting desperately to wipe it away.

"Yes, she is that," said Matthew with a hint of a smile. "Whether you believe it or not, she is going to have the entire estate here in a few minutes, assuming the judge rules in her favor. She will get everything, minus the small bequest to Miss Ida's church and the one to Miss Brewster of course. You, however," he taunted, "will be left with absolutely *nothing*. In addition, the bulk of the inheritance will be used to feed the Kiowa people out West as well as to feed their souls. How is that for God's irony and retribution?"

"But she's not only a woman, she's not white! And only whites can own property. Not half breeds!"

"Oh, here we go again. I told you a minute ago that her father was white, so why do you keep bringing up this lie about her not being white?"

"What about her *mother?* Huh? The Indian that spawned her?"

"Indian? What on earth are you talking about? Her mother was also white."

"Ain't so. Just ask her. Ain't that right?" And he again jerked on her arm, but this time she did cry out. "That pain ain't nothin' compared to what you are going to feel in a little while!"

God, help me! Should I end these lies once and for all? How did he find out? What do I do?

Matthew nodded at her slightly. Was this her sign? Yes, she believed it was!

Alex/Benjamin demanded again, "You'd better speak up now or—"

Mandy suddenly dodged her head to one side, leaving her captor's head exposed behind her for a split second. The knife silently flew through the air straight for the one holding her!

Thunk! It found its target deep in the skull of her assailant, a mere few inches from her own head! The sound of it plunging into his temple was like a cannon going off right in her ear! He just stood there at first, gun hand wobbling for a second. Then the weapon fell to the floor as he slowly released Mandy. When his grip eased, she wrenched away from him, and

Alex Clark/Benjamin Ford fell to the floor, backward, where he lay lifeless at her feet. Instinctively she screamed and stared down at his still body, hugging her arms around her body to stop her shaking. He really was dead and couldn't hurt her or anyone she loved ever again!

The courtroom erupted into chaos! Matthew ran up to grab Mandy's arm to ensure she wouldn't also fall, as Jacob raced forward, followed closely by Nan and Lily. They encircled her and Lily hugged her mother.

"Mama! I was so scared! Are you all right?"

"Oh, Lily, I am now! God delivered me from evil as He promised to do!" Ken-ai-te joined the group and she added, "Along with, with the help of course of, of our dear friend Ken-ai-te!"

She reached out and grabbed hold of his hand, desperately wishing she could do far more, but this would have to suffice for now. How close she had come to having the lies unravel right as everything was finally falling into place! He had saved her in more ways than one.

"How do I say thank you?" she asked him, with tears in her eyes and gazing deep into his own. "You saved my life!"

His eyes said it all. That, and the smile he had on his face. He finally released her hand and reached down beside her to jerk the knife hard to pull it out of the body. Wiping the blood calmly on his breech leg, he put it back in his sheath, as though he did this sort of thing every day.

Nan's jaw dropped. "Ugh! But I guess that's what you do after you kill an enemy, right, Ken-ai-te?"

He nodded but said nothing.

"He was that, and far more, to all of us!" replied Matthew. "Amanda, are you sure you are okay? Do you need to sit down?"

Before she could answer, the judge slammed his gavel down several times in a row and called out above the din.

"Folks, please! Everyone return to your seats. Despite all we have witnessed, this court is still in session, and I need order!" And he punctuated his demand with a couple more swings of the gavel until he had everyone's attention. As they quickly scurried to sit down, silence returned.

"For one thing, I need to issue my ruling before we can be adjourned. I am not sure of the legal procedure on this, after a death occurs to one of the principal parties, but if you will all take a seat, we will find out!"

Mandy found it odd that the body was left where it fell, as a grim reminder of the violent end to one who had brought so much misery to so many. She tried to avert her eyes but since he was only a couple of feet from her feet, she found it difficult to concentrate, to say the least. Shivers continued to wrack her body with each breath. In her mind, she knew he was dead, but her heart feared he might get up from the floor any moment! Was it really all over?

Judge Adams cleared his throat and smiled at everyone.

"That is a hard act to follow, with all the drama and all those confessions! However, now that order is restored, I must say that the long list of crimes committed by the dead man have left me a bit overwhelmed with all that has been going on behind the scenes here in Trenton. Some of it is up to me to handle but some is not. Let's quickly go through each, one at a time. First, we have buried in the cellar the body of a Negro servant, Bessie, right?" And he looked at Nan.

"Yes, sir, Bessie Langston. Only she wasn't a servant, she was a paid employee of Miss Ida's and a dear friend to us both."

"I'm afraid I still don't understand."

"Well, she was a former slave who came through Trenton on the Underground Railroad several years ago, when Miss Ida and I met her at our home."

"Your home?"

"Yes, sir, or rather Miss Ida's. I was living with her at the time. The house was a Depot for that esteemed but secret organization, and we opened our home to runaway slaves for almost a year, as our protest against slavery. Bessie was one of the first to come, and Miss Ida led her to the Lord after her brother, Samuel, died of a snake bite he suffered shortly before they arrived. Bessie was deeply grateful for the care we gave to them both and for spiritual deliverance as well, which is a story for another time. She vowed to return after the war and work for Miss Ida, which she did. Until that vicious monster killed her."

"All right, then. We need to have her body removed to a cemetery."

"If I might request, Your Honor," said Nan, "that it be moved to a plot in the Clark Family Cemetery on the grounds of the house? Her brother is buried there, and we promised her that someday she would lie beside him in that sacred ground."

"Oh, of course. That's up to Mrs. Alton here but as for me, I am fine with that."

Mandy's heart soared. *Did he just say it is up to me if Bessie is buried at the house?*

"Moving on," he urged. "Next we have the problem of a second body in that cellar. Matthew, will you kindly contact the local undertaker and have him take care of that body?"

"Yes, sir, I will. Miss Lawson had no next of kin but I will pay for her burial myself, since she worked for me."

"That is kind of you, since it appears she set out to sabotage your case."

Matthew replied, "It is the Christian thing to do, given the tragic circumstances."

"Next we have the matter of some gold bars. Again, Matthew, I need you to follow up on that with the military authorities, to determine how that is to be disbursed in the estate. It seems that it technically belongs to the US Government, since the Union won the war, even if stolen from the Confederates, so they may have other ideas but that will be up to them. In any case, its current owner is deceased and thus it has legally become the property of the new owner. At least once I have officially ruled in the matter before us today, which I shall do in a moment. Now, have I missed anything? Oh, yes, the whiskey barrels. Those will stay with the house and can be sold, with the appropriate taxes being paid on it, again, by the new owner."

No one said anything further. Mandy's hopes were high by this point!

He continued. "After Mr. Grayson has filed all these documents in Hamilton on Monday, I will also prefer charges against Kendrick and his cohorts for the various crimes they have committed. They should never see the light of day again, given the gravity of what they did, and planned to do."

"Your Honor" said Matthew, "might I make a request of you regarding the custody of Mr. Kendrick?"

"Of course."

"Paul Owens is the Private Investigator I hired to help us interrogate the informants we managed to scour up while searching for Lily Alton. He has in his personal custody the others who were involved in her kidnapping, as well as that of the other girls who were taken, and he and his team are even now hunting down the rest. Might I suggest he also take custody of Mr. Kendrick, since we have no Sheriff to do this for us, and obviously Kendrick cannot remain in that storeroom much longer? With your permission, he and his team can interrogate all of them and carefully build the case needed to prosecute each of them properly. They will thus ensure that they do, indeed, receive the appropriate punishment for their crimes."

"Excellent idea, sir. Thank you for that, and can you contact Mr. Owens to ask if he would be willing to help us in this manner?"

"I certainly shall, Your Honor. I'm quite certain that he will be glad to fully cooperate in this. Thank you for considering that suggestion."

Mandy held her breath. The judge still hadn't said a thing about Alex's dying declaration and she wasn't about to remind him! It might affect how he would rule on her case.

Can a half-Indian woman inherit property in Ohio now? I have no idea and God took Alex out before he could reveal the fullness of my lie. Therefore, I'm assuming I should remain quiet about it, at least for now. Right, Lord? I'm so very tired of all the deceit, though. Show me how I should handle this.

The judge's booming voice brought her out of her thoughts abruptly.

"Therefore, I am now ruling that the Last Will and Testament of Miss Ida Clark is to be upheld in its entirety, with the estate being awarded to Amanda Alton, her niece. Minus the two bequests, of course. One is to go to Miss Clark's church, the other to her friend and companion, Miss Nan Brewster. I have copies of those bequests here which I will sign, along with a document summarizing my final ruling. They will all be filed in the county seat on Monday, as I said. Mr. Matthew Grayson, attorney for Miss Clark and for Mrs. Alton, I am entrusting you to disburse the funds accordingly at that time. As Executor of the estate, it will also be your responsibility to liquidate all other assets and see that all funds go to Mrs. Alton in a timely manner. Is that understood?"

Matthew nodded his head. "I shall be more than happy to do this, Your Honor."

Finally, the judge addressed Dave Harris.

"Sir, you are out of luck, it would seem, on receiving your fees for services rendered. But since those were woefully inadequate, I hope you will take that as a reminder to beef up your knowledge of legal procedure. And what's more, do not ever appear before my bench again this poorly prepared to present a case. In addition, to avoid a repeat of this fiasco, you might reconsider whatever requirements you have for taking on a case, as they seem to have come up quite short in this instance. Is that understood, sir?"

Mr. Harris said, "Yes, Your Honor, I understand. And no, this will never happen again, I promise you that. In fact, I may get out of law altogether. The whole affair has been a most miserable experience for me, knowing the law but being forbidden by my client to follow it. Thank you for not pressing charges against me for what Clark, or Ford rather, did."

The judge nodded and continued. "I believe all that remains now is the body of this Alex Clark or Benjamin Ford, whatever his name was. Matthew, can I again get you to have the undertaker take care of an unclaimed body?"

"Yes, sir, with great pleasure on this one. He will have to be buried in a pauper's grave, I'm afraid, but so be it. That is the expected end for all criminals who refuse to obey the law."

"Well said, sir," said Judge Adams. "One last comment I would like to add to all this drama is to commend the courage and skill of the Indian here—sorry, sir, I still cannot get the hang of your name properly—in protecting Mrs. Alton from deadly harm from Clark or Ford or whatever. I am declaring that there will be no inquest held on his death and the court offers its profound thanks for what you did, sir."

"Thank you, and it's Ken-ai-te, sir." The judge nodded and smiled at his words.

"That being all of the business before this court, I declare this hearing adjourned!" And he brought down his gavel powerfully on the desk before him.

"Matthew, we did it! *You* did it!" Mandy's tears of joy could not be stopped now, Kiowa training or not! "Thank you, from the bottom of my heart!" She hugged him warmly.

"You are most welcome, Amanda. Jacob, Ken-ai-te," he said as he shook their hands, "thank you for all your help. It has been an honor for me to get to know you both. You have quite a gal there, I hope you know!"

"Oh, yes, we are aware of that," answered Jacob.

"She is a special lady," chimed in Nan, hanging onto Jacob's arm with all her might. Her grin was only matched by his!

Lily clung to her mother and wouldn't let go!

The Mallorys came rushing up to congratulate Mandy on the win, and she was thrilled to introduce her friends from Trenton to her Indian Territory "friends." Right after that, Callie Gordon came over to do the same.

Both Jacob and Ken-ai-te were visibly impressed with the many who called out greetings to Mandy as they filed out of the courtroom. If there was ever any doubt that she had made friends here in Trenton, they were put to rest now. People were genuinely thrilled for her! It was an exhilarating feeling for Mandy, after all she had been through.

But one big question remained that the judge had no control over, nor did Mandy, for that matter. Would Ken-ai-te accept her back as his wife? Or continue his anger from their nighttime encounter a couple of days ago? Her heart pounded, in part from the let-down of the whole ordeal but mostly from this anxiety. She held her breath as he walked up to her for one moment, not saying a word. As she gazed into the face of her beloved, Mandy's heart warmed with the kindness and, yes, love she saw shining in his dark eyes. They would have some talking to do together when they got home, but for now at least Mandy felt confident that their marriage was intact and thriving once more. She could hardly contain her joy!

As the group slowly left the courtroom, a not-too-gentle nudge intruded on Mandy's heart. She recognized it well. The Holy Spirit was urging her to put to rest one more vital piece of the whole puzzle before celebrating. It was time for the lies to end!

Mandy took a deep breath. "Matthew, I have something to say to you that all the others here know about already, and it is only fair I share it with you as well. This isn't really the place but maybe outside?"

CHAPTER FORTY-THREE

"And ye shall know the truth, and the truth shall make you free."
John 8:32

May 10, 1867

Guide my tongue, Lord! Mandy's brief prayer had never been more heartfelt than in that moment.

Gathered on the lawn in front of the courtroom building with her closest friends and family, she quickly tried to organize her thoughts as to how to tell Matthew about her lie. She knew he had to be bursting with curiosity. How would he take hearing the truth?

"Matthew, when I made the decision to come here to Trenton, I had a choice to make about a key element. Many times, I've regretted it because it forced me to tell a lie about something important to me, that I'm proud of, and denying it has eaten at my heart the entire time I've been here. But it was necessary for several reasons, which I believe you will see in a moment."

"What a mystery! Please tell me, since you said everyone knows but me!"

"My father was white, as you know, but my mother was a full blood Kiowa."

"What? A Kiowa?"

"Yes. Therefore, that makes me half Kiowa and half white. Alex was closer to the truth than he realized. I believe he guessed on the Indian part but maybe he knew, somehow. I was very, very careful to only confide in one person while here, and that was Nan. Of course, Lily knew, as did Jacob. And Ken-ai-te, who, by the way, is not a dear family friend. That is another lie we told, to support the others, sad to say. Ken-ai-te is my husband!"

"Oh, my! No wonder he was so protective of you, and of Lily! That sure explains a great deal! Ken-ai-te, that makes what you did a while ago in there even more heroic than ever! I would like to shake your hand, as my friend and the luckiest man on the face of the earth!"

They shook with grins on both faces!

"What about your parents, how did they meet?" asked Matthew.

"They met in Indian Territory and fell in love. Eventually Papa led her and her entire family to the Lord. Together, they built a mission dedicated to evangelizing her people. Then I was born. Sadly, my mother disappeared when I was only a few weeks old, so my father brought me back here to Trenton where he and his sister reared me together. He knew if he told Aunt Ida that I was half Kiowa, she wouldn't allow me in her home. At that time her prejudice against people of color was quite strong, but in particular against Indians. That started a lie that had to continue for eighteen years, until I found out the truth after Papa died. It seems my whole life I have been seeking the truth about one thing or another!"

"That is quite a story!" said Matthew. "But you know, your aunt changed dramatically in her attitude on this."

"Yes, I know that now! You have explained a great deal of it to me, as has Nan. Plus, Aunt Ida wrote all those letters to me, taking great pains to share in meticulous detail with me about the spiritual transformation she underwent. But I didn't know anything about all that until after I got here. By then, it was too late to untangle the lie that Lily and I were white. If I had trusted God a little more, I would have come as a Kiowa to see my aunt. But God has given me peace about needing a lie to protect my aunt and myself for a time. My only regret is that I never got to share all this with her before she died. I would have loved that, to see her face when she found out the truth!"

"This, Matthew," added Nan, "is why it was so important that Miss Ida's estate go to Amanda, in order for her to honor Miss Ida's desire to make up in a small way for some of the harm she did years ago. By leaving her money to Amanda to use for the Kiowa people, she accomplished that perfectly. At least she felt peaceful at being able to do that."

"It will be money well used, believe me," said Mandy. "Not only to feed my people who are starving but to share the more important food of the Word of God as well. Without the Bread of Life, they can never fully enjoy the bread for their stomachs. I hope you can understand and forgive my deception, along with all the little lies I had to tell because of the big one I started with. I have hated every second of that! I am proud to be Kiowa and to be married to a Kiowa warrior, as well as to have three beautiful Kiowa children! But I also cherish my white heritage, something I will never, ever forget. It has been essential in making me who I am today. And, by coming here I have learned also to be more proud of it than ever before. God has taught me a great deal during these weeks, and much of it came through my friendship with you. And Nan, of course!"

"I don't fault you one bit. It was necessary, given what you knew," he said in reply. "It is such a shock, though, to realize that a month ago I didn't know any Indians, and today I know an entire family of them! What an honor I've been given, to be friends with all of you."

"We've been through a great deal but I felt you deserved to know the truth. I wanted to scream it out to the judge during the hearing! However, I was fearful it might prevent me from inheriting the estate. I sure didn't want to get this close and lose it all, because I couldn't bear another minute of the lies."

"Yes, it might well have sunk your chances of inheriting," he replied. "Some courts are ruling now in favor of those with Indian blood in a few circumstances but for the most part, that is still not a legal precedent we can count on. The point of a woman inheriting however, as the judge said, has been settled now. The Ohio law will be used by many in cases for years to come all over America until the law in every part of the land fully protects a woman's right to own property. Maybe one of these days the same can be said about protections for the Indians. Meanwhile, it is probably best if we continue to keep this information under wraps for the time being. At least until the papers are all filed and everything is legal and finalized."

Mandy went on. "I understand and agree completely. God directed this, I believe, Matthew, when He allowed Alex to be killed as he began babbling on about me being an Indian! I was praying about revealing my heritage but felt no peace about doing so. And then Ken-ai-te had the chance to end it all permanently. What good would it have done at that point, to tell the judge? However, as I said, I wanted you to know. I'm very weary of all the lies!"

"God honor truth, Prayer Woman," said Ken-ai-te. "Now truth is told."

"Prayer Woman?" asked Matthew.

"That is my Kiowa name," said Mandy with a grin." "What a delight to hear it spoken out loud once more! And by my husband!"

Nan said, "Well, now that this is out of the way, could we please move out of the hot sun? I'm hungry and I have another surprise to share with all of you. This morning before I left the Boarding House for work, Mrs. Wilson asked me what she could do to help all of us, since she was unable to get away to attend the hearing. I mentioned that she might make extra food for luncheon, just in case she 'happened' to have some visitors. She eagerly agreed, saying she hoped it would be a celebration time for what we had all been dreaming about in a favorable ruling from the judge. Therefore, we have a delicious meal waiting on us as soon as we can get there!"

"But Nan," said Mandy, "what about you needing to go back to work?"

"Well, frankly, I no longer need to work! With the bequest, along with my plans to go to Indian Territory soon," and here she grinned at Jacob who returned the smile, "I made a decision while sitting in the courtroom. I promised the Lord that if you won, I would not return to work today but immediately become a lady of leisure! On my way to the Boarding House, I will go by the Emporium to let my boss know. We need to get going, because I don't know about all of you, but my mouth is already watering in anticipation of that food!"

Jacob took her arm and they headed toward the Emporium, happy as could be together! Mandy's heart was deeply warmed to see this, and she wondered again where God was directing this young couple's steps, since they would soon be living far apart.

"Amanda," said Matthew, "I need to talk to the judge one more minute, shouldn't take long. After that, I will join all of you over at Mrs. Wilson's place. Don't worry, I know I didn't use your proper name, but as we talked about, it is probably best if we don't until these papers are finalized and filed properly."

She smiled. "That's fine, Matthew. I love the name Amanda, too! We will go on ahead and see you after while."

After he walked off, Ken-ai-te said, "He right, not Prayer Woman yet but soon! Love Mand-ee, too, though. We go eat."

Mandy walked away from the courtroom building where so much had happened that morning, her heart lighter than it had been in weeks! Lily was on one side, her beloved husband on the other. What more could she ask for?

Mrs. Wilson had put on quite a spread for her guests that day.

"I can't believe you could manage to do all this for us, while also preparing the noon meal for your other boarders," remarked Mandy.

"Well, as it turned out, neither one of them were here! So, I spent the extra time trying to make this very special, by way of saying farewell to my favorite guests and their friends!"

"Yes, well, that," started Mandy, a little nervous. She had never told Mrs. Wilson that Ken-ai-te was her husband, nor the truth about her heritage. No time like the present to do it!

"You see, Mrs. Wilson," she began as they all filled their plates with the sumptuous food, "Ken-ai-te here is not simply a family friend. He in truth is my husband and Lily's father."

"What?" she exclaimed. "My word, what a surprise! No wonder he came all this way. I do understand, dearie, why you felt you had to keep his identity hidden. But, Ken-ai-te, I would have been honored to have you here as my guest even if you were not married to my sweet Amanda."

A knock was heard at the door, and Matthew walked in.

"Welcome, Matthew," called out Mrs. Wilson. "Come on in and have a seat. We were just starting luncheon, and I'm glad you could join us, too."

She turned back to Mandy to ask, "I'm dying to know, do you all live in a tipi?"

Mandy laughed. Everyone seemed to want to know the answer to that one question!

"Yes, we do, with our sons, Spotted Rabbit and Red Hawk."

"Really? What charming names!" She did not have a trace of animosity over all this news. Would she remain so when she found out the rest?

"Thank you. That was their father's choice! I cannot wait to get home to see them again. It seems months instead of mere weeks since I left them, but even that has been far more than I anticipated when we planned this trip. You certainly made it far more comfortable for both of us, when we had to extend our visit by such a lengthy time. We are most grateful."

"Did everyone have the mashed potatoes?" their hostess asked, then turned back to Mandy. "I appreciate you saying that, Amanda. I've told you before that I get attached to all my boarders but you and Nan topped them all. I've already told you this before, but it bears repeating. If I had ever had daughters, I would want them to be exactly like you. And a granddaughter like Lily!"

"Thank you, Mrs. Wilson," she said with a smile. Mandy could tell the compliment had touched her daughter's heart as much as it had her own.

Matthew spoke up. "I talked with the judge briefly and we got everything figured out on what papers need to be filed on Monday. When are you all planning on leaving Trenton, Amanda?"

"I'm not sure but probably in the morning, right, Ken-ai-te?" He nodded, as did Jacob.

"As soon as we can get all packed up after the morning meal," added Jacob.

"That's what I was afraid of," said Matthew. "I'm sorry but I cannot get your money to you before you leave, if you are leaving that soon. I have to wait until after the paperwork is filed in Hamilton, and then I can take a draft to the bank there before I come back here with the cash. But you will already be gone by that time."

"Save it until I come back," said Jacob. He glanced at Nan and she nodded, grinning ear to ear. "Nan and I are engaged to be married, as soon as she can make arrangements to come out to the territory for the big event!"

The room erupted in joy and congratulations to the happy couple!

Mandy gasped, "Engaged? Just like that, Nan?"

"Yes, just like that, Amanda. You said that's how it would happen and it did! I'm so excited to have found Jacob and to know as quickly as I did that he was the right man for me. And, that he felt the same way!"

"This day," said Mrs. Wilson, "is really one of great celebration for sure!"

"Matthew," said Mandy after she caught her breath from the exciting news, "do not worry about getting us the money right away. We will be all right, knowing it is coming very soon."

"All right, Amanda, I wanted to forewarn you is all. I certainly wish you could stay over a few more days but I do understand. Those boys will likely be very happy to see their family return."

"Mrs. Wilson," said Jacob, "would you ever consider moving out to Indian Territory and cook meals for me? I am a terrible cook, and my daughter Hannah really needs to learn from someone who cooks as well as you do, rather than from me!"

"Well, Jacob, I'm a fairly good cook, you know," said Nan. "Oh, wait, you *don't* know, that is the point! I haven't told you yet nor had a chance to cook you a meal."

They all laughed at that one.

"Oh, my goodness, no, to answer your question," said Mrs. Wilson, "sorry about that. I'll leave the travels to younger folks. But I have heard so much from Amanda about it, that it does sound like an incredibly beautiful place to visit."

"Yes, it is," he said. "I'll be back in about two weeks to take Nan there."

"And I can't wait!" she chirped with a giggle, her face glowing in the light of his smile.

"I'm not sure," said Mrs. Wilson, "if you all would like to have a basket or two of food to take with you on the trail home, but I would love to fix some up for you if you feel you would have room for them."

"Oh, Mrs. Wilson, how sweet of you!" said Mandy. "That is a lovely idea, but I'm not sure we can since we are going home by horseback all the way."

Jacob said, "Ken-ai-te and I talked about this, Amanda, and we are going to get a couple of pack horses to take with us. Lily is insisting on taking a few of the books your aunt left to her and we couldn't tell her no! So, I believe there should be plenty of room for the food. At least, I for one intend to make sure there is!"

"And taking food with us, too, for our people back home," added Ken-ai-te. "Sons to think of, plenty of others needing food quickly. Using money you have for that. If any left."

"Yes, actually I do have some left. For one thing, I don't have to keep any back to purchase the railroad tickets now. Matthew has all that right now, so we will get that after luncheon. Is that all right, Matthew?"

"Of course. I will go get it after we eat and get it to Jacob and Ken-ai-te to do just that."

"All right, then," said Mrs. Wilson, "I will get started on pulling things out for my part after I finish these dishes. Is everyone done now, that I might be able to clear the things away?"

"Um, Mrs. Wilson," said Mandy, "before you do, there is a little more to my story than simply the fact that Ken-ai-te is my husband. You deserve to know the truth. The *whole* truth."

"Oh my! There's more? Do tell me, please."

Mandy revealed the facts of her Kiowa heritage and her friend welcomed the news with great enthusiasm, as Mandy's anxiety melted away. It made no difference to her that Mandy was half Kiowa. The relief flooded her heart and she thanked the Lord repeatedly for His goodness in choosing this special lady to watch over her and Lily all these weeks!

Matthew had to get back to the office to get all the papers prepared for the sale of the house as well as those for filing in the county seat in a few days and to get Mandy's money out of the safe. The other two men went to the livery stable to check on their ponies and secure pack horses for the journey, and then use the money to purchase as much food as possible to take with them. Lily went off to finish reading the last book she had borrowed from Ginny, hoping to run it over there later that day in order to also say goodbye. That left Nan and Mandy helping Mrs. Wilson with washing all the dishes. While they worked, they talked about several things including the weather, the next day's menu, what the museum might be like in honor of Ida—anything to keep them off the painful topic in the back of each woman's mind.

"You know," said Mandy, taking a deep breath as they finished drying the last of them, "I am going to have a hard time saying goodbye to the two of you tomorrow. At least I don't have to do that today. I think I'm going up to pack a few things and launder the last couple of items before we leave. I've prayed for this day to come for such a long time; now that it's almost here I find I'm sad! How will I manage even two weeks without you, Nan? And to think I might not ever see you again, my dear friend," and she hugged Mrs. Wilson. "That breaks my heart."

"Nonsense, Amanda! We will all see one another in Heaven someday, don't you forget that! And I won't have to cook another meal, make another bed, or wash another dish. I can't wait!"

CHAPTER FORTY-FOUR

For ye have not received the spirit of bondage again to fear; but ye have received the Spirit of adoption, whereby we cry, Abba, Father."
Romans 8:15

May 11, 1867
Trenton, Ohio

"Amanda," asked Nan, "I mean Prayer Woman—I *can* call you that now, can't I? Do you want this on the pack horse or with you?"

Mandy beamed at hearing her beloved Kiowa name once more spoken publicly!

"With me, please. Thanks! Matthew said we should be cautious about my secret getting out to the general public until the last batch of paperwork is filed on Monday, but no one is here except those who already know the truth. Feel free to use my real name if you want!"

Jacob helped Nan put the last few items into the large canvas bag bound for one of the pack horses. Together they got it strapped on somehow, amid much laughter.

What a joy to watch them, Lord! Who knew that when he came here in response to Your command to help Ken-ai-te, that he would at last find true love as well? And in only four short days! Talk about a whirlwind romance! From what Nan told me, they spent a great deal of the evening last night making plans for their future together!

"Lily," she called to her daughter, "that was sweet of Mrs. Cordon to bring Ginny here to say goodbye to you. I saw you speaking with them but was busy with some last minute packing and couldn't get over there before they left. That must have been hard to say farewell to such a sweet friend."

"Yes, I did appreciate Mrs. Cordon doing that. All she wanted to talk about, though, was who would be living in Great-Aunt Ida's house and who was buying all the furniture. I told her that I didn't have a clue what would happen to all of it. It wasn't really a lie because I wasn't entirely certain at that moment if the Masons were buying it from you or not. Did you get that all worked out with them yet?"

"Not quite but they are supposed to be here any minute so I can sign the papers that Matthew wrote up last night for them. He had some of it done but had to finish it in order for me to sign today. That Mrs. Cordon! Honestly, I am rather glad I didn't get to talk to her!"

"I know what you mean," said Lily with a smile. "Did you know that Ginny whispered to me at the last minute that she is coming to Indian Territory someday to visit me! Thing is, she doesn't yet know that we are Kiowa! What a joke that would be on her mother, to find out her daughter came to visit us and stayed in a tipi!"

"Amanda!" A familiar voice from behind her caused her to turn around with great joy. Mrs. Wilson stood there, loaded down with two large baskets packed high with food!

"Here is the food I promised you yesterday. I only have a minute to drop them off but wanted to again bid you and Lily a safe journey home. Remember, you are always welcome to stay with me if you are ever in town again."

Lily overheard what she said and walked over to greet Mrs. Wilson with a hug. "I hope we can come back someday, as I want to enjoy the beds again! Oh, the sheets, too! I shall miss those most of all. Well, maybe not as much as the food! But almost! I wish you would reconsider coming out to visit us one of these days."

"It must be so beautiful, to hear all of you talk about it the way you do."

"Oh, it is!" she chirped. "The very best place on earth, in fact, because it is home. Well, with Trenton right behind it, that is! We just have to figure out how to fit a bed into our tipi!" That image brought peals of laughter from all three of them. And a deep warmth for Mandy because her daughter could now embrace her homeland without reservation, thanks to the lessons learned while here. Maybe someday she would live out her dream of going to Paris but for now, a tipi filled with her family brought the contentment she had been lacking before!

"The Boarding House," Mrs. Wilson added, "definitely won't be the same without you two there, for sure."

"Well, it will be quieter, at least!" said Mandy and they laughed at that.

"But quieter is not always better," she added. "It was such a blessing to get to know all of you, but I need to rush off now to get the two meals for the rest of the day started for my boarders. Have a safe journey and enjoy the food along the way. My prayers go with you!" Many hugs were exchanged before she took off, as Mandy wiped away a tear. *Thank You, Lord, for such a faithful friend. Bless her richly!*

Mandy's mouth watered at the thought of all those wonderful goodies lovingly tucked into the baskets as she handed them to Ken-ai-te to tie onto one of the pack horses. They were almost ready to head out!

The Masons showed up a few minutes later. Mandy was relieved they had made it in time, as this task was very important to her heart. She signed all the paperwork, handing the documents back to the couple.

"Honestly, I don't know whether to laugh or cry that this piece of business is concluded! You have no idea what an answer to prayer you both are to me."

"And you to us, Amanda," said Alyssa. "We cannot wait to get started on this project!"

"It seems we missed quite an exciting court scene yesterday!" said Crawford. "Our business unfortunately kept us busy all day and we were unable to come to the hearing. We of course were praying and were both thrilled to hear of the outcome when Matthew brought us the papers early this morning."

"Yes, it was that all right. The important part was the judge's ruling, though. That allows me now to sign these papers to give ownership of Aunt Ida's house and property around it to the Trenton Historical Society, to be managed by the two of you. That makes all the effort worth it."

"Matthew told us he would oversee the auction of all the things we do not want to keep and ensure the money gets to you," said Crawford.

"Yes, that's right," said Mandy. "Jacob will be returning in about two weeks to bring Nan out there and at that time, they will load up all the books in a large wagon as well as a few other items I wanted to keep but won't fit on horseback. And of course, to bring the remainder of the money from the estate. Believe me, it will be put to good use to buy food for the Kiowa people, who are most anxious for us to get back there."

"I'm sure they are! If you hadn't come here, no telling what would have happened to that house. How do we say thank you enough for allowing us to honor your aunt in this manner?" asked Alyssa.

"Please ensure that God gets the glory for her life, not her own efforts," replied Mandy. "She would be mortified if the property lifted her up above Him! And I know you both will do as I have asked."

"Absolutely!" added Alyssa. "Well, we will get these papers to Matthew and he will give you your copy later after it is filed officially, with, well, whoever you file these things with! I don't know but he does, so we are trusting him to get this done for us."

As they walked away, Mandy also thanked God for their kindness and desire to honor Ida Clark's memory the way they had. Not keeping the house had tugged at her heartstrings a bit but seeing it to go them made it much easier!

Interesting comment she made that if I hadn't come, the house could not have been purchased by the historical society, and Aunt Ida's contributions would never have been known to future generations. I never thought about it that way, Lord! As difficult as this has been at times, You had a bigger purpose behind it, didn't You?

The hardest goodbye was to Matthew. How sufficiently God had provided for her needs through this man, who had become a dear friend in such a short time. Words failed her a moment as she shook his hand while brushing tears away.

"Take care of Trenton for us, will you? It has taken on a whole new meaning of the word 'home' than ever before for me, thanks mostly to you. And Nan, of course! But you shared so much with me about my aunt and her faith, which helped me better understand her enormous transformation spiritually and emotionally. That helped me grow to love her more deeply than I had ever imagined I could. You will always have a home with us if you ever care to visit Indian Territory! But the mighty way God is using you right here makes me eager to see how He is going to bless you in the future. Your support as you guided me carefully through the mire I encountered when I arrived meant a great deal, along with the kind friendship you offered along the way which I appreciated more than I can express. You were far more than merely my attorney! I hope you know I was praying for you, and it was comforting me often to know you were praying for this case as well."

"Amanda, the gratitude is mutual, as I appreciate what you said more than you can know. I pray God can use me here to pass on the blessings that your aunt gave to me long ago. You are living proof that He is hard at work on that!" He hesitated a moment and smiled.

"I have a surprise for you. Here is the money from Miss Ida's savings that she had entrusted to me," and he handed her a large envelope stuffed full of bills. "And of course, along with it is the money you entrusted to me when you first got here. It is ready cash that I know will come in handy when you get home to buy more food than you could carry on horseback now."

"You had Aunt Ida's savings all along? Where? In your safe?"

"Yes, that's right. I didn't broadcast it for fear someone might try to steal it. But it was there all along, with yours and my personal savings, plus that from several others in town, as I told you the day you put your cash in there. I certainly understand why you wanted a rapid departure today but am disappointed I cannot give you the remainder of the money before you leave, since it will take a few days to bring all that to a conclusion. However, perhaps this will help a bit until the rest arrives."

"Oh, it will!" Her eyes were wide as she peeked inside the envelope, to reveal a great deal of cash inside! "Oh, Ken-ai-te, come see!" she cried. "I cannot believe how much is in here."

He walked over and Matthew explained the money to him, as his eyes joined Mandy's in an expression of pure joy and relief. They hadn't been sure they would have any money to take home with them, leaving as quickly as they decided to do. This blessing overwhelmed them both to the point of being speechless!

Matthew continued, "Looks like Mrs. Wilson has supplied you abundantly with food, but you may have other expenses as well on your long journey."

"Yes, she did give us plenty all right!" said Mandy. "But the food we will purchase with this money will mean life to those starving back in our village. I am eager to get it to them as soon as possible. Our expenses on the journey will be few, so believe me this will be welcomed with open arms and hearts by the Kiowa back home!" Ken-ai-te shook his hand and nodded in agreement.

"Thank you, Matthew," he said. "God bless and keep you."

Matthew nodded. "Same to you, my friend." He watched a moment as Ken-ai-te returned to his task of loading everything up.

"I have spoken with Jacob," he said to Mandy, "about when he can return, and I will make sure to have the rest of the proceeds from the estate ready to take with him at that point. The only one that may take longer is the settlement of the recovered gold. It seems there is some dispute over it brewing, but I have a friend working on that for me."

"There is no rush on it. I'm still overwhelmed with the final tally on what her estate is worth. We will be able to continue our ministry to the Kiowa for many years with this money, as well as to finally defeat the horrible starvation they have been suffering from."

"Another very important outcome of this whole thing," added Matthew, "has been that justice has been served. Bessie, Abigail, and the real Alex himself will rest easier now that the murderer of each of them has been brought to account. I will send a letter with Jacob outlining the resolution of all that later. But with confessions from Kendrick and Barnes, plus the others involved in the conspiracy to kidnap Lily and the other girls, that mess should be cleared up rather quickly. Paul and his men are working hard to tie up all the loose ends to make an airtight case against them. Ford got what he had coming to him for all his criminal mischief. Too bad we can't hang a dead man. But a Kiowa knife to the head is punishment enough for this life, with God taking care of the next one."

"I agree completely." Mandy thanked God again for protecting her from death at the hands of that madman, thanks to the quick action of her husband.

"Judge Adams," Matthew continued, "will dispense with all of this without delay, I'm quite certain. With him having been personally threatened and seeing how much destruction these thugs visited on all of us here in Trenton, he told me he has no hesitation whatsoever in granting the full estate legally come Monday morning with the filing of the paperwork, as he did verbally yesterday. Maybe now with these criminals being removed, we can return to being the quiet town of law and order that we used to be!"

"Thanks to you and to Paul Owens, who also is a hero of mine! Give him my deep appreciation again, will you?"

"Of course. He had to leave town this morning early on urgent business or he would have been here to see all of you off, I know."

That left only Nan, the goodbye she dreaded the most. She watched with a heavy heart as her friend and Jacob were sharing a difficult farewell. Mandy knew her own in a few minutes would flood both of them with many tears. At least some of them would be ones of joy, since Nan would very soon be living her dream once her bequest was in her hands. Thanks to what had happened, now she couldn't wait to come to Indian Territory to visit Mandy and her family—and Jacob, of course, her beloved!

When the fateful moment could no longer be procrastinated, she took a deep breath and hung onto her friend, sobbing. After a few minutes when she could speak again, the words poured forth.

"Nan, how I could have asked for a sister in faith who was any closer to me than a real sister might have been is beyond my understanding! I cannot wait to see you again in a few weeks, but in our village on the prairie. Sharing our Kiowa heritage with you will be so exciting to me!"

"And to me! I cannot wait to get there! Jacob will be back for me in two weeks, and Matthew says by that time he will have everything ready to go with us. I joked that it is going to take a huge wagon to bring it all! Jacob added that he hoped Ken-ai-te could build a tipi big enough to house it all for you and we burst into laughter at that picture!"

"One last thing I want you to do for me," added Mandy. "Take this ring." She took the wedding band off her finger and handed it to her friend, "and keep it until you come out to see us. Then when you and Jacob do marry, he can put it on your finger himself. After all, he is the one who picked it out in the first place. What better use for it than for his new bride?"

With tears in her eyes, she clutched it to her chest. "I will be honored to wear one with that much love behind it!"

"Prayer Woman," said Ken-ai-te gently as he came to say goodbye to Nan, "we need to leave. Day goes quickly. Nan, we see you soon, you put big smile on Jacob's face! Hope you can keep it there!"

"Thanks, Ken-ai-te! With God's help, I'm going to try! Is it all right for me to hug a Kiowa chief? Or is that allowed?"

"I chief, I say law, and I say yes!" And he hugged her enthusiastically.

"One last thing, Ken-ai-te," said Mandy, "before we take off, would you pray for us and for all our friends here in Trenton that we are leaving behind?" He nodded with a smile.

They all gathered around and he prayed, first in Kiowa, then in English as cold chills ran down Mandy's spine for all her blessings, centered in this one man! Whatever the future held for them, she hoped they would never be separated like this again. Yet, she knew now if that did happen, they would never truly be apart!

"Father of us all, guide our steps and keep danger away. Give wisdom and protection for journey. Thank You for taking care of Prayer Woman and Lily here. Bless all who helped them because of You. We thank You for standing with us even when far apart, and for showing us faith of Ida, also healing Prayer Woman's heart. Let all we do praise Jesus! In Name of Jesus Christ, whose Word stands forever, bringing all men together! AMEN."

THE END

ACKNOWLEDGMENTS

My deepest gratitude goes to the following, who all played a vital role in the shaping of this story:

- **To the Lord!** I never intended to write a sequel to *From Now Until Forever* but He obviously had a different idea! He led me patiently onward in developing the plot, until my heart caught up to His.
- **To My Family!** – See the Dedication!
- **To Kelly Curtis Philpot!** When I called the Trenton Historical Society and Museum, this amazing lady answered the phone and it soon became apparent God had divinely put us together! As Co-Curator of it, she became a major resource person for so many details in this story, and there is no way to adequately thank her for all she contributed to this book. Not only did she encourage me every step along the way, she even sent me numerous books to read, all of which allowed me to write about this place in a far more authentic way than I ever could have done on my own. With my not ever having been to Trenton, she filled me in on so much of its history and heritage, including sending me photos of various spots around town to give me a better feel for it. When I stumbled into a potential landmine with a glaring error, she graciously helped me brainstorm for a way to avoid it! In addition, she managed to pull the entire Museum Board in by purchasing autographed copies of the first novel for each one, and they became as excited as she was over the upcoming sequel. Someday I hope I get to visit this lovely town, meet her in person, and walk the streets of this place I have grown to love. She is a fifth generation Trenton resident so knows her stuff, believe me! I only hope I have done her proud!

- **To Kendall Cockrell!** He is a long-time friend and attorney who advised me on the legal terminology and procedure I needed to know in order to write about the court case and in particular the courtroom scene at the end. Many thanks for bearing with me so graciously! Any mistakes I may have made are entirely my own and no reflection on him.

- **To Mary Nichols!** We have been dear friends since we both got out of college and swear somehow we are sisters, even though we are of different races and parents! When I told Mary that I wanted to honor the spirit of those in Ohio who opposed slavery and paid high prices for taking a stand back then in favor of the abolitionist movement, she said the whole concept gave her cold chills and tears of joy as I outlined the specifics. My desire is that the scenes from that time have been an honor to women like Harriet Beecher Stowe and Harriet Tubman, who are highlighted in the narrative and whose passions about slavery mirror my own. In addition, I seek to bring honor to all those brave anonymous people who dared to open their homes to runaway slaves through the Underground Railroad. I pray my portrayal of one such woman, albeit fictitious, has done justice in some tiny part to the tremendous suffering slavery brought to so many for generations. My deep gratitude to you, Mary, for all your loyal support of my writing and many prayers and suggestions along the way! Love you, sister!

- **To John J. Dwyer!** His patience with me as I picked his brain about the history of Indian Territory in the years after the Civil War ended enabled me to discover several huge holes I had in my basic concept for this book. But then he quickly made numerous detailed suggestions on how to work around those mistakes and in fact make the story line even stronger than before. His two-volume book, *The Oklahomans: The Story of Oklahoma and Its People* is a thorough, in-depth look at the state from ancient times through the Civil War years to statehood and beyond, to the present day. His renowned knowledge as a historian and especially of all things regarding Indian Territory helped me enormously to immerse myself again in the Kiowa people's struggles and victories during the time period in which my novel is set. I highly recommend these books to anyone desiring to know more about the state's past and how that has shaped its present-day persona. My husband's cousin Kay Little, herself a well-known historian in her county in northern Oklahoma, is the one who first recommended John to me, and I appreciate very much that tip which so heavily influenced the direction of this novel.

- **To Janice Orvis!** Many thanks go to this dear friend for her continued support of my writing and the many Indian artifacts she has in her home. It is from all this that I have gained so much of my inspiration for these two books. One item in particular has intrigued me for years, a beautiful Indian Prayer Angel, so I wrote it in as an essential part in the plot of this story line. I have tried to trace the artist who envisioned her and brought her to life but sadly have been unable to do so. I hope he/she would be honored to have this breathtaking creation take on a new meaning in my book. Love you, my dear friend, for sharing so freely with me of your own passion for Native Americans, and for gifting me with this sweet figurine which will forever be one of my most treasured possessions!
- **To Dr. Ted Kersh!** When I struggled initially with the idea that the premise of this novel would be based on living a lie, several years ago I consulted with my former pastor, Dr. Ted, and after listening patiently to me explain my conflict, he assured me that the way I intended to handle the lies and the fallout from them should in no way be objectionable to people of faith. Sad to say, lies are a part of life it seems. However, learning to live above them and see through them, showing the result of falling into their traps instead of resisting them, and demonstrating graphically, even in fiction, how much we need to live in truth is a message much needed in today's world. I appreciated so much his encouragement to me and give him many thanks for taking the time to listen!
- **To My Early Readers!** I am deeply grateful for the time each of you took to read the manuscript for this novel and for your kind yet truthful feedback. You have helped make this a stronger book in countless ways!
- **To My Readers!** Last but definitely not least, I want to thank all of you, my readers, for your patience as you awaited the release of

this sequel. It was written through some of my life's biggest storms which delayed its publication considerably. You are the reason I write, and I hope you like this one as much as you did the first one. Thank you always for your loyalty—and let me know what you think!

This novel would not be nearly as believable and authentic as it is without each one who helped in various ways, so I say thank you to these folks for being patient and encouraging when I was stumped and excited alike! Happy Reading to all!

Laura L. Drumb

Called To Hope…To Live In Joy! ~ Ephesians 1:18 – Romans 15:13
www.facebook.com/lauradrumb
www.lauraldrumb.com
AuthorLauraLDrumb@gmail.com

QUESTIONS FOR FURTHER STUDY

1. How could many of the complications of this story been avoided had Mandy chosen to tell her aunt the truth in her letter? Have you ever been tempted to tell a "white lie" in order to save someone's feelings? Do you believe dishonesty is ever justified before God? Can you show from the story how many of the characters became embroiled in the tangles of one so-called "simple lie" and its ramifications, in some cases for years?
2. In what ways does prayer help us practice discernment when dealing with others whose motives might be less than honorable? Have you ever encountered a situation where God kept you from becoming ensnared in a trap that otherwise might have proven disastrous?
3. Have you ever experienced separation for a time from a spouse due to work or other circumstances and yet felt the relationship grow stronger because of it? Why do you believe this is possible?
4. Can you recall from the Scriptures ways in which lies or deceit were used for good? Ways they contributed to great anguish or harm? How could those situations have been different had the truth been the standard instead? In what ways have you learned from lies in your own life that they drag you into a downward spiral that is often compared to a spider web, entrapping you until it becomes almost impossible to get out of its reach?
5. How have society's rules been relaxed or even changed today from the past regarding the business or personal interactions between people of the opposite sex? Do you feel this is a good trend or a harmful one and in what ways?

6. Have you ever gone through any type of spiritual transformation other than salvation itself in which your values or ideas were challenged and transformed, as happened to Ida? How did her change in perspective impact others' lives when she put that into action instead of mere words?
7. What are God's views of such topics as slavery, honesty, trusting in God's plan rather than creating your own, the value of life, overcoming past hurts and being set free from their bondage, and showing compassion toward others? How have they impacted your life personally?
8. When Lily disappears and Mandy faces the horror of perhaps losing her daughter forever, can you relate with anything that has ever happened to you? Did you face it with courage or anger or fear or some other emotion—and why?
9. Do you believe God speaks to us in dreams, as He did to Ken-ai-te in order to alert him to the danger his family faced far away? Why or why not?
10. Explain how the themes of obedience and listening to the call of God on a life can impact the future as well as the present day. Are you struggling with either of these in your own life right now? In what ways does God shape our character, often at the expense of our comfort, to help us become all He designed us to be?

MEET AUTHOR LAURA L. DRUMB

Laura L. Drumb writes Christian historical fiction and always has several ideas in the works. This book is the sequel to her award-winning novel, *From Now Until Forever*. She loves to travel, read, write, and scrapbook. Plus, little thrills her more than being with her two daughters and their husbands, along with her seven amazing grandchildren! Laura and her husband have been married almost 52 years, and are active members of South Tulsa Baptist Church.

You can connect with Laura on her website titled "History Matters" at www.lauraldrumb.com, by email at AuthorLauraLDrumb@gmail.com, or on Facebook at www.facebook.com/lauraldrumb. She loves to autograph copies of her books, if you will contact her at one of the above. If not local to the Tulsa area, she can always mail the books. Be sure to watch the Events tab on her website to discover details on her upcoming book signings or speaking presentations, where she loves to meet her readers personally!

Top on her list of life favorites, however, is the privilege of sharing her faith with others, through her books or in person, as she lives out her Writing Motto.

Called to Hope…To Live in Joy! Ephesians 1:18, Romans 15:13